Dramatists and their Manuscripts in the Age of Shakespeare, Jonson, Middleton and Heywood

This book presents new evidence drawn from manuscript and archival sources about the ways in which early modern dramatists such as William Shakespeare, Ben Jonson, Thomas Heywood, John Fletcher and Thomas Middleton composed their plays and the degree to which they participated in the dissemination of their texts to theatrical audiences. Grace Ioppolo argues that the path of the transmission of the text was not linear, from author to censor to playhouse to audience—as has been routinely argued by scholars—but circular. Authors returned to their texts, or texts were returned to their authors, at any or all stages after composition. The reunion of authors and their texts demonstrates that early modern dramatists collaborated in various ways and degrees in the theatrical production and performance of their plays, and that for early modern dramatists and their theatrical colleagues, authorship was a continual process, not a determinate action.

Extant dramatic manuscripts, theatre records and accounts, as well as authorial contracts, memoirs, receipts and other archival evidence, are used to prove that the text returned to the author at various stages, including during rehearsal and after performance. This monograph provides new information and case studies, and will be a fascinating contribution to the fields of Shakespeare studies, early modern drama studies, manuscript studies, textual study and bibliography and theatre history.

Grace Ioppolo is Reader in English and American Literature at the University of Reading, UK.

Routledge studies in Renaissance literature and culture

Dramatists and their Manuscripts in the Age of Shakespeare, Jonson, Middleton and Heywood

Authorship, authority and the playhouse

Grace Ioppolo

Routledge
Taylor & Francis Group

LONDON AND NEW YORK

First published 2006
by Routledge
2 Park Square, Milton Park, Abingdon, Oxon OX14 4RN

Simultaneously published in the USA and Canada
by Routledge
270 Madison Ave, New York, NY 10016

Routledge is an imprint of the Taylor & Francis Group

© 2006 Grace Ioppolo

Typeset in Garamond by Wearset Ltd, Boldon, Tyne and Wear
Printed and bound in Great Britain by MPG Books Ltd, Bodmin

British Library Cataloguing in Publication Data
A catalogue record for this book is available from the British Library

Library of Congress Cataloging in Publication Data
A catalog record for this book has been requested

ISBN 0-415-33965-0

For Peter Beal

Contents

Figures

Acknowledgements

I began writing this book while under contract from another press to produce a study of how Shakespeare's plays came into print. After finishing the first draft of the book, my general editors discovered that I had written the first four chapters on how Shakespeare's plays were transmitted from author to playhouse and only two later chapters on how Shakespeare's plays were transmitted from playhouse to print. For me, this was a deliberate and strategically planned campaign. Increasingly frustrated by the proliferating number of books on the transmission of dramatic texts that ignored, dismissed or misrepresented the role of manuscripts (and acting companies and playhouses) in this process, I was determined to begin my study at the beginning, not *in medias res*. But even I had to agree that the book no longer suited the series for which it was contracted. I am very grateful that my general editors and the officials at that press graciously allowed me to withdraw from the series so that I could complete the book I needed to write.

I wish to thank the staff of Routledge Press, particularly Liz Thompson and Terry Clague, for their willingness to support the book I needed to write. I am also grateful to the Henry E. Huntington Library, the Folger Shakespeare Library, the British Academy, the British and the American Bibliographical Societies, and the University of Reading for their generous awards of fellowships over the years to support my research in UK and US manuscript archives. I am indebted to the staff at the libraries listed above and especially to those in the British Library Manuscripts Room, who have kindly and courteously indulged my many nagging requests over the years for permission to examine 'vault' or restricted manuscripts and to trace their provenance. I also wish to thank the very helpful staff at the National Archives, Kew, the Victoria and Albert Art Library, Lambeth Palace Library, Hatfield House, Alnwick Castle, and university and college libraries in London, Oxford, Cambridge and Nottingham, as well as National Libraries in Aberystwyth, Cardiff and Edinburgh, and Record Offices in Hampshire, Nottingham, Warwickshire, Cheshire and Wiltshire. I also thank those private collectors who have shared their manuscripts with me. Most especially, I thank Dr Jan Piggott, Keeper of Archives at Dulwich

College, for his patience and generosity in giving me access to Henslowe and Alleyn's invaluable archive and the Marquess of Salisbury for allowing me to cite manuscript material from Hatfield House.

Portions of this book have previously appeared in *English Manuscript Studies*, Volume 11 and in *Blackwell's Companion to Renaissance Drama*. I am also grateful to students at the Universities of Reading, London, Massachusetts, Cambridge and Oxford, and Illinois State University's National Endowment for the Humanities Institute on 'Textual Variants and Teaching Shakespeare: *Hamlet*, *Othello*, and *King Lear*' (led by Professor Ron Fortune) who offered me welcome comments when I discussed my work. With love, I thank my father Gaetano and my late mother Carmela Ioppolo.

Lastly, I wish to thank those scholars who supported or assisted my work on manuscripts and playhouses over the years, including N. W. Bawcutt, J. V. Beckett, Herbert Berry, Peter W. M. Blayney, the late Fredson Bowers, Peter Davison, Marliss Desens, Katherine Duncan-Jones, Andrew Gurr, Christopher Hardman, Peter Holland, Mark Hutchings, Hilton Kelliher, John Jowett, Arthur Kinney, Ronald Knowles, Harold Love, Randall McLeod, Arthur Marotti, the late Jerome McGann, Randall McLeod, Alan H. Nelson, Lena Cowen Orlin, Richard Proudfoot, James Riddell, Carol Chillington Rutter, Brian Vickers, Michael Warren, Stanley Wells, Frances Whistler, Heather Wolfe, H. R. Woudhuysen, Laetitia Yeandle and Georgianna Ziegler. My special, heartfelt, and grateful thanks are due, as always, to S. P. Cerasano, R. A. Foakes and Peter Beal.

Introduction

'What is writ by hand we reverence more'

For the last three centuries, Shakespearean scholars have emphatically argued that the transmission of an English early modern play-text was linear: that is, from author to acting company to theatre audience to printer to literary audience.[1] This type of transmission implies that the author had no further contact with his text or with those who copied, read, used, recited or heard it after its composition. However, significant evidence from dramatic manuscripts, including the handwriting of company scribes, book-keepers and censors alongside that of authors, suggests instead that this transmission was usually not linear but circular and that neither authors nor theatre personnel dissociated authors from their texts. In fact, authors returned to their texts, or texts were returned to their authors, at any or all stages after composition. These reunions of authors and their texts demonstrate that early modern dramatists collaborated in various ways and degrees in the theatrical production and performance of their plays. For early modern dramatists and their theatrical colleagues, then, authorship could be a continual process, not a determinate action.

Dramatists certainly had to contend with their individual or shared artistic interests while working in conditions which had become nearly standardised in the early modern theatrical industry, as documented by authors' contracts, financial accounts, correspondence, depositions, commentaries, and other archival records. The attempts by dramatists to reconcile their concerns with those of their employers, colleagues, critics and audiences may have occasionally caused conflict or required compromise. But, overall, their attempts resulted in collaboration, endowing dramatists with an enduring authority, if they chose to claim it. Much of this evidence about the authority of authors is lost if studied solely in printed form, so it is vital to reinvestigate original manuscript play-texts and records themselves. In both their content and form, these manuscripts allow authors to speak for themselves, not only about creating a play-text but initiating and supporting the processes of theatrical performance and production.

In order to follow this progress of both author and text in the playhouse, I offer in this book a study not of early modern English dramatic manuscripts but of early modern English dramatists and their manuscripts. Authors cannot be separated from their manuscripts, particularly when these manuscripts display the handwriting of their authors as composers, copyists, revisers, correctors, or annotators. Although early modern printed Quarto or Folio editions of plays ultimately derive from their authors, the physical rendering of the texts comes from the hands of their compositors and other printing-house personnel, not their authors. In essence, then, authors are physically separated, or at least distanced, from their printed texts, for they do not actually produce them in a material sense, unless they themselves set the type and run the printing press. But no such separation or distance appears in manuscripts that authors personally create, copy, revise or correct. Quite literally, these manuscripts are the products of their authors' hands.

That the authors of these dramatic manuscripts still have a great deal to say is becoming increasingly evident in early modern drama studies. In February 2002, the convenor of a University of London conference on 'Manuscripts in a Switched On World' proclaimed medieval and early modern manuscripts to be 'hot', because 'researching the archives' has once again become a major, rather than a minor, focus for literary scholars. In reality, the study of early modern dramatic manuscripts had been 'hot' for three centuries, beginning in the early eighteenth century through the work of the earliest editors of Shakespeare's plays, Nicholas Rowe and Alexander Pope. These editors, who appear to have had access to dramatic manuscripts and other documents used in playhouses before and after the reopening of the theatres in 1660,[2] focused on two main arguments. First, manuscripts represented to them the primary stage in the transmission of dramatic texts, and, second, the primary creators and, most importantly, interpreters of such manuscripts were their authors.

But as the eighteenth-century cult of the editor grew to surpass the cult of the author, the successors to Rowe and Pope re-evaluated the second assertion. They debated whether the editor and, in the case of Shakespeare, the restorer of a text, rather than its author, knew best how to interpret it.[3] However, support for the first assertion of the primacy of manuscripts never really waned over the next two centuries, reaching a peak from the early to mid twentieth century in the work of R. B. McKerrow, W. W. Greg, A. W. Pollard and Fredson Bowers, among many others.[4] But these scholars had to confront a rather large obstacle: the manuscripts of the plays in Shakespeare's canon do not survive and those of his colleagues and contemporaries, such as Middleton, Heywood, Massinger and Munday, that do are full of minor and major alterations, deletions and corrections. These manuscripts by Shakespeare's contemporaries did not resemble the idealised view the bibliographers had created of Shakespeare's papers, which scarcely carried 'a blot', according to the 1623 First Folio,[5] let alone strike-outs, cuts and additions in the margins or on inserted sheets of paper.

Perhaps for this reason, Greg and Bowers largely came to derive their theories of textual, hence authorial, production of plays from their work on printed early modern dramatic texts, sometimes exclusively those of Shakespeare, rather than from extant manuscripts of other authors. Greg, in his pioneering bibliographical studies, indeed worked extensively on manuscripts, but this work did not always influence his theories on the authorial production of early modern plays, particularly those by Shakespeare. As Greg finally realised, in the twentieth-century contest between textual scholars, who saw manuscripts as fundamental to the textual transmission process, and bibliographers, who saw manuscripts as incidental or even accidental, bibliographers ultimately moved ahead.[6] In addition, although Fredson Bowers is still cited as the leading expert on dramatic manuscripts, particularly by those who take a theoretical view of such manuscripts,[7] he lacked, by his own admission, both experience and expertise in reading and handling these original documents himself.[8] Rather than working forward by examining the many extant manuscripts of Shakespeare's contemporaries, these scholars worked backward by examining his early printed texts (published as Quartos and in the 1623 First Folio). As a result, many new bibliographers dismissed the less-than-perfect extant manuscripts of other dramatists, marginalising them in the transmission process as unreliable and unrepresentative.[9] This devaluation of manuscripts became central to later generations of bibliographers, who increasingly saw a text as the product not of an author but of a mediating editor. Thus, manuscript scholar T. H. Howard-Hill could state in 1993 that each of Middleton's two autograph manuscripts of *A Game at Chess* 'is deficient as a witness of the text of *A Game* mainly on account of the harmful character of the playwright's own participation in the transcript'.[10] Such a dismissal of the author also became vital to post-modern theorists who argued that a literary text exists for and is created by the reader, if not the editor.

That an author's participation in the circulation of his own text could be seen as 'harmful' epitomises the post-modern fear of direct engagement with an author on his or her own terms. Jerome J. McGann has brilliantly summarised the central doctrine of such a theory:

> Today, texts are largely imagined as scenes of reading rather than scenes of writing. This 'readerly' view of text has been most completely elaborated through the modern hermeneutical tradition in which text is not something we *make* but something we *interpret*.[11]

Perhaps we do not see a text as something we make, but we certainly see it as something an author does not make. Yet a manuscript is a witness to something that was made, and made by an author. When scholars hold an author's papers in their hands they must acknowledge that he or she exists, or at least existed, whether the manuscript records a composition of a new work or the transcription of an old one. But if scholars choose not to examine or recognise the existence of such physical documents they can simplistically argue that 'it is the *manuscript* that is the immaterial abstraction, an enabling figment of the bibliographic and critical imagination'.[12]

The apparent rise of such a theoretical definition of early modern dramatic manuscripts and the genuine decline of required or optional postgraduate courses in manuscript studies have contributed to a current lack of understanding and investigation of early modern dramatic manuscripts. In effect, manuscript study in general may now be 'hot' but the study of dramatic manuscripts in particular is, sadly, still cool.[13] Many scholars of early modern literature are studying manuscripts, publishing their findings, and building electronic or digital archives. Yet the most cited of these are scholars largely working on non-dramatic literature written by women, probably because such literature, as well as that of other ignored or non-traditional writers, was not commonly published in the early modern age. Thus, postmodern privileging of printed texts over manuscripts is not possible in the study of early modern women's literature. Indeed, textual scholars and theorists seem united in arguing that such manuscripts give female authors a 'voice': that is, authority as authors.[14]

While manuscript studies of early modern poetry and prose are currently flourishing and accorded a similarly high status, manuscript studies are not even cited in most of the recent studies of the printing of early modern dramatic texts. Either nearly all early modern drama critics do not know how to handle, read and interpret manuscripts or else they choose not to do so, labelling them 'imaginary and enabling', and speculating on what they must not or should not contain. These scholars also display a marked ignorance of contemporary manuscript culture and of modern, and post-modern, manuscript criticism.[15] Such arguments have not recently been corrected, and their fallacies, accepted as truthful and accurate by those who later cite them,[16] have become almost self-perpetuating.

Simply stated, it is impossible to study, interpret or define the transmission of an early modern printed dramatic text, or its use in the theatre before publication, without studying, interpreting or defining the role of manuscripts in those processes. W. W. Greg wisely noted in 1931 that only when we are 'fully and certainly informed' about the characteristics and circulation of dramatic manuscripts will we be able to 'replace by sound knowledge the subjective and sometimes fantastic criteria which critics have applied in the past'.[17] Yet seventy-five years later we are still immobilised by the sometimes fantastic criteria applied by modern critics,[18] including the lingering assumption that manuscripts are objectified material texts or cultural artefacts that were immediately dissociated from authors after composition.[19] Since at least 1992, scholars have increasingly come to reject the 'death' and accept the 'return' of the author to the production and transmission of literary texts, both as creators and interpreters,[20] but this return is only beginning to be apparent in studies of early modern drama.

New computer technology is revolutionising the study of literary manuscripts: scholars are now making a humanistic discipline truly scientific and thereby claiming some validation (and being awarded generous grant money) from the larger academic community for full-time study of literary texts in manuscript form. The digital age, already underway, will make the many early modern manuscripts available electronically within the next ten to thirty years. Such increased access has begun to expand scholarly interest and study greatly, especially among non-specialists who are discovering manuscript study for the first time. In addition, new fragments or whole manuscripts of plays and masques are still being found in archives and private collections. Digital or real images will be of no use to scholars if they cannot read and interpret them, or if they cannot understand or do not study the context in which manuscripts were created and circulated.[21] Therefore, this is precisely the time to recognise what particular manuscripts and, more generally, the body of extant dramatic manuscripts can reveal about early modern authorship, authority and the playhouse.

We also need to start working forward with a discussion of the culture, creation and circulation of dramatic manuscripts, not continue to work backward from printed texts and selective manuscript evidence or uninformed interpretations of them. Stephen Orgel has claimed that even if a set of Shakespeare's 'magical foul papers' were discovered tomorrow, it 'would not simply declare its secrets to us. We would have to edit it before we could draw conclusions about it.'[22] Actually, we would not need to edit the manuscript at all—that is, *make* it, to use McGann's term; we would simply need to *read* it. As readers and as critics we make and we interpret what others have made and interpreted, so that there is always a history before us or after us. Manuscripts, above all other forms of texts, insist that texts exist before the reader and that the author exists before the text.

Methodology

In this study I offer a new examination and interpretation of the available early dramatic manuscripts written for the professional London stage, as well as related manuscripts, documents and archival records. Although I do not deal in this book with manuscripts made for academic or private performance, including those written by women, I have consulted some of them.[23] The original dramatic manuscripts that I have examined in person include, among others:

United Kingdom

Alnwick Castle, Northumberland: *John of Bordeaux*, *The Wasp*, and several amateur plays by William Percy.
Bodleian Library, Oxford: *A Game at Chess*, *The Renegado*, *The Royal Slave*, *The Witch*.
British Library: *Aglaura*, *Believe as You List*, *Bonduca*, *The Bugghears*, *Candy Restored*, *The Captives*, *The Change*, *Charlemagne*, *The Country Captain*, *The Cyprian Conqueror*, *Dick of Devonshire*, *Edmond Ironside*, *The Elder Brother*, *The Escapes of Jupiter* (also known as *Calisto*), *The Fatal Marriage*, *A Game at Chess*,

Gismond of Salerne in Love, The Governor, The Gypsies Metamorphosed, The Humorous Lovers, Juno's Pastoral, The Lady Mother, The Launching of the Mary (also known as *The Seaman's Honest Wife*), *Love's Changeling Change, The Marriage of Wit and Wisdom, The Masque of Blackness, The Masque of Queens, Between Mustapha, The Tragedy of Nero, The Parliament of Bees, The Poor Man's Comfort, Praeludium, Pyxomaxia, The Queen of Corsica, Raguaillo D'Oceano, Sir John Van Olden Barnavelt, The Swisser, Tancred and Ghismond, Sir Thomas More, Thomas of Woodstock* (also known as *Richard II*), *Time's Trick upon the Cards, Tom a Lincoln, The Second Maiden's Tragedy, The Two Noble Ladies and the Converted Conjuror, Virtue's Triumph, The Whimseys of Señor Hidalgo, The Wizard,* numerous entertainments, fragments, including *The Melbourne Manuscript,* playhouse plots and other supporting documents.

Cambridge University Library: *Mustapha.*

Cardiff Central Library, Wales: *The Welsh Ambassador.*

Cheshire Record Office: *The Tragedy of Amarath, The Wisest have their Fools about Them.*

Dulwich College Library, London: *The Telltale*; a playhouse plot, and a part, as well as extensive manuscript records of Philip Henslowe and Edward Alleyn.

Durham Cathedral Library: *The Wizard.*

National Archives (formerly the Public Record Office), Kew: *The Entertainment at Britain's Burse,* and numerous fragments, letters and supporting documents.

National Library of Wales, Aberystwyth: *Demetrius and Enanthe.*

Nottingham University Library: *Hengist, King of Kent.*

Trinity College, Cambridge: *A Game at Chess.*

Victoria and Albert Art Library (Dyce Collection): *The Faithful Friends, The Honest Man's Fortune, The Parliament of Love, Timon.*

Warwickshire Record Office: *Bajazet* (also known as *The Raging Turk*), *The Humourous Magistrate, Nero* (also known as *The Emperor's Favorite*), *Tancred and Gismond, The Twice Chang'd Friar.*

Wiltshire Record Office: *The Soddered Citizen.*

Worcester College, Oxford: *The Cheaters, The Court Secret, The Feast, The General, The Roman Empress.*

Also various supporting documents at county record offices, including Hampshire Record Office.

United States

Folger Shakespeare Library: *Aristippus, The Beggar's Bush, Belphgor, or the Marriage of the Devil, The Benefice, The Country Gentleman, The Enchanted Lovers, The Fairy Knight or Oberon the Second, A Game at Chess* (two copies), *Gismond of Salerne, Hengist, King of Kent, Henry IV* (Dering manuscript), *Horace, a Tragedy, The Inconstant Lady, La Vedova, The Life and Death of the Great Cham, The Lost Lady, The Lover's Hospital, The Partiall Law, Pompey, a tragedy, Progress from Parnassus, Publius Cornelius Scipio Sui Victor, The Resurrection of Our Lord, Richardus Tertius, Roxana, The Royal Slave, The Shepherd's Paradise, Stiava Imbroglio, The New Comedy of Juli*; and *Julian, Wernerus Martyr, The Woman's Prize, The Massacre at Paris*, and numerous other manuscripts, fragments and supporting documents.

<u>Henry E. Huntington Library</u>: *Arabia Sitiens, A Country Tragedy, The Cuckqueans, The Drinking Academy, The Entertainment of the Dowager-Countess of Derby, The Faery Pastorall, A Game at Chess, The Gypsies Metamorphosed, John a Kent and John a Cumber, King Johan, Necromantes*, numerous fragments, and supporting documents, especially in the Wallace Collection.

<u>William Andrews Clark Library</u>: *Love's Metamorphosis.*

I have also consulted in facsimile or on microfilm a minimal number of other dramatic manuscripts or fragments that are unavailable due to conservation or other reasons. Therefore, my study is not based on selected evidence or printed facsimiles but on as much of the possible evidence and supporting records and documents available in their original manuscript form, and in comparison, collation and context.

Most, if not all, of these texts can be described as one of the following types of manuscript copy: *foul papers, authorial fair copy*, or *non-authorial fair copy*. Fredson Bowers defined foul papers as 'the author's last complete draft in a shape satisfactory to him to be transferred to a fair copy'.[24] He had followed Greg's similarly constricted definition of foul papers as the author's rough draft 'representing the play more or less as the author intended it to stand, but not itself clear or tidy enough to serve as a prompt-book'.[25] Extant dramatic foul papers demonstrate that the text could be full of various types of inconsistencies, alterations, additions and cuts, or the text could be more coherent. In any given case, an author may or may not have cleaned up the foul papers so that they were in shape 'satisfactory' to be 'transferred', or the text, in theory or in practice, could have been suitable for the company book. Also, any given author may or may not have routinely made his own fair copies; if he did, he could easily handle the transference of a difficult set of foul papers, whereas a scribe would have found the task much more demanding. In fact, Bowers's definition of foul papers is too strict to suit play-texts, which went through the hands of book-keepers and censors, although it could suit modern novels or poems that went straight from authors to printers. Instead, *foul papers* should more simply be defined as the working draft by the author(s).

As for fair copies, there are two types: authorial and non-authorial. An *authorial fair copy* is a transcription by the author(s) of an existing text (whether foul papers or fair copy); in making such copies authors could and did revise or alter their texts in minor or major ways. As long as the text was legible it need not have been consistent, regular, perfect, or even visually appealing in format. A *non-authorial fair copy* is a transcription of an existing text (whether foul papers or fair copy) by one or more persons other than the author(s). Such copies would include *scribal fair copies*, made by scribes or professional copyists who were employed to present the text and format as neatly and regularly as possible. Some scribes specialised in dramatic texts or, indeed, were attached to acting companies, sometimes holding the position of book-keeper (the keeper of the company book, or, to use a term prevalent since the Restoration, 'prompter's-book');[26] their fair copies were designed to facilitate the use of the text in the playhouse. Playhouse scribes could and did regularise the text, for example, in making consistent throughout the text the placement and use of entrance and exit directions, speech prefixes, properties and names of characters. While scribes may have lightly annotated the text, they did not usually revise stage directions or dialogue.

Professional or amateur scribes without theatrical experience or expertise also made fair copies. Their transcriptions were often as literal as possible, so that they rendered errors or inconsistencies in foul papers when transcribing those, as well as playhouse notations (for example, to ready stage properties) when transcribing foul or fair copies. Such scribes were paid to present texts as clearly, as legibly and as visually appealing as possible, especially if a copy was designed for *presentation* to a patron or *commissioned* by a paying client. But in reality anyone was capable of copying a manuscript for any possible reason, as transcriptions were not confined to professional or amateur scribes. Any type of copy could have been used in any given case or at any given time as the company book, and/or the copy submitted to the censor, and/or the basis for the transcription of actors' parts.

In this study I therefore assume that it is nearly impossible to distinguish which of the extant manuscripts listed above were used in the playhouse and which were not. There is no reason to argue that manuscripts that still bear, or once bore, the censor's licence or comments, or show annotations of probable book-keepers, are the only extant manuscripts that served as company books.[27] Many of the manuscripts I have consulted suffered from some sort of damage over the years, and some have been cropped or lack opening or closing pages (often due to being bound or re-bound in later centuries) which might have contained censors' licences or annotations by playhouse personnel. Furthermore, it is not certain that a company had only one book from which they acted a play; a company may have locked up its licensed copy for safekeeping and acted the play from another transcript. Or the licensed or other theatrical manuscript may have been revised, lost or damaged and then recopied, so that what appears now to be a fair copy manuscript made for presentation or sale may in fact have been used in the theatre.[28] Any or all types of manuscripts, including foul papers, may have been used in public or private theatrical performances in London or the provinces.

In this study I do not privilege or exclude Shakespeare in discussions of how dramatists worked, but include him with the many others for whom we have extant records. In this way, Shakespeare and his texts are placed within the early modern theatrical world, not above it. The three pages of *Sir Thomas More* which are attributed to him offer an example of Shakespeare at work: this dramatist makes a few strike-outs while in the act of fair copying his original draft. Although the case of *Sir Thomas More* may reveal something about Shakespeare's practice as a collaborator on a specific play, it cannot reveal if his habits changed over the many years when he composed a play wholly by himself. On the other hand, a great deal of collateral evidence exists about how many of his contemporary dramatists, including Jonson, Middleton and Heywood, composed plays alone or in collaboration, as some of their manuscripts and a great deal of collateral material in manuscript form do survive. These dramatists were Shakespeare's collaborators, colleagues, fellow actors, friends and probable mentors and apprentices. However, the numerous records of the production and performance of Marlowe's plays almost all date from after his death in 1593 when his plays were revived and revised by other dramatists working with particular acting companies. The extreme dearth of records of Marlowe's own practices as a working dramatist negotiating terms and conditions with employers such as theatre entrepreneurs and actor-sharers precludes him from this study.[29]

In the early modern age, the circulation of texts in manuscript form was common and constituted a non-printed and often preferable and authoritative form of 'publication' during this period, thereby establishing varying types and degrees of authorship and authority.[30] Thus it was routine to conclude, as Sir Christopher Sibthorp did in 1625, that 'Mens hearts may be poysoned, and seduced, as well by Manuscripts, and written Bookes and Pamphlets, as those that be Printed, especially after they be once scattered and dispersed abroad into diverse mens hands.'[31] More importantly, in the case of plays, performance constituted another type of non-print 'publication'. Whether a play was acted once a month or once a year over a period of 5–20 years (as per the structure of repertory systems), each public playhouse performance could circulate or 'disperse', to use Sibthorp's term, the author's text to 1,000 to 3,000 people at a time. This audience is much larger than that afforded a printed play-text, for which total print runs could average, in total, less than 500 copies.

As John Donne acknowledged, 'What Printing-presses yield we think good store, / But what is writ by hand we reverence more.'[32] Although such reverence for the handwritten document may not be evident in the modern or post-modern ages, it infuses extant early modern manuscripts, whether they are contracts, bonds, indentures, account books, correspondence or play-texts. In this study, I transcribe this manuscript evidence in its original format and spelling, without modernising it, so that readers can see the layered meanings implicit in the original language, as well as the archival 'material text', as written.[33] I trace in as complete and detailed a way as possible the progress of play-texts from author to book-keeper to censor to actor to audience, and the circulation of these texts back to the author in various ways and at various times.

The post-modern contention that 'Shakespeare's own working conditions, the requirements of his playhouse and the fact that his texts were to be spoken by actors, may be considered a form of contamination'[34] ignores a multitude of archival evidence to the contrary. This evidence demonstrates that these precise conditions and requirements, for which the plays were specifically created, allowed authors to collaborate in the theatrical production and performance of their texts. So it is with this material on the working conditions and practices of dramatists that I begin my study of dramatists and their texts. In the succeeding chapters I present a study of how authors wrote, from the composition of foul papers, as exemplified by Heywood, to the transcription and use of fair copies by theatre personnel and censors. The final chapter will present a case study of the composition and circulation of manuscript texts by Jonson, Middleton and Shakespeare, who, along with Heywood, are among the most representative of early modern English dramatists working within an established theatrical profession.

1 'As good a play for y^r publiqe howse as euer was playd'

Dramatists and authorship

In his 1971 book *The Profession of Dramatist in Shakespeare's Time*, G. E. Bentley claimed to examine the 'normal working environment circumscribing the activities of those literary artists who were making their living by writing for the London theatres'.[1] In fact, he depicted as normal an antagonistic working environment in which dramatists lacked 'respect' from their employers and 'control' over their texts, as well as the ability to negotiate their terms and conditions inside and outside the playhouse, particularly with such entrepreneurs as Philip Henslowe. Bentley concluded that only eight early modern dramatists could be categorised as 'regular professionals' or 'attached dramatists', and even they were kept from participating or collaborating in the playhouse transmission and performance of their plays.[2] In effect, Bentley helped to establish the view, recently re-emphasised by Orgel, that the majority of professional dramatists were enslaved, in theory if not in practice, in a theatrical industry that minimised or negated their own interests and concerns and 'contaminated' their texts.[3]

However, the archival records, particularly authors' contracts, bonds, memoranda and correspondence, on which Bentley sometimes selectively drew, show that the 'normal' working environment allowed for dramatists to set out their own terms or to accept or renegotiate those offered by employers, actors, censors and other colleagues.[4] This point is made even clearer when these records are studied alongside dramatic manuscripts themselves. Dramatists and those using their texts worked with and not against each other in the most financially and artistically productive, and cost- and time-efficient, ways possible. By necessity, these relationships between dramatists and theatre personnel were not antagonistic but co-operative throughout the transmission of these texts from author to acting company to censor to audience. In fact, this type of collaboration of authors in the various stages through which their texts moved was routine and widespread, and not confined to only a handful of privileged dramatists. Many dramatists were apparently on short- or long-term contracts with acting companies that gave them the kind of status or authority that Bentley confers upon only eight. It is with this type of collaboration in mind that the majority of London dramatists wrote their texts.

Henslowe and dramatists

The rich theatrical archive of Henslowe (*c.*1555–1616) and his son-in-law and business associate Edward Alleyn (1566–1626) held at Dulwich College, London, does not, in fact, support Bentley's arguments that Henslowe and other employers showed 'no undue respect' to dramatists and refused to allow them to exert 'control' over their texts.[5] Henslowe's Diary offers his financial accounts for his various theatrical businesses from 1592 to 1608, and his other papers, including contracts, correspondence, indentures, bills, receipts and leases, cover the period up to his death in 1616. Alleyn's papers begin in the late 1590s and continue until his death in 1626. As proprietors of the Rose, Fortune, Hope and other theatres (from which they received a percentage of admission fees), and bankers to or investors in the Lord Admiral's, Lord Strange's, Earl of Worcester's and Prince Henry's Men, among others,[6] Henslowe and Alleyn dealt with dramatists on a daily basis. They also conducted theatrical business with many of the leading political and ecclesiastical figures from the 1580s to the 1620s, including monarchs and their families, chancellors, privy councillors and courtiers, church leaders, London civic officials and government censors.[7] All in all, Henslowe and Alleyn dealt with the entire range of national and local officials who authorised, patronised, supported, remunerated, attacked, banned, suppressed, or merely watched and heard seemingly every aspect of theatre in the early modern period, including the employment of dramatists.[8] These same officials were almost certainly applying the same standards and regulations to the other leading companies with which they had dealings, particularly the Lord Chamberlain's Men, which together with the Lord Admiral's Men were specifically named in 1598 by the Privy Council as the two companies allowed to act at court,[9] a duopoly that lasted twenty-five years.[10]

Henslowe's and Alleyn's papers demonstrate that dramatists as well as actors, company managers, theatre owners and other personnel lived in a highly interrelated theatrical business world. These men often moved casually, capriciously or shrewdly among companies, theatres and professions in a seamless way over short or long periods of time. Many of those who began their careers in the Elizabethan theatre often continued in the same or different capacities in the Jacobean and early Caroline theatres. Scholars usually regard acting companies as being composed of at least six actor-sharers, including two responsible for financial management, several boys and hired men, a book-keeper, tireman (i.e. costumer), gatherer (playhouse money collector) and other personnel to take care of stage business.[11] However, dramatists also figure as company members, regardless of whether they were sharers. All these theatre personnel, including dramatists, seem to have negotiated, exploited or accepted the same practices and methods, adapted by necessity to later demands or interests of audiences, playing spaces and employers, with which they began their careers. In fact, the careers of three dramatists, Robert Daborne, Thomas Heywood and Richard Brome, who

figure prominently in this and the following chapter, can briefly demonstrate here the artistic and financial interdependence and interconnection of
the theatrical business throughout the early modern period. These examples
should not be considered unique or anomalous.

Daborne began his theatrical career as a manager for at least one boys'
company, the Queen's Revels, and possibly another, the King's Revels.[12] He
later worked as a dramatist for an adult company, the Lady Elizabeth's Men,
among whom were actors who had worked as boys for the companies
Daborne had previously managed. Later, Daborne also attempted to become
a theatre entrepreneur. Heywood similarly worked and had financial interests in various professions in the theatre industry. A 'covenanted' actor for
the Lord Admiral's Men, he also wrote for them and later for Derby's Men,
and even later became a sharer in yet four other companies: Earl of Worcester's, Queen Anne's, King's and Queen Henrietta's Men, for all of which he
also wrote plays. Heywood thus acted or wrote plays performed at the Rose,
the Curtain, the Fortune, the Red Bull, the Phoenix and the Globe, among
other theatres, eventually working for the theatrical entrepreneur, and his
old friend, Christopher Beeston, who built the Phoenix Theatre in 1617. For
the previous twenty years Beeston had worked as an actor, beginning his
career as a servant to the actor Augustine Phillips, who had worked for Lord
Strange's Men and then the Chamberlain's/King's Men and was an original
sharer in the Globe Theatre. Beeston worked under Henslowe for Worcester's Men, and later for Queen Anne's Men, for whom he became a manager,
and then for Prince Charles's Men. Beeston also later employed Brome, who
may have begun his theatre career as a servant to Ben Jonson in the age of
James I. Brome signed exclusive contracts to write plays for the actors and
theatre owners of the Salisbury Court Theatre twenty years later in the age
of Charles I. Not surprisingly, Brome wrote at least three plays, *The Late
Lancashire Witches* (1634), and the non-extant *The Apprentice's Prize* and *The
Life and Death of Sir Martin Skink*, with Heywood.[13]

These connections, partly documented by Henslowe's and Alleyn's personnel histories, suggest a remarkably interrelated, interdependent and
financially competitive theatrical world from the 1590s to the closing of the
theatres. Surely some, if not many, of these personnel borrowed or adapted
the successful practices of the entrepreneurs for whom they had worked,
including Henslowe and Alleyn. The financial records of the other great
entrepreneurs, James, Cuthbert and Richard Burbage, with whom Henslowe
and Alleyn were most directly in competition, do not survive. Yet that
dramatists such as Daborne could threaten in 1613 to take a play to another
company if not paid a higher rate from Henslowe, his contractor, implies
that Henslowe had to adjust to market competition for dramatists' plays.
Indeed, Henslowe probably helped to standardise dramatists' salaries as well
as their working conditions as early as the 1590s, by which time everyone
already seemed to know everyone else and how they worked and, more
importantly, how much they were paid. Such competition did not end with

Henslowe and Daborne, for Brome not only discussed other companies' rates and offers when negotiating the terms of his 1635 and 1638 exclusive contracts but later sold plays to those competitors, resulting in a lawsuit for breach of promise from his contracted employers. Henslowe's and Alleyn's papers especially provide extensive, detailed, dated and unique information, much of which has not yet been fully interpreted or investigated, about the daily, weekly or annual employment terms and working conditions of dramatists.[14] These documents, therefore, should be scrutinised much more closely in order to understand the standard or 'normal' conditions, practices and 'environment' of dramatists, especially in confirming the extent of authors' authority and 'control' within the playhouse.

'Memorandum tis agreed': dramatists' contracts and salaries

As plays were performed in repertory, in a six-week period, with performance usually six days a week, a play may have been performed only once.[15] An acting company had to have on hand a large supply of new plays, as well as old ones that could be revised into something that looked new, in order to satisfy their regular, returning audiences. G. E. Bentley calculates that professional London dramatists wrote at least 900 plays between 1590 and 1642, most of which no longer survive.[16] Henslowe's potential inventory numbers over 325 plays,[17] thus constituting over one-third of the plays that Bentley calculated were written during a fifty-two-year period.[18] For most of his career Henslowe was acting as agent or intermediary for acting companies; however, he later bought plays himself, retaining financial control and possession of them unless he resold them at a profit to acting companies.[19] Alleyn also bought plays himself that he resold to the Admiral's Men or to other companies or entrepreneurs. As Roslyn K. Knutson shows, the Admiral's Men especially built up a large repertory of new and old plays from 1597 to 1603, noticeably increasing their commissioning of new plays in 1599 and 1600.[20]

E. K. Chambers argued that 1594 to 1598 marked 'a period for which Henslowe records plays only and not authors'.[21] However, entries in the Diary suggest that before 1597, not 1599, Henslowe was earning income from the performance of plays at his playhouses, not from contracting dramatists to write those plays. Thus he lists play titles only before 1597. Prior to that time he was apparently advancing companies the money to buy plays for their sole use and profit. Henslowe apparently first inventoried the plays he had purchased in his *'Note of all suche bookes as belong to the Stocke, and such as I have bought since 3d of March 1598'* with twenty-nine play titles listed.[22] Judging from entries in the Diary for some of these titles, Henslowe wrote out this list some months after 3 March, and thus after 25 March when the new year traditionally started. Hence this list dates from 1598, not 1599, and appears to suggest that he only began buying plays himself, on his own behalf or for others, from 1597. In fact, the first record in the Diary of direct dealing with dramatists occurs on 23 December 1597, when he advanced Ben Jonson 20 shillings (£1) for a play 'he was to writte for vs before crysmas next'.

From 1597, then, in addition to Jonson, Henslowe contracted Antony Munday, Thomas Dekker, Henry Chettle, George Chapman, Thomas Heywood, John Marston, Thomas Middleton, John Webster, Michael Drayton, Samuel Rowley, William Bird, Nathan Field, Philip Massinger and Robert Daborne, among many others, to write new plays or to make 'addicians' to or 'mend' or 'alter' existing plays.[23] Henslowe's Diary shows that his payment to a dramatist or a group of collaborators for a new play in the late 1590s ranged from £5 to £7, but by the 1610s the price had risen to £20. In a 1613 letter, Daborne warns Henslowe that he could collect £25 from another company for his new play rather than the £20 Henslowe had offered,[24] although this may have been an idle threat.

The increase from £5 to £20 over fifteen years may not reflect simply the costs of inflation or of an increasingly successful theatre business but the change in status of dramatists in general. In the earlier period, plays and acting companies apparently attracted audiences; in the later, at least by 1598 when Shakespeare and other authors' names begin to appear for the first time on Quarto title pages of their plays, authors attracted audiences. Those dramatists who had become famous, popular, or, more importantly, desirable to other companies probably demanded higher fees than those who had not, hence the rise in prices in the first decade of the 1600s. In fact, the prices for at least some of the plays listed in the Diary were apparently set not by Henslowe but by dramatists; due to competition, in any given case the price may have been negotiated by the two parties, rather than following a scale fixed by Henslowe. A few pounds for a play may not seem like much, especially as Henslowe sometimes paid more for a single costume than for the text of an entire play. But at a time when schoolmasters made between £6 and £30 a year, £7 to £20 per play was indeed substantial pay.[25] New plays were especially lucrative both for company-sharers and entrepreneurs. As Knutson explains, they could double the admission fee at the opening performance, and by contractual agreement 100 per cent of the fees collected at the playhouse door went directly to the company. Henslowe and his fellow theatre entrepreneurs also benefited from a share of admission fees at the gallery.[26] Revivals of the plays brought yet further income.

An 'addician' to a revived play could consist of new scenes or simply a new prologue or epilogue for ordinary or special performances, as on 12 January 1601/2 when Dekker was paid to add a prologue and epilogue to *Pontius Pilate*. On 14 December 1602, Middleton was paid to add a prologue and epilogue to the old play *Friar Bacon and Friar Bungay* for its performance at court.[27] The job of 'mending', on the other hand, would probably require Henslowe's contractee to overhaul an entire play, working much as an adapter does, making minor and major changes throughout. Mending or altering an existing play took considerably less time and earned less remuneration, as the rate of 10 to 20 shillings seems to have been Henslowe's standard minimum payment for such piecemeal work. Whenever possible, he appears to have sought out the original authors when plays later needed revisions, including additions and mending. For example, he records a 20 shilling payment on 15 May 1602 to 'harey chettel for the mendynge of the fyrste parte of carnowlle wollsey' (i.e. *Cardinal Wolsey*), a play Henslowe commissioned from Chettle in August 1601.[28]

A shrewd businessman, Henslowe employed cheaper occasional or unknown writers, often listing them as 'yonge' in the Diary, but he more frequently used more expensive, experienced professionals. He hired dramatists to work for him on a per-play basis, but paid some significantly more to be on exclusive monthly or yearly contracts. Richard Dutton has recently argued that 'Henslowe's papers reveal no individual enjoying the special position' employed in the type of exclusive contract signed by Richard Brome with the Salisbury Court personnel in the 1630s, and 'apparently enjoyed by Shakespeare'. Dutton further emphasises that 'the Henslowe papers . . . contain no example of anyone employed on this exclusive basis'.[29] However, there are indeed at least two examples of such a contract in Henslowe's Diary and more examples in his other papers. On 28 February 1598/9, Henslowe records in the Diary his payment of 40 shillings to Henry Porter in earnest of his book of *Two Merry Women of Abingdon*. In receipt of that money, Henslowe reports that Porter 'gaue me his faythfulle promysse that I shold haue alle the boockes wch he writte ether him sellfe or wth any other'.[30] Four years later, another such 'band', or bond, stipulates that Chettle will write for Alleyn's company. Henslowe records the sealing of this bond on 25 March 1601/2.[31] Although exclusivity is not noted, it may be implied, at least on Henslowe's part, here and in other notations in the Diary and his papers, especially for those dramatists like Heywood who worked for him frequently or long term. Daborne, who signed formal contracts with Henslowe, certainly saw himself as being under the exclusive hire of Henslowe. Judging from the number of plays contracted simultaneously, many authors worked for him continuously within a given period, leaving them seemingly little time to write plays for any other companies or entrepreneurs. So, Henslowe may have assumed throughout his career that the dramatists he had contracted would work for him on an exclusive basis, and in some cases formally stipulated such exclusivity in their contracts, even if they later disregarded these terms.

If Henslowe did use formal, individual contracts for dramatists before 1613 they do not appear to survive. However, such contracts may indeed be present in the Diary itself but have not been recognised as such, because scholars have drawn their conclusions from printed transcriptions of the Diary without considering the physical characteristics of the original manuscript. Examination of the entries in their original manuscript form suggests that Henslowe employed a consistent system of notation for his payments, including those made to dramatists. In the original manuscript, most of the entries in the Diary are memoranda entirely in Henslowe's handwriting which follow a simple formula, giving the name of the payee(s), whether the payment is 'in earnest' (as an advance) or in full, the date, the play purchased and the amount paid. For advances, Henslowe usually stipulates that the money has been 'lent' to the payee against the total owed, as in this seemingly typical entry in Henslowe's hand for 30 shillings:

> Lent vnto harey chettell the 2 of marche 1599
> in earnest of A Boocke called the 7 wisse } xxxs
> masters th some of ——————————

In fact, this was a second payment for *The Seven Wise Masters*. In the first payment, one day earlier, Henslowe paid 40 shillings to Chettle and his collaborators, noted in this entry, which deviates from the typical format:

> Receavd of m^r hinchlow the 1 of march to paye to
> harry chettell Thomas decker william hawton & Jhon daye } xl^s
> for a boocke calld the 7 wise m^{rs} the some of ————————
>   Wbirde

Unusually, this entry appears entirely in the hand of Bird, who frequently acted as an agent of the Admiral's Men.[32] The final payment of 50 shillings for the completed play appears in Henslowe's hand as follows:

> Lent vnto Samewell Rowly the 8 of marche 1599
> to paye vnto harey chettell & John daye in fulle } l^s
> payment for A boocke called the vij wisse masters
> the some of ——————————————

Appended to this entry is the signature of Rowley, who at this time was an established actor in the Admiral's Men; he frequently recommended, or perhaps brokered, plays to Henslowe on behalf of the company. When making final payments directly to dramatists, Henslowe usually employs the term 'paid vnto', rather than 'lent' as in the entry above. Three further entries in the hands of Henslowe or Robert Shaw list costs for staging *The Seven Wise Masters*.[33] Shaw, who was a sharer in the Admiral's Men, had also worked with Pembroke's and possibly the Chamberlain's Men, and was experienced in theatrical production. Entries that are not in Henslowe's hand are unusual in the Diary; however, in the case of this play they are in the hand of an official surrogate, such as Bird or Shaw, who appears to be acting with Henslowe's authority. Such entries, which include signatures, may not merely represent formal promissory notes for repayment of a debt but a sign that others besides Henslowe could negotiate terms of employment.[34]

Henslowe apparently allowed dramatists to make these same types of offi-

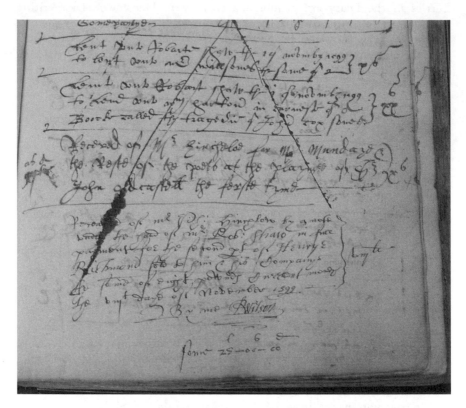

Figure 1.1 Lower portion of f. 65^r, later cancelled with an 'X', showing four entries
  in November 1599 from Philip Henslowe's Diary, Dulwich College MS
  7. The first two entries are in Henslowe's hand and the third is in actor-
  manager Samuel Rowley's hand for 10 shillings in benefit payments to
  'Mr Mundaye & the Reste of the poets at the playnge of Sr John oldcastell
  the ferste tyme' (with a marginal note of 'as A gefte' in Henslowe's
  hand). The last entry is in the hand of the dramatist Robert Wilson, who
  has demanded and received £8 from Henslowe for writing *The Second
  Part of Henry Richmond*. Reproduced by permission of the Governors of
  Dulwich College.

cial entries and negotiations. In a few cases, Henslowe writes out the entry
when contracting a dramatist but leaves blank the name of the author/payee,
and then has the author sign his name in the blank space. This type of entry
may suggest that Henslowe decided on occasion to contract a specific play,
rather than an author, finally asking the author to sign his name when hired.
However, these signatures, as well as those at the conclusion of entries that
Henslowe has written out himself, may indicate that Henslowe needed an
author's signature for particular reasons. In some cases, Henslowe has payees,
including dramatists, write the entire receipt themselves, as in this entry
entirely in the hand of the dramatist Robert Wilson (Figure 1.1):

Receaued of m^r Ph: Hinchlow by a note
vnder the hand of m^r Rob: shaw in full
payment for the second parte of Henrye
Richmond sold to him & his Companye
the somme of eight poundes Current money
the viij^t daye of November 1599
By me R Wilson[35]

viij^{li}

This type of receipt, written in the hand of the dramatist, may represent a formally agreed contract, whether for earnest money or full payment, because it appears to carry the authority of the author to negotiate terms, as in the autograph entries of Bird and Shaw for *The Seven Wise Masters*. In fact, these types of contracts may not have been written strictly at Henslowe's dictation but in the words and terms of the author of the entry, including the dramatist who wrote *The Second Part of Henry Richmond*. This type of entry in the Diary in the dramatist's hand, as well as those in Henslowe's hand subscribed with dramatists' signatures, probably offered not simply a memorandum but a legally binding contract easier to enforce in court than entries entirely in Henslowe's hand. The format of such entries may not, then, have been haphazard but systematic.

Such formal contracts may have been required or demanded by particular authors or by Henslowe or by both parties for a variety of reasons. Perhaps Henslowe used these types of contracts to accommodate his more litigious, troublesome or unreliable dramatists. However, given the apparently large rise in extant records of lawsuits from the early seventeenth century, aggrieved parties may have increasingly turned to the courts to resolve financial conflicts that had been resolved privately or left unresolved in the late sixteenth century. So, Henslowe may have systematically designed the unusual format of these earlier Diary entries written or signed by dramatists as formal, legally enforceable contracts which could prevent or settle potential legal disputes. In any event, these contracts suggest that the author is negotiating his terms and conditions, not simply acquiescing to those of Henslowe.

Whether the Diary entry is in Henslowe's hand or another's, it is usually noted that the commodity that the dramatist(s) will deliver is a 'book', the contemporary term routinely used by those who had commissioned, written or received manuscript documents, such as letters patent, indentures, deeds, grants, contracts or terriers. The term had the distinct and precise meaning of a complete, finished or whole text, as opposed to an informal or preliminary draft, and was used even to describe a document comprising a single sheet of paper or parchment. In this period, then, the term 'book' meant a complete, final or authorised text, irrespective of whether the format resembled one or more stitched quires or a printed book.[36] Thus the type of manuscript 'book' that Henslowe is repeatedly contracting writers to deliver to him is a finished and complete text from which the play was to be acted, not a preliminary draft that required non-authorial intervention or other emendment or amelioration.

Whether or not such a 'book' came to be the official 'book', or master copy licensed and/or used in the theatre, would depend entirely on particular circumstances or conditions. In all his business transactions, Henslowe appears to have been as economical as possible. He would almost certainly have expected or demanded to receive from his contracted dramatists 'books' that were legible and organised enough to go straight to a book-keeper for any necessary theatrical annotations and to the censor for licensing without the extra costs of paying for re-copying: that is, transcriptions. But in any given case, Henslowe's expectations or demands may not have been met. While he, for practical reasons, might have expected to receive a 'definitive' text, dramatists and actors probably knew that there would never be a 'complete', 'finished', let alone a 'definitive' text, only various versions of a text. But, at the least, the text is expected, in theory if not in practice, to be complete, finished and ready to be acted when submitted to Henslowe for final payment.

By 1613 at least, Henslowe had begun to use individual, formally written and witnessed contracts rather than implicit contracts in Diary entries, but he was not the first theatrical entrepreneur to use standard contracts to record the purchase of dramatists' labour. In 1572, two weavers and a barber-surgeon sued Rowland Broughton, whom they had contracted for two and a half years to write 'eighteen seueral plays of the only devise of the said Rowland Broughton and never before played in manner and form'. These entrepreneurs declared that they used a notary to write out a specific contract in the form of an indenture and that they planned to perform the plays themselves with boys hired to fill in the other roles. In terms of fees, the three men agreed to pay their author one-sixth of their income but would charge him the same amount in expenses, hence his salary appeared to have been a one-sixth share in the company.[37] But their project evidently failed due to Broughton's inability or unwillingness to deliver any of the plays. With such a tight writing schedule, requiring him to complete a play approximately every month to six weeks, and his payment in the form of a share, it is evident that this too was an exclusive contract. That this dispute resulted in a lawsuit suggests that, even before the rise of theatre in the next two decades, the legal and contractual bonds between author and employer were as firmly established as with any other legally defined contract of the period between seller and buyer.

Thus the contracts used by Henslowe, and later by the Salisbury Court personnel and the dramatists with whom they worked (see pp. 46–52), were not unusual, atypical or anomalous, but built on the legal conventions and practices of the age and were just as binding and sanctioned as other contracts. The obligations of the author and the rewards of the employer were indeed taken very seriously by all parties concerned. This is made clear in the case of Daborne, whose 1613 contract to write the play *Machiavel and the Devil* for Henslowe begins as a 'memorandum' in Daborne's own hand (Figure 1.2):

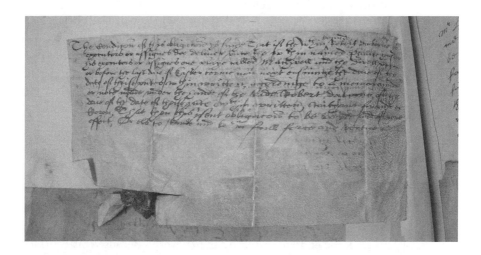

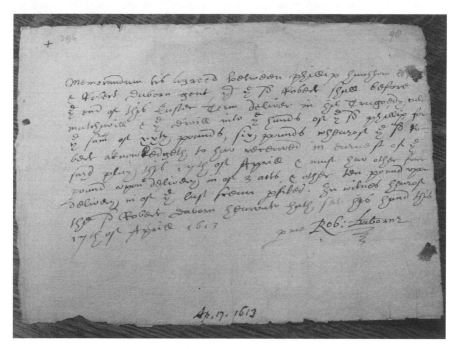

Figure 1.2 The lower portion shows Robert Daborne's 17 April 1613 memorandum which served as the basis for his formal contract to write *Machiavel and the Devil* for Philip Henslowe. The upper portion shows the English translation found on the verso of the formal contract, signed by Daborne and witnessed by the lawyer Edward Griffin, on behalf of Henslowe. Both the Latin contract and this translation appear to be in Griffin's hand. Dulwich College MS 1: Articles 70, 71. Reproduced by permission of the Governors of Dulwich College.

tis agreed between phillip hinchlow esq
& Robert Daborn gent, y^t y^e s^d [i.e. that the said] Robert shall before
y^e end of this Easter Term deliuer in his Tragoedy cald
matchivill & y^e divill into y^e hands of y^e s^d phillip for
y^e sum*m* of xx^{ty} pounds, six pounds whereof y^e s^d Ro=
bert aknowledgeth to hau receaued in earnest of y^e
sayd play this 17th of Aprill & must hau other fowr
pound vpon delivery in of 3 acts & other ten pound vpon
deliuery in of y^e last scean p*e*rfited. In witnes hearof
the s^d Robert Daborne hearvnto hath set his hand this
17th of April 1613.
           *p*er me Rob: Daborne.

Shortly afterwards, a formal Latin contract, with an English translation on the verso page, was drawn up by a lawyer based on the memorandum, and was signed by Daborne and witnessed by the lawyer.[38] Because this contract began as Daborne's own memorandum, he may have proposed in whole or part its terms and obligations.

In any event, Daborne and Henslowe 'agreed' to the terms of Daborne's employment, suggesting that the two men negotiated with each other as partners in a business enterprise, not as a servant indentured to a harsh master, as Bentley generally sees the relationship between dramatist and employer. The Daborne contract also shows the significant rise in prices for play-books. In 1598 Henslowe is advancing authors 10–40 shillings and paying a total of £5–7; in 1613 he is advancing £6, and expecting or is promised the delivery of at least three acts for a further advance of £4, and £10 for the final scene 'perfited' (i.e. perfected), making a total of £20. Such a contract suggests that at least by 1613, and probably earlier, Henslowe was asking for or demanding real collateral—sheets of paper with finished acts written on them—for further advances, rather than simply advancing money on authors' 'promysses'.

Given that Daborne was constantly in debt to him, Henslowe may have reserved his most formal and detailed contracts for his most fiscally irresponsible and unreliable dramatists, or he became increasingly concerned with potential litigation. The contract, or 'bond', also written in Latin and translated into English, likewise survives among Henslowe's papers for Daborne's play *The Owl*. Dated 10 December 1613, it reads:

The Condition of this oblyg*a*con is such that if the aboue
bounden Robert daborne shall deliuer or Cause to bee de=
liuerd one plaie fullie perfected and ended Called by the
the name of the Oule vnto the said Phillip Henchlowe
att, or vppon the tenth daye of ffebruarie next ensuinge
the date hereof w^{ch}: the said Phillip Henchlow shall ap=
prooue alone and accept of that then and from henche=

foorth this present obligacᴉon to bee voyde and of non effect
or else to remayne in full power strength and virtue.

Robert Daborne[39]

If this contract was prompted or preceded by a memorandum, it does not survive. This contract uses formal legal language, especially in the closing lines, probably because by this time Henslowe, his contractees, and the courts saw playwriting as a legally defined form of employment, subject to the same stringent requirements as other partnership deals and financial transactions. Such a contract may have been similar to Henslowe's 1602 bond with Chettle and have arisen from similar legal concerns. However, it is not certain if both buyer and seller were each furnished with his own copy of formal or informal contracts or if Henslowe always kept the sole copy. When Brome's two formal contracts were disputed in court in the 1630s his employers implied that they had kept both in their possession over the years, but either the contracts came to be mislaid or were taken without permission by Brome, and no other copies were available. As buyers, these employers, evidently including Henslowe, who retained Daborne's contracts, considered dramatists' contracts to belong to them, not to the sellers, the dramatists.

'Wheather yu purpose they shall haue the play or noe': terms and conditions

In addition to helping to standardise dramatists' specific contracts and salaries, Henslowe appears to have helped to maintain the general terms and conditions of their employment. His successor, Alleyn, almost certainly continued to use the most successful of Henslowe's business practices. Most of these conditions and practices involved financial recompense for both seller and buyer, although some sellers defaulted on their agreements. As Henslowe would usually offer the dramatist an advance at the time of contracting the play (hence his frequent use of the term 'in earnesste of'), he paid the balance when he received the completed text. For his more hard-up dramatists, he records making a number of small interim payments, always deducted from the final sum owed. However, when convinced he was on to a hot property, such as Wilson's *The Second Part of Henry Richmond*, he appears to have paid in full on the presentation of a summary of one act. But some writers seem to have approached Henslowe simply when they needed a loan, offering an unwritten play which they may not have intended to finish as collateral. The poor fiscal management of some of these dramatists, including Daborne, resulted in their financial ruin or incarceration in debtors' prison, from which Henslowe often obligingly bailed them. His expenses in doing so, for which he expected full repayment, are carefully noted in his papers.[40]

Henslowe records a number of advances to dramatists such as Ben Jonson who did not always fulfil their contractual obligations, as in this entry:

Lent vnto bengemy Johnson at the A poyntment of EAlleyn
& wm birde the 22 of June 1602
in earneste of A Boocke called Richard x^{li}
crockbacke [i.e. Crookback] & for new adicyons for
Jeronymo th some of ————————————————— 41

Here Jonson receives a £10 advance for writing a new play about Richard III (apparently never completed, as no other record, including final payment, appears in the Diary, nor does any text of the play or record of its perform-ance survive) and for writing additions to an old play. This play is most likely *The Spanish Tragedy* (whose main character is named 'Hieronimo'), written by Thomas Kyd around 1587. If Jonson never managed to deliver this new play, Henslowe, or the company, if they had reimbursed him, lost a considerable sum in this advance for *Richard Crookback*. Yet, as Jonson had become quite successful by 1602, Henslowe may have been willing to gamble on him, even though this 'bricklayer', to use Henslowe's term, had killed Gabriel Spencer, a member of the Admiral's Men in 1598, the 'harde & heavey' news of which hurt Henslowe 'greatly'.[42] Nonetheless, Henslowe and Jonson certainly had a professional relationship after 1598; financially, if not personally, such a partnership must have suited them.

To minimise these types of financial loss, Henslowe probably learned to make interim payments to some dramatists only on production of some portion of finished work. On 23 October 1598, Henslowe paid Chapman £3 for 'his playe boocke & ij ectes of A tragedie of bengemens plotte'. This entry most probably means that Chapman has offered up one finished play ('his playe booke') and two acts of another play rewritten from an existing outline of a play ('bengemens plotte') probably written by Ben Jonson. Either Chapman has taken over Jonson's plot, perhaps that noted for the previous December, or he is collaborating with him on the play. Even if Jonson did not deliver *Richard Crookback* or the other play he had already plotted, other dramatists routinely fulfilled their contracted duties. On 5 May 1602, for example, Henslowe enters a £5 payment to Munday and Dekker in 'earnest of a Booke called Jeffae' (i.e. *Jephthah*). Although the text of this play does not survive, the large sum paid suggests that it had already been completed at this time. Sometime between 16 and 18 May, Henslowe spent 20 shillings, 'layd owt for the company when they Read the playe of Jeffa for wine at the tavern'. In the next few weeks, Henslowe also spent several pounds for costumes and properties for the play, and on 4 August he paid Edmund Tilney, Master of the Revels, in arrears for the play's licensing in the previous month.[43]

Henslowe's contracts with Robert Daborne allowed him two months to finish *The Owl* and more than eight months to finish *Machiavel and the Devil*. Daborne's correspondence suggests that he set great store on the latter play, frequently referring to it as his 'Tragoedy', thus probably allowing himself extra time to write it. But the composition of a play could take not much more than a week. The publisher of Beaumont's *The Knight of the Burning Pestle* (printed 1613, but written at least two years earlier) claims that the play was written in 'eight daies'; perhaps over-hasty composition was one of the reasons it was 'rejected' by its audience.[44] Jonson used the Prologue to boast of completing *Volpone* (1606) in a mere five weeks '*in his owne hand without a* Co-adiutor / Nouice, Iorney-man *or* Tutor'. However, in 1602 in *Poetaster*, he had his character Envy, based on his rival John Marston,[45] admit to burning with jealousy for the 'fifteen weeks' necessary for Jonson to write the play, so Jonson's speed of composition obviously varied, if his own accounts are trustworthy. Henslowe's records similarly vary enormously in terms of time allotted for completing a play. For example, on 11 April 1598 Richard Hathaway signed a receipt for 20 shillings 'in earnesst of abooke cald the Lyfe of Artur king of England to be deliuered one [i.e. on] Thursday next following after the date hereof'.[46] Most of Henslowe's other contractees required more than two weeks to finish a new play. Dramatists most likely set their own deadlines for completion dates, frequently, if not usually, based on how quickly they needed final payment.

In addition to their fees for completing a new play, company dramatists could receive a bonus from their acting company of a day's profits from a 'benefit' performance of each play written, a practice apparently established by at least 1601. Authors also received free admission to performances of their plays, a perquisite that apparently at least Fletcher took up (see p. 63). Benefit profits could range from 10 shillings in 1601 to several pounds by the 1630s. In a letter to Henslowe dated 3 August 1613, Daborne discusses receiving the 'overplus' of the second day's performance of one of his plays.[47] Henslowe also records a 'gefte' to Munday '& the Reste of the poets', Drayton, Wilson and Hathaway, of 10 shillings 'at the playnge of Sr John oldcastell the ferste tyme'.[48] After Henslowe's death, when Alleyn has taken over the theatrical businesses, Alleyn records a payment to Charles Massey on 19 November 1621 for 5 shillings 'att his playe', perhaps for a new play or a revival of one of the two contracted by Henslowe in 1602 and 1603.[49] If this amount seems small for the period, Alleyn may have felt that he had gifted Massey enough in other ways.[50]

Not all dramatists were worthy of a reward from Henslowe or Alleyn, for some apparently did not honour explicit or implicit contracts to sell a particular play exclusively to one company. An anonymous satirist (probably a dramatist) chastised Robert Greene in 1592 for 'conny [i.e. cony or rabbit]-catching'; that is, double-dealing. The author indignantly demanded: 'Aske the Queens Players, if you sold them not Orlando Furioso for twenty Nobles [about £6 13s], and when they were in the country, sold the same play to the Lord Admirals men for as much more.' The cony-catcher's response seems to have been that 'there was no more faith to be held with players than with them that valued faith at the price of a feather', as players 'regarded their authors not by desert but by necessity of time'.[51] Henslowe's records certainly suggest that he valued his commodities at more than the price of a feather. He notes only one 1592 performance of *Orlando Furioso* by Lord Strange's Men, although it may have been performed at other times (the 'part', or script, for the title role in Greene's or a related play, performed by Alleyn, survives at Dulwich College). On this occasion, the receipts from performance for the play totalled 16s 6d.[52] If this was the total return on his theatrical investment, Henslowe paid dearly for Greene's 'cony-catching' the play to his company and to the Queen's Men.

Of course, dramatists, including Daborne, certainly exploited the idea of competition to improve their financial terms. On 29 October 1613, Daborne demands to know of Henslowe about one of his contracted plays 'ye determination for the company wheather y^u purpose they shall haue the play or noe, they rale vpon me I hear bycause the Kingsmen hau giuen out they shall hau it'. Daborne apologises for this rumour, assuring Henslowe, 'if y^u please I will make y^u full amends for theare wrong to y^u in my last play before they get this for I know it is this play must doe them good if y^u purpose any to them'.[53] Daborne almost certainly was cony-catching, and not for the first time, setting the King's Men against the company, probably the Lady Elizabeth's Men, for which Henslowe was commissioning plays.

'Their price is eight poundes': working with dramatists

On occasion, Henslowe or Alleyn purchased second-hand play-books from an actor or company-sharer. For example, on 3 January 1588/9, Alleyn bought out Richard Jones's theatrical property, including 'playe Book*es*', but the titles or authors are not listed.[54] At least three other entries suggest that Henslowe purchased used play-books from actors, including Alleyn.[55] However, when buying new plays, Henslowe's standard form of entry is to list the play's title and author, only rarely omitting the name of author. Bentley cites a few cases when play-books were resold without the author's participation to emphasise 'the playwright's lack of control over his own compositions'. Bentley also takes as valid a widow's assertion in 1635 that her actor-husband left her 'things of small value', including four play-books and some household items. As the widow's comments come from a legal deposition, she almost certainly displays the strategy, used by countless other defendants over the centuries, of seriously undervaluing the worth of her property in order to keep it.

Yet Bentley uses this quotation to conclude that 'far from being a sacred holograph, a dramatist's manuscript was often treated simply as another theatrical commodity'.[56] What Bentley does not recognise here is that purchases that bypassed the author were in a minority and were for *used* play-books only, bought second-hand. In fact, other lawsuits valued play-books highly.[57] It is not surprising that any commodity or goods that were resold during this or any period lacked the approval or participation of the original craftsman or seller. In this age before copyright, once an author received final payment for his work he usually lost any further *financial* claim to it, so that a play belonged to whoever had purchased it. This purchaser was free to resell it to another company or agent, or a printer, without consulting the original author(s) or paying compensation.

As the hundreds of entries in Henslowe's papers make clear, the purchase of new play-books almost always involved the participation of authors. These authors show varying degrees of control in their negotiations with Henslowe, so his usual insistence on naming the author or authors he has paid, and, when necessary, any intermediaries who collected the money as guarantors or witnesses, was surely a business and legal necessity. At various times, Henslowe was named in lawsuits over property, leases and other financial agreements or purchases.[58] He clearly realised that he had to record his financial dealings, including debts owed and paid, as fully as possible, thereby forestalling any future claims that someone had not been paid for a material commodity such as a play. He routinely has one or more people 'witness' and sign when he pays dramatists or other personnel; on many occasions these witnesses are other dramatists or actors. To not name the authors and the merchandise they were selling, and not have payments witnessed, would have left Henslowe vulnerable to potential financial problems or lawsuits if disputes arose. Even if such notations were made primarily for business purposes between buyer and seller in Henslowe's records, the acknowledgement of the authority of the seller to negotiate the sale matches that of the buyer. Authors do not seem to be demanding that their 'holograph' be recognised as 'sacred', only commercially viable and worth compensation. It is this same authority to negotiate, as cited by Bentley above, that is transferred to sellers of a small minority of used manuscripts.

On a few occasions, Henslowe notes that he has agreed to buy a play but leaves a blank space for the title. Sometimes he adds the title later, as in mid-October 1598 when he squeezed in the title of Drayton and Dekker's play *Conan, Prince of Cornwall*, and in December 1602 and January 1602/3 when he twice added 'vnfortunat Jeneralle' to the existing title of *The French History*. Or he permanently leaves the space blank, as on 14 January 1602/3, when he advanced 40 shillings 'in earneste of A playe called   vnto harey chettell & thomas hewod'.[59] Chettle and Heywood were two of Henslowe's regular contractees, and Chettle had apparently agreed to a form of exclusive contract in 1602.[60] In the case of the unnamed play, Chettle and Heywood evidently succeeded in negotiating with Henslowe the purchase of a new play, but neither they nor Henslowe had decided on a title or thought it necessary actually to name it at the time. On 12 February and 6 March 1602/3, Heywood was paid an interim and then a final payment for *A Woman Killed with Kindness* (attributed in print solely to Heywood). So it is possible that the unnamed play on 14 January was this one, and that by 12 February Chettle had dropped out as collaborator.[61] Heywood also appears to have paid a tailor the substantial sum of £6 13s for 'A womones gowne of black velluett' (i.e. velvet) that was to be used as a costume in *A Woman Killed with Kindness*, and was reimbursed by Henslowe on 5 February.[62]

Dramatists could, then, take an extraordinary, and hands-on, role in the staging of their plays, even in purchasing costumes. They could also form personal, as well as professional, relationships with those who commissioned their plays, for on 1 September 1602 Henslowe lent Heywood 2s 6d to buy a 'payer of sylke garters',[63] perhaps from the same clothier who sold him the velvet costume.

Throughout Henslowe's Diary and his and Alleyn's contracts, correspondence, memoranda, receipts and other papers it is evident that dramatists worked closely with the acting companies for which they wrote, remaining bound to them in a variety of ways, even after completing contracted plays. For example, on 27 February 1598 Henslowe notes that he has paid Chettle £5 in full payment for his play *Troy's Revenge, with The Tragedy of Polyphemus*. However, Chettle has actually received through the intermediary Thomas Downton, a sharer in the Admiral's Men, only half this sum, 50 shillings, with the other 50 shillings retained, presumably by Downton, in order to cancel Chettle's 'deatte wch he owes vnto the company'.[64] Chettle is very frequently mentioned in the Diary as being paid in 'earnest' of a new play, either alone or as a collaborator, for a particular acting company while still finishing a previously contracted one for that or another company. Thus, he must have been on close working terms for several months if not years with these companies.

In addition, Heywood hired himself as a 'covenante searvante' to Henslowe for two years from 25 March 1598 for the nominal sum of 2 pence 'according to the statute of winshester'. In doing so, Heywood agreed 'not to playe any wher publicke a bowt london not while thes ij years to be exspired but in my howsse' (i.e. his playhouse).[65] Before this period, Heywood had written an unnamed play for Henslowe, receiving at least 30 shillings for it. During the period of his covenant-actor contract, he wrote two more plays, *War without Blows and Love without Suit* (with the last word variously listed as *Strife*), finished on 26 January 1598/9, and *Joan, as Good as my Lady*, finished a few weeks later on 12 February 1598/9. For each play Heywood was paid a total of £5 in two payments, and the exclusivity noted in his concurrent acting contract may have been assumed in the negotiations to write these plays. He did not complete any more plays for Henslowe until 1602, when he wrote several over the next year.[66] It is difficult to believe that Heywood would not have continued to maintain strong ties to the company after he had finished his acting contract and had begun writing plays for them. Many of Henslowe's contracted dramatists, like Chettle and Heywood, were still in the process of writing one play for one company after finishing another and/or being contracted to write yet another for the same or other companies associated with the same entrepreneurs or actors. In addition, actors were frequently present and signed as witnesses when Henslowe made interim or final payments to these dramatists. On occasion, dramatists witnessed Henslowe's payments to actors. These actors and dramatists are therefore working *together* in a variety of ways, and are knowledgeable about each other's specific and general duties, practices, contracts and fees, whether completed or in progress.

Thus, dramatists did not simply hand over a completed manuscript, and their authority, at the playhouse door and disappear with no further contact with the company, its actors, and the play itself. These dramatists, even if not exclusively attached to a particular company, appear to have had nearly continuous contact with the companies for which they worked, especially as many also worked or had worked as actors or in some other capacity for the same or other companies.[67] The overwhelming evidence provided by the Henslowe and Alleyn archive suggests that authors were not forced to surrender all authority in their plays once the manuscripts were presented to agents such as Henslowe or actor-sharers such as Shaw. In fact, many of these dramatists were in the process of writing new plays for a company as their previous ones were still being rehearsed. So the authors could be consulted, or could interfere, when necessary, a point made clear by Daborne, among others. In fact, acting companies frequently sought the advice of authors when casting actors in their plays and continued to turn to authors for other support during readings and rehearsal.[68]

On some occasions, as noted above, the acting company recommended authors or plays to Henslowe, thus acting as a kind of broker to their own broker, Henslowe. Robert Shaw wrote to Henslowe to recommend the play *The Second Part of Henry Richmond*, written by Robert Wilson, probably in collaboration with at least one other dramatist, for the Admiral's Men. Shaw noted, 'we haue heard their booke and lyke yt their price is eight pound*es*, wch I pray pay now to m^r wilson, according to our promysse, I would haue Come my selfe, but that I am troubled wth a scytation'. On the back of this undated letter in another hand is written the outline of five scenes, each with a list of characters, which comprise one act of the play. This hand is clearly Wilson's, for it matches the receipt for the play written entirely in his own hand in the Diary. The receipt, discussed on p. 19, records a full payment of £8 for the play on 8 November 1599 and states that he was referred to Henslowe 'by a note vnder the hand of m^r Rob: shaw'.[69]

In all likelihood, Wilson personally delivered Shaw's letter to Henslowe, on the reverse of which Wilson had already outlined the first act of his play. Wilson then received full payment rather than an advance. Shaw's intervention and recommendation were perhaps necessary, as the play appears to have cost slightly more than Henslowe's standard rate at the time. Clearly, the authors, *not* Henslowe, set the price for the play, for Shaw reported that 'their price is eight pound*es*'. That Wilson showed Henslowe only an outline of a first act does not mean that he and any collaborators had not already completed the play. Wilson had, in fact, collaborated on at least seven other plays for Henslowe, beginning in March 1598, and had also received a loan of 20 shillings in June. It is also possible that Wilson is offering here a sequel to a play already in the company's repertory, even though no play entitled *Henry Richmond* or *The First Part of Henry Richmond* appears in the

Diary or elsewhere. Henslowe must have been able to judge by that November the quality of Wilson's work, as well as his ability to fulfil his contractual obligations and repay his debts. More importantly, the company was able to judge Wilson's work; this play, and possibly others, may have been made to order, written specifically to suit the personnel who would be performing it.

Henslowe was persuaded on 4 April 1601 to purchase another collaborative play, this time on the recommendation of the actor Samuel Rowley, who had handled some of the financial transactions for *The Seven Wise Masters* one year earlier. Rowley advised Henslowe: 'I haue harde [i.e. heard] fyue shetes of a playe of the Conqueste of the Indes & I dow not doute but It wyll be a verye good playe tharefore I praye ye delyuer them fortye shyllynges In earneste of yt & take the papers Into y^r hands & on easter eue thaye promyse to make an ende of all the Reste.' Here Rowley refers to 'papers', not a 'book', which the authors read aloud to the actor; this text is not yet finished or complete. The authors were not as speedy as promised for Henslowe records payments to John Daye, Wentworth Smith and William Haughton from 11 April to 1 September for *The Conquest of the West Indies*. Henslowe eventually purchased 12 ounces of lace and other items for the costumes on 21 January 1601/2,[70] implying that the play was in performance at least eleven months after Henslowe's first advance on the basis of five sheets of paper. Here again is a play that was made to order or commissioned specifically by the actors who would perform it. Such collaboration, with the dramatists as writers and the actors as interpreters, may have occurred regularly for authors who wrote frequently for particular companies, whether or not they were formally 'attached', to use Bentley's term, to those companies.

In addition to taking possession of completed 'shetes' of unfinished plays, Henslowe was also asked to return them. In 1601, Rowley wrote to Henslowe: 'I praye ye let m^r hathwaye haue his papars agayne of the playe of John a gante & for the Repayemente of the monye back agayne he Is contente to gyue ye a byll of his hande to be payde at some cartayne tyme.'[71] Between 24 March and 16 April Henslowe had paid Richard Hathaway and William Rankins advances for writing *The Conquest of Spain by John a Gaunt*, with no final payment noted. It must have been after 16 April that Hathaway asked for the return of the pages of his share in the play's composition; presumably Rankins never finished the play by himself or with another collaborator for Henslowe, or he finished and sold it later to another entrepreneur or company. Whether Henslowe surrendered the papers willingly or under protest is not recorded, but given the sheer volume of plays he was contracting he could have afforded to cancel contracts on occasion. Evidently he could also accede to dramatists' wishes, especially when made through actors' mediation.

At least one other duty of dramatists existed after finishing the play: reading or summarising the play or its outline to the assembled company or listening to them recite it.[72] Although Henslowe does not record these readings for every play he commissioned, such practices may have been common rather than occasional for dramatists who worked closely with particular companies on a short- or long-term basis. Heywood, Chettle, Middleton, Jonson and Shakespeare, among many others, wrote with particular company actors in mind and would presumably want their reactions to new plays; this is exactly what Wilson wanted from the actors to whom he offered *The Second Part of Henry Richmond*. Jonson was also advanced 20 shillings on 3 December 1597 'vpon a Bocke wch he was to writte for vs befor crysmas next after the date hereof wch he showed the plotte vnto the company'. This advance is later cancelled and rewritten (with the same date and payment); evidently Henslowe or Jonson cancelled the first contract and then reinstated it.[73] This may be the plot later taken over by Chapman on 23 October 1598, by which time Jonson has abandoned the play. Henslowe also records payment to taverns in March 1598 'for good cheare' at the reading of *The Famous Wars of Henry I and the Prince of Wales*, collaboratively written by Drayton, Dekker, Wilson and Chettle during a period in which Henslowe had contracted them to write several other plays.[74] One or more of the collaborators, who would also finish the book of *Earl Goodwin and his Three Sons* about two weeks later, would evidently have been present at such readings. Daborne also notes in at least two letters to Henslowe that he will read his finished plays to the company for which he had been contracted.[75]

'His parte of the boocke': dramatists and collaboration

Even those dramatists known for working regularly in collaboration, such as Fletcher, who wrote a number of plays with Beaumont and other dramatists, also wrote plays alone. As Brian Vickers notes, 'every major playwright in this period worked collaboratively at some point in his career'.[76] Heywood famously claimed to have had an *'entire hand, or at least a maine finger'* in 220 plays. Heywood also explained that his plays had never been collected into a printed volume because *'many of them by shifting and change of Companies, haue been negligently lost, Others of them are still retained in the hands of some Actors, who thinke it against their peculiar profit to haue them come in Print, and a third, That it neuer was any great ambition in me, to bee in this kind Volumniously read'*.[77] If his estimate seems high (and he may have included plays by others that he revised slightly for revival, or sometime after composition, such as *Sir Thomas More*), some professional dramatists wrote between thirty and seventy plays each, either alone or in collaboration, during their careers.[78] Shakespeare is credited with thirty-eight plays, although at least one other, *Love's Labour's Won*, mentioned by both a contemporary writer and a book-seller,[79] no longer appears to survive in print or in any other form. He may have written other plays in whole or in part, possibly including the plays *Edward III* and *The London Prodigal*.

But Jonson's boast that he finished *Volpone* alone and *'without a* Co-adiutor/ Nouice, Iorney-man *or* Tutor', also suggests that at least one dramatist, and perhaps his contractors, placed collaborators into hierarchical categories. For Jonson, the main author reigned above co-adjutors (helpers or assistant writers), novices (inexperienced or probationary writers) and journeymen (writers who were newly qualified, having finished their apprenticeships). The definitions of all three positions (adapted here from the *OED*) imply that each served in subservient positions to more experienced masters, such as Jonson. As boy or junior actors were each apprenticed to senior actors, it is worth considering whether 'journeymen' and 'novices' had been or were informally apprenticed to the senior dramatists with whom they worked. Also included in Jonson's hierarchy of collaborators is the 'Tutor', which may have been his rebuke of established dramatists such as Heywood, who later mended or doctored other authors' manuscripts (including *Sir Thomas More*). Jonson was especially irritated when 'second' pens, as in *Sejanus*, later altered or emended his work without his approval.[80]

Whatever their rank, collaborators appear to have portioned off sections of the play by acts or scenes to complete alone and then found a way together or separately to join the scenes (with marginal additions of cue lines, for example) rather than sitting in the same room and composing the entire play together. Before portioning off the play, collaborators almost certainly outlined it together, as noted above in the payments to Hathaway, and in Nathan Field's letter to Henslowe. Field explains: 'Mr Dawborne and I haue spent a great deal of time in conference about this plott, w[ch] will make as beneficiall a play as hath come these seauen yeares. It is out of his loue he detained it for vs.'[81] However, Field's assurance of the high quality of the play is not the main thrust of the letter, as he offers the threat that 'M[r] Daborne may haue his request of another Companie' other than the Lady Elizabeth's Men. Field therefore requests a 'speedie answere' from Henslowe to prevent the play's sale to another acting company, most likely the King's Men. Daborne himself acknowledges that a commission to write a play alone can be renegotiated into a collaborative enterprise, for in a letter to Henslowe about *The Arraignment of London* Daborne explains that he is so pressed for time that he has asked Tourneur to complete one act.[82] In fact, dramatists seem to have chosen their own collaborators rather than accepting those forced on them by Henslowe or other entrepreneurs.

Further evidence of collaborators themselves portioning off plays into acts and scenes comes in a 1623 slander lawsuit against the play *Keep the Widow Waking*, written by Webster, Ford, Dekker and William Rowley. Dekker testified to writing 'two sheets of paper, conteyning the first Act' and 'a speech in the last Scene of the last Act'. Charles Sisson argues that Rowley and Dekker worked the plot out together, then apportioned acts to Webster and Ford, with the four collaborating only in one 'important passage at least reserved for special treatment'. However, the haste in which the authors worked 'precluded anything in the shape of close continuous collaboration' among all four.[83] Jonson may also have portioned off his collaborative plays and entertainments in the same way (see pp. 161–8). As to the charges of slander brought against him, Dekker concludes in his deposition that 'he is no wayes guilty of any crimes specified other then the making part of the sayd play wch he hopeth is no crime'.[84]

Whether or not dramatists joked that the making of a play was a 'crime', some evidently specialised in certain types of scenes, either comic or tragic. William Rowley, for example, provided the scenes of the comic subplot of *The Changeling*, leaving most of those in the tragic main plot to Middleton. Many plays show a marked difference in style or content between collaborators' shares, as in the case of *The Two Noble Kinsmen*, in which Fletcher's scenes seem less polished than Shakespeare's, while other plays are virtually seamless. It is fair to conclude that collaborators who worked together frequently were more adept at assembling their shares of scenes without noticeable differences, especially if, for example, one person wrote the tragic scenes and the other the comic ones.[85] Heywood almost certainly worked as a type of 'script-doctor', to use a modern term, at least in the case of *Sir Thomas More*, in which he was clearly patching up the inconsistencies in Munday's already completed portions of the text.

A fairly typical series of payments in Henslowe's Diary offers further evidence of collaborators working separately. In 1598, Chettle, Drayton and Dekker were collaborating with Robert Wilson on a series of plays, including *The Funeral of Richard Coeur de Lion*. For this particular play, Henslowe advanced

> 5 shillings to Wilson on 13 June;
> 5 shillings to Chettle on 14 June, and 15 shillings on 15 June;
> 15 shillings to Chettle, Wilson and Munday on 17 June;
> 25 shillings to Chettle on 21 June;
> 20 shillings to Munday on 23 June; and
> 30 shillings to Drayton on 24 June.

Also on 24 June, he paid Chettle 10 shillings for 'all his p*ar*te of boockes', probably including the fees due him for *The Funeral of Richard*, and on 26 June Henslowe paid Wilson 30 shillings 'wch is in full paymente of his p*ar*te of the bo*oc*ke' of the play.[86] In total (with the 15 shilling payment on 17 June to Chettle, Wilson and Munday divided equally), Munday earned 25 shillings, Drayton 30 shillings, Wilson 40 shillings, and Chettle 60 shillings for writing *The Funeral of Richard*. This play was probably acted at least once, judging from a shield with two lion heads recorded in the Admiral's Men's properties inventory in 1598.[87] As 20 shillings equals £1, the play cost the company £7 11s, and possibly more in the unlikely event that Henslowe made any further unrecorded payments to Munday or Drayton. The slight increments in pay to each dramatist probably mark the increment in the amount of work produced, or perhaps his status, if the hierarchy that Jonson set up in *Volpone* can be trusted. At least Wilson and Chettle appear to have worked separately in completing this play; each dramatist took full payment for his individual share, not when the entire book was completed but when each had finished his 'part' or portion. In fact, only on one occasion are three of the four collaborators paid at the same time; otherwise these records show collaborators visiting Henslowe separately and demanding and receiving pay based on individual work.

In the last years of his life, when he had ceased to use the Diary or formal contracts as records of his accounts, Henslowe has each payee, whether a dramatist or an intermediary, sign his name upon receipt of the money paid; usually this receipt is also witnessed. However, Henslowe's record-keeping seems to suggest that for each entry in the Diary, although not required to sign, the payee is present at the time of payment, and when payment is made to two or more dramatists at a time the amount received is evenly divisible by the group. The early modern age was, apparently, as egotistical as the modern, and each dramatist would have claimed his fair share of attention and, more importantly, money for his work.

Shakespeare's name is not mentioned in the Diary, probably because he was on an exclusive contract with the Chamberlain's Men by 1597, when Henslowe begins to record his contracting of dramatists. But Shakespeare apparently began and ended his career as a collaborator, writing by himself through the middle of his career. He may have begun as a 'coadjutor' or 'novice', apprenticed to such experienced Henslowe contractees as Munday, chief author of *Sir Thomas More*, on the *Henry VI* plays. Shakespeare then wrote his comedies and tragedies alone, and concluded his career as a collaborator to the apprentice or 'journeyman' John Fletcher with whom he wrote at least *Henry VIII* and *The Two Noble Kinsmen*.[88] So, how Munday and Fletcher wrote offers some insight into how Shakespeare wrote. Henslowe's entries for payments to Munday and to Fletcher, along with their various collaborators, including Chettle, Beaumont and Massinger, help to suggest that most if not all dramatists, including Shakespeare, whether writing alone or with collaborators, worked in much the same ways, sharing the same composing and revising practices. In fact, implicit in a letter from Daborne to Henslowe about the delayed progress of his tragedy *Machiavel and the Devil* is the fact that a play would undergo revision during composition. Daborne tells Henslowe: 'I haue took extraordynary payns wth the end & alterd one other scean in the third act which they haue now in parts.'[89] Evidently he is reminding Henslowe here that he has submitted portions but not all of the play, including a scene in Act 3 which has already been copied out in parts. Even though he is desperate to finish and receive final payment, Daborne's 'extraordynary payns' in reworking the play show authors more determined to craft and perfect a play reflecting their artistic designs than quickly producing an acting text.

Henslowe is meticulous, detailed and comprehensive in his accounts and records. Yet, he does not record any payments made to a scribe (the general name for a copyist) or a scrivener (a copyist or employer of copyists usually specialising in legal documents) to recopy a new or an old play manuscript or to an author to do so. This is remarkable in a businessman who owned or commissioned hundreds of plays, at least some of which would have needed to be recopied at any given time, if only because of wear and tear or accidental damage to the manuscript. Henslowe was known to have employed secretaries and scribes, and certainly knew of the location of at least one 'scryveners shope' by 1603, as he records meeting 'm^r Pope' there to discuss the lease of a theatre.[90] Such shops were plentiful in London. Henslowe also acknowledges the mending of the actor Hugh Davies's coat 'wch was eatten wth the Rattes'.[91] Presumably, rats ate manuscripts too.

Henslowe, at least, almost certainly required dramatists, whether mending, altering or making 'addicians' to an existing play or writing a new one, to supply a legible, coherent text of the play: that is, a fair copy of their foul papers. Hence his dramatists supplied a 'book', a manuscript text complete and finished in itself, a fact that is made clear in Daborne's 1613 contractual obligation for *The Owl* to supply 'one plaie fullie perfected and ended'.[92] If authors did not usually make the fair copies themselves, sitting up late until midnight, as Daborne claims to have done in one letter to Henslowe (see p. 41), they most likely paid a scribe to do so without expecting Henslowe to pay the cost himself. Henslowe would almost certainly not have reimbursed authors for payments to scribes for fair copies, or made such payments to scribes himself, without noting the expenditures in any of his records. In other words, Henslowe apparently took no responsibility for scribal copying of any of the plays that he commissioned as new or for which he ordered altering or mending. In fact, Henslowe may have demanded that his authors supply their manuscripts in 'fullie perfected and ended' fair copy form that could eventually serve as the licensed company play-book.

'The Foule Sheet and ye fayr': Daborne and authorship

Incontrovertible evidence of the practice of supplying Henslowe fair copies, rather than foul papers, appears in a remarkable set of twenty-seven extant letters and numerous contracts, bonds and receipts written from 1613 to 1614 by Daborne to Henslowe.[93] Most of these documents contain Henslowe's autograph notes or his agent's replies subscribed at the end or on the verso, thereby offering a full account of the duties and working conditions, as well as the relationship, of early modern dramatists and their employers. In these manuscripts, Daborne confirms that Henslowe has contracted him to write at least five plays, including *Machiavel and the Devil*, *The Arraignment of London*, *The Bellman of London* (possibly, but not certainly, another title for the previous play),[94] *The Owl* and *The She Saint*. None of these plays is known to be extant in manuscript or printed form, yet all but *The She Saint* are recorded by Henslowe as having been completed.

The relationship between Daborne and Henslowe may at times have been tense but, overall, it was not antagonistic or hostile. Nor did Henslowe consider Daborne to be a hack, 'yong', or amateur dramatist contracted for a one-off or occasional play but an experienced professional contracted for several plays. Contemporary letters from the dramatist Nathan Field show that Henslowe also contracted Daborne, Field and Phillip Massinger to write a collaborative play, possibly *The Honest Man's Fortune*,[95] a later scribal manuscript of which is extant.[96] Daborne thus collaborated with professionally established dramatists who were colleagues or contemporaries of Shakespeare, Jonson, Middleton, and other important Jacobean 'playmakers', to use a contemporary term. Daborne's name does not appear in any record in the Diary itself (which records very few business dealings in these last years of Henslowe's life), so Henslowe may have kept these annotated letters as a type of substitute account-book towards the end of his career.

Daborne's own theatrical career had begun by at least 1608 when he was sued by Robert Keysar, a manager of the King's Revels Children, for a debt of £50, possibly for failing to complete contracted plays. In January 1609, Daborne and the King's Revels dramatist John Mason were charged with robbing a man in Whitefriars,[97] and it is tempting to wonder if their target was a similarly troublesome former employer or colleague. Whatever the circumstances or consequences of this charge, Daborne seemed to have suffered no lasting damage to his reputation. On 4 January 1610, he, Philip Rosseter and other experienced theatrical personnel were granted a patent 'to bring up and practice children in plays by the name of the Children of the Queen's Revels', re-formed from the previous company of that name formerly known as the Children of the Chapel.[98] By 1613 Daborne had moved from managing this boys' company, which performed at Whitefriars, to writing for an adult company, the Lady Elizabeth's Men, which had amalgamated that year with the Children of the Queen's Revels, and played at the Whitefriars, the Swan, the Rose and the Hope.[99] Henslowe became involved in Daborne's financial problems at least by that time if not earlier, for when Henslowe took over the management of the Lady Elizabeth's Men company members were in debt to him.[100] Daborne and his second wife, Frances, rented lodgings from Henslowe, at least for a period in 1613. Thus Henslowe must have been well acquainted with Daborne's personal and professional behaviour by the time they drew up their contracts.

Daborne sent Frances to visit Henslowe five hours before Henslowe died on 6 January 1616 so that she could plead for Daborne to be absolved of his outstanding debts (including the mortgage on his entire estate, which Henslowe then held). Frances Daborne also asked for the return of Daborne's papers, as 'hir husband should be undone by want of those writings yf the said Henslowe dyed'. Henslowe apparently granted both requests. She later served as a deponent when Henslowe's nephew sued Henslowe's heirs, including Alleyn, claiming that the will had been altered while Henslowe lay dying. At that time, Frances Daborne repeated her story that on his deathbed Henslowe had ordered his servant to 'goe fetch all the writings and a Bond of twenty pounds' belonging to Daborne for Frances to take away.[101]

Frances evidently removed 'writings' other than promissory notes, as the 1613–14 correspondence, some of which records still-outstanding debts, was not given to her and remained in Henslowe's possession, being eventually acquired by Alleyn and thence by Dulwich College. Perhaps among the papers Frances carried home to her husband were foul or fair copies of one or more of his contracted plays.

Daborne implies in his letters to Henslowe that they had a surrogate father and son relationship, similar to that of Henslowe and Nathan Field, who signs himself 'yor louing son' in a letter from the same period when asking 'Father Hinchlow' to bail him.[102] In fact these dramatists may have aspired to the same type of affectionate relationship that Henslowe clearly had with his son-in-law Alleyn. Henslowe responds in an indulgent and compassionate way to Daborne's many requests for money, usually supplying the cash the same day that the letter was received. But the depth of their personal relationship is not as interesting as the way in which Daborne sets out, defines and comments on the terms of his financial relationship and contractual arrangements with Henslowe, mostly in an attempt to be excused from them. Here is a documented case of Henslowe's practices with a particular dramatist, but one who collaborated at times with Henslowe's other dramatists, all of whom would most likely have been held to the same conditions and practices.

In his letters, Daborne notes that he has been paid an advance, usually £5 to £10, on his total fee of £20 per play, and often begs for a further advance of 10 to 20 shillings against the remainder of his fee. Only in the contract for *Machiavel and the Devil*, discussed on p. 22, do the two men actually stipulate that some portion of the completed text must be handed in for Daborne to collect interim advances; but the letters also suggest at various places that this is the case for other plays. For example, on 16 May 1613 Daborne tries to reassure Henslowe in a letter:

> y^u shall see one [i.e. on] Tuesday night I haue not bin Idle, I thanke god moste of my trubles ar ended. . . . I will now after munday intend y^r busines carefully y^t [i.e. that] the company shall aknowledg themselfs bound to y^u I doubt not one Tuesday night if y^u will appoynt I will meet y^u & m^r Allin & read some for I am vnwilling to read to ye generall company till all be finisht which vpon my credit shall be to play it this next Term wth y^e [error for 'you'] ffirst . . . I pray . . . ad one xx^s [i.e. 20 shillings] more to y^r mony I haue receaved which makes xi^l [i.e. £11].[103]

Daborne's statement that he will read his new play to the entire company, most probably the Lady Elizabeth's Men, supports the other evidence in Henslowe's papers that dramatists could read their newly finished plays aloud to the actors with whom they are working.

This type of interaction between author and actors suggests, once again, a strong working relationship between them. This relationship could continue after the play was completed, as the author is obviously suiting his material to the general and individual talents of the company for which he is writing. Neither Shaw's nor Rowley's letter to Henslowe about hearing parts of plays read aloud states that he or any other actors served as collaborators in the play's composition, but they probably offered some comments or criticism. Daborne's lack of willingness in this letter to read all of his play appears not to be due to his modesty but to his failure actually to have finished anything at all. He is probably gambling that within a few days he will have written enough to convince Henslowe and Alleyn that he will indeed deliver the entire play on time. But Daborne also seems driven to secure Henslowe's respect for his artistic work.

Determining the type of manuscript copy that Daborne was willing to read 'some' of to Henslowe and Alleyn is important here. In a letter dated thirteen days earlier, on 3 May 1613, Daborne had bartered a fair copy of some of his play for an advance on his payment for it. He writes:

> Mr Hinchlow I am inforced to make bold wth y^u for one 20^s more of ye x^l [i.e. £10] & one ffryday night I will deliuer in ye 3 acts fayr written & then receau ye other 40^s & if y^u please to have some papers now y^u shall but my promise shall be as good as bond to y^u & if y^u will let me haue perusall of any other book of y^{rs} I will after ffryday intend it speedyly & doubt not to giu y^u full content so wth my best remembranc I rest at y^r commaund   Rob. Daborne.[104]

Daborne promises to deliver '3 acts fayr written' to a contractor evidently demanding some proof of the completion or near-completion of the stipulated text (as is witnessed by Daborne's conciliatory comment 'if y^u please to have some papers now'). This deliberate emphasis on fair copy suggests that Henslowe would not have been satisfied with foul sheets: that is, with sheets in draft form. In addition, Daborne seems to imply that he can 'speedyly' rework an old book, plot or story into a new play, although he also seems to be able to furnish entirely new plays. In succeeding letters, Daborne continues to promise Henslowe 'fair' rather than foul sheets of his new play. On 8 May, he writes:

> m^r Hinchlow my trubles drawing to some end haue forcd ~~from~~ me to be trublesom to y^u beyond my purpose bycause I would be free at any rate some papers I haue sent y^u though not so fayr written all as I could wish; I will now wholy intend to finishe my promise which though it come not wthin compass of this Term shall come vpon ye neck of this new play they ar now studyinge, my request is the x^l [i.e. £10] might be made vp whear of I haue had 9^l [i.e. £9] if y^u please to appoynt any horer [i.e. hour] to read to m^r Allin I will not fayle, nor after this day loose any time till it be concluded.[105]

Similarly, on 5 June Daborne writes:

> Mr Hinchlow, the company told me y^u wear expected thear yesterday to
> conclude about thear com*m*ing ouer or goinge to Oxford, I haue not
> only labord my own play which shall be ready before they come ouer
> but giue Cyrill Tourner an act of ye Arreignment of London to write y^t
> we may haue y^t likewise ready for them, I wish y^u had spoken wth them
> to know thear resolution for they depend vpon y^r purpose, I hau sent y^u
> 2 sheets more fayr written vpon my ffayth s^r they shall not stay one
> howr for me.[106]

These three letters demonstrate that Henslowe has been pressuring Daborne
to deliver what has been contracted. That is, Daborne needs to deliver his
own play, *Machiavel and the Devil* (perhaps based on the *Machiavel* play
already owned by the Admiral's Men) as well as *The Arraignment of London*,
now being co-written with Tourneur.

As a money-lender, Henslowe may not have been averse to putting
Daborne into further financial debt by advancing him more and more money
against diminishing collateral, the two still-unwritten plays. However,
Henslowe is demanding a particular kind of proof of that collateral, a fair
copy of the two manuscript plays, as Daborne notes around 13 November
(Figure 1.3):

> Mr Hinchlow y^u accuse me wth the breach of promise, trew it is I promysd
> to bring y^u the last scean which y^t y^u may see finished I send y^u the foule
> sheet & ye fayr I was wrighting as y^r man can testify which if great busines
> had not preuented I had this night fynished S^r y^u meat me by ye common
> measuer of poets if I could not liu by it & be honest I would giu it ouer
> for rather then I would be vnthankful to y^u I would famish thearfor accuse
> me not till y^u haue cause if y^u pleas to p*er*form my request I shall think my
> self beholding to y^u for it hosoeuer I will not fayle to write this fayr &
> p*er*fit the book which shall not ly one y^r hands.[107]

Clearly at this point Henslowe has had enough of Daborne's procrastination
and has idly or seriously threatened to bring a suit for breach of promise
against him for his failure to deliver a fair-copied completed play. In his des-
peration, Daborne has reluctantly surrendered a foul sheet of one or more
pages. That is, Daborne was interrupted in the act of fair copying, apparently by Henslowe's agent, who showed up to collect the promised fair copy.
Daborne delivers an incomplete fair copy, but to prove that he has completed the entire scene he takes the unusual step of sending a 'sheet' from his
foul papers, presumably for the portion he has not yet had time to fair copy
but which concludes the scene. Affixed to each of the letters quoted here,
including this last one, is Henslowe's or his agent's acknowledgement that
he has indeed handed over the requested money to Daborne. Thus, when

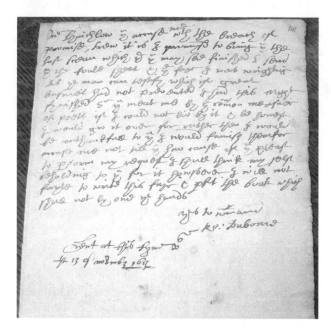

Figure 1.3 Robert Daborne's November 1613 letter to Philip Henslowe, Dulwich College MS 1: Article 89, which Daborne enclosed with 'the foule sheet & yᵉ fayr' from his unfinished play in order to prevent a breach of promise lawsuit. In response Henslowe has subscribed a receipt for a further advance of 10 shillings he 'Lent at this tyme' to the insolvent Daborne. Reproduced by permission of the Governors of Dulwich College.

pressed, Henslowe seems to have made an exception here in taking a foul-paper sheet in lieu of the stipulated and customary fair copy. However, Daborne has also promised of that foul sheet, 'I will not fayle to write this fayr & perfit the book'. He seems determined not to leave any foul sheets in Henslowe's possession and must have retrieved it from Henslowe in order to fair-copy it. Thus the foul sheet has been used as proof that the text was written and not as a substitute for fair copy.

In his complaint that Henslowe sees him in the 'common measure of poets' Daborne may be expressing his wish that he be classed with the most distinguished rather than the common poets. Or Daborne may be suggesting that Henslowe treated all his authors as common; that is, as irresponsible. Numerous entries in the Diary suggest a differing degree of treatment of his authors, with frequently employed dramatists such as Chettle and Heywood receiving special favours from time to time. But given his demonstrated generosity and indulgence in a variety of personal and professional ways to so many dramatists, it would be difficult to view Henslowe as disparaging all dramatists as 'common'. Whether Henslowe considered

Daborne common due to his procrastination and general unreliability, the delivery of fair rather than foul copy obviously seemed infinitely preferable both to contractor and contractee. In an earlier letter on 18 June, Daborne claimed to have 'sat vp last night till past 12 to write out this sheet' of a play enclosed with the letter to prove that he was doing his job.[108] This plea for sympathy suggests that this midnight labour had been required in order to produce a fair copy of his foul sheet.

Daborne's frequent promise to supply a 'perfit' or 'perfited' 'book' implies that a 'perfect' text was a fair copy, without the kinds of strikeouts, marginal additions and other revisions typical of composition in foul papers. This text could be used for licensing and in the theatre, thereby saving Henslowe the expense of having it copied by a professional scribe. By 1613, Daborne had already written one successful play, *A Christian Turn'd Turk* (published in 1612), and was not a novice dramatist. Daborne's letters suggest that dramatists and the company managers who employed or contracted them customarily distinguished between two states of a play manuscript: foul and fair. Henslowe's practices were, in this respect, undoubtedly standard in the period, and what he required of his dramatists almost certainly matched the conditions of other commissioning agents and acting companies, otherwise his business interests and revenue could be severely undercut by his competitors. At least by 1613 this distinction between 'foul' and 'fair' copy was firmly in place, with 'foul' copy as a distinct category for a play manuscript, meaning the completed authorial, working draft.

The foul paper and fair copy manuscripts of the five plays that Henslowe contracted Daborne to write do not survive. If Frances Daborne did not carry any of them away from Henslowe's deathbed, they probably perished along with other play-books owned by the Lady Elizabeth's Men or whatever company finally came to possess them. The 1612 printing of Daborne's play *A Christian Turn'd Turk* was probably set from foul papers, which, judging from his manifest disinclination to foist his foul papers on to his contractors, he had perhaps retained and supplied to the printer himself. In fact, if Daborne had sold this play to one of the companies he managed he had in effect sold it partly to himself, and thus he, and his fellow sharers, could sell it directly to the printer. A scribal fair copy of *The Poor Man's Comfort*, probably copied at one or two removes from Daborne's foul papers,[109] is extant. Daborne may have composed the play by 1614 or 1615, if not as early as 1610,[110] but at least before 1618, by which time, in a significant change of career, he had taken up holy orders, rising successfully to a number of ecclesiastical positions in Ireland.[111]

'Imployd only for yu': some conclusions about Henslowe and dramatists

Daborne's letters, as well as Henslowe and Alleyn's other papers, offer invaluable insight into the contracted role of early modern dramatists. To begin with, authors worked closely with the acting company during a play's composition; in fact, Daborne seems to be using members of the company as the mediators in his disputes with Henslowe. Daborne was also expected to read some or all of his play aloud to the 'general company', but negotiates instead to read what he has finished to Henslowe and Alleyn. Daborne is also familiar enough with the company's affairs to promise that although his play is not finished it will be done 'vpon ye neck of this new play they ar now studyinge'. That is, it will be finished closely following the new play currently being rehearsed, portions of which he may have heard the actors 'studyinge'. Obviously Daborne was aware at this time of the daily routines and future plans of the actors, including their scheduled tour in Oxford. This is not surprising, given that among its members are adult actors who had performed as boys with the Children of the Queen's Revels under Daborne's co-management. He seems particularly unwilling to surrender his authority to the company by dropping off his manuscripts at the stage door and departing to go home to write more scripts in isolation, nor do the actors or managers seem to be expecting or demanding that he do so. In fact, his command of company gossip places him in an even stronger position to tailor his forthcoming texts to suit them.

In a postscript to a letter, Daborne tries to negotiate for pay equal to that of 'm^r messenger' (i.e. Massinger), as well as further advances on this payment. Daborne then advises Henslowe, 'I pray s^r let y^r boy giu order this night to the stage keep [i.e. manager] to set up bills ag^st [i.e. for] munday for Eastward hoe & one [i.e. on] wendsday the new play.'[112] This suggestion may simply be Daborne's way of saying that his new play will be ready for Wednesday, and thus Henslowe's servant can immediately post playbills advertising *Eastward Ho!*, a revived play by other authors, for Monday. However, Daborne's advice about advertising both plays suggests a far wider authorial interest in the company's affairs than has been generally argued. Indeed, this concern would have been second nature to a man who had previously co-managed one or more companies. If Daborne's role is typical for a short-term dramatist, hired to deliver five plays in one year, it would be crucial for a long-term dramatist, such as Heywood, who was attached to Henslowe's companies for several years and collaborated with other long-term dramatists such as Chettle, Drayton and Dekker.

These authors are also on close personal and professional terms with Henslowe. Daborne notes frequently in his letters the number of times he has been to see Henslowe in person, as well as those occasions when Daborne's wife or daughter went in his place, and summarises the agreements made during those meetings. In fact, Daborne's financial dealings with Henslowe did not end in 1614, for in the following year this company manager-turned-dramatist tried to turn into a theatre entrepreneur, or, at least, a theatre landlord, in business with his former employer. S. P. Cerasano has demonstrated that Daborne engineered a 1615 project with some of his previous colleagues in the Queen's Revels Children and current colleagues in the Lady Elizabeth's Men to convert Daborne's father's property in Blackfriars into the Porter's Hall playhouse. This new space was to serve as a replacement for Whitefriars, the lease of which they had lost. Henslowe and Alleyn appeared to have been willing to help finance the project. The Queen's Revels managed to act Beaumont and Fletcher's *The Scornful Lady* at Porter's Hall, but the authorities, probably responding to complaints by local residents, closed the playhouse and had it demolished.[113] All in all, Daborne worked in a variety of positions within the theatrical industry, including acting company manager and would-be theatre proprietor in addition to dramatist. He would certainly have been aware of how the industry operated and what duties were contracted or required in any given part of it.

Dramatists also acknowledged that they could serve Henslowe's interests as well as their own. Daborne notes that Henslowe wants him to peruse his 'books' and use them as the basis for new plays. In some cases, the 'book' in question is an old play to be revived or reshaped or the prequel or sequel to the play Henslowe has contracted Daborne to write. For example, on 3 May 1613 Daborne promises Henslowe, 'if y^u will let me haue pERusall of any other book of y^{rs} I will after ffryday intend it speedyly & doubt not to giu y^u full content'. By 9 December, Daborne is again negotiating to work from an existing book, asking for a loan against a play already finished or 'vpon my other out of y^r book which I will vndertake shall make as good a play for y^r publiqe howse as euer was playd'.[114] On 31 December, Daborne also informs Henslowe that 'one [i.e. on] munday I will come to yu & appoynt for the reading the old Book & bringing in the new'.[115] Here Henslowe seemed at times to be commissioning plays on particular subjects, rather than waiting for authors to bring him possible topics or titles. In any event, the men are clearly working together to suit their individual and shared interests.

Henslowe probably insisted on exclusive contracts with his dramatists whenever possible. As was probably standard, Henslowe had bound Daborne to an exclusive contract to which Daborne only seemed to object when under financial stress. In an undated letter (probably from May or June 1613), Daborne requests yet another loan on the basis that he has forgone his salary in order to repay his debts to Henslowe: 'I pay y^u half my earnings in the play besyds my continuall labor & chardge imployd only for y^u.'[116] That such exclusivity was probably required by Henslowe and offered by Daborne seems clear here, as Daborne is chafing at what he sees as the restrictions under which he has agreed to work as a dramatist. In fact, Daborne pledges in two other letters that he will not break his 'ffayth' to Henslowe,[117] clearly using the word to mean his fidelity: that is, his agreement to write exclusively for Henslowe. Daborne admits in another letter that he sees Henslowe as his 'paymaster': that is, as his financial manager who took charge of his mortgage and other private debts.[118] Like his father, Daborne spent his life in debt to others.[119]

Henslowe and the dramatists with whom he worked could offer each other mutual respect, either generously or grudgingly. At least one of Daborne's letters was wrapped in a blank sheet of paper docketed by Henslowe with the words 'Players priuate debts'.[120] Henslowe may simply have been recycling this wrapper, but his relationship with Daborne is clearly complicated by Daborne's need to be regarded as neither a 'common poet' or hack nor a simple employee. Hence Daborne offers constant reminders to the man who truly holds his purse strings that he would rather 'famish' and would 'forbear a play'—that is, give over playwriting—unless he can make the 'best'.[121] To please Henslowe is one of Daborne's intentions, assuring him at one point, 'S^r if y^u doe not like this play when it is read y^u shall hau the other which shall be finished wth all expedition.' However, to impress Henslowe and himself is Daborne's chief concern, for this offer concludes with the promise, 'for befor god this is a good one & will giu y^u content'.[122] To write a good play, 'as good a play for y^r publiqe howse as euer was playd', that will impress all audiences, including theatre entrepreneurs and actors, becomes the focus and principal ambition of the professional dramatists of the early modern age. That such a desire was worth documenting seems apparent from the fact that Daborne's letters and the rest of the Henslowe and Alleyn material at Dulwich College probably constituted the first English archive for dramatic manuscripts and other materials directly relating to early modern stage performance and production. This archive was further expanded by William Cartwright the younger,[123] whose father William not only acted with Alleyn, financed by Henslowe, in the Admiral's Men in the early 1600s, but profited in the 1610s and 1620s from Alleyn's theatrical investments.[124] Evidently, Daborne was not the only grateful recipient of Henslowe and Alleyn's professional negotiating skills.

2 'You give them authority to play'
Dramatists and authority

Early modern dramatists negotiated their working conditions and contracts, including obligations, duties and fees, and their 'art and industry'—that is, their artistic concerns, needs, requirements and desires—in order to write a 'good' play. Together with Henslowe's and Alleyn's papers, contemporary playhouse and performance documents, bills, memoirs and texts of plays in manuscript or print give authors a voice, sometimes at their own insistence and sometimes by accident. Either way, dramatists speak loudly. If dramatists did not demand or receive full authority over their conditions and texts, they seem to have expected or to have claimed whatever authority they could, subject to negotiation.

'Artickles of Agreem": Richard Brome and the Salisbury Court Theatre

The role of dramatist within and outside an acting company and playhouse could be legally tested and determined. A lawsuit for breach of promise brought in 1640 against Richard Brome, similar to that brought in 1572 against Broughton and that threatened in 1613 by Henslowe against Daborne, offers precise information about the contractual requirements of a company dramatist. Brome acted as Jonson's servant, perhaps as early as 1614, and thus had experience with the earlier generation of dramatists, including those funded by Henslowe and Alleyn, as well as the business in which they worked. Modern scholars who have previously focused on the financial arrangements of the Brome contracts have failed to emphasise the types of authority accorded to the dramatist by both theatre owners and company managers and demanded by the dramatist himself. Nor have scholars analysed the ways in which these contracts closely resemble, or appear to be built on, the type of contract used by Henslowe at least twenty years earlier and by Broughton's employers sixty-eight years earlier.

'His best Arte and Industrye': the Salisbury Court Theatre's contracts with Brome

Two legal documents from 1640 are extant for this case. The first is a bill of complaint brought in the Court of Requests by Brome's employers, Salisbury Court Theatre owners Richard Heaton, John Robinson, Nathaniel Speed and Queen Henrietta's Men acting company members Richard Perkins, Anthony Turner, William Sherlock, John Young, John Sumpner, Edward May, Curtis Grevell, William Wilbraham, Timothy Read and William Cartwright. The second document is Brome's answer. According to the first document, these theatre owners and sharers 'imployed' Richard Brome in 1635 through a specified contract 'to write and Compose playes' for them. After much negotiation (stated as 'many Parleyes and treaties therein') the 'Artickles of Agreem[t]' stipulated that Brome was to use 'his best Arte and Industrye' (Figure 2.1) to write three plays per year for the next three years for his employers, called 'Covenantees' in the documents. However, Brome had to observe the condition that he 'should not nor would write any playe or any *parte* of a playe to anye other players or playe howse, but applie all his studdye and Endeauo[rs] theerin for the Benefitte of the said Companie of the said playehouse'. In return, Brome was to be paid 15

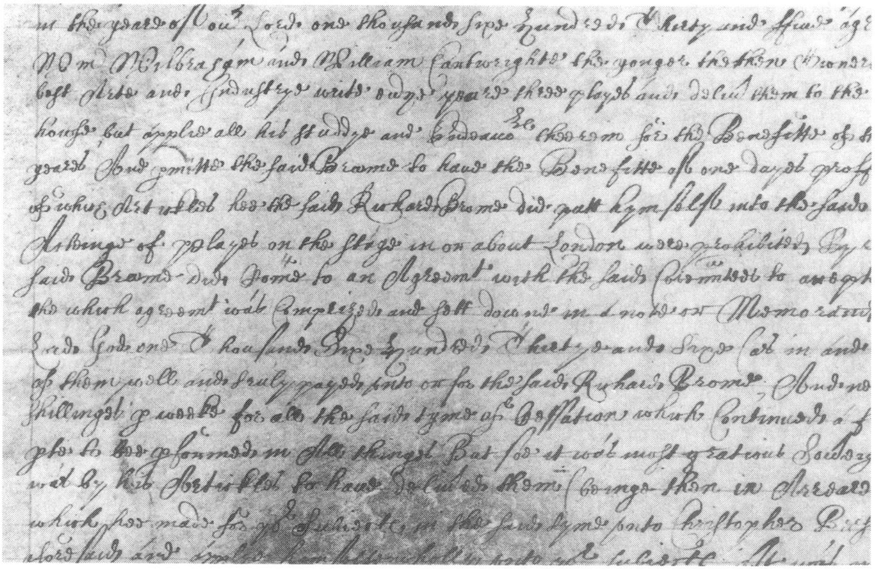

Figure 2.1 Top-left portion of the 1640 complaint, in a scribal hand, against Richard Brome, featuring his 1635 contractual pledge to use his 'best Arte and Industry', and thereby 'applie all his best studdye and Endeauo[rs]', in writing plays solely for the Salisbury Court Theatre and its acting company. National Archives Req. 2/662. Reproduced by permission of The National Archives.

shillings per week, but as outbreaks of plague frequently prohibited playing he was at one point paid £10 in lieu of lost wages.

The employers state that Brome had owed them four plays, having delivered, apparently, only five in the three years covering his first contract. He is also accused of having sold and delivered a Salisbury Court play to William Beeston and his father Christopher, the most important London theatrical figure from 1617 to 1638,[1] who worked with the leading dramatists of the age, including Heywood. In the first two decades of the seventeenth century, Christopher Beeston had performed with the Chamberlain's, Worcester's, and Queen Anne's Men, and from 1617 was the owner of the Cockpit Theatre, which had housed Prince Charles's, Lady Elizabeth's and then Queen Henrietta's Men,[2] for whom Brome wrote, as well as Beeston's Boys. Brome's 'cony-catching', to use a contemporary term, of the play to Beeston produced 'greate preiudice' for his employers at Salisbury Court.

Nevertheless, in 1638 Brome was invited to enter into a second contract for seven years with the Salisbury Court personnel, and he promised to deliver 'three newe playes of his owne Composeinge and makinge within euerye yeare of the said Seauen yeares'. He also agreed that half his salary 'shold be deteyned and kepte from him vntill hee had broughte in such playes as hee shoulde bee behinde and in Arrere with them', and that he had to deliver two plays 'that might bee studdied to bee presented vnto publique veiwe vppon the stage att the said howse' within a specified time. For each play he was to receive 50 shillings from each employer to make up the £5 he claimed he was owed from his first contract. His weekly salary was also raised to 20 shillings, and the two parties agreed to a number of other specific arrangements for payment on delivery of future plays, as well as payment from benefit performances of 'one dayes proffitte of the said seuerall newe playes'.

In return Brome agreed that he should not suffer any of these plays 'to bee printed by his Consent or knowledge priuitye or dirreccion without the Licence from the said Companie or the Maio[r] [i.e. major] parte of them'. To these and other conditions, Brome 'Condiscended vowed and promised the performance'. However, the Beestons 'tampered' with Brome by promising him friendship and higher pay. As a result, Brome refused to deliver the second of the two plays for which he was in arrears, even though he collected his salary from his employers for the next nine months, incurring for them a loss of at least £500. The 'complainants' note that the original contracts and other documents were 'casually lost & mislayed or are Come to the hands of the said Brome'.[3]

'*Best indeavors in wrighting playes for them*': Brome's contracts with the Salisbury Court Theatre

In Brome's answer to the complaint, he states that he was enticed in 1635 to leave the Red Bull Theatre acting company to join the Salisbury Court company 'vpon theire specious pretences and promises of reward and bountifull retribuc*i*on and love'. He confirms that he did 'come and write and compose and make playes for the said Comp^tsl [i.e. Complainants]', and 'upon their Inticements and Inveaglements', which 'proved very fortunate and successfull'. In fact, Brome claims that his play *The Sparagus Garden* had been worth £1,000 and upwards to the company. Brome also professes that he was 'vnwilling to undertake' his duties 'as being more than hee could well performe'. But he was persuaded by the company that they 'neither should nor would exact nor expect' from him any more plays than he 'could or should bee able well and conveyniently doe or performe'. Furthermore, the stipulated number of three plays was used only to oblige him to dedicate 'all his labour and playes totally' to the complainants. At this point in his answer, Brome again stressed that his 'best indeavo^rs in wrighting playes for them should be always accepted, and that they would expect no more from him then hee could well and conveyniently doe therin as aforesaid'.

Brome agreed to the weekly salary of 15 shillings, to be paid every Saturday, as well as 'the cleere benefitt of any one dayes playing vnto himselfe in the space of Tenn dayes after the first playing of any such play' at his own election. He then delivered two plays within nine months, having a benefit for one play only. A plague outbreak put an end to performances and to the 'first and cheefest estimac*i*on accompanyed with very great proffitts and gaynes' for this company. In addition, the promised benefit performance that was to have earned Brome at least £5 did not take place. Nevertheless, Brome set out during this 'vacancy' from playing to write the contracted plays, expecting to be paid his weekly salary, despite the prohibition against playing, but he soon learned that the company did not share this interpretation of the original contract.

Brome then states that in May 1636 he and his employers agreed to cancel his first contract. In financial distress and with a family to support, he accepted an advance of £6 from William Beeston to write one play. The Salisbury Court personnel then pressured Brome to return to them, paying off Beeston in the process, and giving Brome £10 for lost weekly wages. However, even upon bringing them a new play, Brome still found himself in arrears for his contracted salary. A further plague outbreak prevented him, once again, from being paid his weekly wages, whereupon Brome turned to William Beeston. At this point, his employers 'became suitors to Sr Henry Herbert knight Master of the Revells to here and examine the cause betweene them and the said Master of the Revells taking the trouble vpon him'. Herbert ordered the Salisbury Court personnel to pay Brome 'six shillings weekly and ffive pounds for every new play which hee should bring vntill such tyme as the sickness should cease'. However, by October 1637, when the company began to perform again, Brome claims they owed him £11 11s 6d 'or thereaboutes'. Brome stated that he had brought in six plays in the space of three years, performing as well as possible, given his 'sicknes' and other 'hinderance'.

In his 1638 contract he indeed accepted a weekly salary of 20 shillings [i.e. £1], then wrote one new play and 'another new Play written all but parte of the last sceane', yet was treated with scorn and denied payment by his employers. He admitted to being two plays in arrears, but 'hee hath made divers scenes in ould revived playes for them and many prologues and Epilogues to such playes of theires, songs, and one Introduccion'. Brome concludes that such work took up 'as much tyme and studdy as twoe ordynarie playes might take vpp in writing'. As for the play he sold to Beeston, Brome reiterated that the company had evidently retrieved the manuscript and 'acted it and by comon estimacion gott a Thousand pounds and vpwards by it'.[4]

'Bought and provided at very deare & high rates': authors and consent

As Ann Haaker noted, no documents revealing the outcome of this suit against Brome appear to be extant.[5] As in the case of any lawsuit, both the plaintiffs and the defendant saw their grievances subjectively. The Salisbury Court personnel assumed that loopholes in the contracts excused them from having to pay Brome during closures of the theatre due to plague, while Brome assumed that the same loopholes would guarantee his weekly income, regardless of the company's activities. The censor had attempted, unsuccessfully, to mediate the dispute by requiring the employers to pay Brome during plague outbreaks and requiring Brome to produce plays even though they could not yet be acted. Perhaps Broughton failed to complete the plays he was contracted to write in 1572 because, like Brome, he felt himself to be overworked and underpaid, or like Daborne, he suffered from procrastination. In any event, it is clear that Brome, Broughton and almost certainly Henslowe and Alleyn's contracted dramatists and their acting companies saw each other, as well as play-texts, as marketable commodities. However, each party assumed that an author had to use 'his best Arte and Industrye' and 'all his studdye and Endeauo[rs]', to write a play, especially as the original contract signed by Brome probably incorporated his own language here.

That authors' contracts required 'many Parleyes and treaties therein', as stated in the Brome documents and implied repeatedly in the Henslowe–Alleyn archive, suggests that even if dramatists were not engaged in financial struggles with employers, they needed to be wooed or 'enticed', to use the wording of Brome's response. At least by 1638, and probably earlier, given Henslowe's and Alleyn's records, dramatists expected to be able to negotiate their terms of employment rather than acquiesce passively in their employers' requirements or demands. What both sets of legal documents in the Brome case imply is that the owners and actors of the Salisbury Court and of the Cockpit Theatre considered Brome 'desirable' and became suitors to him, suggesting that sellers (i.e. dramatists), rather than buyers, might hold the upper hand in bargains. Thus, authors consented, rather than acceded, to agreements.

Some scholars, including Bentley, have argued that this type of exclusivity and the 'wooing' of dramatists began only from the late Jacobean age when old plays were increasingly revived and fewer new plays were required for repertory companies who increasingly worked in private theatres, attracting smaller and more discriminating audiences. Bentley assumes that at least Shakespeare, Massinger and James Shirley were tied to similarly exclusive contracts with their acting companies.[6] One contemporary anecdote claims that Shakespeare was kept on such a large retainer in his retirement by the King's Men, requiring him to produce only two plays a year, that he could comfortably spend £1,000 a year.[7] Yet, the number of dramatists on retainer or on exclusive contracts was probably much larger at least from the 1590s, given Henslowe's employment of them to write a number of plays simultaneously or in succession.

In fact, Brome's contract should not be seen as atypical, or particular to the 1630s, for he was a product of the earlier theatrical world and had worked over the years with theatre entrepreneurs and acting company managers, actors and dramatists who were also products of the earlier age. Fewer experienced dramatists may have been available for hire and thus able to profit from competition between companies in later years. However, the similarities in contractual obligations and duties of Broughton in 1572, Henslowe and Alleyn's dramatists from the 1590s to 1620s, and Brome in 1635 and 1638 show that exclusivity could financially and artistically benefit both employers and dramatists, so that each party wooed the other when necessary. Brome's contractual terms were probably built on those in the earlier contracts that had become standardised by Henslowe, Alleyn and their contemporary entrepreneurs. Several of the 'complainants' had worked for the Lady Elizabeth's Men some years after Daborne wrote for the company, and presumably his plays had remained in their repertory. One of Brome's 'complainants', Richard Perkins, had worked under Henslowe as early as 1602, and remained a close friend of Heywood.[8] Another, William Cartwright, was the son of the William Cartwright who had also worked under Henslowe and Alleyn and had shared in Alleyn's successful investments in theatres and acting companies. Henslowe and Alleyn's financial and managerial aims, methods and practices did not appear to change drastically in their later years in the profession except in becoming more expensive, and some of their strategies may have been adopted by these later entrepreneurs, including those hiring Brome.

Moreover, Brome's contracts might have been more explicit, detailed and precise because he worked not in a more rarefied but a more litigious age, when recourse was routinely sought through the courts, rather than infrequently as in 1572. In fact, Brome's employers sought redress in the Court of Requests, which from 1492 to 1642 largely handled suits relating to civil jurisdiction in poor people's matters,[9] thus offering legal redress to ordinary citizens. By 1640 this court had evidently established precedents in dealing with theatrical business partnerships, which might have been considered esoteric or unusual in earlier years. In 1572 Broughton's employers sued him by appealing to Sir Nicholas Bacon, Lord Keeper of the Great Seal, and thus most likely to the Court of Chancery, a much more formal and expensive court of equity. So it is not the case that employers routinely held the power in business dealings with dramatists in the earlier age and dramatists held the power over their employers in the later. In all these extant contracts, beginning in 1572, authors and employers 'agreed' and negotiated their terms in mutually advantageous ways, but it was apparently only in later years that the breakdown of such agreements might be more readily redressed through the courts.

Fundamental to these contracts is the author's concern that he write a 'good' play that is a product of art, study, industry and his 'best endeavours'. Such a concern would seem to have suited his employers as well. Like Henslowe's covenanted dramatists, Brome appears to have worked closely and successfully with his acting company, and even five years after his first employment with its members he seems to have known a great deal about their financial and artistic successes and failures. He did not have an antagonistic or hostile relationship with the entrepreneurs and actors until he demanded lost wages during plague outbreaks, a contractual problem that no one had anticipated, and despite these differences Brome entered into another contract with his employers. That the Salisbury Court personnel approached Herbert to mediate contractual disputes also suggests that the censor could be more familiar with the specific operations of acting companies, and employees such as dramatists, than has been heretofore assumed. Authors are therefore seen by theatre owners, actors and the censor to be working in collaboration in a variety of ways in supporting the performances of their plays.

One last crucial issue raised by the Brome case demonstrates that this collaboration continued after performance. In his 1638 contract, Brome was prohibited from allowing any of the plays written for them to be printed. That is, the plays were not 'to bee printed by his Consent or knowledge priuitye or dirreccion without the Licence from the said Companie or the Maioͬ parte of them'. Henslowe and his colleagues probably had the same concern about the printing of plays that were still active in the repertory, as on 18 March 1599/1600 when Henslowe lent Robert Shaw 40 shillings to 'geue vnto the printer to staye the printinge of patient gresell' (i.e. *Patient Griselda*).[10] Indeed, other documents acknowledge that the printing of a company's play could financially and artistically damage the company that owned it. In 1609 a complainant sued to recover play-books and other theatrical property formerly used by the Children of the Revels at Whitefriars. He demanded that 'no man of the said company shall at any time hereafter put into print, or cause to be put into print, any manner of playbook now in use or ... hereafter shall be sold vnto them upon the penalty and forfeiture of £40 sterling'. One play, the non-extant *Torrismount*, was exempted from this stipulation but was 'not to be printed by any before twelve months be fully expired'.[11] Such demands, at the cost of a £40 penalty, certainly derive from the significant loss of income anticipated from the use of the texts by other acting companies and printers.

Such financial concerns did not end in 1609. Heywood claimed as late as 1633 that some of his plays *'are still retained in the hands of some Actors, who thinke it against their peculiar profit to haue them come in Print'*.[12] On 10 June 1637, Philip Herbert, Earl of Pembroke and Montgomery, wrote to the Master and Wardens of the Stationers' Company in his capacity as Lord Chamberlain expressing the same concerns. The Earl noted that the King's Men had heretofore complained to his brother, the previous Lord Chamberlain, that 'some of the Company of Printers & Stationers had procured, published & printed diuerse of their book*es* of Comaedyes, Tragedyes Cronicle Historyes, and the like'. The King's Men stated that they had these repertory plays '(for the speciall service of his Ma^(tye) & for their owne vse) bought and provided at very deare & high rates'. The company further charged that these publications had hurt both the company and the reputation of the dramatists, for 'By meanes wherof not onely they themselues had much p^(r)iudice, but the book*es* much corruption to the iniury and disgrace of the Authors'. For this reason, the King's Men asked the Lord Chamberlain to tell the Stationers' Company 'to take notice thereof & to take Order for the stay of any further Impression of any of the Playes or Interludes of his Ma^(ties) servant^(es) w^(th)out their con=sent*es*'.

On 7 August 1641 Pembroke's successor, Robert Devereux, third Earl of Essex, also wrote to the Masters and Wardens of the Stationers' Company, appending a list of sixty-one plays belonging to the King's Men. In his letter, Essex noted 'that some Printers are about to Print & publish some of their Playes which hetherto they haue beene vsually restrained from by the Authority of the Lord Chamberlain'. Essex himself judges that the King's Men's request 'seemes both iust and reasonable, as onely tending to preserue them Masters of their proper Good*es*, which in Iustice ought not to bee made com*m*on for another mannes profitt to their disadvantage'. For this reason, he writes to the Stationers' Company to insist that 'noe Playes belonging to them bee put in Print w^(th)out their knowledge & consent', and provides the list of plays so as to prevent the acting company from being 'defrauded'.[13] At least five of these plays, *The Mayor of Queenborough* (also known as *Hengist, King of Kent*), *Bonduca*, *Beggars* (possibly *The Beggar's Bush*), *The Honest Man's Fortune* and *The Country Captain* are still extant in manuscript, and others may be extant under other titles.

The survival of so many dramatic manuscripts copied in the 1620s, 1630s and 1640s may be due partly to patrons' or clients' desires to possess the text of a play that was prohibited from being printed. Such enforcement of printing prohibitions may have become noticeably stricter under Pembroke and Devereux, who served as successive Lords Chamberlain from 1626 to 1642. However, companies sometimes had more to gain, such as a small amount of money but more prestige or publicity, from printing a play than they would lose from not printing it, such as exclusive access to the text. Acting companies probably made bargains with the printers with whom they habitually or occasionally worked, with the companies sometimes agreeing to provide an extra play or two from their repertory when they wanted a notorious or highly popular play to be printed. It is only when the acting company's exclusive right to negotiate the sale of their texts to printers is usurped that officials are asked to intervene.

'We heard their booke and lyke yt': dramatists and the playhouse

As these records make clear, government officials as well as theatre entrepreneurs and acting company personnel could be as concerned with preventing anything that contributed to 'the iniury and disgrace of the Authors' as the authors were themselves. This protection and involvement of authors could extend past the circulation and transmission of play manuscripts to other documents produced from them, including theatrical 'plots' (also called 'plats', incorporating the Old French meaning of something flat). Other contemporary comments made by dramatists, as well as audience members and patrons at public theatres or private performances at court or elsewhere, also suggest that dramatists had a lasting connection to and interest in their texts long after composition.

'Enter the prolouge': parts and plots

At least four playhouse plots survive in full: *The Dead Man's Fortune*, *The Battle of Alcazar*, *Frederick and Basilea* and *The Seven Deadly Sins, Part 2*. Three others are extant as fragments: *Fortune's Tennis*, *Troilus and Cressida* (from a collaborative play by Dekker and Chettle) and *Tamar Cam, Part 2*.[14] The title of 'plot' is a misnomer in modern terms, for although broken into acts and scenes, these plots do not provide a summary or outline of the play's scene-by-scene action for the sake of potential audience members. Instead, a plot is an in-house document providing a list of the entrance of characters and properties to be brought on stage for each scene. Plots are written on a single, unfolded sheet of paper, approximately $31\,cm \times 15\,cm$ (12 inches $\times$ 6 inches) in size, and were usually posted backstage to remind actors and prompters of upcoming entrances for each scene and properties, such as a chair or table, to be made ready. For actors who were expected to perform one or more roles in a different play every day in the course of a week or even a month, prompts indicating where to be and when could be very useful.

Strikingly, surviving plots note all character entrances, but exits are marked only when the character exits immediately after an entrance; later exits of characters who have remained on stage are not usually noted. For this reason, at least some of these plots may have been compiled from

entrance stage directions in manuscript play-texts. For example, the plot for
Dead Man's Fortune begins:

The plotte of the dead mans fortune

Enter the prolouge /

Enter laertes Eschines and vrganda

Enter pesscode to him his father

These directions could have been adjusted or expanded from the originals in
play-texts to suit the companies' particular actors or needs.[15] Some of the
plots carry actors', rather than characters', names. Richard Burbage's name
appears in the plots for *Dead Man's Fortune* and *Seven Deadly Sins*, two plays
associated with Alleyn and Henslowe in some way.[16] The name of Robert
Shaw, who convinced Henslowe to buy the collaborative play *The Second Part
of Henry Richmond*, appears in *Alcazar*.

Shaw's 1599 letter to Henslowe about *Henry Richmond*, which contains
Wilson's outline of the first act on the verso, bears a remarkable resemblance
to surviving playhouse plots. Wilson, either as sole author or major collaborator of the play, writes:

~~Enter Richard~~

~~(i se~~
1. Sce: Wm Wor: & Ansell & to them ye plowghmen
            ——————— Q. & Eliza:
2. Sce: Richard Catesbie, Louell, Rice ap Tho: Blunt, Banester
            —————
3. Sce: Ansell Dauye Denys Hen: Oxf: Courtney Bou^{r}chieR &
            Grace to them Rice ap Tho. & his Soldiors
            —————
4. Sce: Mitton Ban: his wyfe & children
~~6. Sce:~~ —————
5. Sce: K Rich: Catesb: Louell: Norf: Northumb: Percye
            ——————[17]

Each scene has been ruled off. The first, centred, stage direction for
Richard's entrance has also been deleted. In the outline of Scene 2, 'Q. &
Eliza' has been interlined with a caret (^) between 'Richard' and 'Catesbie'.
Wilson provides a list of characters without any notation of each scene's
purpose or action. Presumably, Wilson and his collaborators described the
play's action and story to the actors, perhaps because the play was already
finished, making corrections at the opening of Scene 1 and in Scene 2.
Hence Shaw could say that they had 'heard their booke and lyke yt'.

The change in Richard's entrance and the interlineation of the two character names in the second line by Wilson were perhaps simple corrections or additions made after consultation with Shaw and the other actors. The author(s) may have tried to impress the actors, but not by reciting the history of the defeat and succession of Richard III by Elizabeth I's grandfather, a story already narrated in history books and dramatised in Shakespeare's *Richard III* and possibly the non-extant *The First Part of Henry Richmond*. Instead Wilson, with or without the help of collaborators, emphasised the type and number of roles that would be available to the actors. The author(s) may then have been tailoring the story and characters specifically to suit the personnel with whom they were working, producing a custom-made play, working in much the same way as other dramatists that Henslowe contracted. If this outline was not written out in front of the actors, it was probably written out in front of Henslowe, who accepted it as collateral for the £8 he gave Wilson. In fact, this type of outline may simply be reproducing the entrance stage directions for each scene (as in other surviving playhouse plots), rather than a list of characters in each scene.

Thus, Greg's contention that there were two distinct types of plots, the author-plot (or play summary) and the theatrical-plot (or list of actor entrances) may be incorrect.[18] In fact, Henslowe may have used the word 'plot' in his Diary and other papers to denote a list of scenes and characters rather than a summary of the action. It is probably this type of plot that he accepts in exchange for interim payments to some authors, including Jonson.[19] In supplying this plot, the author is immediately contributing to the production of the play by helping the actors to cast and stage it, rather than providing them with a general outline of the play's content.[20] Henslowe and Alleyn may have expected their authors to furnish these plots, whenever possible, so that they could be posted backstage as written, or easily adjusted and then recopied by scribes. If so, dramatists were expected to participate in their plays' performance, rather than simply composing the plays. Henslowe and his contracted dramatists also occasionally note in the Diary or in their correspondence the number of acts of a particular play submitted at the time of an interim payment. These notations probably represent Henslowe's demand that the appropriate portion of the completed text, and not simply an outline, or plot, of its characters, should serve both as collateral for payment and proof of partial or finished composition of the text. Henslowe may have varied his requirements depending on the previously demonstrated reliability of the authors with whom he had worked.

One other form of document used in the playhouse survives as a reminder that dramatists' texts were financially precious. 'Parts' were actors' individual scripts, rolled into a scroll, containing only their own dialogue along with their cue lines. The only surviving 'part' extant is that belonging to Edward Alleyn, evidently for his lead role in the performance of Greene's double-dealt *Orlando Furioso* (or some other version of the play) by the Lord Strange's Men (allied at the time to the Admiral's Men). If this undated scribal document was made for the production recorded by Henslowe in February 1592, it may have been written out in late 1591 or early 1592. A collation of the 1594 first Quarto of the play with the *Orlando* part suggests that the printed text represents a much-abridged and adapted version with a reduced cast,[21] including cuts in Orlando's role. In the part, words written in Alleyn's hand appear in approximately 26 of the 530 extant lines. Although Alleyn has made about ten brief deletions, corrections or revisions in the dialogue or stage directions of the part, the rest of his changes are insertions of one or more words to fill in gaps left by the scribe.[22] Not all of these changes need have been made at the same time; they could have been made for a later or anticipated revival. Some of these added words appear to disturb the sense of the dialogue and may instead be notes or directions that Alleyn made to aid his performance. Most of the other changes seem to heighten the emotional intensity and emphasis of the lines, including such additions as 'inconstant base inurious & vntrue' and 'away w^t thes rages' during Orlando's more frenzied moments. All in all, Alleyn's corrections are minor and sporadic, made possibly in consultation with the scribe who has also made later corrections and insertions into the gaps. Thus even as a lead actor, sharer and contractor of dramatists, Alleyn did not routinely overhaul, alter, adapt or 'contaminate' the texts of parts.

No evidence exists that Greene worked closely with the Admiral's or Strange's Men at any time. However, a few of his other plays eventually came into their repertories as new or were purchased second-hand (perhaps after being similarly 'cony-caught') from other companies for revivals before or after Greene's death in September 1592.[23] If the 'Orlando' scribe had left gaps because he had difficulty reading the foul or fair copy of the play he was using as copy, as Greg posits,[24] or had left them for other reasons, he evidently hesitated in providing substitute dialogue himself. Given that the play came to Alleyn and Strange's Men after its ownership was disputed with the Queen's Men, who apparently acted the play at court on 26 December 1591,[25] it would not be surprising if Greene was not consulted if this part was written a few weeks later. In fact, in light of Greene's notoriously hostile comments about the incompetence of actors in a number of tracts, Alleyn would have had ample reason to dismiss Greene's help in preparing the play for performance in 1592. Alleyn may have purchased the play himself second-hand from the Admiral's Men,[26] thus bypassing any involvement of the author. The possibility also remains that this plot was written out for a revival after Greene's death.

It is not clear why no other parts from professional London plays survive.[27] Given their heavy use and frequent handling over the years, parts may have been more fragile, or worn out, or considered much less valuable than company books, which could be usefully consulted by the book-keeper for a variety of reasons, including prompting an actor who had forgotten his lines.[28] However, the book-keeper may not always have served as the prompter, for in any given case this role may have been taken by another member of the company. Even Shakespeare recognised the occasional use of prompters, as he had Othello proclaim, 'Were it my Qu [i.e. cue] to fight, I should haue knowne it, / Without a prompter'.[29] In any event, because of its importance, the book had to be complete and highly legible; indeed actors' parts were almost certainly copied from it. However, as noted above, once a play was in print, an acting company or printer could use it to the detriment of the rightful owners.[30] That so many play-texts were printed during periods such as the late 1590s in which particular acting companies went bankrupt or broke up suggests that the companies could, of course, have the option of selling off their stock, including parts, to printers and theatre entrepreneurs such as Henslowe. In fact, in some cases, actors or printers may have used 'parts' legitimately or illicitly to reconstruct the text of a play that was not otherwise available.

'Attending your pleasure': authors and audiences

Acting company patrons and audience members, as well as various Masters of the Revels, appear to have had a long memory of particular dramatists' creative output. Some censors or their deputies were financially involved in other aspects of the theatrical profession, including managing acting companies or leasing theatres, at the same time as they were censoring plays, so their relationships with some dramatists were noticeably twofold: employing them and censoring their texts. When George Buc (censor from 1610 to 1622) saw a scribal list of King's Men's plays that had already been licensed he noticed the play title 'The Mayor of Quinborough'. He wrote next to it 'Hengist King of Kent'. Other records suggest that Middleton composed this play around 1619 as *Hengist, King of Kent*, but it later took on the title *The Mayor of Queenborough* when it drew larger audiences for its comic subplot of an eccentric mayor than for its tragic main plot about a ruthless Anglo-Saxon king. Unless someone else drew it to his attention, Buc must have remembered the author's original title for the play from having licensed it, even after it had acquired another name in performance. In this type of non-authorial record appears the voice of the original author, as well as the preservation of his authority against injury or disgrace, long after he finished his foul papers.

In addition to the long memory of censors, audience members sometimes recorded their playgoing experiences or even copied parts of the text down during performance. Numerous extant letters, diaries and personal notebooks, or 'commonplace books', and other documents record snippets, single speeches or whole passages from a wide range of plays and audience behaviour, reaction or gossip. Significantly, these audience members included women, whose manuscripts have only recently been investigated.[31] The most notable, and contentious, theatrical summaries are those of the controversial magus and astrologer Simon Forman who recorded the plot or actions of the performances that he saw of Shakespeare's *Macbeth*, *Cymbeline* and *The*

Winter's Tale in 1611.[32] As his summary of *Macbeth* omits some of the play's most magical action, including the appearance of Hecate, some scholars have used this account, among other textual evidence, to argue that the play was revised or adapted by someone other than Shakespeare after Forman saw it.

Besides these types of audience records, various surviving documents about performance with valuable information about authorial practice include court or government papers, such as legal affidavits, depositions (as in the case of Brome and Dekker) or other manuscript documents.[33] For example, five sharers in Queen Anne's Men, including Heywood, brought a suit against another member for carrying off all the company's play-books.[34] Indeed, these types of government records provide further examples of the professional activities of Jonson, Middleton and a variety of other dramatists. For example, the patronage by James I of Shakespeare's company beginning in 1603 is duly noted in a variety of documents, some of which stipulate that he and the other King's Men sharers were allowed the great honour and appropriate livery to march in royal processions. Numerous other entries in State Papers record payments for Shakespeare, Jonson, Middleton and other colleagues for writing or performing plays or masques at court before Elizabeth I, James I, Anne or Charles I, or for other theatrical duties.[35] Performances of plays and masques at private houses for other aristocratic patrons are also recorded in extensive sets of family papers of such powerful officials as Robert Cecil, Earl of Salisbury and Secretary of State to Elizabeth I and James I, whose muniments are preserved at Hatfield House. Such papers note not just payments to particular authors such as Jonson, actors such as Nathan Field or Richard Burbage, and designers such as Inigo Jones for masques, entertainments or plays, but a close working relationship between aristocrats and theatre personnel.[36]

Documents of this kind can also imply the power of drama to entertain a grieving royal family. For example, a letter dated 19 March 1618/19 and housed in State Papers notes that, after the death of Queen Anne on 2 March, her funeral was delayed, 'to the great hindrance of our players, wch are forbidden to play so long as her body is aboue ground'. A second letter, dated 24 May, records that the first play presented at court after the funeral on 13 May, and to mark the end of this mourning period, was 'Pirracles prince of Tyre'—that is, Shakespeare's *Pericles*. The play was staged at the request of one of James's oldest and closest advisers, the Duke of Lennox, in order to entertain the French ambassador. That this poignant play about the supposed death, over-hasty funeral, and eventual rebirth of Thaisa, a beloved princess, wife and mother, was performed ten days after Anne's funeral could not have been mere coincidence. Instead it suggests that one of King James's senior courtiers, if not the King himself, found solace in the later work of Shakespeare, some of whose plays James, as patron of the acting company, had earlier seen acted at court with the author himself in the cast. At this performance, one audience member reported in astonishment that 'After 2 actes the players ceased till the french all refreshed them wth sweetmeates brought on chinay voyders [i.e. China plates] & wyne & ale in bottells, after the players begann a newe'. Apparently, it was the actors' dexterity in seamlessly rejoining their play after a long interruption, rather than the gluttony of the French, that produced this reaction.[37]

However, Jonson and Middleton, among other dramatists, pushed the limits of the monarch's and censor's indulgence. Jonson's imprisonment for *Eastward Ho!* and his reckless behaviour in writing certain other plays, as well as Middleton's arrest warrant for writing *A Game at Chess*, are duly noted in State Papers, revels accounts and similar documents. Other records include pleas from dramatists for help, support or intervention by these government officials. In the case of *Eastward Ho!* Jonson appealed to Cecil, by then Earl of Salisbury, to help him gain release from jail in 1605, where he was languishing with one of his collaborators, George Chapman. Jonson begged, 'let Mee be examined, both by all my workes past, and this present, and not trust to *Rumor*, but my Bookes ... whether I haue euer (in any thing I haue written priuate, or publique) giuen offence to a Nation, to any publique order or state, or any person of honor, or *Authority*'.[38] Despite his disgrace, Jonson continued to be patronised by Cecil, who paid him to write and perform masques and entertainments at his homes over the years, including one on 24 July 1606, 'on occasion of King [James's] and [the] King of Denmark [coming to] Theobald's', Cecil's country house.[39] Extant are eight lines of the opening of Jonson's text in his own hand which contain three revisions in Cecil's hand; in a sense the two were collaborators, and probably not for the first or last time.

Jonson also performed with his sometime employer and acting fellow, Edward Alleyn, in a 'showe' in front of King James in the library at Salisbury House in 1608. As 'rewards to the actors and deuisors of the showe', Jonson, Alleyn and Inigo Jones were each paid £20. Notably this fee is in line with what Henslowe was paying for play-texts, although it is not clear here if Jonson wrote all or some of this show and whether part of his fee was for acting in it. Also noted in these receipts are the costs of printing and binding in vellum a number of books to be distributed to the audience as gifts.[40] Jonson was paid £13 6s 8d in 1609 for writing *The Entertainment at Britain's Burse*, so presumably the £20 paid for the earlier show also included his fees as an actor. By 1621 Jonson had so redeemed his earlier censorious behaviour that he was considered suitable to judge the censorious behaviour of other theatre personnel. Hence he was granted the reversion of the office of the Master of the Revels, which he did not live to collect.[41]

Only rarely did dramatists leave autobiographical information, but in a revealing series of conversations with his friend William Drummond, Jonson discussed his career and that of his colleagues. Jonson famously bemoaned Shakespeare's command of only '*small* Latine, *and lesse* Greeke' and also faulted him for an ungrammatical line in *Julius Caesar*, not surprisingly ranking him, both as a poet and dramatist, below himself. Jonson particularly noted that 'Sheakspear in a play [*The Winter's Tale*] brought jn a number of men saying they had suffered Shipwrack jn Bohemia, wher y^r [i.e. there] is no Sea neer by some 100 miles'. Jonson confidently concluded of Shakespeare that he lacked 'Arte'.[42] Even if Jonson's sense of his own artistic ambition or status was unusual, this concern of dramatists that they display their 'art', and 'industry', was so common that it was written, most likely at Brome's request, into his contract in 1635. Jonson called Dekker and John Day 'Rogues', and also disparaged Beaumont, Marston and Middleton, among others. Jonson complained to Drummond that 'of all his Playes he never Gained 2 hundreth pounds',[43] perhaps partly because 'half of his comedies were not in print'. In fact, Jonson lost his library when his house burnt down in 1623, probably destroying what remained of any foul or fair copies of his manuscripts. But at least some of Jonson's financial failure can most likely be blamed on his inability to finish plays for which Henslowe, for one, painstakingly recorded having advanced him money 'in earnest'.

'The Poets penne turnes them to shapes': dramatists speak for themselves

Dramatists in this period particularly used the texts of their plays as well as prefaces, prologues, epilogues, poems, essays and other material to set out how they wished to be valued by their audiences and, more importantly, how they valued themselves in particular or general terms. For example, Thomas Heywood's *An Apology for Actors* (published 1612) offers a thoughtful and strongly argued rebuttal of numerous Puritan anti-theatrical tracts of the period that had depicted theatre as the work of the devil, or at least as a violation of moral principles.[44] In his own defence, Heywood claims that 'playing' has 'refined' the previously 'despised' English language and that plays 'haue made the ignorant more apprehensiue, taught the vnlearned the knowledge of many famous histories, instructed such as cannot reade in the discouery of all our *English* Chronicles'. Heywood finally proclaims that plays are written with this aim and carried by this method:

> to teach the subiects obedience to their King, to shew the people the vntimely ends of such as haue moued tumults, commotions, and insurrections, to present the*m* with the flourishing estate of such as liue in obedience, exhorting them to allegeance, dehorting them from all trayterous and fellonious stratagems.[45]

Heywood goes on to list the particular virtues of tragedy, comedy and 'morall' plays. He only discusses the role of dramatists by implication in offering his judgements about their aims in writing plays; and, rather than generally offering an apology for actors, he largely offers an apology for plays.

Heywood appears to have left the particular assessment of the theatrical

role and the cultural value of dramatists to those authors who provided
dedicatory poems to this volume. Forming a kind of induction or prologue,
these poems include Webster's 'To his beloued friend Maister Thomas
Heywood'. As Henslowe records, Webster and Heywood were contracted in
1602 to write at least two plays together: *Lady Jane* (co-written with
Chettle, Dekker and Wentworth Smith) and *Christmas Comes but Once a
Year*. The sizeable payments in each case suggest that the authors had supplied at least half of the texts of the plays at the time Henslowe made these
entries in the Diary.[46] Even if they had not worked together again in the
intervening years, Webster would certainly have known something of
Heywood's writing practices by 1612. In his dedicatory poem to *An
Apology for Actors*, Webster makes clear that he sees Heywood primarily as a
poet (a common term for dramatists, who wrote in verse) and not as an
actor, telling him:

> And well our Actors, may approue your paines,
>   For you give them authority to play;
> Euen whilst the hottest plague of enuy raignes,
>   Nor for this warrant shall they dearly pay.
>
> What a full state of Poets, haue you cited,
>   To iudge your cause? and to our equall view
> Faire Monumentall Theaters recited:
>   Whose ruines had bene ruin'd but for you.[47]

Not only does Webster insist here that the dramatist gives authority to
actors but that dramatists bring historical authority to the process of writing
plays and theatrical production in general. For Webster, performance, and
not print, establishes this authority of authors.

Webster also seems convinced that his belief is one that his culture
shares, a point further emphasised in the commendatory verses by the
astrologer and historian Arthur Hopton, rumoured to have been one of the
most learned men of the age.[48] Entitling his poem 'To them that are opposite to this worke', Hopton advises:

> Wouldst see what's loue, what's hate, what's soule excesse,
> Or woudst a Traytor in his kind expresse:
> Our Stagerites can (by the Poets pen)
> Appeare to you to be the self same men.[49]

Of course, Hopton's conclusion that it is 'the Poets pen', and not print, that
gives 'Stagerites', or actors, the power of expression and transformation was
not new in 1612. It certainly echoes Shakespeare's well-known appraisal at
least twelve years earlier in *A Midsummer Night's Dream* (first published in
1600):

The Poets eye, in a fine frenzy, rolling, doth glance
From heauen to earth, from earth to heauen. And as
Imagination bodies forth the formes of things
Vnknowne: the Poets penne turnes them to shapes,
And giues to ayery nothing, a locall habitation,
And a name.[50]

In fact, Shakespeare is one of many dramatists who used the text of a play itself to comment on the pleasures and perils of their art and industry. In the subplot of *Hengist, King of Kent*, Middleton satirises his own profession, as well as provincial performance, by bringing on the stage three thieves to impersonate actors in Act 5, Scene 1. The old play they perform for the townspeople of Kent, *The Cheater and the Clown*, 'with new additions' (l. 118),[51] is a ruse to gull the foolish mayor into playing the role of the clown and relieve him of his purse. Middleton is less than honest in having the cheated mayor complain of the revised play, 'A pox of your new additions, they spoil all the plays that ever they come in; the old way had no such roguery in't, remember' (ll. 328–30). The entire scene, complete with a Puritan who fears for his soul in being forced to watch a play as punishment for insulting the mayor, suggests that 'roguery' is not a new but a very old authorial device. Here Middleton acknowledges that dramatists can only succeed by gulling their audiences into their power.

Middleton claims in this scene that his cheater-actors 'are anything sir: comedians, pastoralists, humorists, clownists and satirists' (ll. 71–3). Here he is mocking Polonius's claim in *Hamlet* that the newly arrived players are the 'best actors in the world, either for Tragedie, Comedy, History, Pastorall, Pastorall Comicall, Historicall Pastorall, scene indeuidible or Poem vnlimited'.[52] Shakespeare uses this play, as well as *A Midsummer Night's Dream* and its inept actors Bottom and his friends, to emphasise that a dramatist was burdened with an exhaustingly large range of dramatic genres in which he was expected to write. But he also had to endure clowns who ruin the author's text by speaking 'more than is set down for them', a gibe possibly addressed to Will Kemp, the Chamberlain's Men's chief clown until 1599.[53] Evidently Webster, Shakespeare and Middleton were not alone in this view of the power of the dramatist's pen and his dislike of interfering actors who usurped his authority, or at least did not wisely use the authority he invested in them.

Some authors or their acting companies relied on title pages, as in the case of *The Duchess of Malfi*, to advertise changes made to a text in performance, perhaps not just to increase sales. But authors often more directly used prefaces or 'epistles' addressed to the readers of their printed plays to comment on, or complain about, the way texts reached them through print. Although such intervention by the author was more common, and conventional, in prose and poetry works, some dramatists also made their voices heard in this way. In an age before copyright, dramatists could watch their original work being performed or sold several times over without receiving any royalties (such as derive from modern financial arrangements). A preface or epistle might be the only place for a dramatist to state what had happened to a play after the foul or fair papers left his hands. In these prefaces, dramatists acknowledge that writing a play was considered more of a livelihood than an art form, as success was judged not by the literary quality of their play-texts but by the amount of money taken in at their performance. These concerns with the economic viability of their work only intensified when a play moved from playhouse to printing house, as literary audiences were even harder to attract than theatrical ones, and the reader was wooed more heavily than the playhouse audience. Prefaces may therefore have contained exaggerated claims about a play's original form, as did the printed plays' title pages, which were hung up in printers' and stationers' shop windows as advertisements to entice buyers.

However, these prefaces demonstrate that dramatists wanted their audiences to know the extent of their art and industry in composing and maintaining the integrity of their plays, even when subject to non-authorial intervention during performance and printing. For example, Middleton's apparently modest address to the readers of *The Roaring Girl* (1611), co-written with Dekker, begins: 'The fashion of play-making I can properly compare to nothing so naturally as the alteration in apparel.' His plea that 'the book I make no question but is fit for many of your companies' is typical of many other authors' comments. Some, including those by Jonson in *Sejanus* (1605), Heywood in *The Rape of Lucrece* (1608), Massinger in *The Roman Actor* (1629), James Shirley in *Hyde Park* (1637) and Brome in *The Antipodes* (1640), also each offer detailed information about the play's compositions or poor treatment on the stage.

Publishers and printers offered similarly protective comments about dramatists in prefatory material. These ranged from Walter Burre's lamentations that Beaumont's *The Knight of the Burning Pestle* (1613) had been 'utterly rejected' by its audience to Humphrey Moseley's warning in the 1647 Folio edition of Beaumont and Fletcher's plays about cuts made in the texts for performance.[54] Thomas Walkley offered '*commendations*' in *A King and No King* in 1619 of the authors Beaumont and Fletcher and a plea for the '*encouragement of their further labours*', even though Beaumont had died in 1616.[55] Yet Fletcher was evidently successful in later receiving this kind of encouragement and praise from his actors, at least by John Lowin and Joseph Taylor, actor-managers of the King's Men. In the printed text of *The Wild Goose Chase* (first printed in 1652 but acted at court at Christmas 1621), Lowin and Taylor tell readers: 'We wish that you may have the same kind of joy in perusing of it as we had in acting.' They also note that Fletcher's 'innate Modesty' made him suffer from '*Complacency* in his own work' and that Fletcher was '*Himself a Spectator*' at the play, which was well received by its audience.[56]

It would be fascinating to know what Fletcher made of that and other productions of his plays and whether he returned praise to the actors, or offered criticism, when working with the same groups of actors on a regular basis. A great deal of other prefatory material to printed editions of plays, including that of the 1623 First Folio of Shakespeare's works, suggests the same type of close and continuing working relationship between dramatist and actor. Shakespeare provided his own dedications to the first Quarto editions of *Venus and Adonis* (1593) and *The Rape of Lucrece* (1594). Yet, only one of his plays, *Troilus and Cressida*, contained a preface, called an 'Epistle', possibly descending wholly or partly from the author, but it was printed in an issue of the play's earliest text, the 1609 Quarto 1, without being reprinted in the 1623 Folio text. The preface claims that the play went straight from author to literary audience without ever being performed, probably a slight exaggeration to hide the fact that the play had flopped on stage.[57]

'The general scope and purpose of an author': dramatists claim authority

Jonson in particular used many of his plays to assert and defend his authority as author. Some of his comments came later in prefaces, as in *Sejanus*, that he specially wrote for the reading audiences of the printed Quarto and 1616 Folio editions of his plays. However, more remarkable are the comments in the play-texts themselves, which were recited by the 'Stagerites', to use Hopton's term, to whom the poet gave authority and expression. *Epicoene, or The Silent Woman*, written by 1610, was apparently printed then and in 1612, although no copies of these editions are extant. In his dedication of the play to his friend Sir Francis Stuart in the 1616 Folio edition, Jonson claims that *'there is not a line, or syllable in it changed from the simplicity of the first Copy'*.[58] Evidently the two Prologues to the play were presented in the same way to theatre audiences as they appear in print. In the first lines of the first Prologue (ll. 1–8), Jonson has his actor claim,

> Truth sayes, of old, the art of making plaies
> Was to content the people; & their praise
> Was to the *Poet* money, wine, and bayes.
> But in this age, a sect of writers are,
> That, onely, for particular likings care,
> And will taste nothing that is not populare.

The prologue then goes on to assure the audience that 'With such we mingle neither braines, nor brests' as this author wishes to please not the 'cookes taste, but the guests'. In the alternative Prologue, *'Occasion'd by some persons impertinent exception'*, Jonson adapts the theories of poetry proposed by Horace, and filtered through Sir Philip Sidney in *An Apology for Poetry* to contemporary dramatists. Jonson claims, 'The ends of all, who for the *Scene* doe write / Are, or should be, to profit, and delight', acknowledging that

'*Poet* neuer credit gain'd / By writing truths, but things (like truths) well fain'd' (ll. 1–2, 9–10).[59] The 'impertinent' person(s) who objected to the first version might not have been any more impressed with the slight and perhaps more impertinent revision in the second version.

Jonson's generosity of spirit in both Prologues in *Epicoene* shows a marked change from his pronouncements, heavily indebted to Horace, on authorial direction and motivation that appear throughout *Poetaster* (written in 1601), whose title refers to a bad poet-dramatist. In the play, Jonson casts classical poets as his characters and has his hero Horace, apparently based on himself, help to arraign various poetasters, including Demetrius Fannius, based on Dekker, and Crispinus, based on Marston, among a variety of others, who had satirised Jonson in their plays. Crispinus is finally forced to vomit up sheets of his own bad poetry as punishment. But Jonson mocks more than bad poets, for his play loses no opportunity to criticise bad actors, or 'stagers' as well as bad audiences, to whom Jonson also believes he makes a gift of his authority through the process of playwriting. He has the idolised character of Virgil exclaim:

> 'Tis not the wholsome sharpe Morality,
> Or modest anger of a *Satyricke* spirit,
> That hurts, or wounds the body of a State,
> But the sinister Application
> Of the malitious, ignorant, and base
> Interpreter; who will distort and straine
> The general *Scope* and purpose of an *Author*,
> To his particular and priuate spleene.[60]

Like Shakespeare, Jonson was an experienced actor, and at the first performance of *Poetaster* by the Children of the Chapel at the Middle Temple he took on the role of 'Author' in an 'apologeticall Dialogue' at the conclusion. In the Dialogue, Author stingingly berates his audience, almost certainly lawyers and law students, for failing to appreciate his general scope and purpose. He also mocks his actors for failing to make better use of the gift of authority with which he has endowed them.

Johnson's identification of characters in the play with particular men associated with the Inns of Court suggests that he was drawing on previous experiences with a regular audience. Chief among Jonson's complaints about this audience in this Dialogue is that they consider his plays to be 'mere railing' and fault him for being so slow a writer that he can 'scarce bring forth a play a year'.[61] The 'Dialogue' caused such resentment in the audience, who expressed their disapproval by throwing fruit at Jonson, either as himself or as the character Author, that it was prohibited after the first performance. As Jonson indignantly notes at the end of the 1602 Quarto first edition, it was also banned from appearing there '*by Authoritie*'. This may also be a type of authority that Jonson thinks has been usurped from him, as he sees himself as the final arbitrator of the text of his play. This antagonistic relationship between the author and his theatrical audience may not have been typical. However, it does demonstrate that the author was not always subservient to the interests of his audience or acting company but might be primarily concerned with his own artistic interests. Perhaps Brome came to share this attitude of his one-time employer, thereby inserting such a focus on his own artistic merit in his Salisbury Court contracts in the 1630s.

The generosity of spirit, typified by his belief that he is an author who suits general and not 'particular' taste, that Jonson expresses in *Epicoene* may be a form of apology for the insults he had offered about eleven years earlier in *Poetaster*. But even this apology did not extinguish his need for controlling and authorising his audience. Jonson tried too hard to force his audience to recognise and financially remunerate his extensive artistic labour, or perhaps 'his best Arte and Industrye', to quote Brome, in writing a play. On the one hand, Jonson was driven to satisfy his own narrowly defined, and apparently highly egotistical, interests, and on the other, he had to keep from alienating the very audiences that made their power known by attending or boycotting his future plays. This would have been especially important during the periods in which he was a sharer in acting companies and earned a portion of performance receipts.

Four years after *Epicoene* this conflict between what he wanted to write and what his audience wanted to hear may have led him to the drastic action of telling his audience that they must agree to a specific contract with him before they could hear his new play *Bartholomew Fair*. Only two performances of the play are recorded: a public performance at the Hope Theatre on 31 October 1614 and another before James I and his court at Whitehall Palace on 1 November, although other unrecorded performances may have taken place. As the play opens, Jonson sends the characters of the Stage-keeper, the Bookholder (or book-keeper, responsible for keeping track of the company's play-books), and the Scrivener (or scribe trained to copy legal documents) onto the stage. They appear in the Induction, a type of introduction that could explain the circumstances of a play's composition or performance. The Stagekeeper warns that 'these master-poets, they will ha' their own courses'.

But even his long tirade fails to prepare the audience for what happens next when the Bookholder and Scrivener prepare to draw up 'Articles of Agreement', the same term later used in the Brome contracts, between the author and the audience. Here Jonson presents two figures associated with manuscript production: one who supervises the writing out of theatrical books, the other who specialises in writing out legal contracts, and both are in the command of the dramatist. In contracts reminiscent of those used by Henslowe and Alleyn, as well as the Salisbury Court Theatre personnel, signed by Chettle, Daborne and Brome, and probably Jonson, among others, the author of *Bartholomew Fair* sets out the terms to which his already seated and standing audience must 'severally covenant and agree'. Among other things, Jonson promises that he will deliver a play that is 'merry, and as full of noise as sport, made to delight all, and to offend none—provided they have either the wit or the honesty to think well of themselves'. In return, the audience must sit patiently in their seats or stand for more than two and a half hours. But Jonson offers a further stipulation: he accepts as agreed that 'every person here have his or their free-will of censure, to like or dislike at their own charge; the author having now departed with his right'.

Such a contract implies that Jonson had no intention of ever 'departing' with his author's 'right'. At the least he may be mocking Henslowe, Alleyn, Burbage and anyone else with whom he ever signed a contract to write a play and who assumed he would ever surrender his rights or 'authoritie' to a finished work. In fact, the *Bartholomew Fair* contract runs to six detailed paragraphs comprising nearly one hundred lines. Jonson did not include this play in the 1616 Folio edition of his works, and although it was printed with two plays in 1631, *Bartholomew Fair* did not appear in his collected works until 1640, by which time Jonson had been dead for three years. Perhaps the play was not performed more than twice or printed in Jonson's lifetime due to its attacks on the Puritans, but the legal wrangling in the Induction may have been a more obvious source for the play's failure. Even though the Induction was easily detachable from the text of the play, Jonson would probably not have allowed the play to be performed without it. Being forced to agree to such a contract, even in a spirit of good humour, would surely have so alienated or exhausted his audience that some may have been tempted to refuse or leave the theatre rather than agree to the terms. Perhaps Jonson often felt the same way about the dramatists' contracts he had signed.

If the Induction was performed as written in front of James I, Jonson would have audaciously asserted his authority not only over the nobles at court but recklessly over his monarch. In Jonson's view, as audience members, they were all subservient to the author. He provided a separate prologue and epilogue for the court performance, and in the epilogue Jonson admits that King James alone possesses the 'power to judge' the play's success. Yet Jonson cannot resist telling him first:

> *You know the scope of* Writers, *and what store,*
> *of* leaue *is giuen them, if they take not more,*
> *And turne it into* licence, *you can tell*
> *if we haue vs'd that* leaue *you gaue vs well:*
> *Or whether wee to* rage *or* licence *breake,*
> *or be* prophane, *or make* prophane *men speake?*[62]

Evidently Jonson did not feel as compelled to restore this authority to the Hope Theatre audience as he did to James at the play's conclusion at court. Nor does Jonson seem to have been interested in restoring this authority to the owners of the Hope Theatre in 1614, Henslowe and Alleyn, his previous employers and colleagues.

Other dramatists of this period may not have insisted on such a theatrically explicit contract with their audience. Nevertheless, like Jonson they could demand or expect varying control of their texts in performance, even in simply reminding audiences, including critics and other dramatists, of their continuing presence. Massinger certainly showed his indignation after his 'labours' had been maligned by Thomas Carew in commendatory verses to William Davenant's *The Just Italian* (published 1630), a play staged at Blackfriars in direct competition with Massinger's plays at the Cockpit. A manuscript, *c.*1630, preserves evidence of this theatrical row in copies of three verses: Massinger's new Prologue to his play *The Maid of Honour* written in response to Carew's commendatory verses; a critique of this new Prologue written for Carew by an anonymous friend; and Massinger's reply. In the new Prologue, for example, Massinger admits that, as a dramatist, he knows how much 'care and vigilance' he 'owes' to any critic 'that Dares to expose his labours on ye stage'. But he cannot remain 'silent' about this 'Disgrace' and asks his audience to look upon the play and decide if it is 'compos'd of worth & hono^r'.

Evidently, Carew's friend did not come to share this assessment of the play, for in his poem to Carew he condemned the 'Mercenary hand' of the play's 'Mechanicke play=wright', who profits from the degrading behaviour of actors. The friend exclaims, 'How poore a trade is there! Were it not more/ Gentile to squire some prostitutes whore / Then bee a players Brauo?' Here the friend turns Massinger's use of 'bravo' to mean hired assassin in *The Maid of Honour* against him, but Massinger rebuts these charges in his 150-line verse 'A Charme for a Libeller'. He proudly notes that 'a Mechanique playwright' is a 'non=sence name' and argues:

> The stage, yor accademy & what yo^u learne there
> prepares yor entertainem^t: eu^{r}y where.
> Yo^u might sit dumbe & starue else. Is't in mee
> And such as write a crime to take the fee
> Due to our labours & deseru'd?

It is notable that Massinger not only defends dramatists but actors: for Massinger, actors are not just interpreters but caretakers of his work. He concludes with more stinging satire on those capable only of writing bad poems rather than good plays, finally offering his signature with this caustic address to the anonymous author: 'Conceale thy name, I feare not to be knowen'.[63] Clearly, for Massinger there is no such thing as a 'mechanical' dramatist; that is, someone who writes *without* the art and industry that Brome and his employers value in their contracts of a few years later. Nor is it a coincidence that Dekker, in a 1623 lawsuit charging him with slander,[64] and Massinger, in a 1630 attack on his character, both refute suggestions that playwriting is a 'crime', or that Massinger complains of the same type of authorial 'disgrace' as the King's Men in 1637. As Massinger is actually defending himself against another dramatist, Davenant, who may have written the anonymous verse attacking him,[65] the central focus in this personal and professional dispute is bad, rather than just any, playwriting.

Both Massinger and Davenant demonstrate that a good dramatist used his voice and authority to ensure that he was at least recognised, if he could not be appreciated, in performance. Marston had the same concerns when he informed his theatrical audience in the Prologue to *The Dutch Courtesan* (published 1605), that 'If our pen in this seeme ouer-slight, / We striue not to instruct, but to delight'.[66] As the case of Massinger's *The Maid of Honour* proves, prologues and epilogues were certainly detachable from the texts of plays and may have been replaced or cut from performance from time to time. But plays were often cut in other ways, such as when whole scenes or simply the lines of minor characters were excised. Given Henslowe's payments specifically for new prologues and epilogues to existing plays, it cannot strictly be argued that prologues, epilogues and inductions were the first parts of a text to be cut, although they may well have been replaced or updated. All of the comments by Jonson, Marston and their contemporary dramatists in their texts were made for performance and, in most cases, years before these plays came into print. It is possible that these comments and other parts of the texts were occasionally cut by actors in performance, but actors' wholesale alteration or revision of the original text could have placed them in jeopardy of defying the censor's licence of the text as written.

It is not the emergence of the dramatic author in print that gives him authority, nor is it the emergence of print that bestows dramatic or theatrical authority of any kind. It is the emergence of dramatic authors in the playhouse, in front of audiences, and the emergence and circulation of their texts in the playhouse in aural form to audiences much larger than those for print circulation that bestow dramatic or theatrical authority. Dramatists may have feared that their creations would end up serving only one purpose, as 'waste paper to wrap candles in', a worry that is repeated twice in *The Second Part of the Return from Parnassus* (printed in 1606),[67] rather than as a testament to all their study and endeavours. In many cases the authors called attention to themselves, even if they did not perform the role of 'Author' on-stage as Jonson did, in and throughout their plays. If they did not help prepare their texts for performance, authors made palpable their presence, power and authority long after they had completed their foul or fair sheets and submitted them to an intermediary such as Henslowe or directly to the acting company. Even as 'spectators' at the circulation of their texts in performance they could judge how much influence or impact their authority carried.

That potential or real authority of the author is, of course, much stronger and more insistent in a manuscript written in his own hand or in a scribal hand that bears his own alterations or annotations, rather than a text that descends into print. What extant manuscripts reveal over and over again is that most professional dramatists, despite their individual quirks, wrote in much the same way. Those who left manuscript plays wholly or partly in their own hand include Munday (*John a Kent & John a Cumber* and *Sir Thomas More*), Middleton (two manuscripts of *A Game at Chess*, as well as four other scribal manuscripts with Middleton's hand in them), Jonson (*The Masque of Queens*), Massinger (*Believe as You List*), Thomas Heywood (*The Escapes of Jupiter*, *The Captives* and *Sir Thomas More*) and Chettle and Dekker (*Sir Thomas More*). *The Captives*, at least, is a foul paper text, as perhaps are the play fragment found at Melbourne Hall and *The Entertainment at Britain's Burse* by Jonson. Manuscripts that contain a mix of foul and fair papers include *Sir Thomas More*, Heywood's *The Escapes of Jupiter* and Massinger's *Believe as You List*. Enough evidence from these dramatic manuscripts exists to see the same particular characteristics of composing authors at work.

Plays that survive in more than one manuscript or in manuscript and print can reveal even more about an author's practices. Middleton's *A Game at Chess* (1624) exists both in manuscript and in printed form produced during the author's lifetime. Particular comparisons between a manuscript and the printed text of a play indeed reveal what changes or concessions a composing author made in performance and in print to suit others' demands, including the abilities and limitations of the acting company, the censor and the printers. Even so, these authors often show stronger attention to their own artistic concerns than to others' demands. This fact is often overlooked because scholars sometimes spend more time examining variants between texts of the same play than similarities. Such similarities can strongly suggest that the author has worked hard to transmit the features of his original text, proven successful in performance, to later theatrical audiences or to readers.

Authorship, authority, and the playhouse: contexts and conclusions

By 1598, when in *Palladis Tamia* Francis Meres praised Shakespeare's authorship of a number of plays,[68] Shakespeare had already established his authority as a major dramatist. However, by the time he and Jonson had begun writing in the early 1590s, the performance of plays for money had already become an externally regulated and self-regulated industry and remained that way until the closing of the theatres. Actors, dramatists, company managers and agents and theatre owners had already established the boundaries of their professions. The act against vagrancy in 1572 had required all actors who performed for monetary gain to belong to an acting company subsidised and sponsored by an aristocrat or a member of the royal family from whom they derived their patronage and support. By the 1590s Queen Elizabeth, the Lord Admiral, Lord Strange, the Earls of Sussex and Pembroke and the Lord Chamberlain, among others, had given their names and financial sponsorship to London-based acting companies, providing entrepreneurs such as Henslowe, Alleyn, the Burbages and Christopher Beeston opportunities to build small or large businesses.

By 1594 Shakespeare's company, the Lord Chamberlain's Men, and Alleyn's company, the Lord Admiral's Men, had become the two leading adult companies. As acting companies became established in London, venues specifically designed for performance began to be built. Heretofore actors had improvised by using some already existing space such as a dining hall or courtyard or a converted inn such as the Boar's Head or the Red Lion. The first professional purpose-built outdoor playhouse, known simply as the Theatre, was erected in 1576 in Shoreditch, in the suburbs outside the City of London. Other suburban theatres later included the Curtain, the Red Bull and the Fortune. In 1599 the Theatre was dismantled and carried to the south bank of the Thames, further away from the City authorities, and used to build the Globe, of which Shakespeare shrewdly became a shareholder. Other theatres built south of the Thames include the Rose, the Swan and the Hope, providing a thriving entertainment district.

After 1600, actors also began to perform before a more select and wealthy audience at private, indoor theatres such as Blackfriars, leased by the King's Men in 1608, and Whitefriars, used by the Queen's Revels Children from at least 1610, having previously performed at Blackfriars. These private theatres also brought new innovations such as varied staging and seating as well as dimmable lighting and music before the play and between acts.[69] In addition to performing at these public outdoor or private indoor theatres, acting companies could also stage their plays at a variety of other places. These included royal palaces, private houses and stately homes, as well as on improvised stages in small towns and villages in the provinces, especially during outbreaks of plague, as in 1593–4 and 1603–4, when the London theatres were ordered to be closed to prevent spread of the disease.

Therefore, a dramatist had to consider a number of factors when composing, mending or altering a play either alone or with a collaborator. These factors included the type and quality, as well as the strengths and weaknesses, of the acting company for which he was writing. In addition to trying to suit particular roles to the particular actors available, for example, he had to judge the number of roles that could be doubled if the company needed to perform with the least number of actors. He also had to suit the characteristics and vagaries of the many possible audiences and venues for performance; Middleton, for one, was no fan of the Cockpit, claiming 'the / Poor players n'er thriued in it'.[70] Plays performed privately before monarchs at one of their palaces may have been revised in moving to or from a public theatre that had a social mix of audience members.[71] Dramatists may also have reworked plays that moved from public playhouses to the new private indoor theatres, with audiences composed mostly of prosperous law students and aristocrats. In sum, the author had to work *with* the actors, not

against them. It is not surprising, then, that some of the most prominent
and successful dramatists of the age such as Heywood, Fletcher, Dekker,
Massinger, Middleton, Jonson and Shakespeare were also actors and/or
company dramatists with an extensive range of private and public theatrical
experience. They had learned through trial and error how to please differing
types of audiences so that they would pay to return to see other plays.

Thus by the 1590s professional dramatists were usually subject to the
same established, and the most profitable, working conditions and practices:

1   they were attached short or long-term to one of the major acting com-
    panies, although they might also freelance for, or move among, other
    companies, even during periods of exclusive contract;
2   they composed plays that would suit the makeup of the company for
    which they were writing, particularly the prominent tragedians, such as
    Richard Burbage in the Chamberlain's Men and Edward Alleyn in the
    Admiral's Men, and clowns such as Richard Tarleton, Robert Armin
    and Will Kemp;
3   they composed plays that would suit their usual performance venues such
    as the Rose, Globe, Fortune, Phoenix and Salisbury Court theatres;[72]
4   they collaborated by routinely dividing and apportioning shares of a
    play among themselves rather than writing the same scenes or acts
    jointly;
5   they participated in varying ways in preparing their texts for perform-
    ance.

Dramatists also exploited their knowledge of which types of plays attracted
the largest audiences, often by using the most popular of the existing plays
owned by their acting companies or others as sources for, or predecessors to,
their own plays. The original play called *Hamlet* proved popular in the
1580s, so it should not be surprising if Shakespeare used its story or text as
the basis for his own play several years later. In addition, dramatists could
use a notorious contemporary event for inspiration, as in the case of
Chapman satirising the affair of a young heiress with three simultaneous
suitors who sued her for breach of promise in *The Old Joiner of Aldgate*, performed by the Children of St Paul's in 1603. Chapman, in fact, received a
larger than average payment of £13 6s 8d for writing the play. Not surprisingly, the satirised figures then sued Chapman and his colleagues,[73] and presumably the notoriety before and after the play was performed helped attract
audiences.

Also, companies could commission sequels, and what is now termed 'pre-
quels', to existing popular plays. For example, a company already possessing
history plays dealing with the middle part of the reign of Henry VI could
commission its company dramatists to write preceding and succeeding plays
on the first part of the reign of Henry VI and the reign of Richard III. This
is precisely what Shakespeare and his colleagues did for the Chamberlain's

Men.[74] In fact, if a single play proved popular it could also produce a sequel. Shakespeare wrote the play now known as *Henry IV, Part I* simply as *Henry IV*. It took on its later title when he was evidently prompted by its success to write *Henry IV, Part 2*. Conveniently, he could write the sequel to it in *Henry V* and then see it performed as part of a four-play cycle, beginning with his existing play *Richard II*. In fact, this cycle would in turn encourage the composition of a comedy, *The Merry Wives of Windsor*, extending the stage life of one of the main characters.

In fact, as noted in records such as Henslowe's, plays written as part of a cycle could be performed on successive days, thereby guaranteeing that an audience would return to watch the cycle continue.[75] Thus Henslowe's repertory of plays also shows a number of English history plays apparently written as sequels to earlier plays; for example, performances of the plays *Uther Pendragon* in April, May and June 1597 and 'henges' or *Hengist* in June followed the performance of the play *Vortigern* in January. At one point, *Uther Pendragon* and *Hengist* were performed nine days apart.[76] In April 1598, Henslowe paid Hathaway to write, within two weeks, *King Arthur*. As a variety of English chronicles make clear, the English monarch Vortigern was threatened by the Saxon invader Hengist and deposed by future English monarchs Aurelius and his brother Uther Pendragon, father of King Arthur. The four plays, and possibly others purchased by Henslowe, thus offered a coherent history cycle. The companies, including the Admiral's and Worcester's Men, for which Henslowe was acting as agent, banker or sharer, used the same strategy in contracting plays as those working for the Chamberlain's/King's Men. Neither was Jonson above exploiting or writing sequels or analogues to his previous comedies, hence his composition of *Every Man out of his Humour* (1599) after the success of *Every Man in his Humour* (1598). Nor was Middleton averse to writing a play based on the same story that had proved popular for another dramatist: his 1619 version of *Hengist, King of Kent* must surely have owed something to the 'henges' play noted in Henslowe's records in 1597.

In fact, it was financially sound to base new plays on existing sources, for which reason Henslowe and Alleyn, at least, each kept some type of library from which they could provide 'books', either printed or manuscript, for commissioned writers like Daborne to adapt into new plays. With or without existing source plays, Shakespeare and his collaborators and colleagues usually based English history plays and Roman plays on historical sources such as Holinshed's *Chronicles* (which furnishes the Vortigern, Hengist, Uther Pendragon and Arthur material) and Plutarch's *Lives of the Romans*. For comedies, romances and tragedies they could use literary sources such as novellas, prose pamphlets, poems, and even epic romances such as *The Faerie Queene* and *The Arcadia* (used, for example, by Shakespeare in writing *King Lear*). Thus dramatists would usually have had a complete story from which to work before they began writing, and may have worked in some cases by rewriting each scene sequentially. Or dramatists could begin by writing out an outline of a new play, sometimes reading it to the actors for their reactions, comments or approval, as Henslowe records.

Many of Shakespeare's plays printed from foul papers show errors in the early scenes and corrections in later ones (as in Quarto 1 *Love's Labour's Lost*).[77] This same feature is common in extant dramatic manuscripts, suggesting that authors wrote each scene in succession, rather than starting in the middle of the play or with the conclusion. They often changed their minds about character or plot by the end of Act 1, or even as far along as the beginning of Act 5, as in the case of Fletcher's *Bonduca* (see pp. 76–8). Sometimes dramatists went back and fixed their inconsistencies, though more often than not they, like Fletcher, did not correct their foul papers but made changes to later transcripts. Despite Jonson's boast that he completed *Volpone* in a mere five weeks, the composition of a play could take anywhere from a few weeks to several months. In addition to suiting the needs of the theatrical entrepreneurs and their actors and playhouses, these dramatists also kept a close eye on, as Jonson put it in *Poetaster*, 'the general scope and purpose of an author'—that is, their own artistic aims and desires.

3 'The fowle papers of the Authors'
Dramatists and foul papers

Whether writing alone or in collaboration, dramatists began by writing out their draft, called 'foul papers', a term now used generically and incorrectly to mean the last complete, rather than completed, draft of a play in the handwriting of the author or authors. Paul Werstine, among others, has argued that there are no extant foul-copy early modern dramatic manuscripts and attacks Greg's conception of the company book. However, as N. W. Bawcutt has persuasively demonstrated, Werstine ignores or misinterprets significant evidence in dramatic manuscripts of the period.[1] The writer who gave the title of 'Book' to the wrappers for the *Sir Thomas More* and *John a Kent and John a Cumber* manuscripts may have assumed that each text could or would be submitted to the censor, thereby coming to serve as an official licensed copy. Whether that writer also assumed that the text would be used in performance or stored for safekeeping would have depended on a variety of factors, including the practices or experiences of various theatrical personnel. What that writer, and probably the numerous others of those manuscript wrappers which are now lost, means is that the text is as complete as it needs to be at the time.

'Transcribed from the fowle papers': fair is not foul

As to what constitutes foul and fair copy, Daborne made clear in 1613 in his letter to Henslowe that he would be sending him a 'foule sheet' of the play that Daborne had not yet had time to copy. In his further correspondence with Henslowe, Daborne repeatedly uses the term 'fair' copy to indicate a more polished draft than the 'foule' one. For Henslowe and his dramatists, 'foul' and 'fair' copy denoted two different types of copy, otherwise Daborne would not have repeatedly insisted on using the two distinct terms, especially without ever defining them. This distinction between foul and fair copy may have been one he was accustomed to using during his previous years as patentee and co-manager of the Children of the Queen's Revels, for whom he and his co-managers must have commissioned and purchased plays. Some of the authors with whom Daborne presumably dealt during that time were Jonson, Chapman, and Beaumont and Fletcher, whose plays were performed by the Children between 1610 and 1613.[2] Daborne was already the author of *A Christian Turn'd Turk* and perhaps *The Poor Man's Comfort* when he signed his contracts with Henslowe. If *A Christian Turn'd Turk* was not written and performed for the Children of the Queen's Revels, the play may have belonged to the King's Men,[3] who later in the 1613–14 period were so eager to poach the plays Daborne was writing for Henslowe. Thus, by the time he was using the terms 'foul' and 'fair' copy distinctly with Henslowe, Daborne was an experienced purchaser of plays by leading dramatists, an author of his own plays, and a collaborator with Tourneur, Massinger and Field in other plays. Daborne must surely have known how business affairs with dramatists were handled, at least between 1610 and 1614. His definition of terms was almost certainly familiar to those, including Jonson, Chapman, Beaumont, Fletcher, Tourneur, Massinger, Field and Henslowe, who worked with him in theatrical businesses.

In fact, the second explicit use of the term 'foul' papers is exactly the same as Daborne's and is almost certainly by Edward Knight, an experienced playhouse scribe and official book-keeper of the King's Men's acting company from at least 1624 to 1633.[4] However, Knight appears to have been in the employ of Henslowe some years earlier, for he witnessed a contract between Henslowe and a group of actors in March 1616 and may also have been familiar with Daborne when he was under contract to write plays for Henslowe.[5] In his manuscript of Fletcher's play *Bonduca*, copied in part or in whole from Fletcher's foul papers of the play, Knight begins writing out the act–scene notation in Act 5, Scene 1, in the usual way: '*Actus Quintus: Scaena: pri*ª'. He then offers the text not of the next two and a half scenes but the following:

~~*Here should be A Scane of the Solemnitye of Panius his ffunerall mournd by Caractieus*~~

Here should A Scaene. be between Iunius. & petillius: (Iunius mocking petillius for being in loue wth Bonducas Daughter that Killd her selfe: to them: Enterd Suetonius: (blameing petillius for the Death of paenius:

The next scaene. the solemnitye of paenius his ffuneral mournd by Caractius:

The beginning of this following Scaene between petillius & Iunius is wanting.—the occasion. why these are wanting here. the booke whereby it was first Acted from is lost: and this hath beene transcribed from the fowle papers of the Authors w^{t}h were found:[6]

The scribe then transcribes what appears to be the rest of Act 5, Scene 3. That the first two scenes and the beginning of the next are 'wanting' in the author's own foul papers suggests that Fletcher had only outlined them when composing the play and wrote them out more fully by providing dialogue and stage directions in a later copy. Or the foul papers contained more than an outline but not enough coherent text for the scribe to transcribe, so he summarised them instead. It is also possible that Fletcher wrote the play with a collaborator who had not yet supplied the two scenes and the cue or transition lines in the third scene of Act 5, and that these scenes were added later to the fair copy and not to the foul papers. Yet one other possibility for Knight's failure to transcribe the missing scenes in *Bonduca* is that Fletcher or a later reviser provided them as 'new additions', to use Middleton's term in *Hengist, King of Kent*, sometime after the play's original performance.

However, a similar summary appears at the end of Act 4 in the scribal manuscript of Fletcher's play *The Faithful Friends*, although the scribe appears to be describing a comic masque with songs rather than a scene with dialogue.[7] So Fletcher may have been used to leaving gaps in his foul papers that he filled in himself or worked with a scribe to fill in later in a fair copy. Fletcher died in August 1625, and if Knight's transcript of *Bonduca* was made after that time he would have had to consult the actors for a summary of the scenes if this particular outline had not appeared in the foul papers. Knight also copied the manuscript of the collaborative play *The Honest Man's Fortune* (a play possibly co-written by Daborne), and annotated Massinger's autograph manuscript of *Believe as You List* and the scribal manuscript of *The Soddered Citizen*, a play now attributed to John Clavell. Knight would evidently have been on familiar terms with company dramatists and actors.

Knight does not reveal where he found Fletcher's foul papers of *Bonduca*. That the King's Men, their dramatist Fletcher, or his heir had kept the original foul papers would not be an unusual occurrence. In 1621, William Drummond acquired a manuscript with an incomplete text of Samuel Daniel's masque *Hymen's Triumph* from his kinswoman to whom it was presented. Drummond then wrote to Sir Robert Kerr, who had been bequeathed the dying Daniel's manuscripts, and asked him to look for a 'more perfect coppye among the Author's papers'. Drummond states that Kerr has also been given some of Donne's manuscripts to keep,[8] evidently in the same way that Fulke-Greville was given those of Sidney after the poet's death.[9] According to a contemporary anecdote, Shakespeare entrusted his manuscripts to his favourite daughter Susannah who gave them to her daughter, who could not manage to preserve them.[10]

Knight's outline in *Bonduca* bears some resemblance to that of Wilson and his possible collaborators in *The Second Part of Henry Richmond*, including the ruling-off of scenes (a common convention in completed dramatic manuscripts). So it would not be surprising if Fletcher included such an outline, especially as it appears at the beginning of an act, while he was composing the play. If writing alone, Fletcher was still outlining the act in his foul papers and was unsure how many scenes he would complete in Act 5. Knight has struck out the first summary:

~~Here should be A Seane of the Solemnitye of~~
~~Panius his ffunerall mournd by Caracticus~~

However, rather than striking out his own errors here, Knight may be deliberately transcribing what he found in the foul papers: a summary written and then struck out by Fletcher. The author may have begun Act 5 with the scene of Penius's funeral but changed his mind and decided that he needed to present a scene previous to it. In this previous scene, Junius mocks Petillius for having been in love with Bonduca's daughter, and Suetonius angrily confronts Petillius over Penius's death. Still uncertain about how to present this material, Fletcher outlined a second scene with the funeral, and then moved on to the third scene, perhaps beginning either at the opening of the scene or somewhere further on.

Significantly, in the first text of the play printed, apparently from the previously lost company book, in the 1647 Folio edition of Beaumont and Fletcher's plays, the two scenes appear in reverse order. Scene 1 presents the funeral and Scene 2 the mocking of Petillius by Junius and the confrontation between Suetonius and Petillius. Even if he was writing with a collaborator, the striking out of the first scene in the manuscript text, and the reassignment of the two scenes in the company book and the text printed from it, almost certainly stems from Fletcher's reworking of the play during and after composition. As the manuscript of *Bonduca* shows, foul papers could represent a completed draft but could be less than complete. Hence Bowers's definition of foul papers once again proves to be inappropriate, as Fletcher's apparent outline of Act 5 did not leave it 'in a shape satisfactory to him to be transferred to a fair copy',[11] including Knight's fair copy. In fact, Bowers's definition implies that the author would not need to work with a playhouse scribe, and that each worked independently of each other, with the result that the author had no further involvement with his text after finishing it. On the contrary, authors and scribes could work closely together in preparing a text for production and performance.

The term 'foul papers' or 'foul sheet' was in use by playhouse personnel eleven years after Daborne cited it. It was probably in use eleven years or more before he cited it. Daborne repeatedly used 'fair' copy in his correspondence, and the theatrical censor Sir Henry Herbert used it at least once. In his licence at the end of Walter Mountfort's 1633 autograph manuscript of *The Launching of the Mary*, Herbert insists that the next copy of a manuscript play presented to him be 'fayre', not 'fayer' (i.e. fairer) as most modern scholars have misread the word.[12] Herbert evidently considered *The Launching of the Mary* manuscript to be foul papers, and its frequent illegibility and general untidiness would support his judgement. 'Foul' therefore seems to have been the contemporary descriptive term for authors' own papers, sheets or copies of the working draft of a play and was most probably a term, like 'fair' copy or sheets, that Jonson, Shakespeare, Heywood and Middleton also knew and used.

The problems of Bowers and succeeding critics with the term 'foul' papers arises from their failure to understand that Pollard, Greg, McKerrow and other first-generation new bibliographers drew their theories about authors' practices from scribes' practices, largely because more scribal manuscripts are extant than authorial manuscripts. Some later scholars indeed formed most of their theories about how authors wrote or copied their plays from manuscripts that were produced by scribes. In fact, a close examination of nearly every extant dramatic manuscript, fair and foul, authorial and scribal, written for the early modern London professional stage demonstrates that authors may have worked as scribes but that scribes did not work as authors.

In fact, it is vital to make some clear distinctions. First, it is incorrect to assume that scribes who were fair copying, that is, copying authors' manuscripts, wrote them out in the same ways that authors wrote their foul papers. Second, it is wrong to assume that scribes who were fair copying authors' manuscripts wrote them out in the same ways that authors wrote out their fair copies. Above all, manuscripts fair-copied by authors are not by their nature necessarily perfect or cured of all errors or inconsistencies, nor often are those fair-copied by scribes. Knight, at least, did not attempt to recall or even compose himself the missing dialogue in the first three scenes, nor did he write out someone's full or partial report of the dialogue. Instead he wrote out a brief summary of it, even though he appears to have been making a new company book or a presentation copy of the play for a patron or a copy commissioned by a client. As a theatrical scribe he would know that in some respects he had defaced the integrity and usefulness of the manuscript in providing such a bare and inconsistent outline. Evidently he thought it better to adhere exactly to what Fletcher wrote than to alter the text, even though thereby embellishing the manuscript's appearance and increasing its value.

In sum, for dramatists and those for whom they wrote, 'foul' papers meant the working draft of a new play, full of the types of cuts, additions, revisions, confusions, false starts, incomplete outlines and loose ends and inconsistencies commonly made in composition. These foul papers could contain *currente calamo* changes (that is, changes made during composition), or later changes made after the scene or entire play was finished. Extant foul paper or fair copy manuscripts such as *The Captives* (in Heywood's hand), *John a Kent and John a Cumber* (in Munday's hand) and *Believe as You List* (in Massinger's hand) show such revisions made interlinearly, in the margin, and on inserted, pinned-in or glued-in sheets of paper. Writers sometimes signalled cuts by crossing out lines of text, as in those portions of Munday's text of *The Book of Sir Thomas More* which were replaced by a collaborator's contribution. But writers more often marked these cuts with a simple vertical line in the margin next to the text.

The 'secretarie Alphabete': early modern handwriting

In his 1618 book *The Pens Excellencie*, Martin Billingsley provided illustrations of the major contemporary handwriting styles, including 'sett', 'facill' and 'fast' Secretary, 'Bastard-Secretary or Text', Roman, Italian (or Italic), Court and Chancery. Billingsley noted that the 'rounded' facile and fast secretary were the 'onely vsuall hand of *England*', with the more 'square' set secretary reserved for formal documents, and bastard-secretary used for 'engrossments' (text in large letters, as in legal documents), epitaphs on tombs and book titles.[13] In his 1658 handwriting manual *The Pen's Triumph*, Edward Cocker, a long-experienced 'teacher of the art of writing', more clearly defined these hands, concentrating on 'running' or 'coursary' secretary, which may be equivalent to Billingsley's fast hand. Cocker discusses the difficulty of writing any of the secretary styles, as the writer should not affect 'a conjunction of Letters in the writing of this hand, but rather that every Letter thereof be made distinctly by it self, unless they run naturally one to another'. He also notes that Italians write their hand with 'unimitable dexterity', probably because they are 'generally more airy then we'.[14]

The seemingly standard hand of the late sixteenth century, the fast or running secretary hand, began to give way in the early seventeenth century to a mix of secretary and italic letter forms. By the end of the seventeenth century, secretary letter forms had all but died out, so that a kind of rounded italic hand, from which modern handwriting evolved, became the standard. In the early modern age, middle- or upper-class men, those most usually taught to read and write, were thought capable of mastering all the various hands. Yet women were most commonly taught, as Billingsley notes, Roman or Italian hand,[15] suitable for the type of occasional writing women did, rather than the daily writing represented by secretary hand.[16] However, as it is secretary hands that pose problems for both readers and writers, it is important to reconsider their forms and styles in order to understand how early modern dramatists transmitted their texts and how theatre personnel received them.

The 'secretarie Alphabete' in the top half of Figure 3.1 shows how elaborate the capital, or 'majuscule', letters are, especially **A, E, H, R, S,** and **Y. J** or **j** is absent as it is usually interchangeable with **I** and **i** at this time, although **i** can be written as **j**, particularly at the end of Roman numerals, as in the number **xiij**.[17] Some of the small, or 'minuscule', letters, however, are so elaborate to a modern reader that they are illegible.[18] This is especially true for the first small **a** (called a 'spurred' **a** due to the diagonally slanted and extended line on its left side) and for **d, f, g, h, k, m, n, r, s** (including 'long' **s**), **t, v, w** and **z**. While modern writers are taught to write capital letters so that flourishes remain above the line (as in modern italic **R**), many of these capital secretary letters descend below the line (as in secretary **R**). Even more noticeable is the number of secretary small letters with elaborate flourishes below the line (as in secretary **h**) or above the line. Such flourishes could partially or wholly obscure letters on lines below them.

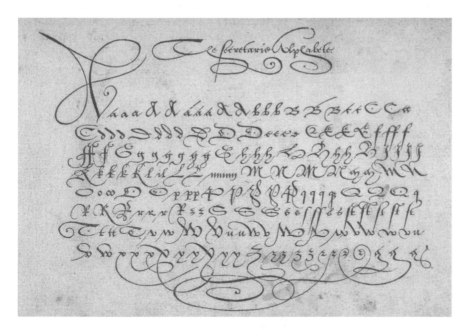

Figure 3.1 Woodcut engravings of 'The secretarie Alphabet' and 'Secretary' Hand. In the last line of text in the latter, the engraver has mistakenly written 'there' as 'thete', and an owner of this copy of *A Booke Containing Divers Sortes of hands* by John De Beau Chesne and John Baildon (1571) has also had trouble copying out the minuscule letters featured as models. Reproduced by permission of The British Library.

Although secretary hand was intended to create a uniform handwriting style that would be legible to all readers and writers, some authors wrote a careless or sloppy form of it, especially in the heat of composing, or failed to conform strictly to all the standard letter forms. This was not usually true for scribes or scriveners who were paid to transcribe a new or an existing document. For example, Jonson's 'Scrivener' who wrote out the author's contact with the audience in *Bartholomew Fair* would have had to produce a legible document or forfeit his fee. In the top and bottom of Figure 3.1, some small secretary letters are highly distinct and stylised, such as the **h** or **d** (particularly if used at the beginning or end of a word), but other letters were not so distinct and could easily be confused. A small **f** is often indistinguishable from a long **s** ($\int$), especially if the horizontal bar on the long **s** protrudes on the right side through the vertical one. Both letters could be indistinguishable from a **t** or **l**, especially if the writer gave his **t** or **l** a too short 'ascender' (or upward stroke). As Cocker notes, 'sometimes in the making of a Secretary f, t, or k, you must hold [the pen] as for a downright stroke [or 'descender'], when you make the blot or right line through those letters. Let not your Breast lie on the Desk you write on, nor your Nose on the Paper, but sit in as majestical a posture as you can'.[19] Some dramatists, notably Heywood, apparently did not heed this kind of advice, and their hands produce letter forms that were indistinct or illegible, perhaps even to a trained scribe.

Some forms in this alphabet, by convention, are only to be used in the initial or medial position in a word rather than in the final position, as in the case for **s**, with the long **s** (the uncrossed **f**) used in the initial or medial position and another **s**, which looks like an upside-down italic **e** (∂), used only at the end of the word; **u** was almost never used in initial position but in the medial one, with **v** used mostly for the primary letter. Thus, **us** would be written as **vs** but **thus** written as **thus**. In addition, some secretary letter forms signalled standard abbreviations, including a capital or small **p** with a bar or cross-stroke at its descender (þ) serving as an abbreviation for **per** or **pro**. Thus the word **property** could be spelled **proþty** or **þperty** and **part** as **þte**. In addition, a tilde (~) or macron (-) placed over a letter signified that another letter had been omitted in the word; for example, words containing a double **m**, such as **common**, could be written as **com̃on**, and those missing an **m**, such as **thẽ**.

There are numerous other variants from the forms listed in Figure 3.1, including an elongated italic-looking **e** for **es** or **is** (e) and **yᵉ** and **yᵗ** for **the** and **that**, with **y** as a holdover from the Anglo-Saxon 'thorn' (þ), the letter representing **th**. Other common abbreviations using superscript letters include **Mʳ** (for **Master**) and **Mʳⁱˢ** (for **Mistress**), **Sʳ** (for **Sir**), **wᵗʰ** and **wᵗ** (for **with**), **wᶜʰ** and **wʰ** (for **which**) and **yʳ** and **yᵘ** (for **your** and **you**). Proper names could also be abbreviated, including **William** as **Wᵐ** and **Thomas** as **Tʰᵒ**. Such abbreviations are sometimes punctuated with a colon (:) below the superscript letter, as in **yᵘ:**. Any type of word could be abbreviated; for example y^r LL: (or y^r ll:) was a common abbreviation for your Lordship or Lordships, also abbreviated as LL^{shp} and LL^{shps}, and Ladyship, for example, as La^{pp}. That a word was abbreviated did not mean that it had carried less honour, status or force than non-abbreviated words, for even the monarch could be addressed in standard abbreviated letter forms. For example, in his private letters Robert Devereux, second Earl of Essex, frequently addressed Queen Elizabeth as 'y^r ma^{tie}' ('your Majestie').[20] Henslowe was often creative in using non-standard and inconsistent abbreviations.

All these variants, including unusual letter forms, abbreviations and superscript letters, could perplex a reader of secretary hand. More problematic are 'minim' letters that were simply short vertical lines that were not connected with horizontal strokes. While some authors would formally write a letter like n or m using the secretary form in Figure 3.1, others would use a series of minims with no connection between the vertical lines, such as ıııı. For example, two minims in a row could signify an n or a u (or even ii if the author forgot to dot them); three in a row could signify an m or a w or an ni or in or iu or ui or iii (among other combinations of letters). It is especially common for early modern writers to dot an i one or two letters before or after it. As Cocker indicates, writing out as well as reading lines of text in secretary hand, with its elaborate flourishes and embellishments, particularly in capital letters, required a great deal more time and energy than italic hand. For this reason, writers began to adopt a mixed secretary hand, particularly using italic form for the letters that were the most elaborate or troublesome in secretary hand for majuscules such as C, S, T and minuscules such as c, h, f, r, s and medial and final e. As the italic hand was a humanist attempt to imitate ancient Roman texts, the letters are unlinked and clear, and thus look neater and more regular on the page. These letter forms are also less inclined to carry over into, and obscure, a letter on the previous line with an ascender or the next line with a descender.

The use of punctuation was also significantly different from the modern age, in which writers in English generally adhere to the same rules, such as periods at the end of a complete sentence, a comma to separate certain clauses or modifiers, or a colon to introduce a proposition. Early modern dramatists used much lighter punctuation and were often inconsistent when they did punctuate. Judging from extant dramatic manuscripts, writers often failed to use any punctuation to mark the end of a complete sentence, especially if it concluded at the end of a line of text. When they did use punctuation at the end of a sentence it was not usually a period (.) but a semi-colon (;) or virgule (/). Question marks (?) are often used interchangeably with exclamation points (!). A hyphen was often represented by an equals sign (=), especially at the end of a line, rather than a short dash (-). However, when correcting, rather than composing, a dramatist could insist on heavy punctuation. One example is Middleton, who used pencil to correct a partly scribal transcript of *A Game at Chess* by adding commas and other punctuation marks on nearly every line as well as to correct a few words in the portions of the text not in his own hand.[21] However, he may not have been typical, as he was clearly correcting a scribal copy of his own work, even though he did not correct the lightly punctuated portion of the text that he had transcribed himself.

Most authors, including dramatists, used both a separate secretary and an italic hand; in many cases the secretary hand was used for composing (that is, cursive or fluent) writing and italic for more formal copying. For example, Jonson used a predominately italic hand in writing his presentation or commissioned transcripts, as well as his inscriptions in printed books, probably more for decoration than for legibility. However, in his letter to Cecil asking for release from jail for writing *Eastward Ho!*, Jonson's cursive hand is largely italic but with some secretary letters, though no example of a literary text written by Jonson in entirely secretary hand appears to survive. Each writer's hand, whether secretary or italic, could change over time, as Henslowe's and Alleyn's various papers amply demonstrate. Even Jonson altered his hand noticeably after he began to suffer from palsy in 1626. Some dramatists used a hand that was entirely or predominantly italic for all their writing, although such a hand did not guarantee legibility, including the case of Middleton, whose failure properly to form many italic letters often renders his handwriting illegible. The legibility of a dramatist's cursive hand may have had some bearing on whether he routinely copied his own foul papers; however, dramatists other than Jonson routinely used a neater version of their usual cursive hand, rather than a calligraphic italic, to copy their texts. Daborne's sometimes sloppy cursive secretary hand may not have improved much in his fair copies, for his hand in his more formally written memo to write *Machiavel and the Devil* is only slightly more legible than that in some of his more rushed letters to Henslowe.

By convention, writers of dramatic manuscripts using secretary hand wrote act–scene notations, stage directions, speech prefixes, proper names, dumb shows and other specialised material in italic hand in order to call attention to non-dialogue material. While it is usual to see this formal use of italic in scribal manuscripts, especially in copies of reading texts to be presented to patrons or clients, authors in the act of composing frequently use one standard hand throughout the text. Professional scribes were paid to write a uniform secretary hand in order to present in the best possible way the documents that they were being paid to transcribe. But literary or dramatic authors certainly would have felt no such compunction, especially when they were in the act of composing a new text, not transcribing an existing one. Thus, composing authors might have been somewhat careless about their handwriting, punctuation and the conventions, especially if, like Daborne, they made their own fair copy of foul papers, or if they knew that they or the theatre company would pay a scribe to do so. An author would be assumed to be making decisions and changes in the act of writing foul papers or fair copies, thereby introducing further errors or problems into the text as he wrote.

Another issue affecting legibility would be spelling, which was not standardised until Dr Samuel Johnson published his *Dictionary* in 1755; hence early modern authors had no one standard source by which to check spelling. Although writers may have been taught to use the spellings already available in texts they had read or studied, they often adopted idiosyncratic spellings, probably based on phonetic pronunciation. In the case of homonyms such as 'there', 'their' and 'they're', all three words could be spelled in the same way, either as 'theere' or as 'theire' or as 'theyre', for example, or in any variety of ways or interchangeably at any given time. The meanings of such words would be distinguishable only by their context and not by spelling alone, and in some cases they would be entirely indistinguishable. R. B. McKerrow argued, definitively as he saw it, that a writer of this period chooses one particular spelling of a word and 'sticks to it', so that 'the more a man writes the more would his spelling tend to become fixed'.[22] However, such a generalisation cannot be supported, as writers may actually have preferred variety rather than uniformity. Inconsistent spelling is common in Henslowe's papers and in those of Alleyn, as well as in dramatists' manuscripts. For example, Henslowe is not unusual in offering such spellings as in this notation: 'leafte in the Rome of this peticote the sceartes of tufed tafitie of a womones gowe'. As he is inventorying the costs of stage costumes, he seems to mean, 'left in place of this petticoat the skirts of tufted taffeta of a woman's gown'. In other entries a few months later, he varies his spelling of peticote to 'peticot', 'peaticot' and 'pettecotte'.[23]

In addition to using unusual spellings for common words, Henslowe manages to spell the names of his authors in a variety of ways. Dekker, for example, is referred to as 'Dickers', 'Deckers', 'Deckkers' and 'Dyckers', even in entries that Dekker must have witnessed. Similarly Heywood's name is recorded as 'Hawode', 'Hewod', 'Hewode' and 'Hewwod'. Henslowe confronted his own name in a variety of ways, spelling it himself or seeing others spell it as 'Hensley', 'Hinchley' and 'Hinchlaw', as well as 'Hinchlow', the spelling favoured by Daborne and Field. Daborne also referred to Alleyn as 'Allin', with others spelling the name 'Alen' and 'Allen' or, of course, 'Alleyn'. The name was most likely spelled phonetically and was thus pronounced, as Daborne, Henslowe and others frequently spelled it, as 'Al-en', rather than 'Al-ane'. In fact, the pronunciation of vowels was shifting during the early modern age, so applying modern pronunciation to any vowel of this period may result in mispronunciation.

Given the lack of standardised spelling and punctuation and the frequent deviation in handwriting from standard letter forms and conventional usage, early modern readers, including theatre personnel and the censor, could have been left bewildered in reading a particular manuscript text. Heywood's admission to mending so many other dramatists' plays, including, presumably, *The Book of Sir Thomas More*, suggests that he must have been adept in reading others' writing even while, ironically, writing a sloppy and nearly illegible hand himself. If Chettle wrote Greene's *A Groatsworth of Wit* rather than merely transcribing it, Chettle may have been coy in noting, '*it was il written, as sometimes Greenes hand was none of the best: licensd it must be, ere it could bee printed which could neuer be if it might not be read. To be brief, I writ it over, and as near as I could, followed the copy.*'[24] First as an apprentice and later as a master printer, Chettle would surely have had to decipher printer's copy written in difficult or illegible hands. As McKerrow also notes, 'it is unsafe to take the spelling of any ordinary printed book as representing that of its author',[25] as compositors could impose their own spelling on the texts they typeset, often depending on the pieces of type available to them at any given time.

It is important to recognise all the factors involved in reading and writing secretary and italic letter forms before attempting to trace the source of errors, confusions, variants, and/or revisions in the manuscript texts of Heywood, Massinger, Jonson, Middleton and other dramatists. This is especially the case for the printed texts of their colleagues whose manuscripts do not survive. For example, knowing that an l could be confused with a t may explain why the word **flecked** (spelled **fleckted**) could be printed as **fleckeld** in one line of *Romeo and Juliet* and as **fleckted** in another. However, knowing that Shakespeare had distinctive ways of writing certain letters, including a 'spurred' a (*ᴀ*), would suggest that confusions in handwriting were not responsible for other variants. Shakespeare's standard o would have been markedly different if from his standard spurred a, demonstrating that **sallied** and **solid** were probably not variant because the F *Hamlet* printer mistook an o for an a but because that text contained **solid**, not the **sallied** of Q2. These types of variants resulting from misreading hands may be minor individually, but, in combination, unclear or imprecise letter forms, abbreviations, punctuation and spelling could have a major impact on the ways in which an early modern dramatic manuscript was transmitted from author to playhouse.

'Take three Ounces of Galls': early modern paper, pen and ink

Although parchment (usually made from sheepskin) and vellum (usually made from calfskin) were still used for some official handwritten documents such as legal deeds and the like, by the 1500s paper was the common material used for writing. Rather than modern mass-produced and machine-made 'wove' paper composed of wood pulp, early modern 'laid' paper, usually imported from France or Italy, was handmade from linen rags which were reduced to pulp and laid in wooden frames, trays or other moulds strung with wires. When the paper dried, the wires across these moulds would leave a series of parallel indentations called 'chain lines'. The mesh of wires in the middle of the mould could leave a watermark: a symbol such as a pot, a bunch of grapes, a fleur-de-lys or a set of initials used both as decoration and as a logo to identify the papermaker (some luxury modern paper is still made with watermarks). Some papermakers seemed to take particular pride in their products, providing distinctive and elaborate watermarks and even countermarks by which to call attention to their particular work.

A standard sheet of paper, amounting to the size of a papermaking mould, less the trimming of edges, would be approximately 61 cm × 40.5 cm (24 × 16 inches). When folded vertically down the middle this would form a single bifolium (i.e. two conjugate folio leaves forming four pages). If folded yet again, smaller units of paper could be produced.[26] Although most bibliographers would argue that paper produced for print and for handwriting were the same, some recent research suggests that they were distinct and different.[27] According to one 1585 account, the cost for ten sheets of paper was roughly one pence;[28] thus paper was not inordinately expensive. Because scribes could calculate how much paper they would need in order to make another copy of the finished manuscript in front of them, they could begin by making up manuscript books containing several numbered pages. Binding the book would involve sewing thread through the gatherings of paper to make a spine.

However, a composing dramatist or other author usually worked with one sheet of paper at a time. The sheet could be left unfolded and used to create two pages, one on each side. But it would have been much more economical and convenient for the writer to fold vertically this large and unwieldy sheet once into a bifolium; in fact, some paper may have been sold pre-folded in this way. Each half sheet would create two pages, for a total of four pages, with two recto ('upright' or 'straight' in Latin) or right-hand pages, and two verso ('turned' in Latin) or left-hand pages. This type of format in which the sheet is only folded once is now termed 'bifoliated'. Even more economically, the writer could fold the sheet once more (thus folded twice altogether) and turn it sideways to make eight pages, and so on.

After being folded two or more times, the sheets would have to be slit across the top and/or sides so that they could be opened. If not folded, the paper could be trimmed to any size, although it was most economical to fold rather than trim paper so as to use as much of it as possible. How the paper was folded can still be determined by checking the placement of watermarks: for example, in the gutter of a bifoliated sheet, or in the top or bottom corners of a manuscript in quarto format. However, given that the paper may have been trimmed, or other single sheets inserted later into manuscripts, watermarks may appear in a variety of places. A half sheet would be the appropriate size for playhouse plots which were posted backstage to aid actors. Actors' parts, rolled up as scrolls, could be made up of folio- or smaller-sized sheets pasted together lengthwise (writers of this period also used pins or stitching to join pieces of paper). On the other hand, an author who wanted to make up a manuscript book that would be small enough to carry around in his pocket would fold his sheets into octavo size.

However, the common format of surviving dramatic manuscripts, whether written by the author or a scribe, is folio, with each four-page bifolium laid on top of another folded sheet. This implies that each bifolium was completed before the next was used. Had all the sheets been folded at the same time and placed inside each other or 'quired', the author would have been much more restricted in making significant changes and would have been less able to rip out sheets to make corrections.[29] Some authors or scribes also pleated the bifolium again vertically. That is, by folding twice, they could create a small column to the left for the speech prefixes, a larger column in the middle for the dialogue, and a smaller column on the right for the exit directions. In this way, the text of each column would be neatly lined up in the same place on each recto and verso page. Such columns, which could eventually be smoothed out but would still be noticeable, would aid the writer but could detract from the embellished form of any manuscripts transcribed as presentation copies for a patron or commissioned copies for a client. In any event, creating columns by folding twice or even once through pleating is simply an option and is neither typical nor atypical of authors or of scribes.

Those who were writing for their own purposes could treat paper in a much more casual way, even recycling it on occasion. At some point, Henslowe turned his Diary upside down and started writing again from the reverse end; that is, from the back page forward to the front. He also wrote in empty margins of already used pages.[30] Many of his correspondents used a portion of a larger, previously used sheet when writing to him, and in some cases their deletion of existing material is still legible. Even Alleyn wrote a 1597 contract for Henslowe and his covenant servant William Kendall on the verso of a portion of a larger piece of paper that listed some accounts which Alleyn had crossed out.[31] These writers may have recycled material strictly out of convenience, not because they were too poor to purchase more paper. George Buc, Master of the Revels, was apparently not financially strapped when he began writing his *History of King Richard III* on the verso of sheets that recorded his accounts for licensing plays.[32]

The chief writing implement available to Shakespeare, Jonson, Middleton, Heywood and their colleagues and collaborators would have been a quill. As Cocker advises, 'procure the first, second, or third Quill in the wing of a Goose or Raven', then sharpen the point with a penknife. If 'you intend to write Italian hand therewith, the nib must be small, and almost round, with a long slit: For secretary it must be broader; for large Italique, or that which we call Italian Text, it must be of a greater breadth'. The penknife could be used both to erase errors (by scraping off dried ink) and to resharpen the pen point when necessary, possibly every page or two. Cocker also notes, 'You may rule your paper with black-lead, and with white bread, or the paring-dust of white Leather, clearly fetch those lines out again.' In practice, such rulings were often made discreetly and faintly so they would not be immediately apparent after the text had been written out. If the paper was too rough, it could be polished with the penknife or a bookbinder's folding stick.[33]

Some dramatic manuscripts in this period show the use of red ink or red pencil (often used to rule off margins) as well as regular plumbago pencil, but the bulk of the manuscript would be written in ink that would dry as brown or black. Ink was made from a variety of natural ingredients, as in Cocker's recipe:

> Take three Ounces of [oak] Galls which are small and heavy and crisp, put them in a vessell of three pints of Wine, or of Rain-water, which is much better, letting it stand so infusing in the Sun for one or two dayes; Then take two Ounces of Coppris, or of Roman Vitrial, well colour'd and beaten small, stirring it well with a stick, which being put in, set it again in the Sun for one or two dayes more. Stir all together, adding two Ounces of Gum Arabique of the clearest and most shining, being well beaten.

To make it more lustrous, Cocker advises adding pomegranate or sugar and boiling it gently.[34] Once armed with his ink, his sharpened pen, his polished paper and a 'pounce-pot' or 'sander' to help blot or dry the ink on written pages, the writer was ready to begin. Although a few women, such as Elizabeth Cary, wrote amateur plays for their own entertainment,[35] all professional dramatists of this period were male, hence the use of 'he' throughout the rest of this chapter in describing the process for an author working alone or in collaboration after plotting out the play.

'Incipit actus primus'

The dramatist would begin the composition of a play by taking a sheet of paper and folding it in half vertically, producing four pages in total, with two on each side (thus producing a 'bifolium'). The writer began his text on the first page made from folding it, the right (or recto) side of the first half of his sheet, as is still common when printing the first page of a book. Before beginning to write the text, he may have ruled off the top and bottom and the left margins of each page, either in red or black ink or in pencil. However, dramatists usually wrote without ruling off margins, and only very occasionally would they rule off lines on which to write the text, and even then only in faint pencil so as not to be visible once written over in black ink. Although scribes such as Ralph Crane sometimes vertically folded or pleated each page two or three times to create neat columns to begin speech prefixes, dialogue and exit directions, extant authorial manuscripts suggest that authors only infrequently followed this practice.

Some dramatists would begin writing with the words 'Incipit actus primus' ('Here begins Act 1' in Latin) and/or 'Scena Prima' ('First Scene'), with 'Prima' sometimes written as 'Pr^a' or '1^a'. Otherwise, the first lines written would probably have been the entrance stage directions, usually centred here and throughout the text (but occasionally written from a flush-left margin). Exit directions were usually written flush right, either on the last line of dialogue for the character making an exit or on a separate line below it. Writers were most inconsistent in providing exit directions for characters; of all stage directions these are the ones most frequently omitted. However, a writer often added or corrected stage directions after writing out the dialogue (perhaps in re-reading), as many exit and other directions such as 'a noise within' are written one or more lines above or below where they belong, usually due to lack of space on the correct line. Thus an entrance direction may appear after a character has entered and begun speaking, or an exit direction for a character a few lines before he has finished speaking, or a direction for a noise or shout several lines before or after it occurs. When this type of text is printed, compositors usually set these misplaced directions on the lines in which they found them in the manuscript.

Act and scene divisions may or may not be included within the text, although opening and closing pages usually contain 'Incipit actus primus' and 'Finis'. While many of Shakespeare's texts evidently printed from foul papers lack act and scene notations, it is not uncommon for dramatists of this period to use them sparingly or occasionally, often letting them drop as the play progresses. Shakespeare, like other dramatists, also seems at times to have used simultaneously vague and descriptive directions, as well as including 'ghost characters', as in *Much Ado about Nothing*, for which he never developed dialogue or action. The composing author may have had a 'plot' to consult, so he would know who would be in the scene but not what each character would do or say.

After completing the first entrance direction, the dramatist would write the speech-prefix (or heading) for the first character with dialogue. Speech-prefixes were usually set off in the left margin, with all dialogue, even that without a speech-prefix, set in columns to the right of it, in order to maintain the empty left margin. Sometimes, speech-prefixes were centred on a separate line, but most dramatists knew that centring them required a much greater and more expensive use of paper, so if they began this way they often abandoned this pattern early in the manuscript. On occasion, authors may have written out a series of speech-prefixes before going back to write in the dialogue. A fair-copied passage in the collaborative manuscript of *Sir Thomas More*, for example, shows one speech-prefix within a scene with no dialogue next to it. This suggests that the author forgot to fill it in, or was waiting for someone else to do so, before moving on to the next character's dialogue. A few other speech-prefixes occur without dialogue in manuscripts of this period. In the scribal manuscript of *The Lady Mother*, speech-prefixes are slightly out of alignment with the text, which suggests that they were added after each page of text had been written.[36] Such misalignment could also result from the scribe copying the speech-prefixes out first. On the whole, a composing author would have written each speech-prefix and then the dialogue for that character before writing the next speech-prefix. After finishing the first character's dialogue he would then draw a short horizontal line or 'rule' below it in order to separate it from the next character's dialogue. Authors were fairly consistent in ruling off each character's dialogue in this way.

Dramatists were accustomed to using italic hand for stage directions and speech-prefixes and the usual secretary hand for all the dialogue, but some dramatists did not bother with a separate italic hand and wrote the entire text in their usual hand. In writing the dialogue, some writers italicised characters' names within the text. This is not common however, as switching to italic hand would have interrupted the composing dramatist's fluency. Occasionally, a writer could not fit the entire pentameter line of his verse onto one line and continued on the next line, indenting it slightly from the left margin, or writing it somewhat flush with the left margin. Although scribes often mislined when copying a verse line, it is unusual for authors to do so as they were accustomed to thinking out dialogue in verse lines and tried to maintain the look and integrity of their lineation. However, they do not usually capitalise the first letter in a verse line. Like punctuation, capitalisation was not standardised in this age, and whether a word, such as a proper noun, was capitalised was often a random decision rather than a marker that the word required extra emphasis. Some words are capitalised strictly because a particular small letter, for example secretary c, used in the primary position in a word in secretary hand might be difficult to read.

This lack of uniformity in writing, spelling, capitalising and punctuating different parts of a play-text may have created confusions and problems for both the writer and his readers. But if a dramatist provided a fair copy of his own play (because his foul papers were usually messy or illegible at points), he was probably much less concerned with being neat and legible than an author who usually handed his foul papers over to someone else to copy. Company dramatists would have had some experience with the company book-keeper, such as Edward Knight, the copyist of Fletcher's *Bonduca*, who, no doubt, developed a system to cope with each dramatist's writing quirks. Scholars have debated whether Shakespeare wrote out his own fair copies of his foul papers.[37] In the case of the Q2 *Romeo and Juliet*, apparently printed from Shakespeare's foul papers written very early in his career, his first draft was so messy as to be illegible at points. The apparent condition of these foul papers suggests that if his handwriting had not improved as the years went by Shakespeare might have needed to prepare his own fair copies or insisted a scribe do so in consultation with him.

After finishing the first scene, the dramatist would continue writing the succeeding scenes immediately below it in much the same way as he had done the first scene. Because of the cost of paper, or as a matter of convenience, a dramatist did not usually begin a new scene or a new act on a fresh sheet of paper but continued from the point at which he stopped. After finishing an act, he may on occasion have surrendered it to Henslowe or another eager contractor who wanted it as immediate collateral against an advanced payment. The Master of the Revels was required by his employer, the monarch, to read a play in its entirety before actors could begin to rehearse any of it; he would cut any politically contentious speeches or characters or other offensive material such as political or religious satire. Yet Henslowe's Diary and Daborne's correspondence show that on occasion the first completed acts or scenes were immediately copied as parts and distributed to the actors even before the entire play was finished, and the actors then began 'studyinge' the early portions of the text. As noted earlier, it was not unusual for a dramatist to read portions, if not all, of his new play aloud to the assembled actors, either in front of Henslowe or his business partners such as Robert Shaw, who persuaded Henslowe to buy *The Second Part of Henry Richmond*.

Evidently, Henslowe, at least, assumed that actors could alter any material they had already learned and to which the censor later objected. Or perhaps Henslowe and his fellow entrepreneurs considered the submission of the completed text to the censor a mere formality rather than the required first step in the rehearsal and performance process. As he often paid the censor in arrears, Henslowe and the co-managers of the acting companies with which he worked may have established a mutually beneficial relationship with the censor that depended on trust rather than formal inspection of the manuscript. An experienced dramatist would certainly know whether he needed to proffer acts of an unfinished play to Henslowe or someone else. Such early and hasty dispersal of the text probably depended on particular circumstances, such as the author's need for interim payment or the actors' need to rush rehearsal of a new play. But it may also imply that dramatists, entrepreneurs, actors and censors saw the production of a play as a collaborative act in which they all worked together, either directly or indirectly, throughout composition, licensing and performance.

After finishing the play, the author most likely read it over, making corrections (rectifying errors) and revisions (deleting, rewriting or adding text) when necessary. However, some surviving manuscripts are so messy or disordered that it looks as if no one ever re-read them. The fragment of the recently discovered 'Melbourne' manuscript (attributed to John Webster's hand) and of the manuscript of Jonson's *The Entertainment at Britain's Burse* (perhaps partly in Jonson's hand) are both nearly illegible at points.[38] Neither manuscript shows indented columns for dialogue or clearly marked-off speech-prefixes or stage directions. The authors of both of these manuscripts may either have planned to make their own fair copies or to assist the scribes who did so, in which case correcting the foul papers would not have been a high priority for them.

Whether carefully re-read or not, the manuscript could then be bound or left loose; if bound, each folded sheet would be placed on top of each succeeding folded sheet, forming a book, and sewn or pasted together along folds at the spine. Very occasionally an author would have correctly anticipated how many sheets he would need to complete the play. But this was not the usual practice, as it limited the writer's ability to add or cut sheets in the act of composing (if required he could pin or glue in extra sheets or small fragments). Some dramatists or book-keepers recycled paper, especially at the beginning or end of a manuscript. It is not unusual to find a dramatic manuscript wrapped up in a vellum leaf that was once part of a medieval or early Renaissance manuscript with the handwriting still legible, as with the 'Books' of *Sir Thomas More* and *John a Kent and John a Cumber*. However, most foul paper manuscripts were probably left unbound immediately after completion, at least until a decision was made as to whether they would be fair-copied or, occasionally, to be passed along to the censor as they were.

Extant manuscripts may vary in their legibility, size, binding or other features. But most manuscripts in the original authors' hands suggest that dramatists tried to present their text in a coherent way, for they knew that they would directly or indirectly have to provide legible copies of their plays to the censor and playhouse personnel. Censors complained loudly when presented with copies not 'fair' enough to read (as in the case of *The Launching of the Mary*), so illegible foul papers would have been fair-copied, either in whole or in part. As mentioned earlier, actors were given only their own lines and the cue lines to them in order, among other things, to prevent them from selling copies of the entire play. Thus the only complete copies of plays available would be those kept by the author, if he retained the foul papers or a copy of them, and the acting company's copies. At least some early modern dramatists, including Daborne, attached little or no importance to their foul papers if they could not exchange them for payment. Once sold, authors who were not company sharers considered foul or fair copies the property of their purchasers, unless tempted to 'cony-catch' them, whether to the acting company or the printers who used them to set their texts into type. Many manuscripts may have been destroyed after fulfilling the companies' or printers' purposes, and few were stored in conditions to ensure preservation over the centuries.

For these and other reasons very few foul paper copies of plays survive. Even Ben Jonson, who was adamant in his lifetime about keeping samples of the various stages of his texts, transmitted through to the twenty-first century only one theatrical manuscript wholly in his own hand, and it is of the privately performed *Masque of Queens*, not a commercial play. Variant manuscript copies of the same text also suggest that most dramatists did not value foul papers more highly than scribal copies or theatrical transcripts of them. Middleton participated in the transcription of at least six manuscripts of *A Game at Chess*, either in copying out all or parts of the texts or reading through them and making small corrections or dedicatory comments. He did not seem unduly concerned that no two of these manuscripts were exactly alike. He did not distinguish among the early, intermediate or later copies but treated them all as equally valued copies of his play, even if they uniquely cut or added material. Middleton also did not note or remark that the two manuscripts partly or wholly in his handwriting were superior to the other four written out by scribes, probably because he seemed to have read over or corrected all the scribal manuscripts himself.

Authors could revise their plays in the act of writing the foul papers, or after completion of them at any stage, during rehearsal, after early performances or some months or years later, or at the time of a revival, for example. Signs of authorial revision are, for instance, deletions or additions within a line of text as well as changes written in the top, bottom, right or left margin, or on inserted sheets of paper. What seems clear from the extant manuscripts of Shakespeare's colleagues and collaborators is that dramatists saw revision as a normal part of the writing process, both before and after completion of foul papers. Numerous dramatists returned to their plays (sometimes twenty years later in the case of John Bale, who rewrote his play *King Johan* for a planned performance before Queen Elizabeth). Even if dramatists surrendered their financial claim to a play by selling it to an acting company they did not surrender their artistic claim to it, especially if they still worked with the company performing it. Jonson, Middleton, Dekker, Heywood, Fletcher, Massinger, Shakespeare, Daniel, Shirley and many other dramatists were practised and ardent revisers. Many of these authors may have learned the art of revision by 'mending', 'altering' or making 'addicians' to other authors' plays for Philip Henslowe or James or Richard Burbage. But these dramatists were also keen revisers of their own plays for artistic reasons. Dramatists not only revised when compelled to, as a result of censorship or of the desire to pass an old play off as a new one, but when they wanted to.

'Enter mr Raphael a yonge marchant': Heywood's foul papers

Heywood's 1624 autograph manuscript of his play *The Captives* is a foul-paper text that offers a full example of an author in the act of composition.[39] Other foul-paper manuscripts also survive although they have not always been recognised as such, including Mountfort's *The Launching of the Mary*, and the manuscript of *The Wasp or Subjects President* (i.e. Precedent).[40] Heywood apparently knew that his handwriting was often illegible, as it proves to be in the manuscript of *The Captives*. Even the printers of his prose work *The Exemplary Lives and Memorable Acts of Nine the Most Worthy Women of the World* (1640) offered a postscript to the volume 'Excusing the Compositor, who received this Coppy in a difficult and unacquainted hand, and the Corrector who could not bee alwayes ready in regard of some necessary employments'.[41] Heywood's secretary hand looks sloppy in *The Captives*, but it is a fast, cursive hand that is still engaged in the process of composition. Although E. A. J. Hongimann speculated that this manuscript is a fair copy 'fouled' by free composition, his case is based largely on seeing a significant number of 'eyeskip' errors in copying.[42] When this manuscript is compared with Heywood's partly foul and partly fair copy of *The Escapes of Jupiter* (a comparison Honigmann makes), and to his foul paper contributions to *The Book of Sir Thomas More* (a comparison Honigmann does not make) it proves indeed to be foul papers.[43]

Judging from all his extant manuscripts, Heywood routinely tried to avoid copying his foul papers whenever possible, finding his original compositions and revisions satisfactory. In fact, Heywood's characteristics as a composing dramatist can clearly be seen in his own additions and in his occasional revisions to Munday's portions of *More*, a manuscript that also serves as an example of extant mixed foul and fair copy. That is to say, the fair-copied portions of *More*, in the hands of all his collaborators, show very little revision or alteration in the act of writing and instead show much more coherence, consistency and fluency typical of a copied text. Heywood's marginal additions which correct Munday's fair copy are, by nature, foul papers, but his other additions are also uncorrected, cursively written, and the least legible of all the hands.

In his own manuscript of *The Escapes of Jupiter*, Heywood recycled material from two of his previous plays already in print, *The Silver Age* and *The Golden Age*. Even though he could have pasted in and annotated the printed portions of the texts he was reusing, he chose to copy them out in order to revise as he went. One other partly foul-paper and partly fair-copy manuscript, of Massinger's *Believe as You List*, also combines the composition of new material and the revision of existing material.[44] Massinger shows that he satisfied the censor's earlier objections by altering his potentially dangerous use of modern Spanish characters and settings to those of the less threatening ancient world. In all these manuscripts and *The Wasp*, *The Entertainment at Britain's Burse* and *The Launching of the Mary*, the sections in which the author is composing, rather than recopying existing material, show *currente calamo* alterations and confusions typical of foul papers.

In his manuscript of *The Captives*, Heywood is obviously in the act of composing, not copying, unsure as he writes which characters will appear in which scene, at what point they will enter, what they will say, and even what relationship they bear to one another. The manuscript has some light notation (in act–scene breaks, signalled by a ruled line, and in stage directions, mostly signalled by the word 'cleere' written at the end of scenes) by another hand, most likely a playhouse scribe responsible for keeping the company book. But this does not disqualify it from the category of foul papers. It is lightly annotated foul papers and certainly not a company book. The reasons that a dramatist would make a fair copy of his text, as Heywood's foul paper manuscript of *The Captives* suggests, might be many. His handwriting while composing might be illegible to others, or the text might have had so many changes (including marginal additions written any which way, and not on the line where they belonged) that it would seem confusing, or else a combination of these or other reasons. It was probably a rare dramatist who wrote his first draft so legibly and fluently that it could be passed along to his theatre company without being copied. The playhouse scribe who tried to use Heywood's foul papers of *The Captives* to make a company book (largely by adding occasional stage directions) or a copy for the censor evidently did not succeed. This manuscript lacks the censor's license, suggesting instead that a fair copy of it was made for him to read, and certainly it remains often too illegible to have served for the book-keeper in the theatre.

The first page of the manuscript, in Heywood's hand (f. 52^r: Figure 3.2) without non-authorial marks, excepting one asterisk and ruled line next to it to mark an entrance direction towards the bottom of the page, offers foul paper characteristics. At the top of this first scene, Heywood has centred the notation, 'Actus primus. Scena pr^a' (with the last two words damaged or cropped sometime later to 'Sce pr ') and below which he has written the opening stage direction, 'Enter m^r Raphael a yonge marchant mr Treadway his companion and ffrend, Etc'.[45] The act–scene notation is in italic, but the stage directions and the speech-prefixes are written in secretary hand, suggesting that this composing author ignored the convention of using italic hand for all directional sections of a play-text. Or he began with the intention of using italic for such material but quickly abandoned it. The stage directions are at the same time descriptive and vague, especially the last part, 'his companion and ffrend, Etc'. The audience who will eventually hear and see this play will not have any access to the stage directions. The description of Mr Raphael as a 'merchant' is for the benefit of the author, who is still establishing how the characters will be linked, not for the audience. Heywood's description would also signal to the acting company how to costume Raphael and to the actor how to fix his accent and demeanour (probably as regional and 'trade'). Heywood's language here obviously represents what Leslie Thomson refers to as that of 'the tiring house, for players and book-keepers rather than general readers'.[46]

The word 'Etc' in the stage direction is another authorial signal. Either it suggests that Heywood has not quite worked out what else he needs to put into this direction because other, unspecified characters may appear here, or he has left it for the company to decide. The first option seems the most probable, because by the bottom of the page, the Clown has a line of dialogue that is preceded by a squeezed-in stage direction, 'Enter the Clowne' (later marked with an asterisk by the book-keeper to make it more noticeable).[47] 'Etc', in fact, appears frequently in various types of early modern manuscripts to signal authors' indecision or uncertainty, or even the lack of any need at that stage to determine certainty. Heywood was probably undecided at the start of the scene as to whether the Clown should enter then or later, and began his dialogue before writing an entrance for him, requiring the squeezed-in entrance direction. Were this fair copy, as Honigmann argues, Heywood would not have needed to squeeze in this direction as he did in the original. He would also have been more certain from the beginning of the scene when the Clown enters. Clearly Heywood is still composing the scene in his mind as he writes it. As Alan C. Dessen and Leslie Thomson note, although theatre personnel and their audiences shared a common language, the language used by professional dramatists in theatrical manuscripts differed from that of book-keepers and scribes as well as

Figure 3.2 Heywood's foul paper manuscript of the first page of *The Captives*, British Library Egerton MS 1994, f. 52ʳ, showing *currente calamo* revisions in the act of composition. Reproduced by permission of The British Library.

other writers, including dramatists revising for literary readers. In fact, even so-called 'permissive' directions designed to allow as much leeway as possible in staging proceed from 'the playwright's original conceptions rather than actual staging'. As Dessen and Thomson conclude, 'most stage directions are authorial in origin'.[48] The manuscript of *The Captives* serves as a representative example of these types of stage directions in authorial language.

But this type of authorial sign of indecision could have been corrected once the manuscript came into the hands of the acting company itself, which needed as much precision as possible in determining which actors enter when. Several other authorial characteristics of Heywood appear on this page:

1   He has written the speech-prefixes in a flush-left margin.
2   He has neatly set off the dialogue in an indented column (following the folds in paper that he has made).
3   He has drawn a short horizontal line after the last line of dialogue for each speaker; this is most noticeable after Raphael's second set of dialogue, underneath the word 'Alls'.
4   He has not capitalised the first letter in each new line, even though he is writing in verse.
5   He has separated from the text the first stage direction and the later one for the Clown by ruling it off with a long horizontal line.
6   He has made a few *currente calamo* changes in the act of composing. These are most noticeable in Treadway's third line of dialogue, 'no consequent', which is followed by the crossed-out line 'ffor instanns, who so ffond'. It looks as if Heywood tried to rub or scratch out the line before the ink dried.
7   He has made some major cuts in Treadway's and Raphael's early speeches by simply drawing a vertical line close against the margin to signal deletion. He has, in fact, not put a giant X through the entire passage or crossed out each individual line with a horizontal line (as modern writers are accustomed to doing). These deletions are also *currente calamo* because they begin with the deleted half line 'for instanns, who so ffond', which was rubbed out while the ink was still wet. However, Heywood probably added the second horizontal line (further to the left) to mark deletion sometime later when he realised the first deletion line might not be clear enough.
8   He has used very light punctuation, only occasionally supplying a period at the end of a character's dialogue, and is especially stingy with his use of commas necessary to make sense of many of the lines.
9   He uses some distinctive spellings for certain words, including 'know', twice spelling it as 'knwe', and spelling 'unknown' as 'vnknwne'. In all these instances, he has omitted the *o*. But he is inconsistent in spelling other words, such as 'lady', spelling it 'Lais' in one line and the plural 'Ladyes' in the next.

As Woudhuysen has demonstrated, a scribe could easily abandon a sheet when he had made too many errors and begin writing again;[49] an author could have done the same. If Heywood is fair copying here, rather than composing in foul papers, his deletions are early enough in the text that he could easily have abandoned this sheet and started over rather than continuing on the same sheet. Instead he marks the cuts, thereby introducing some confusions into the text, showing that he is still engaged in the act of composition.

The manuscript shows many other signs of a composing author at work besides what can be recognised from this single page, including loose ends, false starts, duplications, and other minor errors, inconsistencies, and confusions in plot, characters or setting, especially between early and later scenes. Most of these categories that signal the patterns of a composing author can be found in the manuscripts of Massinger and Fletcher, among others.[50] They are also evident in the 'Melbourne' manuscript fragment attributed by Felix Pryor on stylistic and circumstantial grounds to John Webster, examples of whose hand are not extant.[51] When discovered, the fragment had been used as wrapping paper for letters by Sir John Coke. The manuscript shows the same types of indecision, inconsistencies, false starts and *currente calamo* additions and revisions as in Heywood's *The Captives*. Such foul paper characteristics also survive to some extent in the Quarto and Folio texts printed from the foul papers of Fletcher and Shakespeare, among other dramatists.[52]

Henslowe employed Heywood at various times between 1596 and 1602 to write plays, and as a 'covenant servant' (i.e. actor) for two years between 1598 and 1600. Heywood was probably as illegible a writer earlier in his career when he worked for Henslowe as he was at its conclusion. Henslowe would probably have known better than anyone that promises by Heywood to supply his own 'fayr' copy probably would not have been fulfilled. But supplying a fair copy of this foul paper manuscript would have been a necessity. For this reason Heywood's manuscripts were almost certainly copied by a scribe who would have had to work closely with him throughout the transcription. Daborne was probably too penurious or destitute to pay a copyist; hence his constant complaints to Henslowe about the extra labour of fair-copying his foul sheets himself. Heywood apparently wrote *The Captives* for the Lady Elizabeth's Men,[53] the same company for which Daborne had been contracted by Henslowe to write plays. *The Captives* was performed at the company's home, the Cockpit, run by Heywood's friend and colleague, Christopher Beeston, who would later attempt to poach Brome's play from the Salisbury Court company. There was, in fact, no degree of separation between dramatists and theatre personnel or between authors and their texts in the early modern age. The text could return to the author at any or all stages of transmission: after the scribe had copied it; after a censor had licensed it; after the book-keeper had prepared the company book; after its rehearsal and performance; before one or more later revivals; and after it was printed. In this foul paper manuscript, Heywood is at the primary point of this circular transmission of his text.

4 'A fayre Copy herafter'
Dramatists and fair copies

As soon as the dramatist finished his foul papers he faced a decision. If they were legible, he could tidy them up and correct them; if they were illegible, due to sloppy handwriting, marginal or interlinear cuts, additions or corrections, or even the insertion of added sheets, he or someone else would have to recopy them. This 'fair' copying was usually done before the play was submitted for licensing, although in some cases foul papers were probably submitted to the censor. The majority of the dramatic manuscripts that survive in authors' hands indeed look like fair rather than foul papers, and thus scholars tend to draw their theories about authorial foul papers correctly or incorrectly from authorial fair copies. While recopying a manuscript the author could make minor as well as major changes in parts or in the whole of the text.[1] However, scribes were much more conservative when copying an author's foul papers, usually confining themselves to regularising performance features of the text, as were book-keepers and other theatre personnel, including actors. Although dramatists worked collaboratively with these personnel and censors to prepare a text for performance, this collaboration left the responsibility for the composition and revision of the play's content, including dialogue, plot, characters and structure, entirely up to dramatists.

'Sʳ I sat vp last night till past 12 to write out this sheet': authors' fair copies

For only one play performed in the London professional theatres is more than one autograph fair copy extant: Middleton's *A Game at Chess*, with the Trinity College, Cambridge manuscript entirely in his hand, and the Huntington Library manuscript partly in his hand. Neither manuscript appears to be foul papers, due to its neatness, consistency and lack of correction. Because the texts in the two manuscripts vary so much, it appears that neither descended from the other or from the same manuscript. The differences between the two texts, and from the other four entirely scribal manuscripts of the play that Middleton checked or annotated after transcription, suggest an author rewriting slightly in the act of copying from foul papers or another fair copy, as well as making some major revisions. Middleton may have made such changes in both of these autograph manuscripts, rather than in one or neither. He evidently, then, made at least two different sets of changes, without being noticeably concerned that the two texts were not identical. Many of the other surviving authorial fair copies almost certainly underwent the same process in being copied by the author from foul papers.

Anthony Munday's play *John a Kent and John a Cumber* survives in a manuscript fair copy in his hand, at the end of which is his signature subscribed to the end of the last line of text.[2] However, this last page suffered damage and only one quarter of it remains. Munday must have completed this transcription by the time the notation of 'Decembris 1595', not 1590 or 1596 as previous scholars have misread the date,[3] was written below Munday's signature in another hand and followed by a flourish typical of scribes. The manuscript has been very lightly annotated by a book-keeper working in ink darker than Munday's who has scored out a few lines and made a few marks of 'X' in the margin (as on ff. 5^v, 8^{r-v}). However, in two other places (ff. 6^v, 7^r) another hand, most likely the censor's, whose licence probably appeared after the flourished date, has made two much larger notations of 'X' in the margins. Munday has not used scene divisions but has provided act divisions for all five acts.[4] Although the text is neatly copied for the most part, Munday wrote a major marginal addition sideways in the margin at one point and at others heavily deleted passages he had just written out. Such alterations show that authorial fair copies were not perfect or flawless in format or content.

The manuscript's wrapper gives the title as 'The Book of John A kent & John a Cumber', suggesting that Munday's fair copy indeed served as or derived from the company's book. As the last scene of the play is set in West Chester, E. K. Chambers followed Greg in arguing that this manuscript records the text of the play known as *The Wise Man of West Chester*. Henslowe notes three performances by the Admiral's Men of this play in 1594, nineteen in 1595, six in 1596 and three in 1597. Henslowe later bought the book second-hand from Alleyn on 19 September 1601,[5] implying that Alleyn was the original purchaser. If the two plays are the same, Munday presumably would not have needed to produce a company book for a play that had already been in performance a year earlier unless he revised it in 1595, thereby producing this fair copy in the process. Or he may have made this manuscript as a presentation copy for a patron or even a commissioned copy for a client, perhaps Alleyn, who sold this particular manuscript to Henslowe six years later.

However, there is no indisputable evidence that the two plays are the same. In fact, *John a Kent and John a Cumber* may be some sort of sequel or companion piece to the earlier play, for which no text survives, but which appears to have been one of the Admiral's Men's most popular and most revived plays between 1594 and 1597. The wrapper of *John a Kent and John a Cumber* was formed from a portion of the same vellum leaf of an earlier manuscript used to wrap *The Book of Sir Thomas More*, and the titles of both are probably in the same hand. This suggests that if Munday had not supplied both wrappers at the time he made the fair copies, the plays acquired the wrappers while simultaneously in the possession of someone else. As both plays probably came to be owned by the Admiral's Men, the book-keeper of that company may have supplied the wrappers and written the titles. His hand may also be that found as book-keeper and reviser in the manuscript of *Sir Thomas More*, and possibly as the copyist of the plots of *The Seven Deadly Sins* and *Fortune's Tennis*. If Munday supplied both wrappers, or oversaw the book-keeper who did, he went to similar lengths when copying both sets of his fair papers. He also protectively had his texts wrapped in old, heavy vellum.

What Munday's foul papers looked like is not clear from the fair copy of *John a Kent and John a Cumber*. The other surviving manuscript in his hand, the original pages of the book of *Sir Thomas More*, to which Chettle, Dekker, Heywood and, apparently, Shakespeare added scenes or passages, is also a fair copy. In fact, judging from examination and collation of all manuscript pages, all these collaborators except Heywood submitted fair rather than foul papers of their work in this particular case. Taken together, the *John a Kent* and *More* manuscripts suggest that Munday wrote out his own fair copies, rather than having a scribe do so. He probably made the copies himself because his foul papers were difficult to read, or he wanted to make changes in copying the play again, or he was contracted to do so by his employers, or for a variety of other reasons. Perhaps he simply wanted to impress his readers, including theatre personnel, with the form as well as the content of his manuscripts, as well as to aid their use of the text as an exemplum for further copying (of parts, for example) and in rehearsal and performance. In any case his careful transcriptions of these two plays imply that he is proud of both these texts; they are the products of his hands. Other dramatists also appear to have slightly or greatly revised their texts both in the acts of copying them out and afterwards. For example, Francis Jaques's 1642 fair copy of his play *The Queen of Corsica* shows later, 'literary' additions in his own hand.[6]

'Why yo" must need be straingers': Shakespeare's fair copy

At least on occasion if not regularly, Shakespeare, like his colleagues and collaborators Munday, Middleton and Jonson, apparently made his own fair copies of foul papers, working in the same way as the others. That is, he probably made minor changes and refinements and cleared up whatever inconsistencies, errors or false starts that he recognised. But it is also possible that he undertook major revisions in any or all parts of a play, including setting, plot, characters, structure, dialogue and stage directions. The early printed texts of at least three plays, Quarto 1 of *The Merchant of Venice*, Folio *Antony and Cleopatra* and Folio *Coriolanus* were probably printed from

Shakespeare's fair copy of his foul papers. The manuscript behind the *Antony and Cleopatra* text, for example, has been described as having been 'in a more finished condition than most of Shakespeare's foul papers, but shows no sign of originating in a prompt-book'.[7] Basically this means that the text is sufficiently clean and free of errors but still preserves authorial spellings, speech-prefixes and/or stage directions.

That Shakespeare had to have his foul papers fair-copied is suggested by the difficulty the compositors had in reading his hand in his disordered foul papers of *Romeo and Juliet*, from which they set Quarto 2. On at least one occasion, they consulted the Quarto 1 text, even though it was printed from a heavily cut text used for provincial performance, to fill in Q2's gaps, possibly because a leaf in the copy they were using to set the type was missing.[8] The compositors had evidently encountered the same kinds of problems apparent in Heywood's foul paper manuscript of *The Captives*, including generic (or otherwise inconsistent) speech-prefixes, variant character names, and vaguely descriptive and misplaced stage directions, as well as loose ends, duplications and false starts. Like the scribe of *Bonduca*, the compositors did not compose dialogue to fill in the missing text, but instead sought out or were furnished with what was assumed to be another copy of the play as performed.

However, manuscript evidence of Shakespeare's possible practices after composition appears in *The Book of Sir Thomas More*.[9] Scholars have not been able to agree that the hand termed 'Hand D' in the collaborative manuscript of *Sir Thomas More* belongs to Shakespeare. But they usually accepted the theory that the three pages (on one and a half leaves) in this hand constitute 'foul papers' rather than a 'fair copy'. For example, W. W. Greg staunchly argued that

> the Shakespearian pages in *Sir Thomas More* and Heywood's *Captives* alike prove than an author's foul papers may be reasonably free from alteration. Supposing the former to be in this respect a fair sample of the manuscripts that Shakespeare handed over to the players, while it may be a matter of opinion whether Heminge and Condell were justified in describing these as containing scarcely a blot, there can be no doubting that they prove the author's ease of composition. This fluency was, we may readily believe, common to other writers of the time, and the unblotted papers became a literary tradition.[10]

In addition, palaeographers have independently agreed with Greg's viewpoint. Although Anthony G. Petti did not state that these pages are foul papers, his typical assessment of the hand in his *English Literary Hands from Chaucer to Dryden* as 'facile/rapid Elizabethan secretary'[11] implies a composing author writing quickly.

Greg's circular and interdependent arguments about the manuscript being in Shakespeare's hand because they are foul papers supported his contention that Shakespeare did not need to revise his text after composition, as his colleagues and collaborators commonly did. This is because he was supposed to have written without blotting or alteration, as Heminges and Condell's preface boasted to readers in the 1616 Shakespeare First Folio in what surely must have been and continues to be a shrewd sales ploy. In order to institutionalise such a theory, thereby isolating Shakespeare from his colleagues and collaborators who routinely practised widespread authorial revision, Greg had to insist that Hand D in *Sir Thomas More*, which used a minimum of alteration and blots, was Shakespeare's. Succeeding scholars who have examined the manuscript in person have largely accepted Greg's claims that Hand D represents Shakespeare's foul papers and that he acted as an original collaborator or later reviser, like Dekker and Chettle, of a text primarily written by Anthony Munday, probably in the early 1590s.[12] Two other hands, including that of a book-keeper, are also found in the manuscript,[13] as is that of the censor Sir Edmund Tilney, whose comments and cuts show that he was not satisfied enough with revisions he originally and later demanded to be made to approve the play for performance.

Munday, Chettle, Heywood and Dekker were, of course, regularly contracted by Henslowe to write plays for the Admiral's Men and other companies, either alone or in collaboration, and thus would have been experienced both in writing for acting companies and in dealing with the censor. Both Dekker and Shakespeare, at least, also wrote for the Chamberlain's/King's Men. The manuscript's wrapper terms this copy of the play the 'Book', so the text eventually came to be termed a complete text, intended to be used in the theatre, most likely as the company book, by the person providing this wrapper and the wrapper for *John a Kent*. Thus the *More* manuscript was to have been used by the company book-keeper, not only to transcribe other copies of the play and to prompt actors during performance but to copy out the playhouse 'plot' and actors' 'parts'. Yet the many inconsistencies, incomplete corrections and confusions acquired as the play was repeatedly revised to suit the censor has led scholars to conclude that the entire *More* manuscript was largely untidy, incomplete foul papers.

However, close and repeated examination of the original manuscript in its entirety suggests that the three leaves usually ascribed to Shakespeare are, like the portions of the play written by Munday, Dekker and Chettle, authorial fair copies of foul papers, rather than the foul papers of Heywood's additions.[14] This argument rests on three sets of evidence:

1   Hand D's secretary writing is not rapid or cursive, but slow, measured and flourished, requiring both time and leisure to write out. The hand also shows a relatively high number of unlinked, hence non-cursive, letters, typifying the perfect hand that Cocker acknowledges as being too laborious to write out fluently and quickly.

2   Some of the deletions, additions and other alterations in Hand D's portions sometimes attributed to the author as a sign of *currente calamo*

changes during composition are, in fact, in another hand or are authorial corrections rather than revisions.

3   Some of the remaining alterations made by Hand D are a result of eyeskip error. This suggests that as he was copying out the text from another text, he occasionally lost his place and transcribed a few letters or a word in the wrong place; upon realising his error, he deleted incorrect words or letters and wrote them out correctly.

Thus, Petti errs in arguing that 'though not especially distinctive or aesthetic, the hand is firm, even-stroked and very cursive, and ably combines boldness and freedom with compactness and economy. Particularly noticeable is the large number of different forms of letters, especially *a, b, g, h, p, s,* and *t*, though this might be expected from a fairly rapid hand.'[15] Using variant forms of letters is not a practice confined to composing authors writing rapidly, for numerous extant dramatic manuscripts fair-copied by authors and scribes show the use of variant letters, even in the same line of text. Examples of such are numerous, but can be found, for example, in Munday's authorial fair copy of *John a Kent and John a Cumber* and Ralph Crane's scribal fair copies both of *Demetrius and Enanthe* and *The Witch*.[16]

The elaborate and stylised letter forms with a large number of flourished ascenders and descenders suggest that the author of these three *More* pages is writing slowly, carefully and methodically, not cursively. The author is very concerned not just with being legible but with being impressively, and unnaturally, elegant. Thus he is probably not in the act of composition, in which he must write quickly or lose his train of thought. Instead, these letter forms show an author at work recopying an earlier text before him rather than composing and writing out a new text still in his mind. Some speech-prefixes in these sheets were added later, another possible sign of a copyist rather than a composer. Above all, these types of correction imply that the author had an exemplum of his text in front of him when writing out these three pages.

Numerous examples of this recopying appear on Folio 9* (Figure 4.1), the only page of the three not obscured by tissue paper applied in the modern age to preserve the manuscript. The 'spurred' *a*, used repeatedly in primary and medial positions, the descenders on the *g* and *y* on 'forgyven' (l. 234), the *h* in 'earth' (l. 256), and the *y* in 'by' (l. 264) would require extra time and effort to make, as they and many other letters are not linked to letters before or after them.[17] In many places the hand looks semi-calligraphic, not cursive. It is possible that the author, almost certainly Shakespeare judging from an examination of six examples of his hand, wrote a highly stylised hand, both when composing and rewriting, and therefore the hand in these pages may reflect a composing hand. But many of the texts (including Quarto 1 *Romeo and Juliet* and *King Lear* and Quarto 2 *Hamlet*) printed from his foul papers show errors resulting from the compositors'

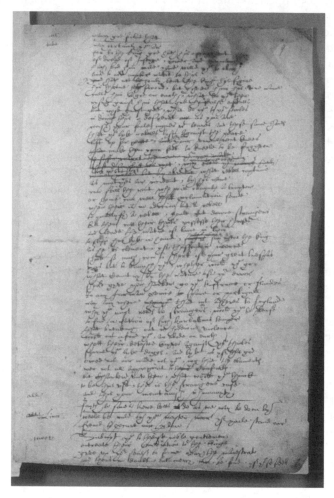

Figure 4.1 Hand D in *The Book of Sir Thomas More*, British Library Harley MS
7368, f. 9*. Reproduced by permission of The British Library.

failure to read his hand accurately. This suggests that his usual composing
hand was not as legible as in this manuscript, which is consistently clear and
legible, almost exaggeratedly so. In essence, this author writes like a scribe
rather than an author. The use of abbreviations (for example a crossed Þ to
signal 'per' or 'pro') or superscript letters (as in 'yoʳ' and 'yoᵘ') do not signify
a rapid hand, as numerous abbreviations appear in fair copy manuscripts of
poetry and prose writers as well as dramatists.

Almost none of the signals of Heywood as composing author in *The
Captives* and in *More* can be found in Hand D's pages of *Sir Thomas More*. In
fact, most major alterations in these three sheets are in the hand of a book-

keeper, playhouse scribe or other acting company member who has changed some speech-prefixes and cut some lines, in order to regularise the scene and thereby fit these three pages into the existing collaborative manuscript. In the only major revision here, the book-keeper or another scribe has deleted three lines and replaced them interlinearly with another line in his own hand. However, the author also made an interlinear revision, which was deleted by the book-keeper, most likely after the book-keeper's first attempt to revise the lines by deleting them. In these 147 lines of Hand D, there are approximately 19 single words (or parts of single words) altered by the author. These consist entirely of deletions of incorrect words and substitution of the correct words, and not revisions. Of these nineteen corrections, only one multi-word addition (ll. 22–3) may be a later revision. All the occurrences of revision are typical of extant manuscripts such as Massinger's *Believe as You List* and Heywood's *The Escapes of Jupiter* in which a book-keeper has lightly annotated the authors' mostly fair copy.

The strongest evidence that Hand D is copying an already completed text in front of him comes by virtue of the fact that of the nineteen words corrected, at least five (and probably more) resulted from eyeskip. For example, line 79 appears as:

and yo^u in ruff of yor ~~yo~~ opynions clothd

The deletion of the seventh word is almost certainly due to correcting the inadvertent repetition of either the second or sixth word in the line while the author was looking at the original copy. That is, he wrote out 'yor', glanced at his original text (but at the wrong place) saw either 'yo^u' or 'yor' and accidentally began to copy this incorrect word. When glancing back at his original copy, perhaps to check if he needed to finish his word with an *r* or *u*, he saw his error and struck out the 'yo', replacing it with the correct word, 'opynions'. This type of eyeskip error is more apparent in lines 129–30:

nay any where ~~why yo^u~~ that not adheres to Ingland
why yo^u must need be straingers, woold yo^u be pleasd

Here we can see that the author recopied the first two words, 'why yo^u', from the following line, into the wrong place, after 'nay any where'. He deleted these misplaced words and copied out the correct words in their place. The substituted words are not a *currente calamo* revision or a change of mind but a correction. Other obvious corrections are also among the nineteen authorial alterations, for example, 'ar' corrected to 'or' (l. 34) and 'mv' corrected to 'nvmber', with the *v* representing a *u* (l. 51).

However, some alterations may indeed be authorial revisions, for example in this confusion in ll. 21–4, the only place the author does not adhere to the margin he has already set for the beginning of dialogue:

```
Seriaunt        yoᵘ ar the simplest thing that euˈ stood in such a question
```
_____

```
                now prenty
Lin   how say yoᵘ prentisses symple down wᵗʰ him
```
_____

```
All             prentisses symple prentisses symple    X
```

Here the 'now prenty', added interlinearly, and 'how say yoᵘ', added marginally, are probably a revision or addition in response to the book-keeper's mark of 'X' to alter or cut the following line or to resolve what he may have seen as too much repetition. 'Now prenty[ces], how say you?' is used to replace 'prentisses symple' and perhaps 'down wᵗʰ him' in Lincoln's speech. Other corrections may also be subtle revisions. In fact, such alterations are typical of authorial fair copies, in which an author makes slight and subtle, and only occasionally major, revisions in recopying his foul papers. The idea that authorial fair copies, however neatly written, not to mention foul papers, would be perfect or even without 'a blot', as Heminges and Condell claimed of Shakespeare, cannot be substantiated in any of the authorial fair copies of Massinger, Heywood, Middleton, Dekker and Chettle, among others. What other fair copy manuscripts show repeatedly and continually are the types of small fine-tuning that appears in these three pages of *More*.

Most importantly, this author does this fine-tuning *after* the book-keeper has read through the text. These three pages in *Sir Thomas More*, as well as many others, show the dramatists working *with* the book-keeper and responding to his corrections. In fact, Shakespeare's methods of working here suggests the following:

1   He made or accepted changes in theatrical business that the book-keeper and other colleagues offered or imposed.
2   In working as a collaborator on portioned-off sections of text, he showed a concern with accommodating his writing to suit the manuscript as a whole.
3   He presented the text in such a way to make it as easy to read and to use as possible, not only for the censor but for his fellow collaborators, the book-keeper, and, ultimately, the actors.
4   In effect, he did not simply compose his text but helped prepare it for production and performance; that is, he 'perfected' the text as much as possible.

These dramatists were evidently expected, as part of their contractual duties or for their own artistic interests, to 'perfit' the text, to use Daborne's term, even after it entered the playhouse. However, they did not always consider changes made between foul papers and fair copies as 'improvements', nor are fair copies necessarily 'better' than foul papers.

While the first page of Heywood's *The Captives* shows some errors, it also presents a particularly coherent text of a play in the heat of being composed. The same can be said of passages in the foul paper text behind Q2 *Romeo and Juliet*. Foul papers are not the bottom of the transmission process but the source of it, and authorial fair copies are the next stage. Daborne's insistence that he will indeed give Henslowe fair and not foul copies of plays he was contracted to write, but could not deliver, may be a convenient excuse for being late rather than a moral judgement that only fair copies were acceptable texts. What is clear from extant autograph foul paper and fair-copied manuscripts is that texts could continue to evolve or change, and the author participated in that evolution or change when the text reached the playhouse.

'Theatrical Business': scribes and authors' copies

Scholars have not only failed to recognise the differing characteristics of authorial foul and fair papers but have extrapolated evidence about authorial practice solely from scribal manuscripts or printed texts. To begin with, the stricture that authors would routinely create blank manuscript books, as some scribes did, before they began writing,[18] is highly questionable. Most extant authorial dramatic manuscripts were written on successive individual folded sheets and bound later. Also, the contention that authors would always pleat manuscript pages to create columns because scribes did so cannot be supported. In fact, comparison of scribal and authorial manuscripts demonstrates a number of other differences in format and size and in the treatment of paper. The comparison of scribal manuscripts made for the theatre and those made as reading, presentation, or commissioned copies shows even more differences.

Some arguments about scribal practice are drawn so consistently from Shakespeare's printed texts, rather than from extant manuscripts of other dramatists' plays, that they ignore valuable evidence. Those who recognise the existence and importance of manuscripts may see Shakespeare's manuscripts as unique from those of his colleagues. For example, Stanley Wells, Gary Taylor, William Montgomery and John Jowett, the editors of *William Shakespeare: The Complete Works*, constructed their edition from two unsustainable arguments about scribal copy. They repeatedly set out these arguments in *William Shakespeare: A Textual Companion*, which has now largely supplanted W. W. Greg's earlier books as the standard reference guide on the transmission of Shakespeare's texts. First, these editors argued that any manuscript copy that contained act notations could not be authorial but must be scribal prior to 1609, when they assume Shakespeare's company moved into the private Blackfriars theatre at which music was played between acts.[19] Second, they argued that scribes routinely introduced 'interference' into the manuscripts they were copying, either by extensively adding their own or cutting the author's material.

As for their first argument, extant authorial manuscripts before 1609 such as *John a Kent and John a Cumber* show the use of act division, even if the numbering drops out after the first or second act. Henslowe commissioned both freelance and company dramatists to provide individual scenes or acts of a collaborative or revised play, thus his writers were more than accustomed to noting act or scene divisions. It would have placed a huge burden on book-keepers to have had to find each act and scene division in a manuscript and supply it both in the company book and in the plot. Book-keepers would have expected or hoped that authors supplied act notations themselves. Furthermore, such dramatists as Daborne, Wilson, Chettle, Munday, Drayton, Chapman, Webster, Ford, Dekker, Tourneur and Samuel Rowley, among others, signed contracts, correspondence or legal depositions before and after 1609 specifying that they had each produced an act, scene or some other closely delineated portion of a play. Thus they were accustomed to dividing their text into acts and scenes. Shakespeare apparently used act divisions at least on occasion and, like his colleagues, may have dropped the numbering of later acts in the heat of writing. Dramatists may have been more regular in formally noting act divisions than scene divisions, as the end of a scene may simply have been noted by 'Exit' or 'Exeunt' directions which left no characters on stage. Authors of this period followed what they took to be the classical convention of writing a play in five acts, with one or more scenes per act. Not using act or scene divisions would have violated this convention, or simply caused chaos in assembling a play consisting of separate acts or scenes by different collaborators.[20]

As for 'scribal interference', the role that many scholars imagine for scribes of Shakespeare's plays violates evidence found in extant scribal manuscripts, many of them written for Shakespeare's company. For example, Stanley Wells argues that it would be 'an unreasonable expectation that someone preparing a "literary" transcript of the prompt-book [of *Twelfth Night*] would preserve theatrical annotations such as the names of particular actors, marginal notes about props, or added early "warning" directions'.[21] However, two different scribes, each of whom transcribed a 'literary' copy of Middleton's *Hengist King of Kent* from the company book, did indeed copy out three minor actors' names and marginal symbols next to directions for properties or actors to be made ready.[22] In fact, one of the scribes was so concerned that he match the manuscript from which he was copying that he redrew one of the marginal symbols when he failed to copy it out in the right dimensions the first time. These two scribes were so precise in following their copy that their two texts, written separately and individually, show almost no substantive variants. Although scribes certainly varied in their practices, they were more likely than not to edit lightly the grammatical features of the text they were copying rather than to 'interfere' in it seriously, as the two *Hengist* scribes demonstrate and Edward Knight proved to a fault in his copy of *Bonduca*.

Far too many Shakespearean or early modern drama textual scholars, then, including the editors of *William Shakespeare: A Textual Companion*, have seen scribes as 'interfering', 'careless', 'sloppy' or 'cavalier', in order to protect Shakespeare from his own textual cruxes, inconsistencies and occasional bouts of sub-standard writing. Suppositions about scribes and their practices should be reasonable and non-moralistic. In 1928 Eleanore Boswell claimed that the 'formal and distinctly legal' shape of the manuscript of *Edmund Ironside* could make one 'imagine the manuscript having been written by a broken-down scrivener's clerk'.[23] Her conclusion evidently had the approval of Greg, who checked her edition. Such an 'imagination' derives from the still institutionalised view of the new bibliographers that scribes were 'broken-down' hacks or interlopers always acting independently from authors in the textual transmission process.

One last issue about the new bibliographic imagination needs to be addressed here. William B. Long has argued that 'theatrical personnel seem to have marked the book only in response to problems', and attacks the 'tenacious notion of the supposed existence of clean, complete, and well-ordered "promptbooks" filled with at least dozens if not hundreds of theatrical alterations'. He holds Greg responsible for such a notion, yet accepts Greg's contention that fifteen extant manuscripts served as 'playbooks', including *The Captives*, but adds one other to the list.[24] However, it is impossible to know for certain how many of the more than one hundred extant dramatic manuscripts cited in the Introduction to this book were used in some way or at some time as play-books. So Greg's count is faulty, especially as one, *The Captives*, is not a play-book at all but annotated foul papers. In addition, most non-authorial annotations in manuscripts do not respond to 'problems' but to practical theatrical business. Not every play-book was neat and tidy, but this does not mean that none was; surely the competence, efficiency and organisational skills of playhouse book-keepers and scribes were as varied as were those of the dramatists themselves.

'Barre ready': book-keepers and authors' papers

As Beal, Woudhuysen, Love and Marotti, among others, have demonstrated, the employment of scribes was such a routine practice by lawyers and government officials as well as by literary authors that 'scriptoria' (professional copy houses) could be readily found in London in this period. Bowers argues from the evidence of a few plays of this period sold directly to a printer that 'some authors seem to have retained possession of their foul papers, a situation which could arise only if a fair copy were made for the theatre'.[25] Yet the scribe who found Fletcher's foul papers of *Bonduca* was apparently writing after Fletcher's death, and may have found the foul papers among the company's inventory of theatrical stock. Whether or not they kept possession of their foul papers on occasion, dramatists depended to varying degrees on scribal assistance throughout their careers. Shakespeare, Jonson, Middleton and their contemporaries were more than accustomed to handing over first or later drafts, if they were not going to recopy them, to someone paid to transcribe them as literally as possible. Virtually anyone who could write a fluent secretary or italic hand could be pressed into service when necessary. Scribes could specialise in copying legal documents, as most scriveners did, or work more generally in copying literary and other documents. Whether working for private clients or freelance or employed by scriptoria, scribes were trained penmen and were expected to act responsibly in their employment.

Professional theatre companies could employ scribes working for a scriptorium or on a freelance basis to make copies of a dramatic manuscript. Or the companies could use scribes who sometimes doubled as book-keepers and prompters, or even scriveners pressed into writing the type of contract outlined in *Bartholomew Fair*. Peter W. M. Blayney's estimation that the transcription of a play of average length would have cost between 2 and 3 shillings (24 to 36 pence),[26] seems too low. Using Peter Beal's calculation of scribal copying costing at least $1\frac{1}{2}$ to 3 pence a page,[27] the transcription of a dramatic manuscript of approximately 44 to 50 pages would cost approximately 5 to 12 shillings. The very experienced printer Humphrey Moseley noted in the 1647 Beaumont and Fletcher Folio: 'Heretofore when Gentlemen desired the copy of any of these Playes, the meanest piece here ... cost them more [in scribal copying] than foure times the price you pay for the whole Volume.'[28] Whether it is true that in 1647 scribal copying of one play cost four times the price of buying the Folio (£1, or 20 shillings, and upwards),[29] this statement makes clear that manuscripts were more expensive commodities than printed books.

Scribes did not act as editors or as authors, although they may have regularised mechanical or formatting features such as spelling, lineation, speech-prefixes, act–scene notations and stage directions. While they may have relocated stage directions, they would not usually rewrite dialogue or in any other way change plot, structure or any other content in the play. Extant scribal manuscripts look neater and are more formal than an authorial manuscript such as *The Captives*, for scribes were paid to make writing look good, clear, presentable and, most importantly, legible. Scribal manuscripts belong, by their very nature, to a visual medium.

There is no professional London play known to be extant in both a foul paper manuscript and a scribal fair copy. However, at least two wholly or partly foul paper manuscripts were corrected or annotated by playhouse scribes: Heywood's *The Captives* and Massinger's *Believe as You List*. This latter manuscript was the product of a complex set of circumstances, as well as the intervention of a scribe connected to a few other manuscripts. *The Captives* is a more direct case in which Heywood and a scribe worked together to try to turn the foul papers into the company book without having to fair-copy them. The fact that this second hand annotates the manuscript specifically for theatrical practice suggests he was a playhouse scribe or book-keeper rather than a freelance or scriptorium copyist. Indeed,

Heywood and the scribe apparently did not succeed in making it legible enough to serve as the 'book' or to submit to the censor, so eventually another copy was made for the censor.

Although Heywood made copious changes and alterations to this manuscript when it was in his hands, the scribe, who writes in a different hand and ink, was more conservative when the manuscript reached his hands. As Arthur Brown has concluded, *The Captives'* book-keeper has

1   regularised the Act 2, 3, 4, and 5 notations (which Heywood neglected to write out in full after Act 1), placing them clearly in the left margin;
2   called attention to major character entrances by drawing a star opposite them in the left margin;
3   separated the names of each character in many of the entrance directions by using vertical strokes;
4   highlighted some directions by drawing rules above and below them;
5   written some actors' names in the margins, in order to remind himself to make them ready to appear;
6   added some necessary or missing stage and entrance directions;
7   made a number of cuts, removing two minor parts in the last scene and assigning some of the lines to one of the surviving characters (probably to reduce the number of actors required);
8   added directions for scene division, sometimes writing 'clere' or 'cleere' to signal that the stage is emptied;
9   clarified other stage directions.[30]

What these conclusions demonstrate is that the book-keeper's only substantive changes to dialogue and content are his cutting of two minor characters and their speeches in one scene. This particular book-keeper, at least, did not act as author but largely confined himself to editing stage directions and other stage business, such as readying properties and actors, for which he would be responsible during performance. His major changes were surely made in consultation with the company, the Lady Elizabeth's Men, who perhaps wanted to save the expense of using two actors in minor roles in the final scene. These changes were probably made in consultation with Heywood, given his close working relationship at the time with the company and especially his friend Christopher Beeston, to whom Heywood supplied the play.

As a collaborator in the composition of a play-text, this book-keeper serves only a minor function of correcting errors, although he has overlooked some others, thereby allowing them to stand. This copy of *The Captives* demonstrates that play-texts were not made perfect, consistent or correct after being annotated by the author, scribe or book-keeper. As Leslie Thomson notes, 'book-keepers were most concerned with what they could control from the tiring house—such as entrances—and with what was not the players' responsibility—such as large props, music, and *entr'acte* entertainment'.[31] Brown argues that this book-keeper, nearly as illegible as Heywood, annotated the manuscript 'for the guidance of the scribe by whom the official "book" was to be prepared'.[32] If this was the case, Heywood may have checked and approved the book-keeper's changes, and the book-keeper cannot be seen as part-author in the play's composition. Rather than preparing the manuscript for another copyist, it is more probable that the book-keeper attempted to turn the manuscript into the company book, but he finally realised that he could not succeed in making any or all of it legible enough to submit to the censor.

The exact nature of the book-keeper's corrections is apparent on one page (f. 70ᵛ; Figure 4.2) in the manuscript. On the line above the authorial division 'Actus 5ˢ' (i.e. Quintus), 3ᵃ (i.e. Terza), the book-keeper has twice written '/clere' (also spelled 'cleere' elsewhere), in the left and right margins, to remind himself that the stage is to be emptied before the next scene starts. He has also drawn an asterisk in the margin of three entrances for the characters of Mildew, Gripus and Godfrey, and he has deleted 'and Sarlabois' from the entrance for Mildew. He then cancels the two occurrences of Sarlabois's speech-prefixes and dialogue on the page, using vertical lines, and also deletes one speech of three lines for Mildew, effectively cutting all mention of the character of Sarlabois. In essence, the book-keeper has reduced a two-person dialogue to a soliloquy.

He has further clarified stage directions by writing and ruling off 'Barre ready' in the right margin of Sarlabois's first cancelled speech in order to remind himself to get a property ready, most likely a staff or fishing pole for the soon-to-be entering Gripus. The book-keeper then changed his mind and deleted the direction for the 'Barre' by scoring through it, or he added the direction before deleting Sarlabois's character and dialogue, and then deleted it. The book-keeper has added and ruled off 'to him' (i.e. towards Mildew) at the end of the stage direction 'Enter gripus the ffisherman', signalling to himself the opposite of 'clere'. This character does not enter on a cleared stage but on one already occupied by one other character, Mildew. The book-keeper has done the same with the entrance for Godfrey, writing 'to them' (i.e. towards Mildew and Gripus), and has written and ruled off 'godfry' in the line above the character's entrance, again to remind himself to make the actor ready to enter.

Greg claimed that 'with the possible exception of the wholly exceptional *Launching of the Mary*, acted by some unidentified company, no instance survives of an original draft being used as a prompt-book'.[33] Yet there is no evidence of which texts, bearing the licence or otherwise, were actually used as the company book. Acting companies may have locked up their valuable licensed copy (usually signed by the Master of the Revels on the first or final page) after making another transcript of it to serve as the company book, or they may have used the licensed copy itself as the book. A number of extant manuscripts, including a scribal fair copy of the collaborative *The Honest Man's Fortune*,[34] still carry the censor's licence (although the signature appears to have been removed by a collector). This particular manuscript of

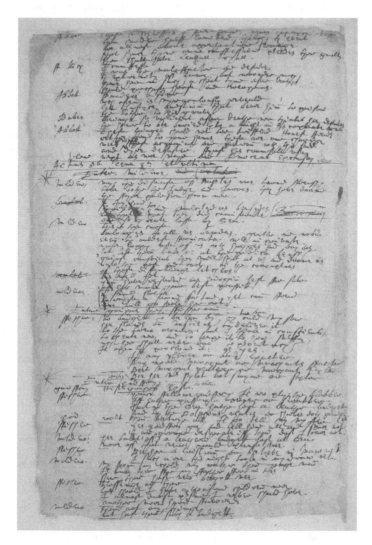

Figure 4.2 Heywood's foul paper manuscript of *The Captives*, British Library Egerton MS 1994, f. 70ᵛ, showing a few emendations by a book-keeper or theatrical scribe. Reproduced by permission of The British Library.

an 'olde' play was evidently recopied for submission to Herbert, who 'real-lowed' it on 8 February 1624/5, 'the original being lost', and accepted as payment a printed edition of Sidney's *Arcadia*.[35] This and other licensed manuscripts do not show the typical added marginal notations made by the book-keeper. Some licensed copies were *not* used as the company book but were fair-copied by a freelance or company scribe or the author to make the book. The *Bonduca* scribe's complaint that the company book of the play was lost and that he had to find the foul papers to make his transcription implies that he had no other licensed copy to consult at that time. Some licensed copies were probably locked up for safekeeping while others may have been used as company books, depending on circumstances, experience or company practice.

Although it does not bear the censor's licence, portions of the manuscript of *The Captives* could have been used in rehearsal or at any performances of the play to prompt actors. It could also have been used to copy out some actors' parts or as the basis for another theatrical transcript. If *The Captives'* book-keeper were merely cleaning up the foul papers for another scribe, as Brown suggested, he would not have needed to add actors' names, among other things. The company book later made from this manuscript was probably the copy submitted to Herbert for his approval, which he noted on 3 September 1624.[36] Heywood's difficult handwriting would probably have pre-empted him from transcribing himself the copy seen by Herbert. Given the often confusing and illegible nature of this manuscript, Heywood would almost certainly have been consulted by the scribe who made Herbert's reading copy. Heywood may have made required alterations after the book returned from the censor, thus putting his hand to the text once again.

This type of consultation between author and scribe was apparently also done in the case of the scribal copy of *The Second Maiden's Tragedy* in which the scribe faltered at times in reading the foul papers of the authors.[37] As with the *More* manuscript and a variety of others, this manuscript contains a number of additions written on extra slips, which are marked for insertion at the appropriate points. The manuscript bears a number of hands, in addition to Buc's, including one of the collaborators and the playhouse scribe or book-keeper. None of those writers, other than the collaborator, revises the text, except in making cuts to suit censorship. Scribes seem to defer to the author when dealing with another scribe's transcript. Edward Knight appears to have consulted the author, probably John Clavell, and the reviser (if he was not Clavell) in annotating the scribal manuscript of *The Soddered Citizen*.[38]

Knight was not alone in consulting the author whose text he was preparing for the playhouse. The heavily revised authorial manuscript of the anonymous play *The Wasp or Subjects President* (i.e. Precedent) shows the dramatist reworking the play on his own, making changes, most likely in writing these foul papers, as well as changes made by a book-keeper.[39] As in the case of *The Captives*, that this set of foul papers shows annotations by a book-keeper does not mean that the manuscript should not be classed as foul papers. In *The Wasp*, the book-keeper, who also appeared to have annotated the manuscript of Glapthorne's *The Lady Mother*,[40] regularised or added stage directions for actor entrances, stage properties and music (including the note for 'Recorders'). As J. W. Lever notes, the book-keeper made these annotations and corrections on at least three different occasions, judging from the colour of the ink. He also inserted the names of actors who were members of the King's Revels in the 1630s, the same company for which *The Lady Mother* was written. Thus the *Wasp* book-keeper marks the play as the property of a professional London company, who performed at the Salisbury Court, the contentious, contractual home of Richard Brome. Lever's impressive study of the manuscript leads him to conclude that not only was the book-keeper working with the author to incorporate his revisions more fluently into the text, but, more precisely, the book-keeper was present while the author made his revisions.[41] Another contemporary hand has made some slight alterations. The manuscript lacks the censor's licence, but the possibility remains that some of the revisions were due to anticipated censorship.

When confronted with a less chaotic manuscript, scribes who were regularly employed in the playhouse may have confined themselves to the purgation of oaths, especially after the 1606 Act against Abuses, and other censorable material. Their alterations were probably made in anticipation of the kinds of cuts they expected from the censor. Hence, for the 1633 revival of Fletcher's *The Woman's Prize, or The Tamer Tamed*, Sir Henry Herbert noted to the King's Men book-keeper Edward Knight on 21 October: 'In many things you have saved mee labour; yet when your judgment or pens fayld you, I have made boulde to use mine. Purge ther parts, as I have the book.' It is not clear here if the actors' parts had already been written before the play was licensed, as Herbert may be anticipating that Knight would be less than careful in writing the parts out afterwards. In any event, the two men must have been judicious in their cuts, for Herbert reported that when the play was performed on 28 November before Charles I and Henrietta Maria, it was 'Very well likt'.[42] Clearly Knight is expected to make the same cuts in the existing actors' parts for this play, but his role is confined to a censoring editor, not reviser or collaborator.

'The changes are very few and as brief as possible': scribal fair copies

One possible stage of dramatic manuscript transmission is the foul or fair copy annotated by a scribe, but another is the scribal fair copy of foul or fair copy. Although Edward Knight's hand has been identified, those of other freelance or attached playhouse scribes have not. W. W. Greg, G. R. Proudfoot, Peter Beal and H. R. Woudhuysen, among others, have done invaluable work in identifying which dramatic documents are in the hands of the same known or unidentified scribes.[43] Two examples, copied by the same, probably professional, playhouse scribe are the manuscripts of Dekker's play *The Welsh Embassador* (c. 1623), and Massinger's *The Parliament of Love*, licensed in 1624 (although it lacks two leaves at the beginning, the rest of the manuscript is largely intact). In *The Welsh Embassador*, the scribe, almost certainly a book-keeper or other person with experience in the playhouse, added marginal directions for properties and/or characters to be made ready, including 'bee redy Carintha / at a Table', 'bee redy Clowne / & Eldred', and 'sett out a Table'.[44] The scribe also had to make some *currente calamo* corrections in the act of copying, and made a number of large cuts.[45] But he also introduced errors, as in this alteration, which he later corrects:

> *Eld*: I lay farr off from Pendas regiment
> nor know I what fate followes him
>
> ———————
>
> *Edm*: nor I ~~from Edmonds tent I come~~
>
> ———————
>
> *Eld*: from Eldreds tent I come   (f. 3ʳ)

The word 'Eldreds' in the last line has been written over in at least the first letter. The deletion, alteration and reattribution of this line may proceed from the scribe's having difficulty making sense of the author's marginal or interlinear addition. But it could have been due to the scribe's uncertainty about the opening stage direction for Act 1, which he copied fourteen lines earlier (it is now damaged and incomplete at the end of line 2):

> *Enter the Duke of Cornewall, the Earles of Chester*
> *and mercia; and Edwin; // Elfred and Edmond yᵉ Kings broth*
> *disguizd like souldiers*

Evidently the scribe was confused, writing the name 'Eldred' in the stage direction as Elfred (or recopying it as the author wrote it). Then, as he began to write the speech-prefixes, he perhaps mistakenly assumed that 'Eld.' was one of the unnamed '*Earles of Chester and mercia*' and not the King's brother. At any rate, the scribe recognised that the line he had copied for Edmond made no sense and deleted it; when he reassigned it to 'Eld' it was similarly incorrect, but he let it stand. This scribe cannot solve the puzzle offered him in his copy, and evidently gives up on his second try, letting stand an obvious mistake. Perhaps this is why Henslowe paid established authors to make even the smallest 'addicians' to a dramatic manuscript.

The manuscript of *The Parliament of Love* similarly has a number of passages marked for deletion by scoring through the entire line in each passage.[46] This scribe wrote out the text in the same way that an author usually worked, by writing on loose sheets,[47] not in an already assembled manuscript book. This copy once bore the censor's licence at the end, but it was later neatly cut out. Judging by the removal of censors' signatures here and elsewhere, later collectors may have valued a Master of the Revels' autograph more than an entire dramatic manuscript. This manuscript then, is the official, licensed copy of the play, but it does not contain any of the playhouse annotations found in *The Captives*, for example. So it was probably kept locked up by the company and was not used as the company book. A previous editor of the manuscript has noted the characteristics of this professional scribe in making a fair from a foul copy:

The scribe was economical of paper and left no margin at top or bottom, but the fortunate absence of prose prevented him running into the right margin. He averages nearly 70 lines to a page, but his writing grows somewhat larger as he proceeds. . . . The lower portion of fol. 8^b was left blank, by accident it would seem, and subsequently filled with cross hatching to indicate that there was nothing lost.

Although wasting space here, the scribe continues to attempt economy with paper and placement. Above all, he tries to be regular and consistent in his practices:

The play is divided into five acts, but not into scenes: no space is left between the acts. There are the usual short rules separating speeches. Entrances at the beginning of an act are centred, otherwise they begin in the left margin between rules. Short stage-directions appear in either margin between rules; longer ones in the right only and without rules.[48]

This scribe has also punctuated lightly, although he may simply be using the punctuation of the author, Massinger.

The lack of scene division may appear puzzling in a manuscript intended for use in the theatre. Yet, this scribe has been diligent in writing exit markers at the end of scenes, so he may have relied on these to denote the end of one scene and the beginning of another, as may have Shakespeare. Or the scribe may be copying *verbatim* from foul papers lacking scene divisions. Unlike *The Captives'* annotator, he saw no need to write 'clere' between scenes. Although this scribe has corrected his own errors in transcription, another contemporary hand appears in the last two acts, making several cuts by scoring out lines and making substitutions of a few words here and elsewhere. These changes may have been made by the company book-keeper before or after its submission to the censor, Herbert, or at a later point, such as a revival. While cuts to a text would be allowable after licensing, additions would not, but these slight additions would not have been noticeable. These cuts would most likely have been made during rehearsal or after early performances, as they speed up the action as the play comes to a close, as is the case with the cuts in the last three acts of the Folio *Hamlet* text.

The annotator here acts as an editor but not as an author; he rearranges existing material rather than composing new material. For example, he is confronted with this difficult passage in a speech of Cleremond:

I neede not
so well I am acquainted wth yor vallor
to dare in a good cause as much as man
lend yo^u encoragm^t & should I ad
yor power to doe, wch ffortune, then not blind
hath euer seconded, I cannot doubt

> but victorie still sitt vppon yo[r] sword
> & must not now for sake yo[u]

The annotator alters the passage with deletions and interlinear additions to this:

> I am so well acquainted wth yo[r] vallor
> to dare in a good cause as much as man
> I need not lend yo[u] encouragm[t] & your Courage fortune
> hath euer seconded, I cannot doubt
> but victorie still sitt vppon yo[r] sword
> & must not now for sake yo[u].

The annotator makes the deletions and revisions after, rather than before, copying them out, apparently literally, from his foul paper copy; this suggests that he was hesitant to revise on his own accord as he was copying. He may, then, have worked out the proper sequence of phrasing here and emended the text, or he revised it at the later direction of the author. The annotator makes only three other one- or two-word additions in the rest of acts 4 and 5, as well as the cuts of a few lines here and there. This scribe, probably the book-keeper, makes cuts to reduce playing time. However, what is striking about his alterations is that they are sometimes 'clumsily' made,[49] often showing no understanding of verse flow or character. That is, the non-authorial editing of the text is obvious in this case.

Another scribal copy showing annotations and later revisions by a co-author and various theatre personnel is the manuscript of a play now known as *John of Bordeaux*,[50] but whose original title was probably *The Second Part of Friar Bacon*. The manuscript appears to offer a shortened version of the original text. It displays the hands of at least two playhouse scribes or book-keepers, including the hand that annotated *Edmund Ironside* and *The Two Noble Ladies*, and the hand that may have written part or all of *Thomas of Woodstock* (also known as *Richard II*).[51] Significantly, all three of these manuscripts are bound, like *The Captives*, in the British Library's Egerton MS 1994 volume, which the actor William Cartwright donated to Dulwich College in the seventeenth century, probably as part of an existing or planned theatrical archive. Greg and W. L. Renwick argue that the *Bordeaux* manuscript was copied for a company already familiar with it, as it contains such stage directions (in the primary scribe's hand) as 'Exeunt Bacon to bring in the showes as you knowe' and 'Enter the seane of the whiper'.[52] However, these directions may refer to comic set pieces used and adapted by the company.

The manuscript carries the name of an actor associated with two of the companies, Strange's and Pembroke's Men, with which Henslowe worked. The play's probable predecessor, *Friar Bacon and Friar Bungay*, was written by Robert Greene; it was acted by Strange's Men in 1592 and by the combined Queen's and Sussex's Men in 1594, as Henslowe notes in his receipts.[53] Henslowe's papers contain no record of a sequel, unless, as Renwick posits, some of the records of *Friar Bacon* refer to the *Bordeaux* play. If the *Bordeaux* manuscript represents a sequel also commissioned by Henslowe in the same decade, it would explain the presence of the hand of Chettle, a frequent contractee of Henslowe. The play was apparently composed by Greene and was revived after his death, when Chettle was paid to add one speech of a dozen lines only,[54] in the same way that Middleton was paid in 1602 by Henslowe to add 'a prologe & A epelogue for the playe of bacon for the corte'.[55]

This addition suggests that the scribe and the three other hands of theatrical personnel in the manuscript were not considered appropriate to do even such minor composition or revision and that companies called upon established dramatists to do so instead. Chettle may have had some part in the play's original composition, given the types of records kept by Henslowe and Alleyn that show them contracting original authors to mend or alter existing plays. In fact, the manuscript of *John of Bordeaux* demonstrates, once again, that acting companies drew a very clear line between what theatrical personnel on the one hand, and what dramatists, on the other hand, were allowed to do to a play-manuscript. Perhaps not ironically, Hamlet understands this distinction. He asks the newly arrived players to insert a 'speech of some dosen or sixteene lines' into the old play of *The Murder of Gonzago*, but he writes the lines himself, rather than asking the actors to do so.[56] Perhaps Hamlet's insistence that he serve as author reflects Shakespeare's own concern over any possibility of losing control of his texts to actors. Whether it was Chettle or Hamlet supplying the addition, even a speech of 'some dosen lines' had to be composed by an author, not by actors or scribes.[57]

'Suche as they shall thincke meet to be played': dramatists' manuscripts and censorship

Some of the alterations, rewriting, cuts, or other signs of indecision, clumsy or otherwise, in these foul and fair copies may have been made due to anticipated or actual censorship. Authors and scribes wrote with the knowledge and experience that their texts were to be recited to or read by the Master of the Revels before they could be rehearsed or performed. He decided which plays would be licensed, and thus performed, in exactly what state, down to each word. As an appointee of the monarch, the censor was responsible also to the Privy Council, composed of the monarch's chief ministers, as well as other government officials such as his superior, the Lord Chamberlain, who could overrule him, and did so, on occasion. All in all, the censor had a number of people to please, from the monarch down in descending hierarchical rank, but he did not have to please theatre and company sharers, actors and dramatists. Instead these personnel had to please *him*. In only one or two cases in this period, apparently, did a company perform an unlicensed play;[58] thus the censor's demands, strictures and dictates were in theory, if not always in practice, to be obeyed. Authors knew both that the censor would effectively collaborate in the production of a text and that they would be required to deal with any changes that such collaboration required.

Theatre performance had begun causing offence long before an official censor had been established. A manuscript dated 3 October 1550 complains that 'the players playe abrode in everye place', with the result that 'euerye lewd sediciouse fellowse deuise to the daunger of the kynge and his counsaylle'.[59] The position of the Master of the Revels became official in 1581 and was held by four men in the early modern period. Sir Edmund Tilney served from 1578 to 1610, followed by his relative (by marriage) Sir George Buc, from 1610 to 1622; Buc also licensed printed plays from at least 1607, and continued in this role after becoming censor.[60] John Astley then served briefly in 1622, and was succeeded by Sir Henry Herbert from 1623 until 1642, assisted at times by his deputy William Blagrave. At Tilney's formal appointment in 1581 he was officially authorised to warn, command and appoint

> all and euery plaier or plaiers with their playmakers either belonginge to any noble man or otherwise bearinge the name or names of vsinge the facultie of playmakers or plaiers of Comedies Tragedies Enterludes or what other showes soever from tyme to tyme and at all tymes to appeare before him with all suche plaies Tragedies Comedieis or showes as they shall haue in readines or meane to sett forth and them to presente and recite before our said Servant or his sufficient deputie.

Tilney and his deputy were further given the power to 'order', 'reform', 'authorise' and 'put down' whatever they thought 'meete or vnmeete' in the plays and playhouses and to imprison those who 'obstinatelie' refused to obey specific censorship demands.[61]

However, the Privy Council specifically intervened in theatrical censorship in 1589 due to the satiric staging of material central to the Martin Marprelate tracts, which had attacked the principles of episcopacy.[62] The government appeared not to have been satisfied with entrusting censorship only to the Master of the Revels to contain this controversy, for on 12 November of that year the Privy Council wrote to the Archbishop of Canterbury to ask him to help form a committee to aid Tilney. A recently rediscovered letter shows that the Council claimed that in certain plays and interludes performed in and about the city of London, 'the players doe take vpon them to handle in their playes certen matters of divinitie and of State unfitt to be suffred'. The Council wishes to appoint 'some persones of Judgement and understanding' to view and examine plays before they can be presented 'publickly'. The Archbishop is therefore commanded to appoint someone schooled in divinity as well another person appointed by the Lord Mayor to join the Master of the Revels. These three will then be ordered

> Jointly and wth some spede to viewe and consedir of suche Comedies or Tragedies, as are and shalbe publickly played by the Companies of Players in and bout the Cittie of London, and they to geve their allowance of suche as they shall thincke meet to be played, and to forbydd the rest.[63]

No later evidence exists to document that this trinity of censors was actually formed or that such officials exercised any joint theatrical censorship. That the Privy Council sought in 1589 to add both a religious and a local government censor to the one already appointed by the Queen suggests that Tilney had either been ineffective or overwhelmed in censoring the increasingly large number of plays performed in London. This document verifies both that the censorship of publicly performed plays (and shorter interludes or entertainments) was a matter of serious concern to the government and that, at least by 1589, the government did not see itself as having as much influence over plays as their authors and performers had. The Marprelate controversy emphasised that the content of plays must have had a great deal of real influence over their audiences, something of which professional dramatists would have been well aware, endowing them with a power that scholars may still not fully appreciate.

Although Tilney was supposed to have had more assistance from 1589, the few surviving records for him and his successor, Buc, are scarce. As G. E. Bentley notes, the large increase in acting companies and new plays by the 1590s prevented actors or authors from reciting new plays in front of the censor; instead the plays were presented in manuscript to be read at the censor's leisure.[64] At least by 18 October 1633, Herbert demanded of acting companies that 'the Master ought to have copies of their new playes left with him, that he may be able to shew what he hath allowed or disallowed'. Perhaps Tilney and Buc had not made the same demand, for Herbert notes that 'in former time the poetts tooke greater liberty than is allowed them by mee'.[65] Herbert would presumably have known the exact extent of that liberty, as he possessed the licensing books of his predecessors.[66] That the majority of extant fair copy manuscripts date from 1624, coinciding with the early years of Herbert's employment, suggests that he enforced this demand for extra copies to be made and kept for him, even if the copies were for some reason later dispersed. Such a demand would have led to a proliferation of manuscript transcription. This may be one simple explanation why dramatic manuscripts written before 1624, including Shakespeare's own, do not as readily survive.

In theory, the censor was responsible for licensing both new plays and old plays that had been revised or updated; both types of books were to be submitted for his approval. But in practice Tilney and Buc seem to have confined themselves to licensing new scripts. Herbert was much stricter, and more contentious, in enforcing the censorship of old, revived plays, possibly because he was suspicious of plays originally licensed by his predecessors. He notes in a series of entries in October 1633 that two members of the King's Men, probably John Lowin and Ellaerdt Swanston, lost their temper when Herbert censored the old, and previously licensed, play of Fletcher's *The Woman's Prize, or The Tamer Tamed*. Herbert told them that 'it concernes the Master of the Revells to bee carefull of their ould revived playes, as of their new, since they may conteyne offensive matter, which ought not to be allowed in any time'. Lowin and Swanston apologised some days later to Herbert in the presence of their two colleagues, probably after being scolded by Herbert.[67] However, Herbert also acknowledges that he recorded licences for a few plays without his 'name'; that is, he may not have signed the licences or may not have seen the texts before performance.[68]

Surprisingly, the censor did not usually demand to see a play again in order to prove that an acting company had indeed incorporated his demands—for example, to leave out all oaths. With the exception of the book of *Sir Thomas More*, which never seemed to have satisfied the censor no matter how many hands tried to improve it, there are no extant manuscripts with censors' licences demanding that the play be submitted again after the required changes have been made. Herbert's transcribed records, however, do survive for plays not approved upon first submission, including *Believe as You List* which *was* resubmitted after revision. While a dramatist and censor may have trusted each other to operate under a set of mutual guidelines, each or both were apparently lax, or even complicit, on occasion. Whether acting companies usually obeyed the censor's demands in his conditional licences, or usually gambled that he would not remember every contentious word or passage in the enormous number of plays for which he was responsible, is not certain. However, as Henslowe and, most likely, the Burbages, had running accounts with the censor over a period of several years, they probably encouraged some informality or favouritism that helped to ensure that the risk of prosecution for them and their acting companies was low. But the issue may simply have been resolved through the familiar relationships of the censor with particularly co-operative dramatists and playhouse book-keepers and scribes, as noted in the extant records of Herbert. As in the case of Fletcher's *The Woman's Prize*, Herbert thanked Edward Knight, with whom he frequently worked, for his careful purgation of censorable passages before the text was submitted for licensing, stating, 'In many things you have saved mee labour.'

Of course, the acting company paid the censor a fee for his services in licensing old or new plays, as did playhouse owners. Henslowe records an average payment of 7 shillings per play to the censor in the late 1590s. As Foakes and Rickert suggested in 1961, Henslowe stopped listing his daily and weekly receipts from plays after 1597, suggesting that he had only made such records to provide evidence for the censor of actual performances.

After 1597 Henslowe kept records for the censor in other ways.[69] In fact, in his running account with the censor, Henslowe paid Tilney £100 on 2 January 1594/5 'in full payement of what soever is due from the daie above wrytten vntill Ashwednesdaie'. At other times he paid the censor monthly or per play, for example, paying 9 shillings for the licensing of two books in January 1597/8 and then 21 shillings for three more books in July 1598; 7 shillings remains the standard per play payment from 1598 to 1600.[70] The monthly payment of £3 in August 1602 includes five named plays, making the per-play cost 12 shillings.[71] However, this monthly fee may be part of the running account that would let under- or over-payments ride from month to month until the account came out even.

In general, Henslowe's payments for licensing a play follow by some weeks or months his payments for commissioning them, suggesting that he gave a completed copy of the play to the censor. But implicit in Henslowe's accounts is his apparent generosity for past or future favours rendered, and it would not be surprising if Tilney, or later, Buc agreed, on occasion, to license a play without having actually read, or indeed received, a copy of it. In fact, none of Henslowe's payments to Tilney specify that the censor has read prologues, epilogues or other new material added to previously licensed plays being revived. Henslowe may have assumed or been told that such products of 'mending' or 'altering' an old play were to be tacitly approved without the censor's actual attention or knowledge.

These types of per-play payments to the Master of the Revels, which had increased to £1–£2 in the 1620s and 1630s, as noted in Herbert's records, would have supplemented the yearly salary given to him by his employer, the Crown, to defray his costs. For example, Tilney's salary for 1600 to deal with plays only (and not playhouses for which he was also responsible) was £66 6s 8d,[72] a sizeable sum. Herbert also records receiving 'benefitt' fees, similar to those paid to dramatists, of £12 4s from the second day's performance of a play.[73] If Henslowe paid Tilney approximately £3 every month, as he did in August 1602, Henslowe's annual payments of £36 would equal more than half the censor's annual wage from the monarch, without individual licensing or benefit fees, at this time. More extensive records are extant for Sir Henry Herbert than for Tilney and Buc, as Herbert's detailed notes were transcribed in the late eighteenth century, although Herbert's original manuscript was subsequently lost. His per-play licensing fees ranged from £1 in the 1620s to £2 in the 1630s.[74] Herbert records, for example, relicensing in 1623 a later copy of *The Winter's Tale* without rereading it, admitting that he took the word of John Heminges that 'there was nothing profane added or reformed, thogh the allowed booke was missing'.[75] It is not clear if Heminges presented Herbert with a printed copy of the play taken from the newly published Folio edition, and now being used by the actors as their book, or offered him a transcript of the lost manuscript book.

'They should then had their ears cutt & noses': dramatists and censorship

Much of what modern critics have assumed about the censor's requirements has been drawn from Herbert's accounts of the 1620s and 1630s. However, the practices of professional London theatres, as well as audiences' political and religious attitudes and alliances, had changed significantly from those in the Elizabethan and Jacobean ages, especially with the increasingly wide-spread support for Puritanism, often safely satirised in the earlier period. So there would have been a great difference between what would have caused offence to the censor in 1590 and in 1630. While the matter that required censorship may have shifted, Herbert's accounts relate that the manner of censorship had not altered much since the periods of Tilney and Buc. Herbert complains at various times that he particularly objects to 'oaths, prophaness, and ribaldrye'.[76] But the censor read through the manuscript, quill pen in hand, looking for any material that could be considered offensive, insulting or dangerous to the English monarch, friendly foreign monarchs, the Protestant clergy, or favoured aristocrats. In a defiantly Protestant country, however, Catholic religious or political figures, if they were not personal friends of the monarch, were often welcome targets for satire or abuse, and the presentation of them as foolish, wicked or licentious usually provoked no censorship. Thus the majority of the censorship involved political, royal or religious issues that would threaten or offend the establishment or incite the audience to challenge current authority.

As for obscenity, most professional dramatists were usually adept at keeping bawdy material from stepping over the borderline from acceptable to obscene. Thus a play title such as *The Knight of the Burning Pestle* (with the last word pronounced 'pizzle' and meaning 'penis') was considered comic rather than obscene. Of course, obscene words were not allowed, and Shakespeare may only have been allowed to include passages such as Princess Katherine's English lesson in *Henry V*, in which she so mispronounces some English words that they sound obscene, because the character was French, traditionally ridiculed on stage at this time. Jonson also built *double entendres* that border on obscenity into *Volpone*, *The Alchemist* and a number of other comedies.

However, after the Act against Abuses in 1606, 'oaths', largely confined to phrases referring to God, Jesus Christ, the Holy Ghost or the Trinity, such as 'by Jesus's wounds' or 'by God', were banned from publication, and probably, but not certainly, from performance. Thus texts, including those of Shakespeare, written before but printed after this date will often have a hypermetrical or hypometrical line of dialogue in which 'by God' has been changed to 'by Heaven', or 'O Lord', for example, is simply deleted. In 1633, Charles I personally intervened in lessening the severity of Herbert's purgation of oaths by reading the company book of a play by William Davenant, at the request of Davenant's patron.[77] It is intriguing to wonder if his father James ever did the same. However, Charles also took action when other dramatists had crossed the line. On 5 June 1638, Herbert reported that Charles censored Massinger's *The King and the Subject*, for when 'readinge over the play at Newmarket, he set his marke upon the place with his owne hande, and in thes words, "This is too insolent, and to bee changed"'.[78] These two documented instances of royal contribution to the transmission of a play-text from author to audience suggest the extraordinary cultural power and status of dramatists by the 1630s.

In spite of the Privy Council's 1589 letter, personal satire in plays often produced a more dangerous rebuke from the censor than religious or political satire. Jonson in particular faced punishment for his frequently reckless satire, which did not keep him from being granted the reversion to hold the office of Master of the Revels, although he died before the position could come to him.[79] He was prohibited by the censor or some other authority from performing or printing the 'Apologetical Dialogue' in *Poetaster* for fifteen years (it was finally printed in the 1616 Folio text), because it had so insulted the audience at the first and only performance of it in 1601. Either the censor had not recognised how offensive the passage was when licensing the play, or Jonson added the material after licensing. Or perhaps it was Jonson's arrogant performance of the role of Author in it that incited the riotous response.

Jonson was punished more severely at other times in his career, particularly after the early performances in 1605 of *Eastward Ho!* which used a possibly unlicensed company book indirectly attacking the Scottish nationality of James I. For this act Jonson was imprisoned and sought Robert Cecil's help (see p. 59). Jonson later boasted to his friend William Drummond that

> he was delated by S[ir] James Murray to the King for writting something against the Scots jn a play Eastward hoe & voluntarily Imprissonned himself w[t] [i.e. with] Chapman and Marston, who had written it amongst y[m] [i.e. them]. The report was that they should then had their ears cutt & noses.[80]

This anecdote concludes with Jonson claiming that he 'banqueted all his friends' after his release from prison, at which time his mother informed him that she would have sent him poison if the sentence had not been commuted. Jonson's narrative is certainly aggrandised, as there is no evidence that Marston had been imprisoned with the others, nor is it likely that Jonson would have 'voluntarily' subjected himself to imprisonment.[81] It was only Jonson's friendship with Thomas Howard, Earl of Suffolk, the current Lord Chamberlain, who could overrule the Master of the Revels, that saved Jonson from further action, including mutilated ears and nose.[82] The play was printed a few months later with the offending passages removed, and it remained in the repertory of the boy's company for which it was written. That the play went through three Quarto editions in the latter part of 1605 suggests that royal censorship and its attendant notoriety were good for business for the printer, as well as the acting company, which would continue to draw audiences eager to watch or read a notorious play.

However, the greatest benefit of a censorable play may have been for the dramatist who could increase both his fame and his salary, so that the threat of punishment may have been a worthwhile gamble in return for larger fees and more artistic control within the company in the future. As Richard Dutton notes, 'there is no record of any dramatist being prosecuted or threatened with prosecution on the basis of a manuscript as it was submitted to the Revels Office—that is for its *ideas*, as distinct from things later found offensive in performance or print'.[83] The willingness of company or established dramatists, often under royal patronage or holding crown-appointed offices, to cross the censor appointed by their ultimate patron, the monarch, often seems flagrant. This may be why Tilney was apparently so overwhelmed in 1589 that the Privy Council decided that he needed two assistants.

Other dramatists and their acting companies blamed actors for so corrupting a play that it caused offence with the Master of the Revels. This was the excuse of Thomas Nashe, whose play *The Isle of Dogs*, which does not survive, was finished by Ben Jonson in 1597. Nashe improbably claimed that he wrote only the Induction and the first act, the other four acts 'without my consent, or the least guesse of my drift or scope, by the players were supplied'.[84] Nonetheless, Jonson and 'some of the players' were briefly imprisoned for their part in this 'lewd' play, 'contanynge very seditious and sclandrous matter', while Nashe conveniently fled.[85] Jonson later claimed to Sir Robert Cecil that since his 'first Error'—that is, co-writing *The Isle of Dogs*—he had so 'attempred' his style that he had 'giuen no cause to any good Man of Greife; and if to any ill, by touching at any generall vice, it hath alwayes been wᵗh a reguard, and sparing of particular persons'.[86] Nevertheless, Jonson wrote these words while imprisoned for *Eastward Ho!*

Herbert notes in 1632 that 'the first that offends in this kind, of poets or players, shall be sure of publique punishment'.[87] He also agreed with the players of Jonson's *The Magnetic Lady* in 1633 when they laid the 'whole fault' for the play's notoriety on themselves and not the censor or the 'poett'.[88] Dramatists may have given actors opportunities to alter the play to suit them; for example, Robert Kean Turner argues that in the 1624 case of *A Wife for a Month* Fletcher gave the King's Men's actors 'an imperfect text expecting them to alter it as they chose'.[89] As a company dramatist, long-experienced with these actors, Fletcher would have known that the actors would work with and not against him. But Jonson's attribution of blame to actors or later adapters, championed by Herbert, for many of his problems implies that he, like Herbert, was incapable of always controlling his theatrical colleagues.[90] Nevertheless, it is more likely that this excuse masked Jonson's regular willingness to test the limits of censorship.

In 1605, Samuel Daniel admitted his own responsibility for the politically dangerous play *Philotas*, reminiscent of the second Earl of Essex's rebellion against Queen Elizabeth I in 1601. Daniel told his patron the Earl of

Devonshire that the first three acts had been written before Essex's 'troubles' and that 'the Master of the Revels had perused it'.[91] Ironically, Daniel himself had been allowed to act as Master of the Revels solely for the Children of the Queen's Revels, the company which had performed his contentious play, despite the obvious conflict of interest.[92] Daniel also breached his duties as censor with such notorious plays as *Eastward Ho!*, *The Isle of Gulls* and Chapman's two-part play *The Conspiracy and Tragedy of Charles, Duke of Byron, Marshall of France* (1608), all performed for the Queen's Revels.[93] In the case of the *Byron* plays, the French ambassador to England noted that he had succeeded in having them prohibited from playing, yet, during a period in which the court had left London, the players staged the plays with the insulting matter left intact. The ambassador states: 'At my suit three of them were arrested, but the principal person, the author, escaped.'[94] Sir Thomas Lake, Clerk of the Signet, later reported to Sir Robert Cecil that King James had ordered that the actors 'should neuer play more but should first begg their bred and he wold haue his vow performed And therefore my lo*rd* chamberlain by himselfe or your ll. [i.e. Lordships] at the table should take order to dissolue them, and to punish the maker besides'.[95] Yet Chapman, the maker of the plays, seems to have escaped having to beg his bread or any other form of permanent censure, even though he was 'the principal person' who remained responsible for his text even after performance, for which he probably prepared it himself.

'I like not this': censorship of manuscripts

Although some censorship of plays and productions occurred after performance, most took place, or was supposed to take place, at the time of licensing. Manuscripts such as the *The Book of Sir Thomas More* (*c*.1590) show heavy interference by the censor, in this case Tilney, who demanded a number of cuts. Tilney, appointed by Elizabeth I, objected to passages overly sympathetic to More, executed as a traitor by Elizabeth's father, Henry VIII, and to other controversial material. Tilney has drawn vertical lines, like those used by Heywood for deletion, in the margins of the offensive passages, writing on the first page, for example:

> Leaue out ye insurrection wholy & ye Cause ther off & begin w^t [i.e. with] Sr Tho: Moore att ye mayors sessions w^t a reportt afterwards off his good servic don being Shriue [i.e. Sheriff] off LondoN vppon a mutiny Agaynst ye Lumbards only by A shortt reportt & nott otherwise att your own perriles.[96]

The 'insurrection' to be cut in this case is an allusion to riots during More's time against foreign merchants in London. But other numerous comic complaints in this opening scene about London, as well as slanders against the Mayor and his wife, would have contributed to Tilney's demand that the entire scene be cut. At other points in the text, Tilney has marked his objections with the terse comment, 'Mend this'. No records exist of the play being performed, and it is unlikely that the manuscript could have served as the basis for acting in this form. This manuscript serves as one example of a play that failed to secure the censor's licence despite apparent numerous later alterations and additions in an attempt to make it licensable.

Other examples of the Master's wrath at offensive passages appear in a few surviving censors' licences in foul or fair copy manuscripts. Buc seemed to take personal offence at the presentation of rudeness to the Prince of Orange in the scribal company book of *Sir John Van Olden Barnauelt* (*c*.1620), complaining:

> I like not this: neith^or
> do I think y^t [i.e. that] the pr. [i.e. prince] was
> thus disgracefully vsed.
> besides he is to much
> presented ~~her~~.[97]

Buc also demanded 'reformations' to the 1611 play that he named *The Second Maiden's Tragedy* 'for it hath no name inscribed', as did William Blagrave, Herbert's assistant, to the 1635 manuscript of *The Lady Mother*. After reading the 'book' of *The Launching of the Mary, or The Seaman's Honest Wife*, Herbert granted his licence on the condition that all the

> Oaths left out In ye action as they are crost In ye booke &
> all other Reformations strictly obserud may be acted not
> otherwyse. this 27 June. 1633.

The 'crost' out passages were mostly allusions to the Dutch torturing and killing eighteen Englishmen, a subject that proved sensitive in 1633 when the English government was involved in negotiations with the Dutch. Below the licence, Herbert angrily added a note:

> I commande your Bookeeper to present mee wth a fayre Copy heraft[er]
> and to leaueout all oathes, prophanite & publick Ribaldry as
> he will answer it at his perill.[98]

This foul copy manuscript in the hand of Walter Mountfort has enough *currente calamo* revisions and somewhat later, pre-licensing additions to make it illegible at points. It also contains a number of small sheets of paper, pinned over censored passages, which contain the post-licensing additions by the author.[99] Here again is an example of a play recirculating to the author before and after licensing.

Herbert finally licensed Massinger's *Believe as You List* in 1631. But he did so only after refusing this or an earlier copy a licence the first time in

1630 'because itt did contain dangerous matter, as the deposing of Sebastian king of Portugal, by Philip the [Second,] and ther being a peace sworen twixte the kings of England and Spayne'. In banning the play, Herbert demanded his usual fee, 'notwithstandinge, which belongs to me for reading itt over, and ought to be brought always with the booke'.[100] Apparently Herbert was not a subscriber to the type of credit system used by Henslowe for the earlier Masters of the Revels. After Massinger replaced the contemporary story of the modern Sebastian with the more ancient one of Antiochus, Herbert allowed the play without any further changes.

The censor would usually sign on the last page of the text, immediately below the last line of dialogue (or the notation 'Finis', if it appeared), but it is possible that he sometimes signed elsewhere, such as on a separate sheet or title page. The censor would keep a record of his licensing of the play in his account book. Some of the extant manuscripts that no longer bear a licence may once have done so. That a play was supposed to have been licensed before the actors began rehearsing it seems often to have been ignored, judging from contemporary comments, including Daborne's remark to Henslowe that the actors already had 'parts' of one scene before the entire play was finished.[101] It is not certain that Daborne is referring to actors' 'parts' in the theatrical sense, as he may instead simply mean that the company has started rehearsing from an incomplete script. But given Henslowe's running account with the censor, it would not be surprising if the actors working in Henslowe's or Alleyn's companies usually observed the same laxity about rehearsing the play, already copied out in parts, before it was licensed. The widespread flouting of this regulation over several decades may be why Herbert attempted to enforce stricter observance of this requirement in 1633, warning that 'The players ought not to study their parts till I have allowed of the booke.'[102]

Tilney, Buc and Herbert usually marked offending passages sparingly, with marginal crosses, vertical lines, brackets or rules, and occasional brief comments. Some manuscripts that have been through the censor's hands show very little actual censorship, other than an 'X' or a vertical line here and there without marginal comment, so the task of reading through a play may not always have been as burdensome as it now seems. In fact, the censor may have skimmed, rather than comprehensively read, the text routinely or on occasion. In any event, these three censors, at least, did not do wholesale editing, writing or rewriting, or otherwise heavily mark up the manuscript except in making cuts.[103] Nor did they give advice on dramatic, thematic or grammatical elements of the plays or make additions.

Herbert and his deputy William Blagrave both invested in theatrical businesses as owner-sharers in acting companies or theatres, and thus must have been knowledgeable about what type of plays would attract audiences. But, curiously, or perhaps shrewdly, they did not concern themselves with the artistic or commercial merit of the play-texts they read, including, apparently, those of the dramatists they directly employed. The only type of correction that Buc made consisted of offering play titles on occasion, for example in writing out the alternative title of one play, *Hengist King of Kent*, in a 1619 scribal list of plays and inventing another for *The Second Maiden's Tragedy*. He presumably used this title because he remembered that a previously licensed play had been titled *The Maid's Tragedy*.

Shakespeare may have seen first-hand the contentious problem of pleasing the censor when he collaborated in the censored 'book' of *Sir Thomas More*. Evidence from the early Quartos of *Richard II* and the two parts of *Henry IV* suggests that Tilney, or his deputies, also reprimanded or cautioned Shakespeare about politically dangerous material in these plays at least. The deposition scene (Act 4, Scene 1) in *Richard II* did not appear in the first three Quartos (1597–8) and was first printed in the 1608 fourth Quarto five years after Elizabeth's death. It is not certain whether the deposition scene had been cut from all or some of its court, private and public performances during her lifetime. The Earl of Essex and his followers, who attempted to overthrow Elizabeth in 1601, paid the Lord Chamberlain's Men to stage a play about Richard II (whether Shakespeare's play or another one) at the Globe the night before the rebellion.[104] If it was Shakespeare's play, presumably Essex would have asked the Chamberlain's Men to include the deposition scene, if it had not already been banned on stage by 1597 when the play was first printed without it.

Shakespeare was apparently also considered politically provocative in the later plays in this history cycle. The epilogue of *2 Henry IV* and a few stray uses of 'Oldcastle' as a speech prefix or character name in *1 Henry IV* imply that Shakespeare had originally written the clown figure as Sir John Oldcastle, a well-known Protestant martyr of the 1550s, in both *Henry IV* plays. Evidently he had been forced after early performances of the first or both to alter the name to satisfy the complaints of Oldcastle's aristocratic descendants. Thus Oldcastle became Falstaff, as the epilogue speaker in *2 Henry IV* makes clear: 'Olde-castle died Martyre, and this is not the man'.[105] No records exist, as in the cases of Jonson, Nashe and Middleton, that Shakespeare was ever called before the censor or the Privy Council to be reprimanded or punished for offensive material for his plays, although it is possible that he was. However, that Shakespeare's company was patronised until 1603 by the Lord Chamberlain suggests that the actors directly under his patronage would receive special consideration or protection on occasion from their employer, as well as his subordinate, the censor. Such consideration might also have extended to their next, and much more powerful, patron, James I.

No matter the dramatist, Herbert's accounts demonstrate that he expected the text to return to the author after it left the censor's hands. In the case of James Shirley's play *The Ball*, Herbert noted on 18 November 1632 that he would have 'forbidden' the play except that the company and theatre manager Christopher Beeston promised that the many things with which Herbert found fault should be left out. Herbert stated, uniquely in this case, that Beeston 'would not suffer it to be done by the poett any more, who deserves to be punisht'.[106] This statement strongly implies that the poet was generally expected to have done such mending and alteration after the censor had made his decisions about the state of the text, but Shirley had proved unco-operative or unreliable in this case. Less than a year later, Herbert could not resist complimenting Shirley on lessons learned from the censorship of *The Ball*. In his records for licensing Shirley's new play *The Young Admiral* on 3 July 1633, Herbert described his 'delight and satisfaction in the readinge' of the play, for it was free of 'oaths, prophaneness or obsceanes'. Herbert then offered a tutorial, in the terms Jonson would surely have understood in his Prologue to *Volpone* and the Induction to *Bartholomew Fair*, on the aims and objectives of authorship. Herbert recommended that *The Young Admiral* 'may serve for a patterne to other poets, not only for the bettring of maners and language, but for the improvement of the quality, which hath received some brushings of late'.

More importantly, Herbert noted in his records that he had repeated all this information in the play's licence in or attached to the manuscript. He had done so because when 'Mr Sherley hath read this approbation' it will 'encourage him to pursue this beneficial and cleanly way of poetry' and serve as an 'example to all poetts that shall write after the date hereof'.[107] An author himself, Herbert is clearly praising the cleanness as well as the quality of the play here, although his tutorial focuses primarily on making his job as censor easier and only secondarily on making Shirley a better dramatist. But thanks to Herbert's 'approbation', which he has included with the returned manuscript, it is certain that he fully expected this manuscript to come back to the author, and that Shirley would reread this text of *The Young Admiral*. This Master of the Revels, and almost certainly all of his predecessors, knew that dramatic manuscripts would return to the author after the Master had fulfilled his duties, including providing an occasional lecture on clean living and writing.

5 'Plaide in 1613'

Authorial and scribal manuscripts in the playhouse

After the Master of the Revels contributed to the transmission of a play-text, and, perhaps, to the moral responsibility of its author, licensed manuscripts could pass into rehearsal, performance, and later revival. For dramatists, writing a 'good' play was not their only aim, nor was it 'the bettring of maners and language', as Herbert described it, for at least one other aim was to help guide their plays through production. A dramatist seems not to have needed the 'approbation' of the censor or anyone else to 'encourage him to pursue this beneficial and cleanly way of poetry'. Instead dramatists seemed to share a contractual or personal duty to participate in the staging of their plays, even in co-ordinating with actors and other theatre personnel the use of the text in the playhouse.

Authors' and scribes' manuscripts after censorship

The manuscript of *The Honest Man's Fortune* reveals the entire and common process of authorial circularity. The play was written collaboratively by Nathan Field, Philip Massinger and John Fletcher for the Lady Elizabeth's Men[1] and first printed in the Beaumont and Fletcher 1647 Folio. If the contract Daborne signed along with Massinger and Field to write a new play for Henslowe refers to this play, he may have been another collaborator. The surviving manuscript of the play, which was apparently not used to print the Folio text, is in the hand of Edward Knight, the King's Men's book-keeper.[2] It has a few marks in another hand and notes on its title page that it was 'plaide in 1613', perhaps for the censor's benefit, as Herbert's licence at the end states, 'This Play being an olde one, and the Originall lost was real-lowd by mee this 8. Febru. 1624' (i.e. 1625). Thus this manuscript is a later transcript made at some stage of the play's transmission, and could have been copied from the foul papers, an intermediate fair copy, the licensed and/or company book or another transcript, or from some combination of them. However, this manuscript need not have been copied in 1625 for a revival in that year by the King's Men but at some earlier point.[3]

The manuscript lacks Act 5, Scene 3, found in the 1647 printed text, and presents a different final scene. Cyrus Hoy argues that 'F1 gives us the earlier, pre-1625 version of the play', printed from foul papers. However, he states that the manuscript represents 'a somewhat altered version prepared for the 1625 revival', with cuts and alterations to the two scenes made to shorten 'a long play' and to replace the original ending's 'indelicacy'. The manuscript has a number of strikeouts, using vertical or circular strokes through the lines of contentious material, as well as cuts, mostly in the last two acts, marked by vertical lines in the margin, some of which agree with those in the printed text. The manuscript shows signs of playhouse editing because it contains the names of three actors in its stage directions. Hoy notes that Knight, and most likely a stage adapter, made editorial changes 'to straighten out the grammar or the syntax of the authors, to adjust the dialogue to accommodate a projected cut, to modify a word or phrase that might seem to give offence'. Hoy argues that other changes may either be 'sophistications' by Knight or the other adapter, or they may indeed be authorial revisions.[4] If these changes do in fact proceed from one or more of the authors, this manuscript has taken at least two circular journeys. The first was in 1613, when it was composed and licensed, and then adjusted by the authors. The second was in 1625, when it went through almost the same process for revival, with possible revisions by Fletcher, who died of the plague later in the year, and by Massinger, whose writing career continued into the 1630s. Knight's editing is light and non-intrusive, and the other changes may demonstrate that authors collaborated in, or at least oversaw, the transmission of their texts, even up to twelve years after composition.

Knight and his colleagues provide other significant evidence of an acting company's handling of dramatists' texts. In addition to transcribing the manuscript of Fletcher's *Bonduca* (carrying his anxious note that he had to find the foul papers, as the company 'book' was lost), in 1625 Knight copied *The Faithful Friends*, a play written by Fletcher, possibly in collaboration with others.[5] In *Bonduca*, Knight used italic hand for speech-prefixes, stage directions and proper names, again dividing the play into acts but not scenes, and was consistent in drawing rules before and after stage directions and between speakers' dialogue. He may also have purged some oaths in the act of copying, if not already cut by the author or the original book-keeper. In *The Faithful Friends*, Knight left gaps in his text when confronted by a number of words he could not read in the foul papers,[6] demonstrating that this professional scribe, at least, took pains not to 'interfere' with the text he was copying, even in minor details. This manuscript also shows alterations, corrections, additions and deletions, most likely by a collaborator who reworked portions of the manuscript sometime after composition.

Yet this collaborator did not fill in the blank passages, perhaps because Fletcher had originally composed those portions of the text. The collaborator and Knight may have assumed, then, that Fletcher would eventually fill in these passages, but Fletcher died suddenly of the plague. This may explain why another dramatist, possibly Massinger,[7] revised the manuscript later but did not fill in the blank passages. Knight probably employed the same strategy in leaving gaps in the first three scenes in Act 5 of *Bonduca* if, like *The Faithful Friends*, it was copied in early 1625, and Knight was forced after Fletcher's death to offer summaries of the scenes instead. Knight also annotated two other manuscripts of plays from the King's Men's repertory: *Believe as You List* (*c.*1631), in Massinger's hand, and Clavell's *The Soddered Citizen* (*c.*1632), in the hand of a scribe who consulted the author during transcription.[8]

Knight may not have been the only conscientious playhouse scribe or annotator who intended to defer to an author. An authorial fair copy manuscript of *Charlemagne* similarly shows conscientiously slight annotations in four other hands, including that of the book-keeper who has added marginal cues for music and properties.[9] George Buc has also altered the term 'reverend' to 'priests' and marked a few passages for deletion; two other hands added one-word marginal additions.[10] However, judging from ink colours, the original author has also made later additions to the text, possibly after Buc's reading of the manuscript and its return to theatre personnel. The scribal manuscript of *The Telltale* (*c.*1630–40) may have been copied from a company book (written *c.*1605), but this scribe similarly leaves a gap, in this case of $2\frac{1}{2}$ pages in Act 4, Scene 2. He ends the transcription in the middle of a line and continues it after the gap in the midst of the same scene.[11] The scribe may have expected at some point to fill in this gap after consultation with the author(s) or later reviser. Perhaps this is why he provides at the conclusion to the text an elaborate anagram of his initials (with *H* and *N* as the primary, interlocked letters and *COS* as the other letters). This anagram serves the same function as the 'notarial mark' or 'paraph' used by members of the Company of Scriveners to identify themselves.[12] He was obviously proud of the transcript, or at least would be when the gap eventually was filled in, and wished to be identified with it, even if now his identity is unknown.[13]

Massinger's autograph manuscript of *Believe as You List*, however, reveals the most about the often frequent, if not routine, circular transmission of a play-text. When Herbert refused to licence the play in 1630, it was indeed revised by the author and resubmitted in the next year. According to C. J. Sisson, the surviving manuscript, in the author's hand and carrying Knight's annotations and Herbert's licence, shows 'all the processes through which the copy passed on its way from the author to the prompter'.[14] The manuscript, like that of Heywood's *The Captives*, can best be described as foul papers, in this case censored by the Master of the Revels, and annotated by the book-keeper for the stage. But as the play was revised and some of it recopied from the first version, it is also partly fair papers, containing both errors from copying, including from eyeskip, and *currente calamo* corrections and revisions in the newly written portions, as in Figure 5.1.[15] The manuscript still retains the pre-revised layers of the story of the Portuguese King Sebastian which Massinger was forced by the censor to alter to the story of the classical King Antiochus. As in the case of *The Captives*, the book-keeper

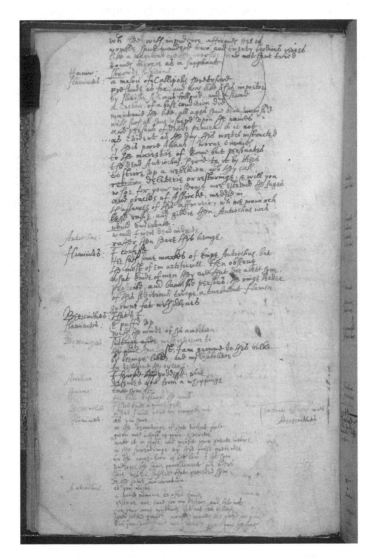

Figure 5.1 Massinger's foul paper and fair copy manuscript of *Believe as you List*, British Library Egerton MS 2828, f. 12ᵛ, showing a change of pen and ink and *currente calamo* and/or later revisions. Reproduced by permission of The British Library.

attempted to turn a somewhat illegible author's draft into a company book suitable for presentation to the censor and/or for use in the theatre without employing a scribe at that stage to make a fair copy. Because Massinger's composing hand is somewhat more legible than Heywood's, this book-keeper largely has succeeded where Heywood's did not.

In his careful editing of the manuscript, Knight chiefly confined himself to emending stage business by regularising speech-prefixes and stage directions. He also corrected some passages of dialogue, particularly those still carrying vestiges of the pre-revised first draft or other such confusions or inconsistencies, and he wrote out the title page. He also fair copied the prologue and epilogue and placed them at the end of the play after it had been licensed. It is also possible that Massinger wrote (or rewrote) these portions only at or after the successful licensing in 1631, and that Knight then transcribed them. Given the King's Men's problems in securing Herbert's approval of the play, the inclusion of the prologue and epilogue suggests that he authorised them at some point. In the case of Fletcher's *The Woman's Prize* two years later, Herbert thanked Knight for his efficiency in purging oaths, so the two men may have had the same type of familiarity in 1631. On the back of the last sheet Knight listed some required properties for the actors, including 'A letter. for M*r* Robinson'.[16] In sum, Knight made corrections, including recopying a song in a more convenient place,[17] that would enhance his ability to read or consult the manuscript at any point, including during performance. Herbert made at least one marginal note before licensing the play. After this second, and the first successful, licensing of the play, Massinger made further changes to the text.

Thus the progress of this *Believe as You List* manuscript was not linear (simply from author to scribe/book-keeper to censor), but circular (back to the author). More precisely, the alterations and additions, made at different times, demonstrate that this manuscript moved in this way:

1   from the author to the book-keeper;
2   back to the author;
3   back to the book-keeper;
4   then to the censor;
5   back to the author, at least to write the prologue and epilogue; and, finally,
6   back to the book-keeper, who fair-copied the prologue and epilogue but may not have made any further changes.[18]

In fact, the first manuscript of the play also moved from the author to the book-keeper to the censor and back to the author. The progress of *Believe as You List*, among many other plays, proves that a dramatist attached on a short- or long-term basis to a company did not always or usually surrender interest or participation in his text after the foul papers left his hands. Instead, he rechecked and refined the manuscript even after it reached the hands of the censor and the book-keeper, working closely with them and with his company to suit all of their interests in the play, effectively preparing it for production and performance. Massinger did not act unusually here but in the same ways as other King's Men's dramatists, including Shakespeare, Jonson and Middleton. So many of Henslowe's entries in the Diary appear to duplicate interim or final payments for contracted plays that he most likely withheld some of his payments, or inadvertently recorded them twice, until the authors had made the changes required by the company book-keeper or the censor.

For Massinger at least, it was not the case that once a manuscript reached a playhouse it became a collaborative object, bereft of authorial control or interest. An early modern poetry or prose manuscript could acquire a form of publication by being passed among a select group of readers, some of whom could make additions, deletions or other changes to the text, as well as their own copies, without its being returned to the author for his final approval. Woudhuysen meticulously documents this type of circulation of the texts of Sidney before and after his death, for example. These readers in fact acted very much like collaborative authors as well as distributors of further copies.[19] However, dramatic manuscripts took a significantly different series of routes in their transmission and were more deliberately controlled. Dramatists wrote play-texts to be performed on stage, not printed, and the text was guarded from those who might try to act or print it without permission.

In addition, poetry and prose manuscripts were only subject to censorship before publication, not after composition, as was the case for dramatic manuscripts. Once a manuscript was approved and/or marked for cuts or alterations by the Master of the Revels, it would return to the author(s) or company personnel who remained responsible for its contents. To circulate the manuscript after licensing to indiscriminate readers who could add to or revise the text as they liked, regardless of the censor's concerns, would have had potentially disastrous consequences and have been against the interests of the company. Dramatic authors would not have allowed their manuscripts routinely to be circulated among friends or patrons outside the playhouse while the plays were still in repertory. It was the dramatist Chapman, after all, who was held responsible as 'the principal person' for the text of the *Byron* plays *after* their performances caused official complaints. Within the playhouse, dramatists were expected by company managers, book-keepers and, especially, the censor, to be the principals who would reclaim the text at various points to make corrections, alterations, revisions or any other changes.

As with the autograph manuscripts of *Believe as You List* and *The Launching of the Mary*, the scribal manuscript of *The Second Maiden's Tragedy* travelled back to the hands of its original author(s) after it had been fair-copied.[20] It also circulated back to the author(s) after having been read by the censor, and possibly again after it had been annotated by one or more book-keepers.[21] The autograph manuscript of Henry Glapthorne's *The Lady Mother* (1635) took the same route of transmission. The play was probably written for the King's Revels Company at Salisbury Court,[22] the same theatre for which Brome signed his 1635 and 1638 contracts. After Glapthorne finished his first round of revision, the manuscript returned to the scribe, most likely a book-keeper, who added some stage directions and warnings of actor entrances. It was then submitted to William Blagrave, Herbert's deputy, who, like his superior, was also a sharer in theatres and acting companies, including the Salisbury Court Theatre, seemingly a conflict of interest in this case. Blagrave made minor alterations in the text, including adding the preposition 'as' to a line clearly lacking it. On at least one occasion, then, the censor concerned himself with ungrammatical elements which happened to strike him rather than with purely censorable content. The manuscript returned to the author, who made a thorough revision of it, giving it back to the scribe to incorporate his and the censor's changes and to refine it for stage use, probably without showing it again to Blagrave.[23] That only company dramatists such as Brome who were on exclusive contracts could contribute to the preparation of texts for performance is, therefore, not correct. His colleague at Salisbury Court, Glapthorne, whose 'amateur' writing career appears to have been limited,[24] offered the same services as Brome. In sum, dramatists, no matter what their status, experience or contracted terms, appear to have contributed to the transmission of the texts of their plays in the playhouse, particularly by preparing them for performance.

Authors and financial authority

What has rarely been emphasised before is that as a financial investor in three different consortia—the Chamberlain's/King's Men and the respective owners of the Globe and Blackfriars theatres—Shakespeare sold his plays to *and* derived income in theory or in practice from consortia that included himself. This meant that almost certainly he did not relinquish the artistic control or financial interest that non-sharer dramatists did in selling plays to a company. To be more specific, in the case of the Globe, there were most likely two corporate bodies or consortia from 1599, with the first composed of Cuthbert and Richard Burbage, who may have owned up to 25 per cent each, and five actors, including Shakespeare, who owned at least 10 per cent each. This consortium owned the real estate of the Globe.

The second consortium was composed of Chamberlain's/King's Men's players, including Shakespeare and all but one member of the first body. Formed in 1594 by actors who had shifted their allegiances from a variety of other companies, including the Admiral's, Strange's and Pembroke's Men, for the next four decades the Chamberlain's/King's Men became the most stable of all its competitors. At its core by 1596 were at least eight equal sharers, including Richard Burbage, Will Kemp, Christopher Sly, John Heminges and Shakespeare. The company also included numerous 'hired' men and boys who were paid a wage for their work. By 1603, when Henry Condell and Robert Armin, among others, replaced sharers who had left, and the company became the King's Men, the number of sharers remained at twelve until the company dissolved in 1642 with the close of the theatres.[25] The unusual stability and consistency of its sharer personnel, particularly from 1594 to 1616, suggest that the Chamberlain's/King's Men adhered to the same patterns and practices for its actors and dramatists over the years. Shakespeare remained an actor-sharer from 1594 to 1614 with one-eighth to one-twelfth of a share in the company, most likely also on an exclusive contract as dramatist. This consortium bought plays and produced them, in effect renting the use of the Globe from the first consortium.

The third consortium, composed of the Burbages, Shakespeare and four others, owned from 1608 the real estate of Blackfriars, which, like the Globe, was rented by the second consortium. This second consortium again 'paid all the costs of producing plays, including their own wages' in using this theatre.[26] Thus, the second consortium, of which Shakespeare was a member, was most likely paying him to write plays and offering him wages when those plays were produced and later sold to printers. In addition, this second consortium also paid the first consortium 50 per cent of the money taken in from the gallery, box, and tiring house doors of the Globe, and retained the other 50 per cent and all the money paid at the outer doors. As a member of the first consortium, Shakespeare also earned a percentage of the money taken in at each performance of his plays at the Globe. In addition, as a member of the third consortium, he profited from similar financial arrangements from the second consortium when using Blackfriars.

None of Shakespeare's contemporary dramatists became investors simultaneously both in theatres and acting companies, and thus none served in his quintuple role of Globe-sharer, Blackfriars-sharer, Chamberlain's/ King's Men-sharer, Chamberlain's/King's Men-dramatist and actor. It is possible that if Shakespeare was on an exclusive contract with the company to write plays, it may have precluded extra wages as a member of the three different consortia. But as such an arrangement would have cost Shakespeare a great deal of extra income over the years, it is likely that he would not have agreed to such restrictive contractual terms. In fact, as in the case of Brome and some of Henslowe's contractees, dramatists needed to be wooed or enticed with financial incentives in order to agree to an exclusive contract. The likelihood is that Shakespeare would have demanded a contract in which he received the wages due to him as a member of each of the three consortia and in any other capacities, especially when earned from the production of his own plays. Thus, Shakespeare would *not* in general or in particular cases have been obliged to surrender control of his play-texts once they reached the theatre, watching helplessly as his play-texts acquired alterations by interfering actors and book-keepers. In fact, he would have had tremendous financial incentive to help prepare the texts to the best advantage for production and later for publication, from which as a company-sharer he also derived income.

In addition, theatre companies of this age lacked the figure now called a 'director', and instead it appears that a company's chief actors, book-keepers and/or other theatrical personnel directed plays. But as Andrew Gurr convincingly argues, Shakespeare, like Jonson in such plays as *Cynthia's Revels*, surely participated in staging his own plays, probably discreetly advising even his most important fellow-actor and friend, Richard Burbage, how to play the roles Shakespeare wrote for him.[27] As Gurr also demonstrates, from the 1580s to the early 1600s the honour, fame and power associated with the theatre shifted from companies' clowns to their tragedians, but by the early 1620s it had already shifted again to actor-dramatists and actor-managers.[28] By the end, if not the beginning, of Shakespeare's career, his role of actor-dramatist and actor-sharer had secured him an increasingly strong and influential position in his company. In fact, when Shakespeare sold a play-text to his acting company, he could, in effect, retain a percentage of the rights to it, possibly one-eighth to one-twelfth, depending on the number of sharers.

Actors, including sharers, were accused of everything from saying more than was set down for them, as Shakespeare complained, to writing four-fifths of a scandalous text, as Nashe complained, to causing a dramatist to be imprisoned, as Nashe and Jonson complained. It would be an overstatement to argue that actors routinely collaborated in the early, later or final version of a play-text, but it is more than probable that they did make changes or improvements. Alleyn, for one, made some minor cuts, alterations and corrections to his 'part' for *Orlando*, mostly, it appears, to heighten the emotional intensity of the lines. But these alterations were probably made during a period in which Greene, the author of the play, was not working with the company. Generally, actors appear to have made cuts, which is not surprising, given the nature of the repertory system in which actors, performing at least six days a week, may have repeated a role only infrequently. Hence actors would have confronted the 'new play they ar now studyinge', to use Daborne's words, more frequently than in the modern age, and they probably welcomed cuts.

The editors of the Beaumont and Fletcher 1647 Folio also claimed in their preface that when the plays had been acted on stage 'the *Actours* omitted some Scenes and Passages (with the *Authours* consent) as occasion led them'. The manuscript that served as printer's copy for *The Knave in Grain* was, according to R. C. Bald and Arthur Brown, marked for cutting, as 'some passages have been lost altogether, although there are clues to suggest that other passages marked for omission were set up by the printer. As a result, there is a good deal of confusion, and, inevitably, a number of loose ends.' The manuscript also had a number of additions on inserted leaves, and the printer 'did not always realize just where the new episodes were to be inserted, but went solidly forward from the foot of one page to the top of the next'.[29] Manuscripts could indeed be rendered chaotic after use in the theatre.

For this reason, not all authors seem to have been as agreeable about cutting as Beaumont and Fletcher. Richard Brome, who agreed in 1635 to use 'all his studdye and Endeauo[rs]' as well as 'his best Arte and Industrye' to write plays, later complained about those actors who did not appreciate such endeavours and industry. In his preface to the 1640 first Quarto of *The Antipodes* he attacked some of the original players who 'pretended' that the play's 'superfluous length' required necessary cuts. It is worth considering whether other complaints about cuts came from authors. The title page of the anonymous *Damon and Pithias* (1582) notes that the text was the same as 'shewed before the Queenes Maiestie, by Children of her Graces Chappell, excepting (only) the Prologue which is somwhat altered for the proper vse of them that hereafter shal have occasion to plaie it, either in priuate, or open Audience'. Other Quartos, including those of Jonson's *Every Man Out of his Humour* (1600) and *Sejanus* (1605), and Webster's *The Duchess of Malfi* (1623), have similar warnings or advertisements that a play had been cut or adapted in performance.

Shakespeare and Jonson, among others, note in their texts that the performance of a play could take between two and two-and-a-half hours. This suggests that the average 3,000-line play (with a performance time of at least three hours) would have been significantly cut to meet this reduced playing time. However, plays were not always cut in the same places or in the same ways. Cuts may have been made at least occasionally with the collaboration of the entire company, including the author and the actors. A scribal manuscript of Jonson's masque *The Gyspies Metamorphosed* offers a composite text, recording three different sets of performances before James I.[30] In the margins of the original text appear additional speeches substituted at each of the two later performances. Another scribal manuscript records the text of the last performance. Jonson's supervision of the transcription of these manuscripts, which offer three separate states of composition and authorial revision, cannot be doubted.[31]

Jonson, Heywood and Shakespeare were experienced actors as well as dramatists, and the probability of their fellow actors substantially altering or mangling their plays was probably very low whenever they were sharing the stage. However, these dramatists and their colleagues could probably do very little to actors, or others, who later absconded with or appropriated his play-texts, in whatever form. Like other dramatists, they apparently had little or no control over 'reported', stolen or otherwise incomplete copies of their texts. These texts could have been assembled either by actors from 'parts' or from memory or from a text cut for provincial performance, or from some other 'report' of it. Or audience members or theatre personnel could have copied the text by dictation during performance and then sold it for publication. For example, Heywood complained in the preface to his 1608 Quarto of *The Rape of Lucrece* that some of his plays 'copied only by the eare' had been printed in 'corrupt and mangled' texts. Whether dealing with his employers or his texts, Brome similarly insisted on asserting his authority.

Scholars have recently questioned whether these types of mangled texts really resulted from theft, piracy, report or memorial reconstruction, rather than the carelessness of, lack of interest by, or collusion between authors, acting companies and printers. Yet all of these routes of authorised and unauthorised transmission remain a possibility, especially for Shakespearean Quarto texts termed 'bad'.[32] The most 'mangled' of Shakespeare's texts, Q1 *Romeo and Juliet* (1597) and Q1 *Hamlet* (1603) appear to have been assembled from company books already cut substantially for provincial touring or from sometimes incomplete actors' parts. At any stage after completion of a play, including during or after rehearsal, performance (public or private), or a later revival, Shakespeare and any other dramatist could once again pick up a play-text and rework it. Indeed, extant manuscripts demonstrate that not all revision was done in the playhouse by other hands and that dramatists did return to their texts some weeks, months or years after composition and original performance to make their own revisions, as in the case of Shirley's *The Court Secret*.[33]

For example, Heywood rewrote portions of his existing plays *The Golden Age* (printed in 1611) and *The Silver Age* (printed in 1613) as *The Escapes of Jupiter* (c.1624), which survives in manuscript in Heywood's hand (with the alternative title of *Calisto*).[34] This play is not merely an adapted or pasted-together version of the two old plays but a thorough revision of them into a new creative work. As with the manuscript of *The Captives* and his share of *Sir Thomas More*, in *The Escapes of Jupiter* he appears to be a composing author at work. Heywood could simply have amended or added handwritten sheets to the relevant printed portions of the 1611 and 1613 Quartos of *The Golden Age* and *The Silver Age*.[35] But he must have believed himself to be writing a new play rather than condensing two existing plays. Greg concludes that at least some of Heywood's revisions were due to changing taste of the author or his audience, positing that 'such revision was habitual with Heywood'. While Greg elsewhere eschewed the theory of such habitual revision by Shakespeare, he uses this case of *The Escapes of Jupiter* to argue against 'continuous copy', the nineteenth-century scholarly notion that Elizabethan and Jacobean plays were continually picked up, revised and/or mangled by a succession of non-authorial agents.[36]

However, Greg does not explore whether Heywood and other dramatists used such revision for theatrical effect, examining only whether the revisions make the play more literary. This manuscript of *The Escapes of Jupiter* looks like a text to be used in the theatre, not printer's copy for a book. After a space of ten years, Heywood would have been more than knowledgeable about what had or had not worked in the theatrical presentation of his two previous plays. He does not appear to have believed that their literary publications in 1611 and 1613 enshrined, elevated or fixed the plays' artistic or literary meaning forever, nor did he cease by 1624 to have an interest in or ownership of *The Golden* Age and *The Silver Age*. In his preface to *The English Traveller*, he may imply that he is ashamed of, and would rather not acknowledge, some of those two hundred and twenty plays in which he only had a 'maine finger'. However, he may be writing honestly rather than modestly when he claims there that '*it neuer was any great ambition in me, to bee in this kind Volumniously read*', perhaps because as an actor-dramatist he preferred the circulation of his plays in performance to publication. In revising *The Golden* Age and *The Silver Age* in major and minor ways, especially in copying out a new manuscript by hand, he demonstrates that he could reclaim portions of his own texts previously purchased by a printer and revise them for his theatrical, not his literary, audience.

Massinger, who annotated and inscribed a 1623 Quarto of his play *The Duke of Milan* as a presentation copy to a friend, similarly returned to his plays after their publication. He made thirty-three corrections, including at least one revision, to a Quarto copy of his text as printed from his own heavily revised manuscript. Massinger also made handwritten corrections, at least, to copies of a 1624 Quarto of *The Bondman*, a 1630 Quarto of *The Renegado*, a 1632 Quarto of *The Emperour of the East*, a 1629 Quarto of *The Roman Actor* and a 1630 Quarto of *The Picture*.[37] Such meticulous corrections and revisions to printed editions years after their original composition and performance demonstrate that this author considered his play-texts to be fluid documents that he could reclaim as his own. His corrections prove that the exact state of a text, word for word, was of enormous concern to a dramatist, even years after surrendering foul papers to the acting company that had commissioned them. Such concern is borne out by the King's Men's complaint to the Lord Chamberlain in 1637 that 'corruption' in the texts of plays printed without the company's permission led to 'the iniury and disgrace of the Authors'.[38]

'Those who own'd the *Manuscripts*, too well knew their value': manuscript copying

Other hands could, of course, copy out a play manuscript, long after its original composition, specifically to make reading copies either for presentation to a patron, for example, or for commission to a purchaser. The Portland manuscript of Middleton's play of *Hengist, King of Kent* still bears its original cover, written in the hand of the scribe who copied the entire manuscript. The scribe has written the number '52' in the centre of the upper half of the cover, suggesting that the manuscript was copied to order, taking the place of 52, either at page 52 or number 52, in an already assembled collection.[39] Extant presentation or commissioned copies such as this one often show a text that has been nearly flawlessly written and beautifully bound in vellum, with elaborate title pages, and, occasionally, leaves that were already gilt-edged at the time of transcription.[40] Jonson appears to have thought it necessary to present similarly fine, beautifully transcribed presentation copies of his works to royalty, personally fair-copying *The Masque of Blackness* and inscribing it for Prince Henry, elder son of James I.

As dedicatees or commissioners would be given copies of plays they had admired in performance, their copies apparently offered the text as used in the theatre. As Moseley notes about some of the plays in the Beaumont and Fletcher 1647 Folio, private copies had previously been transcribed for friends from acting texts. In fact, such copies were prized and expensive, 'for those who own'd the *Manuscripts*, too well knew their value to make a cheap estimate of any of these pieces'. Moseley knew from experience that the recopying of manuscripts for sale was preferable to actors' loaning company manuscripts to their audiences, for he notes that such a loan to 'a *Person of Quality*' resulted in the loss for several years of the company's only manuscript of *The Wild Goose Chase*.[41] As a result, the play could not be included in the 1647 Folio of Beaumont and Fletcher's works. Only afterwards was the manuscript text apparently recovered and used for the first printed edition in 1652.

Among the recipients of these kinds of manuscript was an amateur dramatist. The poet William Percy (1575–1648), son of Henry Percy, eighth Earl of Northumberland, wrote a number of plays for the Children of St Paul's or another professional London company,[42] although there is no evidence they were acted. Percy may have become interested in collecting or modelling his work on manuscripts from the professional London theatre, hence the Percy family's acquisition of the theatrical manuscripts of *The Wasp* and *John of Bordeaux*. But as they lack dedications, these manuscripts were probably purchased or acquired in some other way, rather than being presented to Percy. In any event, he acquired one set of foul papers (*The Wasp*) and one theatrical fair copy (*Bordeaux*), providing him with examples of two stages of the transmission of a dramatic text.

A presentation or commissioned copy is a fair copy, showing neatness and consistency, and its material form, including its binding and gilt-edged pages, makes it a literary and not a theatrical object. Nonetheless, only the form, and not the text itself, has been adapted for a reader. William Warburton famously claimed that he had amassed fifty-eight plays in manuscript, including *The Woman's Prize*, which were 'unluckely burnd' when used by a servant to line pie-tins.[43] Greg and other critics have assumed that Warburton was exaggerating or lying about his collection, possibly drawing play titles from the Stationers' Register.[44] However, Warburton, like Pope and other eighteenth-century editors of Shakespeare's plays, worked with theatre personnel and book dealers to examine or purchase original documents used by Shakespeare and his colleagues. Sir Edward Dering collected at least 221 printed 'playbooks', as he called them, between 1619 and 1624, and he may have also had a collection of dramatic manuscripts that were later damaged or dispersed.[45]

That so many scribal copies and the two autograph copies of Middleton's plays survive may suggest that he, and those who kept control of his texts after his death in 1627, also occasionally supplied patrons and collectors with copies of plays. These included an infamous but banned play, *A Game at Chess*, as well as popular or topical plays not yet in print, *The Witch* and *Hengist, King of Kent*. The two *c.* 1640 manuscripts of *Hengist, King of Kent*, probably commissioned, were written by different scribes, each of whom is carefully and conscientiously copying from the same company book or a playhouse manuscript with actors' names and signals for properties in the margin, details which both scribes also transcribe. One of the manuscripts has lost its title page and was further damaged by later binding. However, its original form may have been as visually appealing as the other manuscript. Dramatic texts could move out of the theatre to the literary reader with a minimum of transformation and continued to be valuable documents in their non-print, material form.

'Raph' Crane and his scribal copies

Transcripts of manuscripts could also be made for preservation within the company or for revival, or specifically for printer's copy.[46] One of the most prolific King's Men's scribes, who prepared some of the printer's copy used for the 1623 Shakespeare First Folio, was Ralph Crane, who signed his name 'Raph' (thus pronouncing it 'Rafe') in at least one manuscript, *Demetrius and Enanthe*. Although there is no evidence that he worked in the theatre as a book-keeper, he appears to have acquired some knowledge of playhouse practices. He made all but one of his surviving manuscripts as presentation, commissioned or, possibly, printer's copies as they are Quarto-sized rather than the more common folio size used in the theatre. Crane made his one exceptional folio-sized manuscript of Fletcher and Massinger's *Sir John van Olden Barnavelt* for an acting company. He copied this play and Fletcher's *Demetrius and Enanthe* (later published in the Beaumont and Fletcher 1647 Folio as *The Humorous Lieutenant*), Middleton's *The Witch* and *A Game at Chess* between 1624 and 1625. All of his manuscripts show a master copyist at work.

Crane most likely worked under the supervision of Middleton for both *The Witch*[47] and *A Game at Chess*, but Crane may also have worked with Fletcher and Massinger in transcribing their plays. Unusually for a scribe, Crane added an elaborate and personal dedication of his own to Sir Kenelm Digby, to whom he gave *Demetrius and Enanthe*.[48] This dedication carries the date of 27 November 1625, approximately three months after Fletcher's death from the plague, although Crane might have copied the text of the play at some earlier point. Digby may have commissioned it, but it is more likely that Crane decided to present it to Digby, as implied in Crane's dedication. He begins, 'Worthie Sir. I know that to a Man of yo^{ur} religious Inclination, a *deuine Argument* would haue byn much more wellcom; And such a one (*good Sir*) haue I vpon the Anvile for you, but it requires some=what a more *Consolatorie time* to fashion it.' Clearly this manuscript is a substitution for another on a '*deuine Argument*', which Crane has not yet finished, and he asks Digby instead to accept 'this *Comedie*' as 'a Matter *Recreatiue*'. This substitute manuscript may have only been available because Fletcher asked Crane to copy it under his direction, without stipulating the recipient, and it was still in Crane's possession after Fletcher died, hence this scribal appropriation of an author's right in the dedication. This is the only apparent case in which Crane wrote a dedication to a play, and he most likely did so because Fletcher could no longer claim possession of the text or the manuscript.

Crane's *Barnavelt* manuscript bears not only Buc's censorship marks of crosses in pencil and pen as well as the marginal note, 'I like not this...', although the final licence is now lost, but also annotations by the King's Men's book-keeper, probably not Edward Knight.[49] Particularly noticeable are the lines inserted interlinearly, in the margins and on inserted sheets, to replace those marked for deletion by Buc, as in Figure 5.2. T. H. Howard-Hill terms the manuscript 'the product of co-operation of the scribe, censor, and book-keeper to prepare a play acceptable for performance on the public stage', but does not speculate on the extent of Fletcher and Massinger's co-operation other than submitting to the scribe the revisions required by Buc.[50] But the two authors would most certainly have consulted this manuscript after its return from the censor in order to make these extensive revisions. Although Howard-Hill finds 'nothing in the manuscript that suggests that it was actually used in the playhouse', he argues that it may have been recopied as the company book,[51] especially as it once bore the licence. Before he began copying this manuscript, Crane pleated each page vertically three times to provide three columns for speech-prefixes, text and marginal directions, in order, as Howard-Hill has noted, to 'centre the text on the page and to align the recto and verso'.[52] Crane did the same in his manuscript of *Demetrius and Enanthe*, which apparently was not made to be used in the theatre.

Crane is known especially for the neatness and order of his copies; for example, in *Demetrius and Enanthe* and in *The Witch*, he anticipates his text by writing entrance directions a line or two before they appear. In various other ways, he can be noted as a 'fussy' or precise scribe.[53] As a temporary or long-term employee of the King's Men, Crane also worked with Shakespeare's manuscripts or the transcripts made from them. For the copy he almost certainly transcribed of *Measure for Measure* for the Folio printers, for example, he consistently introduced or regularised apostrophes, colons and parentheses, act–scene divisions, speech-prefixes and 'massed' stage entries. He also hyphenated compound words and deleted oaths, if the company had not done so by 1606.[54] In effect, Crane corrected or regularised grammar in this play, introducing incidental variants, but he did not change the dramatic features of the text, such as plot, setting, structure, character or dialogue, thereby introducing substantive variants, even though he had good cause to do so. *Measure for Measure* contains a number of obvious inconsistencies in dialogue and plot (including the 'nineteen' years mentioned in Act 1, Scene 3 and the 'fourteen' mentioned in Act 1, Scene 4 since the Duke enforced the laws against fornication) and duplications, but Crane did not correct them. As appeared to be his practice, he added a list of *dramatis per-*

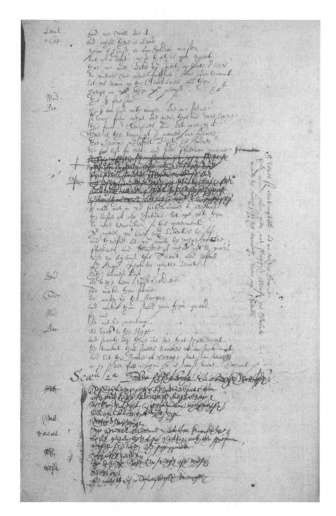

Figure 5.2 Ralph Crane's fair copy of Fletcher and Massinger's *Sir John van Olden Barnavelt*, British Library Additional MS 18653, f. 8ᵛ, showing revisions inserted by Crane due to censorship, marked by crosses, by the censor George Buc. Reproduced by permission of The British Library.

sonae to the end of the play, writing in the unnamed Duke's first name as 'Vincentio'. Crane may not have taken any creative liberties here but instead copied the name that he heard used by the players.

Crane also apparently copied out the manuscripts used to print the Folio texts of *The Tempest*, *The Two Gentlemen of Verona* and *The Merry Wives of Windsor*, in addition to *Measure for Measure*. These plays were the first four printed in the First Folio, suggesting that the King's Men planned to provide the Folio printers with fresh transcripts of each of the plays to be printed, later abandoning the idea either due to pressures of time or cost or other reasons. Crane may have produced some other transcripts used for the printing of Folio plays, including *Cymbeline* and *The Winter's Tale*.[55] In fact, Crane may have been contracted to make fresh transcripts of all the texts, and either he or his employers, or both, ended the agreement for some reason after only some texts had been copied.[56]

Scholars have used Crane's extant manuscripts and those of other scribes to suggest that only one copy of a particular text was made at a time, and that few plays existed in more than a few copies, largely because copying plays cost money. For example, Richard Knowles concludes that only two manuscripts, the company book bearing the censor's licence and another non-theatrical transcript, of *The True Chronicle History of King Leir* (the source play for Shakespeare's *King Lear*), would have been available to the 1605 printer because manuscript copying was too expensive.[57] However, there is no evidence that only two manuscripts of the play were extant at a given time, and Knowles may be much too strict in assuming that an acting company made one or two copies of a manuscript at most. Considering the thousands of manuscript pages left by Henslowe and Alleyn in their archive, theatrical personnel evidently did not ration or eschew the purchase or use of paper, ink or writing implements. That Henslowe and Alleyn did not separately record the costs of such copying does not mean that they subsidised or expected others to pay for it; they may have included or subsumed the cost of fair-copying in authors' fees.

In at least the case of Daniel's entertainment *Hymen's Triumph*, John Pitcher notes 'we can only guess' how many manuscripts of the text were needed and therefore made, beyond that presented to the bride. Pitcher assumes that there 'were surely no less than three others—one for vetting at court, one for Daniel to work with (perhaps ultimately printer's copy for the 1615 edition), a master-copy for the actors (who might want further part-copies for individual roles) and so on'.[58] The sheer volume of play-texts, at minimum 325, that Henslowe contracted or owned would suggest that at least some would need recopying due to wear, damage, loss or theft, or to suit changes in venue or personnel—for example, for provincial touring or for later revival. As Pitcher notes, acting companies or authors made as many copies as they 'needed', even if that meant four or more.

Lastly, on rare occasions, manuscripts were circulated to readers in part or in whole, as in the case of the lost manuscript of *The Wild Goose Chase*. Perhaps to prevent such a catastrophe, when Lucius Cary, Viscount Falkland, asked to borrow a manuscript of *The Shepherd's Paradise*, he was lent only part of it.[59] Nevertheless, a song from that play was copied again and widely circulated.[60] Such copies could be repeatedly made and dispersed. Peter Beal records that in addition to two extant scribal manuscripts of Jonson's masque *The Gypsies Metamorphosed* there are at least fifty-eight extant manuscript copies of songs or passages from it, copied either from manuscript or printed texts in the first three decades of the seventeenth century.[61] Such a large number, actually much less than that for copies of poems by Donne, for example, demonstrates that manuscript copying was not always subject to need or to save costs but was done for other reasons, including to circulate the text.

This type of circulation was particularly evident between 1624 and 1642, the period from which many extant dramatic manuscripts date. Some of these transcripts may have been made as extra copies to furnish Sir Henry Herbert, who as censor demanded that he receive two copies of a play, one for him to license and return and the other for him to keep in his files.[62] However, such a flurry of recopying may have been due to at least three other reasons. As is probably the case for Massinger's manuscript of *Believe as You List*, companies were accustomed to recopying and updating their repertory plays, as the majority of professional performances in this period were of old, revived plays, rather than new and original ones.[63] Some of these manuscripts managed to survive the closure of the theatres and the interregnum, and were later kept in the repertory of the newly opened or reopened Restoration companies and theatres. Theatrical personnel may, in fact, have begun to anticipate by the late 1630s that the Puritan threat to theatrical performance would decimate their stock, including company books, and thus paid for fresh transcriptions of their texts in order to safeguard their survival. Yet another reason for this extraordinary copying of texts, as suggested by the later history of the manuscripts of *Hengist, King of Kent*, is that clients specifically commissioned transcripts of plays that had been prohibited from publication and, later, from performance due to closure of the theatres.[64] In fact, at least some of these manuscripts were eventually donated in the seventeenth century by William Cartwright and other theatrical personnel to Dulwich College Library, a growing repository for theatrical papers, but later partly dispersed to other libraries and private collections. Most of these manuscripts do not appear to have served as printer's copy and were probably made as theatrical documents instead.

Shakespeare and the 'Book'

The extant manuscripts discussed thus far suggest that early modern dramatists and their colleagues saw the transmission of a play as a circular process. While various people, including a playhouse scribe, censor, book-keeper, actor and literary scribe, could contribute to a play's form, the author could remain responsible for its content at various stages, including during licensing, rehearsal, performance, revival and transcription for readers or printers. Given this knowledge, it is now time to work forward, not backward, by looking at some Shakespearean printed texts in the context of the manuscripts and working practices of his collaborators and contemporaries.

At least three Shakespearean texts were printed from authorial fair copies, including Q1 *The Merchant of Venice*, F *Antony and Cleopatra* and F *Coriolanus*. In order to make this argument, scholars draw their evidence from inside the text, looking for signs of authorial practice, including unique spellings or syntax or diction, which appear in an apparently clean and corrected text. For example, scholars generally agree that F *Coriolanus* was printed from Shakespeare's fair copy manuscript that had not served as a company book. As G. B. Evans notes, the text also preserves typically Shakespearean spellings: 'one' for 'on', 'shoot' for 'shout' and 'Scicinius' for 'Sicinius' (Shakespeare also added a 'c' to the beginning of 'silence', spelling it 'scilens').[65] Some passages are mislined, either due to the fondness of compositors or Shakespeare for not splitting half-lines in order to save space.[66] However, the supposed cleanness and regularity of the manuscript does not mean that it was completely legible, as the two compositors who set the type had difficulty at points reading Shakespeare's hand, resulting in some nonsensical passages. The most notable fair copy features of this text are the regular appearance of descriptive and complete stage directions, required entrance and exit directions, and non-varying speech-prefixes. The direction in 1.3, '*Enter Volumnia and Virigilia, mother and wife to Martius: They set them downe on two lowe stooles and sowe*', is distinctly authorial in the first part and distinctly theatrical in the second.

Other numerous occurrences of these types of directions and the consistency of the text suggests that when Shakespeare prepared his own fair copy from foul papers he served as a kind of book-keeper, using practices similar to those seen in the manuscripts discussed in this and the previous chapters. Like Heywood, Shakespeare also helps to define his characters through directions, as in, for example, '*Enter Martius Cursing*' (Act 1, Scene 5), '*Enter Cominius as it were in retire*' (Act 1, Scene 6), and '*They all cry, Martius, Martius, cast up their Caps and Launces: Cominius and Lartius stand bare*' (Act 1, Scene 10). No Quarto edition of the play exists with which to compare this Folio text, so it is not possible to document the variants that would suggest later authorial revision. This text shows a theatrical sophistication and smoothness that are not typical of Shakespeare's foul paper texts. Folio *Antony and Cleopatra* has some of the same characteristics as the *Coriolanus* text, and as both plays were written in the last years of Shakespeare's career, he may, according to Greg, have had more time to produce the 'very carefully written' and 'elaborately prepared' manuscript behind *Antony and Cleopatra*.[67]

However, Shakespeare was evidently as careful and elaborate in making fair copies early in his career. Fredson Bowers assumed that Heminges and Condell's boast in the First Folio of having received Shakespeare's papers without blots meant that Shakespeare routinely wrote out his own fair copy, revising it in the process.[68] Judging from the numerous cases in which compositors found Shakespeare's foul papers to be difficult to read, Shakespeare was probably aware of the untidiness or illegibility of his hand when composing. He may have been accustomed to supplying his employers with fair, rather than foul, copies of his new plays, at least on most if not all occasions, as in the case of his portion of *Sir Thomas More*. At the same time, Shakespeare also made minor or major changes in writing out his fair copies, so they would not have been entirely without blots, as Bowers imagined, but would have contained the kinds of alterations and corrections seen in his three pages of *Sir Thomas More*.

Judging from his experience with *Sir Thomas More*, Shakespeare not only acceded to changes in theatrical business that the book-keeper and other colleagues made but worked painstakingly to copy out the text in a form that made it as easy to read and use as possible. This is the type of concern for preparing the text for performance that is repeatedly evident in his contemporaries' extant manuscripts. That so many of the early Quartos of Shakespeare's plays were printed from foul papers may at first suggest that he or the Chamberlain's/King's Men saw no need to retain foul papers for use in the theatre once he had submitted the fair copy. But more probably, Shakespeare and his fellow actor-sharers themselves sold the foul papers to publishers, as each sharer, including Shakespeare, would have received a percentage of the selling price, possibly one-eighth to one-twelfth, depending on the number of sharers at a given time. Even if this sum was one-eighth of 40 shillings (thus 5 shillings), a contemporary rate for purchase of a playtext, the money was legally his. In foul and fair copy stage and afterwards, then, authors could prepare their texts not only for performance but print.

So, it is time to abandon the entrenched cultural notion that Shakespeare was such a natural genius that everything he wrote was produced flawlessly and brilliantly the first or second time. He was a working man of the theatre and worked as his colleagues and collaborators worked. He composed a text, rewriting or rethinking it before and after it was read by the censor and after performance, copying it again, and in the process sometimes polishing and refining it and sometimes allowing it to stand with errors or inconsistencies. When texts were printed from foul papers it is clear that printers acquired them with the owners' permission. As the papers of Henslowe and Alleyn show, all the theatre personnel in this age worked in a tightly interconnected and interrelated business. That printers could hoodwink or pirate texts in such a world, in which everyone seemed to know each other's personal and private affairs, including the terms of their contracts and any monies earned, is impossible to accept.[69] That Shakespeare would have allowed his texts to be printed without his participation and co-operation, when as sharer he still partially owned them, is equally hard to accept.

It is not possible to re-examine here all of the early printed Quarto and First Folio texts in order to question whether more were printed from fair copies than has usually been posited by modern textual scholars. However, Shakespeare can be seen in the context of the major dramatists of this period, especially as an authorial fair copy, sometimes still containing errors or inconsistencies, could serve as the possible source of any printed text. For example, the 1598 Q1 *1 Henry IV* was reprinted from another 1600 Quarto, now known as Q0, of which only one sheet of one copy is extant. Those arguing that Q0/Q1 was printed from a scribal, rather than an authorial, fair copy have drawn their evidence from both inside and outside the text. The play was censored after its early performances because of its portrayal of Sir John Oldcastle as a clownish companion to Prince Hal. Shakespeare would have had to rework his copy meticulously to alter the 330 occurrences of this name and the two others, Harvey and Russell, that had apparently given offence, to Falstaff, Bardolph and Peto, the names appearing in Q1.[70] These extensive changes, made either in the foul or fair papers or in the company book, would have probably rendered the manuscript illegible. Thus Shakespeare or a scribe might well have made a new fair copy from one or more of these texts and included the required (and possibly other) changes.

In any case, the censorable, original foul papers and the original fair copy, and the original company book made from either, would have been prohibited from being used as printer's copy as well as being performed on stage after Oldcastle's descendants had complained. Although Greg argued that Q1 was printed from foul papers, Jowett argues for scribal papers instead.[71] However, there are still some remnants in the censored text that Shakespeare may have overlooked in making the required changes (and that he or the scribe did not correct). These include a pun on 'my old lad of the castle' and a stage direction with 'Haruey' and 'Rossill' in it in 1.2 as well as three speech-prefixes for '*Ross*' in 2.5. If a scribe fair-copied the manuscript used to print Q1, he did not perfect the text he was copying; the other possibility is that Shakespeare made this fair copy.

Scholars have seen the same textual inconsistencies in Q1 *2 Henry IV*, yet they seem to agree that it was printed from foul papers. It too has a few traces of the names of Oldcastle and Russell. As no evidence exists to suggest that this play was censored after performance (as *1 Henry IV* apparently was), if Shakespeare had not censored the names as he was composing he probably did so before the play was performed. The entire scene of Act 3, Scene 1 (in which Hal seizes the crown from his sleeping father) does not appear in the first issue of Q1 but does appear in the second issue (printed in the same year, 1600). If the scene already existed when the first issue was printed, it may have been misplaced or withheld by the company or overlooked by the printer. But it is also possible that Shakespeare wrote it during or after the printing of the first issue.

Yet comparison of the Q1 and F texts provides evidence that Shakespeare was extensively revising this play during or after completing the foul papers (perhaps when required to censor the Oldcastle material). He probably made the revisions, and added the scene, as he transcribed the foul papers into a fair copy, later used as the company book. As a sharer in the Chamberlain's Men, Shakespeare may not have been concerned that he and his colleagues had released a somewhat incomplete version of the play when giving the Q1 printers his foul papers. Thus Shakespeare most likely worked in the same way as the authors of many of the extant manuscripts discussed earlier, including Middleton and Heywood, who assumed that their papers, however variant, presented texts with which they were satisfied. Shakespeare was probably given or retrieved the foul or fair copy of *2 Henry IV* after it had been examined by the censor, making his adjustments to it before transcribing or returning it to a company scribe.

Shakespeare's fair copies were probably not flawless, completely legible or perfect, but like his fair copy of the *More* passages occasionally contained a few *currente calamo* or later changes and eyeskip errors. The scholarly belief that authorial foul and fair copies can be easily distinguished because the first will be messy and the second completely clean is based on a false premise. Fair copies could be far from fair, and could contain a few, or some, or many cuts, alterations and revisions. That a manuscript such as the one behind Q2 *Romeo and Juliet* is foul papers seems clear due to its major confusions, false starts and the type of glaring inconsistencies which would show in performance.

But there is no such stable argument for the same type of manuscript behind Q1 *2 Henry IV*, a much less problematic text. The text is authorial, but may be foul or fair copy. In the discussion of the Folio text *2 Henry IV*, Jowett provides a harsh assessment of scribal, as opposed to authorial, practice. He argues that F was printed from a scribal transcript of the company's book, prepared with a great deal of interference from a 'cavalier' scribe who 'must be responsible for hundreds of minor variants. In F, contractions are expanded, colloquialisms and solecisms are formalised, and irregular aspects of syntax are regularised.' This scribe also used massed entries for stage directions.[72] However, Greg sees these variants as normal book-keeping practice: 'the cuts are restored; the Epilogue rearranged; directions are drastically pruned, made explicit, and generally tidied up; ghosts and mutes disappear, and many entrances and exits are added; character-designations and speech-prefixes are largely normalized and made consistent'.[73] If Shakespeare, both as company sharer and company dramatist, consented to such changes in the preparation of the company book from which this scribal copy was prepared, there would in fact be nothing 'cavalier' about the changes. The changes are instead made at Shakespeare's own direction or with his permission. Jowett's argument sets up an antagonistic relationship between playhouse scribe/book-keeper and author, especially one who has distanced himself from his text. Instead, it seems to have been routine practice for scribes and company dramatists to work closely together, evidently without antagonism, in order for both to succeed in their individual jobs and to suit the company and entrepreneurs as a whole. Such collaboration would be especially profitable when the dramatist was himself also an entrepreneur, as Shakespeare was.

Other evidence of scribes working with and not against authors comes in the manuscript of William Cavendish's play *The Country Captain*.[74] The text appears to be a scribal copy made by the same copyist of the manuscript of James Shirley's play *The Court Secret*.[75] *The Country Captain* shows corrections by another scribal hand, as well as the restoration of a scene cut from the text in the hand of Cavendish's secretary John Rolleson, and further revisions and cuts by Newcastle himself. Rolleson had also copied the prologue to Cavendish's copy of a scribal manuscript of Jonson's masque *The Gypsies Metamorphosed*.[76] The manuscript of *The Country Captain* may represent a fair copy made specifically to serve as printer's copy and then adapted and cut, for political reasons, for a later production of the play. The play was first written in 1641, and the transcript appears to date from the mid-1640s.[77] Ralph Crane worked closely with Middleton in these same ways in making fair copies of his manuscripts, and it is worth considering whether Crane had such a role, or had been promised one, with Shakespeare at the time of his death in 1616. Crane's copies of Folio plays may not have been made at the behest of the King's Men but at that of Shakespeare himself.

Some of the changes to the manuscripts used to print the Folio may indeed have been made after Shakespeare's death or after the end of his financial involvement with the King's Men. But others may have been made with his consent, especially as he was frequently staging these texts with his Chamberlain's/King's Men colleagues. Scholars have identified other Shakespearean texts as being set from scribal, rather than authorial, fair copy, although these arguments need to be reconsidered. For example, Greg argues that F *Twelfth Night* (written by 1602, probably revised by 1606) was printed from the company's book largely because it is an 'unusually clean text'. The play has been purged of oaths, and a song appears to have been reassigned from Viola to Feste in 1.2.[78] The fact that the text is 'clean' actually cannot prove that it was printed from a scribal rather than authorial manuscript, however. A play could circulate back to the author at a variety of stages, including a later revival.

F *Henry VIII*, collaboratively written by Shakespeare and Fletcher, shows enough signs of having been printed from a scribal fair copy as it has regular and consistent use of character names and entrance and exit directions. However, in this case the fair copy may have been necessary because the foul papers were collaborative, although it is possible that Fletcher and Shakespeare each submitted fair copies of their portions to the company. Judging from Heywood's messy annotations to Munday's portions of the *Sir Thomas More* book, some authors may have made their collaborators' portions of a text less than legible. Folio *Julius Caesar* appears to have been printed from the company book with directions calling for music, sound effects and other theatrical features, as well as signs of character doubling of Cassius and Ligarius.[79] Yet the text also preserves signs of Shakespeare's foul papers, including an uncorrected duplication in 4.2 in which Brutus offers the news of Portia's death to Cassius and, forty lines later, shows astonishment when told of her death by Messala. Here even in the company book is the strong presence of the author.

The Folio text of *Macbeth* seems also to have been printed from the company book, but as it is the shortest play in the Shakespeare canon it may have been cut at some point. Its stage directions and character names are regular and consistent. The text also contains two cue lines to the songs found in Middleton's *The Witch* (composed *c*.1616). That *Macbeth* contains only the cues and not the complete songs suggests that the songs were already familiar to the book-keeper and probably the actors. Thus the songs were recycled from another company book or text, not added on this occasion by Middleton who would otherwise surely have transcribed the songs in their entirety. The Folio text of *As You Like It* was probably also printed from the company book or a transcript of it.

As noted earlier, Herbert had to relicense *The Winter's Tale* in 1623 because the 'allowed' or licensed book had been lost. Thus the King's Men had to make new theatrical manuscripts on occasion, recopying them from whatever sources could be found if they did not substitute printed copies for company books. During recopying, play-texts could be updated, altered, cut, added to or changed in a variety of ways, particularly in regards to suiting current theatre personnel, performance venue, topical issues or audience taste. If a company acquired plays that could be performed in sequence with their existing plays, the old or new plays could undergo some adaptation or revision to fit all the plays together. A variety of types of manuscript, and even printed copies, could have been used in the theatre and could have carried equal weight to the first, original, licensed book made when a play was new. Many different kinds of copy, foul papers, authorial or scribal fair copies, and previously printed Quartos, were used during Shakespeare's lifetime to print Quarto editions of his plays. This suggests that the Chamberlain's Men, and later the King's Men, were flexible about the types of manuscripts and printed texts that they commissioned and kept.

The theory that Shakespeare revised his plays some years after their original composition was successfully re-examined in the 1980s, using the Quarto 1 and F text of *King Lear* as a test case. Modern scholars had been nearly unanimous in arguing that Shakespeare had revised *Othello* after composition. Yet the idea that he had revised any of his other plays often provoked angry debate, largely because some scholars saw later authorial revision as an admission that the texts as originally composed had been faulty. The recent debate about revision in *King Lear*, and the subsequent scholarly acceptance that Shakespeare revised that play, and probably others, including *Hamlet*, after composition, has encouraged scholars to re-evaluate the sources of major and minor variants between Quarto texts or between Quarto and Folio texts of the same play. These variants may just as likely signal authorial revision rather than non-authorial interference, especially if done in a way that maintains the artistic coherence of the play. The changes made between Q1 and F *Lear*, for example, show an author returning to his text to make well-thought-out, consistent and intelligent changes to his major characters, notably Lear.

Gary Taylor has argued that 'as a class, the heavily revised plays all date from after *1 Henry IV* (1596), when Shakespeare was securely established as the leading dramatist of the capital's leading company', and thus that extensive literary revision was a 'luxury' practised in the later part of his career.[80] However, numerous early and late plays show the same kinds of later revisions, most likely partly if not wholly authorial, and revision was most certainly not a 'luxury', as Henslowe's papers can confirm. These revisions can be catalogued by looking at the surviving texts of the same play printed in Quarto and Folio form, the first apparently from foul papers and the second from the company 'book' or another manuscript used in the theatre at some point. Early plays in this category include *Titus Andronicus, A Midsummer Night's Dream, Love's Labour's Lost, The Merry Wives of Windsor, Much Ado About Nothing, The Merchant of Venice, Troilus and Cressida*, parts 2 and 3 of *Henry VI, Richard III, Richard II*, the two parts of *Henry IV, Henry V*, and *Romeo and Juliet*. Later plays, from the period in which Taylor claims Shakespeare had more time for the 'luxury of revision', include *Hamlet, Othello* and *King Lear*. Plays not printed in early Quartos but in the Folio for the first time may also shows internal signs of later revisions (not just revision during composition), including *The Tempest, Coriolanus, Julius Caesar, Antony and Cleopatra, Twelfth Night* and *All's Well that Ends Well*.[81]

The relationship between an experienced dramatist and those who regularly handled and used his texts was apparently not antagonistic but was in fact necessarily co-operative and co-ordinated. Most notably, Shakespeare worked in the same way as his collaborators and colleagues. Scholars may single him out among Elizabethan, Jacobean and Caroline dramatists as unique in the achievement of a great artistic vision and genius: that is, as unique in the quality of matter he ultimately produced. However, he cannot be singled out among these dramatists as unique in his manner of composing and circulating this matter. It is only through print that Shakespeare and his contemporary dramatists begin to lose control, unless they corrected proofs or printed copies themselves. The surrender of the acting company's text to the printer marks the beginning of the end of the recirculation of the text back to the author.

6 'It sprang from ye Poet'
Jonson, Middleton and Shakespeare at work

As the work of Heywood in *The Captives*, *The Escapes of Jupiter* and *Sir Thomas More* has particularly demonstrated thus far, even in the act of composing, dramatists had to anticipate how their texts would evolve past the page to the stage at any given point. By way of conclusion, this chapter presents three further examples of this circulation for Jonson, Middleton and Shakespeare along with the consequences for performance, inside and outside the playhouse. Each time a play or theatrical entertainment circulated, it moved within the interconnected and circular theatrical world that entrepreneurs such as Henslowe, Alleyn and their colleagues, including dramatists, did so much to build and, ultimately, record.

'Speeches, songs & inscriptions': the manuscript of Jonson's *Entertainment at Britain's Burse*

Jonson probably treated his foul papers in much the same way as Daborne and Heywood. In his autograph copies of poetry and prose, Jonson used a calligraphic italic hand, as in his fair copy manuscript of *The Masque of Queens*, written for Queen Anne, his dedication to Prince Henry in the scribal fair copy of *The Masque of Blackness*, and various epigrams and inscriptions. However, this exceptionally neat, orderly and error-free calligraphic hand differs noticeably from the largely italic hand mixed with some secretary letter forms that he used for two 1605 letters to Sir Robert Cecil and a *c.* 1635 letter to Sir Robert Cotton.[1] Even more remarkable is that the hands in the two 1605 letters are somewhat different from each other, and it is not certain that either or both letters to Cecil are fair copies. Jonson's annotations in his own copies of printed books, which are numerous, vary from being neat to slightly rough; however, his hand always remains legible. No foul paper copies of any of Jonson's plays appear to survive. If Jonson followed the same requirements set down by Henslowe for Daborne he may have turned over his fair copies of the many plays he was commissioned to write for the companies for which Henslowe acted as commissioning agent; thus Jonson would have retained his foul papers.

However, Jonson's foul papers of another performance work may indeed survive. In 1997 James Knowles announced his discovery of a hitherto lost manuscript of an entertainment written by Ben Jonson among Sir Edward Conway's papers in State Papers at the National Archives, Kew. Knowles produced an edition of the entertainment in 1999.[2] This entertainment was apparently that performed on 11 April 1609 at the opening of the New Exchange, then known as 'Britain's Burse', in the Strand.[3] The entertainment, with designs by Inigo Jones, had among its audience King James, Queen Anne, Prince Henry and Prince Charles, and Princess Elizabeth, as well as numerous members of James's court. Although the manuscript of the entertainment was lost until 1997, documentary evidence has existed since April 1609 about the celebration for which it was performed. Cecil funded the building of the New Exchange, begun in 1608 and built adjacent to Salisbury House, Cecil's London home, as a shopping arcade. The materials to build the property had been partially pilfered from Durham House, previously occupied by Sir Walter Ralegh, who had by then been consigned to the Tower on the orders of the King through Cecil, the financial backer of Jonson's entertainment. Jones had also designed much of the building's façade, numerous drawings of which survive in the library of Worcester College, Oxford.[4]

The evidence for this event chiefly consisted of Cecil family accounts and bills, now held at Hatfield House, and a dispatch by the Venetian ambassador, who attended the entertainment, now among State Papers.[5] In this translation, the Venetian ambassador reported that Cecil

> has fitted up one of the shops very beautifully, and over it ran the motto: 'All other places give for money, here all is given for love'. To the King he gave a Cabinet, to the Queen a silver plaque of the Annunciation worth, they say, four thousand crowns. To the Prince he gave a horse's trappings of great value, nor was there any one of the Suite who did not receive at the very least a gold ring. The King named the place Britain's Burse.[6]

In addition to this report, there exists a notice of the entertainment in Stow's *Annals* (1616) as consisting of 'pleasant speeches, gifts and ingenious devices'.[7] The Cecil Papers also contain a letter dated 31 March by Thomas Wilson to his employer Cecil describing the plot nearly two weeks before the performance. Among other things, Wilson reminds Cecil that he 'invented' the subject of the entertainment and had told Wilson to instruct Jonson and Jones that 'the deseigne is to haue three persones only actors according to yo[r] lo[ps] conceit'. In other words, this entertainment was made to order by Cecil. In addition, Wilson noted that the three roles were of a 'Keeper' (who would respond to criticisms of the building's construction), a Mountebank and his apprentice. The Mountebank was to wear a vizard, which he would take off to reveal himself as the Merchant who offers his gifts to the audience.[8]

Bills in the Cecil Papers show that Nathan Field was paid £4 for playing the Keeper, William Ostler £5 for the Mountebank, and Giles Cary (or Gary) £2 for the Mountebank's boy. In 1609, all three were or had been members of the Children of the Queen's Revels, the company for which Daborne became a co-manager in the following year. By 1610, Ostler joined the King's Men, and by 1611 Cary was a member of Lady Elizabeth's Men,[9] for which Daborne later wrote plays. As a young man, Field had been mentored by Jonson as his 'Schollar', according to Drummond, and Field acted in *Cynthia's Revels* (1600), *Poetaster* (1601) and *Epicoene* (1609), as well as plays by other authors. By 1613, when the Queen's Revels merged with the Lady Elizabeth's Men, Field also began working as a collaborator with Daborne, among others, in writing plays, as his correspondence with Henslowe records. By 1609, presumably Field would have already been very familiar with Jonson's assertions about dramatists and their authority.

For the entertainment at Britain's Burse, Jonson 'the Poett' and Jones (the designer) were each paid £13 6s 8d, although Jones's staging expenses amounted to an extra reimbursement of £9 12s. A much larger and remarkable sum of £96 was spent on properties, including hired costumes and the foreign shop goods or commodities displayed by the characters, all of which were given away to members of the audience. Wilson also notes payment

> To Ionson's man and anoth[er]
> feld that satt upp all night wryt[ing]
> the speeches, songs & inscript[ions].

Whether this 'man' was Richard Brome, known to be Jonson's servant by 1613, is not clear. That 'feld' is Field is clear enough. McMillin concluded from this evidence and from the lost manuscript that Jonson had prepared without any collaborators 'a particularly mercantile show', which prefigured *The Alchemist* (written the following year), celebrating Jonson's rendering of his 'satirical impulse'.[10]

McMillin took as truthful Wilson's account of the plot and the bill's implications that the play had been transcribed by Field and two others, even though the bill actually suggests they may have been collaborators who 'wryt' the play rather than scribes who copied it. In 1959, Lawrence Stone had already drawn conclusions similar to McMillin's, particularly in accepting Wilson's account of the plot.[11] Knowles's examination of the National Archives manuscript led him to conclude that, although there are slight discrepancies between the text as described and the actual text, the manuscript is indeed the Jonson Entertainment.[12] Knowles originally named the Entertainment *The Key Keeper*, as this notation is centred at the top of the first page. However, the notation is clearly a speech-prefix only, not the text's title. One of the bills in the Cecil Papers calls it *The Key Keeper*, but it is usually referred to as 'the Entertainment at Britains Burse' in most receipts, thus its true title is *The Entertainment at Britain's Burse*; in his later edition, Knowles, in fact, adopted this title. Knowles originally decided that:

The manuscript is clearly a contemporary copy, written in three different scripts, and enclosed in a letter to Conway. Although it starts with a neat italic, generally resembling Jonson's calligraphic italic, the presentation gradually deteriorates. Whereas the opening leaves are carefully arranged, allowing proper spacing for the speech headings, a straight margin and level lines, towards the end of the manuscript there are signs of speed and carelessness and erratic line-spacings. On one sheet, all three scripts appear in succession. These factors suggest that the text which survives here is unlikely to be a presentation copy, but an *ad hoc* version provided for an interested outsider—hence its lack of stage directions.[13]

Knowles later concluded that the manuscript is written in four hands, with the fourth possibly by the same writer whose hand appears first.[14] In any case, this fourth hand is responsible for copying only two words in the manuscript.

Knowles originally claimed that despite the notation by Wilson that the text was copied out by 'Jonson's man', Field and another person, 'palaeographical evidence cannot clinch the argument, since the copy's hands do not match those of either Jonson or Field'. Knowles adds that 'the likeliest candidate for Jonson's "man", Richard Brome, cannot be verified due to the lack of manuscripts for comparison'.[15] Knowles noted the text's obvious stylistic, linguistic and contextual links to other Jonson works, including *Volpone*, *Epicoene* and *The Alchemist*. In his edition, Knowles later considered whether the hand of the first copyist was Jonson's, but decided that 'we cannot *prove* that this MS includes Jonson's hand', as 'the only comparable draft', the 1606 entertainment for the King of Denmark,[16] 'employs differing forms and layout from this MS'.[17] However, the 1606 entertainment is not the 'only comparable draft' in Jonson's hand to which to compare the manuscript of *Britain's Burse*. Knowles's reservations appear to derive instead from lack of familiarity with transcripts of texts that were written to be acted, especially play-texts.[18]

To begin with, Knowles confidently stated in his edition of the manuscript that 'its layout resembles the private transcripts of the period'. However, in comparison with the many autograph or fair copy manuscripts examined and discussed throughout this book, the manuscript of *The Entertainment at Britain's Burse* does not resemble private transcripts of such texts or even copies used in the theatre or other playing spaces. This manuscript differs from most dramatic manuscripts in many respects. First, as noted by Knowles, it has three (or possibly four) hands transcribing the text on one of its pages (see Figure 6.1), which is unusual. But more unusually, and not noted by Knowles, is the way the hands change mid-sentence. Fair copy manuscripts in more than one hand studied throughout this book usually show a change in hand between completed passages, if not pages. The distribution of the hands in *The Entertainment* appears as follows (using the manuscript's stamped page numbers rather than either set of the pencilled ones):

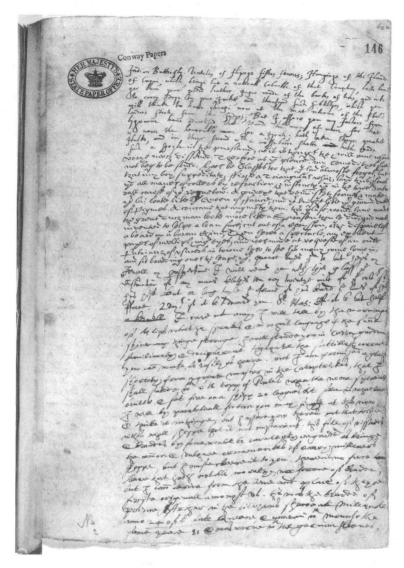

Figure 6.1 The Entertainment at Britain's Burse, National Archives SP 14/44/146, showing Hand A and at least two other hands at work as copyists or co-authors in portioned-off passages. Reproduced by permission of The National Archives.

144 recto:	Entirely in Hand A (an italic hand)
144 verso:	Entirely in Hand A
145 recto:	Entirely in Hand A who ends halfway down the page in mid-sentence, and the rest of the page is blank (also an unusual characteristic; the standard argument among manuscript

	scholars is that because paper was expensive it would not generally be wasted or left blank)
145 verso:	Blank
146 recto:	Hand A picks up in mid-sentence and completes ten lines; then Hand B (in a formal secretary hand) takes over in the first third of the line (in mid-sentence) and writes out fourteen lines; then Hand C (in a sometimes illegible secretary/italic hand mix) takes over mid-line and completes the rest of the page, another twenty-five lines
146 verso:	All in Hand B
147 recto:	All in Hand B

The distribution of the hands and the curious stopping mid-page on 145^r seems to suggest that the manuscript is a transcript of another copy, possibly foul papers. After the completion of 145^r (with a blank verso) the manuscript was relinquished to someone other than a scribe copying out this text.

Most likely, the first three transcribed pages, 144^r–145^r, consisting of two sheets, were to be delivered to Conway immediately upon the completion of 145^r, and the scribe was in such a hurry to get the text to Conway that he stopped mid-sentence. In fact, the blank verso of page 145 contains the notice, 'for Sr Edward / Conway knight', obviously serving as a delivery address. This conclusion is also supported by the fact that the manuscript consists of two bifolia (each was later pasted onto a guardstrip). The leaves were evidently meant to be put together sequentially like this (if viewed with the manuscript lying on its spine):

VV

rather than nested or 'quired', with one inside the other, like this:

V
V

This latter arrangement would require some special care in transcription, especially for a manuscript that was passed among three people. That the manuscript was first organised as two bifolia in sequence would suggest that it was a casual manuscript not originally intended to be bound as a formal product. But as the fold lines of all the leaves match up, the manuscript was eventually sent off as a complete text. However, the possibility remains that Jonson had intended to send off this portion by itself but that either he or the other copyists later held these leaves back until the others were finished. The transcription in Hand A and the sequence of the manuscript suggests that the manuscript was copied in haste. It was probably not made as a presentation copy to Conway, an influential statesman, Member of Parliament, and ambassador to The Brill. The transcription of the rest of the manuscript, which sometimes is fairly sloppy and even illegible, would also support this conclusion.

But the question remains as to why would Jonson have to rush a partial copy to Conway after *The Entertainment* had already been performed. It seems that his haste would imply instead that the partial copy was to be sent to Conway *before* its performance, possibly for his approval. John Pitcher discusses a similar type of haste in the case of Samuel Daniel's 1614 masque *Hymen's Triumph*: 'Daniel was still adding new material to the play (the Prologue and three of the choruses) only a short time before the performance... This might explain why the manuscript presented to Lady Roxburgh was left incomplete, and why it was copied, with some signs of haste, by two scribes.'[19] A manuscript reference in a letter of 3 January 1609/10 from Sir Richard Verney to John Coke notes that Conway was in 'principale imployment in the Barryers of oʳ Younge prince this twelue tyde'.[20] That is, Conway, among whose papers the *Entertainment* was found, was involved in the tilt for Prince Henry on 6 January 1610, for which Ben Jonson wrote *The Entertainment at Prince Henry's Barriers*, subtitled *The Lady of the Lake*. A number of manuscripts with extracts from this text, as well as other relevant material, also record this event.[21] Rather than acquiring the manuscript of *The Entertainment at Britain's Burse* some point after its performance, either directly or indirectly, from Jonson, as Knowles posits, Conway was probably 'employed' in some way in this entertainment before it was performed. This would not be surprising, given that nine months later he was involved in another of Jonson's entertainments.

More importantly, the manuscript of *Britain's Burse* may not be a transcription of an earlier copy but the original, working draft; that is, foul papers. Knowles assumes that the first hand is not Jonson's because it does not entirely resemble Jonson's calligraphic hand in copying out the fair copy of *The Masque of Queens* or in writing a formal dedication in a printed copy of *Sejanus*. Knowles does not consider that the text may not be a fair copy but foul papers, showing Jonson's fluent, cursive hand in the act of composing. His hand varied throughout his life, most obviously after he began to suffer from palsy in 1626. Although there are no other samples of Jonson's cursive hand in his literary manuscripts, some of the majuscule and minuscule letter forms in this manuscript match those in the hand he used for composing or writing quickly. This hand appears most readily in his marginal comments made in a number of books which he owned, now in the British Library and elsewhere,[22] as well as the letters to Cecil and to Cotton. However, a few other letter forms, notably a minuscule 'p' with a high ascender at the left (used mostly in primary position in a word), do not appear to resemble Jonson's usual letter forms. But the possibility remains, as it must do until an example of a working draft by Jonson comes to light, that Hand A is Jonson's.

As for Hands B and C, at least Hand C is not the hand of a professional scribe, because it is very difficult to read. In fact Hands B and C may not be scribes at all but collaborators. Hence they could be authors. That Hands B and C, neither of which appears to be Field's,[23] took over mid-sentence from others may at first suggest that they continued copying from a manuscript in front of them. However, the literary quality of the passages in their hands differs markedly from the passages in Hand A. Hands B and C may have been collaborating at the same time. Possibly, Hand C proved so inept that Hand B took the manuscript away from him and finished it. Most importantly, the passages in Hand A suggest a type of *currente calamo* fluency typical of composing authors, and hence also the lack of stage directions, as composing authors tend to provide only very sparse or ambiguous directions. These passages and those in the other hands show no sign of being corrected or cleaned up, which would certainly have been the case if this manuscript represents a formal transcript. Jonson, a notoriously self-conscious reviser and perfecter of his own work, would almost certainly have made necessary corrections were he making or supervising a fair copy, particularly one to be presented to a patron.

In addition, the passages in Hand A are not written in the typical format found in so many dramatic manuscripts which have set-off speech-prefixes as well as dialogue indented from the left margin with noticeable spacing between lines and passages. In all three hands, the dialogue is written flush left and flush right with the speech-prefixes centred above the dialogue. At one point on 146^r, which contains all three hands, two speech prefixes for the Boy and his Master (the Mountebank) are written by Hand C within the same line as the dialogue, making the entire text look very cramped. If Hand C were a professional scribe he would surely have set off the speech-prefixes. The writer of the first three pages does set off and centre speech-prefixes, so the fact that Hand C does not also set off the speech-prefixes suggests that he, even if an inexperienced scribe, is not copying from Jonson's foul or fair copy. Hand C may here be a composing author, albeit an inexperienced one. There are no further speech-prefixes in the text; however, Hand B very formally sets off the various lines of the text's concluding poem or song on the final page.

If it is partial or full foul papers, or even an entirely fair copy of foul papers, *The Entertainment* reveals new evidence of Jonson's practices as a composing author. Most notably, he wrote just like all his contemporary dramatists, including many with whom he collaborated; or they wrote just like him. So Jonson was not atypical in his composition practices and in his insistence on 'perfiting', as Daborne put it, and reclaiming his later texts. This text shares many of the characteristics of a foul paper text such as Heywood's manuscript of *The Captives*, including sentences that digress, lose track, or run on without focus or correction. Such sentences seem to be very uncharacteristic of the standard view of Jonson, who was fastidious about demonstrating his grammatical fluency, even attacking Shakespeare at one point for an ungrammatical line in *Julius Caesar*.

That Jonson would want this manuscript to serve as anything but a preliminary, uncorrected copy is very difficult to accept. For example, a portion
of the text on 144^Y, which seems to be written by a composing author, gives
these lines to the Keeper, who is discussing the types of people who have
complained that the New Exchange should be used for another purpose,
other than for shops:

> A seuenth woulde needes haue it Tippers
> office; And many a fayre front builte onely to grace the streete, and
> for noe vse; wher I wonder how such men could keepe theyr braynes—
> from being guilty of imagining it; rather, a place to twiste silke in, or
> make ropes, or, play a shittlecocke, better then nothing. Well if theyr
> igno=raunce healpe 'hem not to mercy I know not what can. I may
> feare—myne owne proper too, iustly, for hauing bene thus impertinent
> about 'hem.

The text of *The Entertainment* consists largely of a succession of lists—of
people's reactions, of wares for sale, etc.—which often digress or which have
unclear antecedents for later references. The literary quality of the passages
in Hand B is not as good as the passages in Jonson's apparent hand. The
quality of the short passage in Hand C seems to be amateurish; however,
both B and C demonstrate an understanding of the plot and characters in
Jonson's section. *The Entertainment*'s concluding poem, in the Hand of B,
seems to be poor in comparison with Jonson's other poetry.[24] As for identifying these two other hands, Wilson's note (damaged on the right side) states
that payment was made

> To Ionson's man and anoth
> feld that satt upp all night wryt
> the speeches, songs & inscript[25]

This suggests that these men served as collaborators, not scribes, and the
placement of Field's name on the second line may suggest that he is not the
'another' to whom Wilson refers in the previous line. Given his intellectual
tutelage by Jonson, and his contracts with Henslowe a few years later to
write plays with collaborators such as Daborne and Massinger, Field may
have acted as an annotator or contributor to the text, especially as he was to
play the role of the Key Keeper.

For these reasons, Hands B and C may represent Brome and another collaborator. This receipt for payment is dated 16 April, five days after
performance, but it is written at the bottom of a bill for all the participants,
which was submitted fairly quickly after the performance. As noted above
(p. 59), Jonson, Alleyn and Inigo Jones were each paid £20 as 'rewards to
the actors and deuisors of the showe' performed earlier on 6 May 1608, with
no breakdown noted of the number of devisors. In the same way, the fee of

£13 6s 8d, simply noted for Jonson the 'poett' for *Britain's Burse*, may not strictly define his role as its only devisor. In fact this record simply means here that he did not act in the entertainment, as Ostler, the boy Cary (or Gary) and Field did. Or it means that Jonson was commonly known by this time, perhaps at his own request, as a 'poet' when receiving money due him, in order to distinguish him from actors or other theatre personnel.[26] Jonson's fee here is significantly smaller than the £20 he earned for the earlier show, perhaps precisely because he was a collaborator rather than actor and sole author.

The conceit and invention for *The Entertainment* came from Cecil, who apparently dictated both the plot and the characters' roles, not from Jonson. Also, Wilson's summary of the plot may, in fact, have been written before all or part of *The Entertainment* was composed or completed. His letter is dated 31 March and *The Entertainment* was performed on 11 April, so it may have been unfinished until even a few days before its performance. This scenario would fit the haste with which the manuscript was apparently written by men sitting up 'all night', according to at least Wilson. The text may indeed have been written all on a single night, possibly even in the early morning hours of 11 April, hence resembling Daniel's haste in copying *Hymen's Triumph* and Daborne's in writing out his new play for Henslowe at midnight. It would not be surprising if Jonson was with his 'man' and the one or two others at the time, and that the second part of *The Entertainment* was written collaboratively. It does not seem atypical for Jonson to take entire credit for writing the play, especially if he believed himself to be working with those he considered 'co-adjutors', 'novices' or 'journeymen', all of whose lack of experience can be seen in this manuscript. Jonson himself may have supplied Wilson with the information on who was involved in 'wryghting' the copy. If so, *The Entertainment* was written by Jonson and at least two collaborators, with Jonson portioning off the text, so that he would write the first half himself and give the second half to his junior collaborators. As Knowles suggests, the payment to Field may have been made for subsequent copies of the speeches and lyrics 'to be offered to the audience as synopses or souvenirs', not the text of this manuscript.[27]

As Daborne and Field made clear in their correspondence with Henslowe, some collaborators spent a great deal of time in 'conference' about the play they were co-writing. Cecil, who outlined the plot of *The Entertainment at Britain's Burse*, should be considered a partial if not the primary devisor. As in the case with the 1606 entertainment he commissioned for the King of Denmark, Cecil may have slightly revised this text after composition. In any event, if the first hand in the manuscript represents Jonson's composing hand, it is his voice and practice that are prominent and insistent here. If it is not Jonson's composing hand, Hand A, as well as B and C, must be slavishly recopying the signs of the same type of incomplete and irregular foul papers written by Jonson's contemporaries, including Heywood.

This manuscript surely demonstrates that Jonson's theatrical world was as interrelated as that recorded by Henslowe's and Alleyn's manuscripts. Not only does Jonson's *Entertainment at Britain's Burse* make use of actors who had worked or will shortly work with Henslowe and Daborne, but Jonson's principal actor in his 1608 *Entertainment at Salisbury House* was Edward Alleyn himself.[28] So it would be exceedingly difficult to argue that Jonson is anomalous or atypical in *any* of his practices. These would include producing foul sheets that were nearly as difficult to read or as incomplete as those of Daborne, who, not ironically, had probably already become involved with the acting company from which Jonson cast *The Entertainment at Britain's Burse.*

Middleton and his manuscripts

Of all the early modern dramatists, Middleton has had the most success in directly or indirectly ensuring the survival of the manuscript texts of his plays. He not only left the largest number of manuscripts of his plays in total, but he left the largest number of a single play. These manuscripts include a remarkable six manuscripts of *A Game at Chess*, two manuscripts of *Hengist, King of Kent* and one manuscript of *The Witch*. So it is appropriate, finally, to confront T. H. Howard-Hill's contention that each of Middleton's two autograph manuscripts of *A Game at Chess* 'is deficient as a witness of the text of *A Game* mainly on account of the harmful character of the playwright's own participation in the transcript'.[29] These are the Trinity College Cambridge manuscript, entirely in his hand, and the Bridgewater–Huntington manuscript, partly in his hand (in Act 2, Scene 2 and most of Act 5).[30] The scribal portions in the hands of two unknown scribes in the Bridgewater manuscript contain hundreds of corrections of punctuation marks in pencil and a few interlinear corrections, which also appear to be in Middleton's hand. The other four manuscripts show his corrections or participation in other ways. Three—Lansdowne, Malone and Archdall—are in the hand of Ralph Crane.[31] Middleton wrote out a dedicatory page in Malone and made corrections to Archdall. The Rosenbach manuscript is in the hand of two other unknown scribes, with a title page in Middleton's hand.[32] As Howard-Hill argues, there must have been other contemporary manuscripts made, including those used as printer's copy for Quarto 1 and Quarto 3.[33]

The circumstances of the performance of Middleton's scathing satire on the corrupt Spanish court and its ambassador to England, Count Gondomar, are well documented in contemporary records. This notorious play, unusually, was acted 'nine days to gether at the Globe on the banks side' in August 1624 (as noted in the first Quarto, printed sometime afterwards), possibly twice a day,[34] packing in 3,000 people at each performance. In a letter dated 27 August 1624, the Earl of Pembroke, the Lord Chamberlain, outlined the entire episode to the Privy Council. He noted that the play contained 'some passages in it reflecting in matter or scorne and ignominy upon yᵉ King of Spaine some of his Ministers and others of good note and quality'.³⁵ The Privy Council took action 'to fynd out yᵉ originall roote of this offence, whether it sprang from yᵉ Poet, Players, or both'. The Council demanded that the play 'bee not onely antiquated and sylenced, but yᵉ Players bound as formerly they were and in that poynt onely never to Act it agayne'. Nor were the players allowed to act any other play, and, in fact, they had to bail themselves at the cost of £300.

An earlier letter, dated 21 August, from the Privy Council to Sir Edward Conway, the man to whom Jonson had sent *The Entertainment at Britain's Burse*, by then one of James I's principal secretaries of state, fills in the story. Only when the Council decided that the actors had had enough punishment for their 'scandalous Comedie' and their 'Insolency' would they be allowed to begin performing again. Providing that they agreed to act only 'any common play lycensed by authority', the ban would be lifted so that they could improve their financially desperate 'livelyhood and maintenance'. Even though summoned to explain himself before the Privy Council, Middleton declined to appear and sent his son in his place. The younger Middleton and the actors, also summoned, appeared before the Council. They 'produced a booke being an orriginall and perfect Coppie thereof (as they affirmed) seene and allowed by Sʳ Henry Herbert knight, Mʳ of the *Reuells*, under his owne hand, and subscribed in the last Page of the said booke'. When the Council demanded 'whether there were no other part*es* or passages represented in the Stage, then those expressely contained in the booke, they confidentlie protested, they added or varied from the same thing nothing at all'.³⁶ The Councillòrs also reported: 'The Poett they tell vs is one Midleton, who shifting out of the way, and not attending the Board wᵗʰ the rest as was expected, Wee haue given warrant to a Messinger for the apprehending of him.' Herbert's records note that he licensed this same book on 12 June 1624.³⁷

Perhaps the reason that Middleton did not present himself to the Council was not because he was too frightened but because he was too busy faircopying his manuscripts or instructing scribes on how to do so. Of the six extant manuscripts, none appears to be foul papers or even the company book, suggesting that at least eight manuscripts would have been in existence at some time. In fact, the company book was confiscated by the Privy Council, as they note in their letter, so that they could certify 'what passages in the said Comedie we should finde to be offensiue and scandalous'. They enclosed 'the booke it self' with the letter to Conway on 21 August for his and others' inspection so that they could call Herbert to account. Thus the company book probably made its way to the Earl of Pembroke, who reported his answer on 27 August.

However, there seems to have been no clear decision on the part of any official as to whether the 'poet' or the 'players' were responsible, and the censor, Herbert, seems to have had no blame attached to him. Nor was Middleton, then holding the position of London city chronologer, ever jailed, although a crude poem supposedly written by him as he languished in prison, circulated widely. No records exist to show that the play was ever performed again professionally. All six extant manuscripts seem to have been made between early to mid-August 1624 (Archdall is dated 13 August, when the play was still in performance) and 1 January 1625 (the date of the dedication page in Malone). However, all may have been copied in a shorter period of time if the January dedication was added later. Strikingly, these fair copy manuscripts all appear to be copies made for presentation to a patron or commissioned by clients. As in the case of *Demetrius and Enanthe*, bearing Crane's ingratiating dedication to Sir Kenelm Digby, it is often impossible to determine if manuscripts were presented as favours or sold for cash.

In any event, Middleton simply ignored the censorship and banning of his play and he immediately began to circulate and hence publish it in these manuscripts and in print, including three quartos by 1625. Although some manuscripts follow the same or similar lines of descent, each varies substantively from the others, and the three quartos represent two other versions of the text. Hence eight of the nine surviving early modern texts each represents a substantively different version. All of them were sanctioned or supervised in some way by the author.[38] Richard Dutton accepts Howard-Hill's argument that Crane worked 'somewhat independently' of Middleton in making his transcripts of *A Game at Chess* and 'censored' the Lansdowne manuscript himself.[39] However, as the manuscripts were made to order, Crane was clearly working with and for Middleton, not against him, both here and in transcribing *The Witch*, in which Crane copied Middleton's dedication to Thomas Holmes. If the Crane transcripts were censored it would have been at Middleton's direction or with his permission.

An examination of the same passage from Trinity and from Bridgewater written in Middleton's hand reveals the type of alterations he made in fair-copying his texts. In Act 5, Scene 3 of Trinity (Figure 6.2a), he writes:

> Bl. Kt. how? I how? how came they thether thinke you?
> Huldrick Bishop of Ausburge in his Epistle
> to Nicolas the first can tell you how,
> maye bee hee was at clensing of the Pond;
> I can but smile to thinke how it would puzzle
> all Mother-Maydes that euer liude in those parts
> to Knowe theire owne childes head, but is this all?   (f. 49ᵛ)

In Bridgewater (Figure 6.2b), he writes:

> Bl kt. how? I how? how came thether thinke you?
> Huldrick Bishop of Ausburge ins Epistle
> to Nicholas the first can tell you how
> maye bee hee Was at clensing of the Bond:
> I can but smile to thinke how it would puzzle
> all mother-Maydes that euer liude in that place
> to Knowe theire owne childes head? but is this all? (f. 52ʳ)

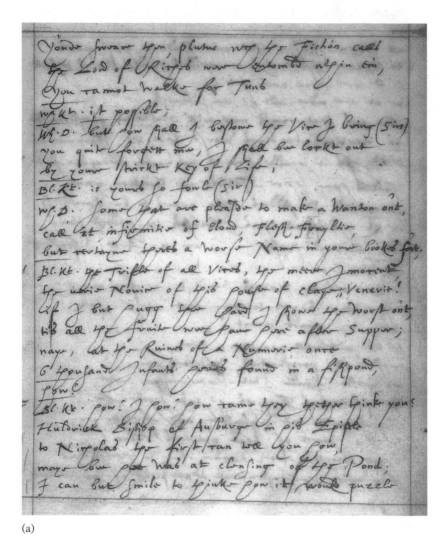

(a)

Figure 6.2 Middleton's autograph copies of the same passage in Act 5, Scene 3 of *A Game at Chess* in Trinity College, Cambridge, Library MS O.2.66, f. 49ᵛ (6.2a) and Huntington Library MS EL 34.B.17, f. 52ʳ (6.2b), showing variants between them. Reproduced by permission of Trinity College Cambridge and the Henry E. Huntington Library.

Middleton introduces incidental variants, such as 'in his' and 'ins', in line 2 of each passage, which do not change the meaning, although the second helps regularise the meter; nevertheless, in each line the passage is still hypermetric. Middleton also introduces substantive variants, which do change the meaning, as in line 4, with 'Bond' and 'Pond'. Such variants do not matter at all to those who read it or hear it performed.

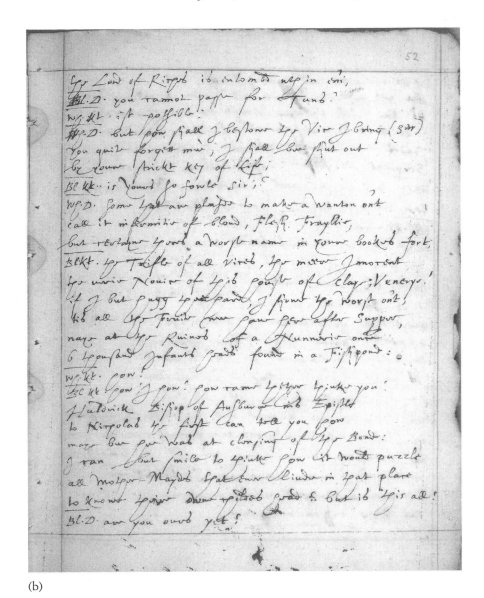

(b)

Figure 6.2 continued

Once the textual transmission and descent of the manuscripts of *A Game at Chess* are unravelled,[40] it becomes clear that Middleton was revising the play as he wrote it, after he wrote it, as he recopied it, and after he recopied it. The eight versions derive in varying degrees from manuscripts that Middleton wrote, copied and revised in whole or in part, or which he supervised, reread or corrected in whole or in part. Like any other dramatist of the period, he probably assumed that he could alter his plays or make them suitable for different theatrical or reading audiences, or because revising was habitual to him. He was not used to copying his text mechanically, like a scribe, but constantly tinkering with it, like an author. For him, and surely for Jonson, Heywood and Shakespeare, a play was always a work in progress.

Middleton's wholly autograph Trinity College manuscript is not 'deficient', nor does it show him as 'careless' or 'harmful', to use Howard-Hill's terms, especially as Middleton had enough time and energy over a period of at least five months to produce commissioned or presentation copies. Instead, this particular manuscript marks him as a working dramatist responding to the needs or demands of his audiences, actors and himself, writing in the kinds of changing conditions that were first detailed by Henslowe and Alleyn. The two manuscripts that he wholly or partly copied, as well as those he had recopied by scribes, eloquently demonstrate that this text returned to the author, even when the play was banned from stage, print and manuscript circulation. This same type of circular transmission, although less politically fraught, can also been seen in the scribal copies of Middleton's *Hengist, King of Kent*.[41]

'*Enter* Romeo': Shakespeare as composing dramatist

Shakespeare's texts printed from foul papers show his own idiosyncrasies while composing: for example in Q *King Lear* and F *Antony and Cleopatra*, in vague stage directions, generic speech-prefixes and unusual spellings. He repeatedly uses generic speech-prefixes for certain types of characters, referring to Shylock as 'Jew' and Edmund as 'Bastard' in speech-prefixes in the texts of *The Merchant of Venice* and *King Lear*, apparently printed from foul papers. So Shakespeare probably continued to think of his stock characters generically when it came to writing speech-prefixes, even as he developed major roles for them. This characteristic can even survive scribal copying. In Crane's transcript for the Folio text of *Measure for Measure*, he continues to refer to Pompey and Mistress Overdone as 'Clown' and 'Bawd' in the speech-prefixes even though both are referred to by their character names in the dialogue given to these speech-prefixes.

One particular text almost certainly printed from Shakespeare's foul papers shows him at work. The title page of the 1597 Q1 *Romeo and Juliet* advertises the text as it 'hath been often (with great applause) plaid publiquely, by the right Honourable the L. of *Hunsdon* his Seruants', the title used by the Lord Chamberlain's Men for a short period in 1596 and early 1597. Thus Shakespeare completed *Romeo and Juliet* no later than early 1597. However, Q1 was apparently not printed from foul papers but from a non-authorial manuscript, with a text which reported a provincial performance of the play. This text, evidently heavily cut and otherwise mangled, is not very close to Shakespeare's original. The 1599 Q2 was probably printed almost entirely from Shakespeare's foul papers and represents the play as first written. The title page of Q2 seems a correction of that in Q1 with the statement, '*Newly corrected, augmented, and amended:* As it hath bene sundry times publiquely acted, by the right Honourable the Lord Chamberlaine his Seruants.' Here appears to be an authorised publisher's notice at being beaten into print by an unauthorised competitor, but this advertisement—of a type not unusual in itself—may not be the publisher's alone.

While there is no direct evidence that Shakespeare collaborated in or supervised the publication of his plays, there is no evidence that he did not do so. As an actor-sharer, he and any other professional dramatist in the same position derived income twice, rather than once, from the sale of his texts. As a sharer in the Globe and Blackfriars playhouses, Shakespeare also received a portion of receipts of every play performed (as Henslowe did in the Rose, Fortune and his other theatres), including his own. In effect, he was re-paid for writing a single play every time it was performed. Henslowe's and Alleyn's records, and those of the Salisbury Court personnel, show that when they lost income due to competitors performing, selling or printing poached plays, the entrepreneurs could take legal or other action to recover the loss. Shakespeare and his fellow sharers, including the Burbages, would probably have done the same. They were almost certainly aware of what happened to their plays when printed. They could have been so concerned about the 'injury and disgrace of the Authors' or loss of revenue of reported or unauthorised texts that came into print that they later sold a corrected and authorised one. If the title pages of Q2 *Hamlet* and *Romeo and Juliet* are correct, this is exactly what the sharers, including Shakespeare, did in the case of this play.

Some of the signs that the printer's copy for Q2 *Romeo and Juliet* was in the author's hand are its generic (and sometimes inconsistent) speech-prefixes, variant character names, and vaguely descriptive stage directions, as well as its loose ends, duplications and false starts. At times, the printers were apparently unable to read the foul papers properly (possibly because they were partly illegible or out of order), and on at least one occasion they consulted Q1 to fill in Q2's gaps, possibly because a leaf in the copy they were using was missing.[42] Therefore, modern editors may argue that Q1 has 'some authority' even though it is not particularly 'Shakespearean'. The Folio text appears to have been printed from a slightly corrected copy of the 1609 Q3, itself a reprint of Q2, and shows no signs of having a text behind it that served as the company book.

Some specific signs of the composing Shakespeare appear in Quarto 2, particularly, as with Heywood, in authorial (as opposed to a book-keeper's) stage directions. The play's first stage direction reads: '*Enter* Sampson *and* Gregorie, *with Swords and Bucklers, of the house of* Capulet.' The last part of the direction '*of the house of* Capulet' seems straightforward: Shakespeare is trying to establish, either in his own mind or in the audience's, that the two characters are allied to the Capulets. He may simply be thinking that they should be dressed in clothing or carrying objects associated with the Capulet family. But more probably he is trying to plot out which characters will serve which functions, as Heywood did with 'Enter m' Raphael a yonge marchant mr Treadway his companion and ffrend, Etc'.

The stage directions become more confusing and disordered as the play progresses. At the beginning of Act 1, Scene 3, appears '*Enter* Capulets *Wife and Nurse*': here should be the more precise name of 'Lady Capulet' rather than the non-specific 'Wife'. However, Shakespeare will also variously refer to her simply as 'Wife', 'Madam' and 'Mother' in stage directions and speech-prefixes throughout the text. He knew to whom he was referring at any given point, but a book-keeper would have had to make changes to clarify and regularise the text and avoid confusion. Another authorial entrance direction appears in Act 1, Scene 4: '*Enter* Romeo, Mercutio, Benuolio, *with fiue or sixe other Maskers, torchbearers.*' While it is typical for a composing author to be imprecise about the number of minor characters coming on stage, such as masquers and torchbearers, the acting company would require a more precise number. This direction would probably therefore have been corrected by the book-keeper who would have been responsible in performance for knowing exactly how many actors were to enter the stage at this point.

Other signs of a composing author at work, such as misplaced or missing entrance or exit directions, also appear, or disappear, early in the play. For example, at the end of Act 1, Scene 4, which opened with the imprecise stage direction for Romeo, Benvolio and Mercutio and their uncertain number of companions, Romeo finishes a speech of eight lines, and then Benvolio speaks one line: 'Strike drum.' It is not clear to whom he has given this order—one of the five or six masquers or someone else such as a musician (no musicians are listed in any entrance direction in the scene). Perhaps it is a misplaced stage direction, rather than a line of dialogue. These directions follow Benvolio's line:

> *They march about the Stage, and Seruingmen come forth with*
> *Napkins.*
>   *Enter* Romeo.

But this entrance direction for Romeo makes no sense, as he is still on stage, unless he made an exit by himself (or with Mercutio and Benvolio) after '*They march about the Stage*'. If this was the case, the direction should have read '*They march about the Stage and Exeunt*'. Then Romeo would re-enter with this direction. But it is much too awkward to have him make an exit and then return; it seems then that he continues marching around with his two friends while the servants enter. So the erroneous entrance direction, '*Enter* Romeo' should be for one or more of the servants, for they are the only characters who speak after this direction and are described in the speech-prefixes as 'Ser.', '1', '2' and '3'. Four servants, at least, enter, yet the direction in the previous line, '*Seruingmen come forth with Napkins*', already serves as an entrance direction for them. As only one of the servants is referred to in the speech-prefixes as '*Ser*', perhaps this direction should have read '*Enter* Seruant', so that he can enter the stage on which Servants 1, 2 and 3 have already 'come forth with Napkins'. Here is a composing author at work, not primarily concerned about such details in the throes of composition and thus slightly and momentarily confused about who is, and is not, on stage.

But the confusion does not end there, as after the erroneous '*Enter* Romeo' direction, the four servants (or the chief 'Servant' and his three lower-ranked 'Servingmen' in Shakespeare's probable conception of them) speak thirteen lines of dialogue, after which appears the direction '*Exeunt*'. This is followed by the direction '*Enter all the guests and gentlewomen to the Maskers*' and then begins the dialogue for Lord Capulet and his male cousin (identified as '1 *Capu*' and '2 *Capu*' in the speech-prefixes) who welcome the guests and discuss the dances they attended in their youth. But it is not clear who has left the stage in the direction '*Exeunt*'. The exit should be for all the servants and Romeo, Mercutio and Benvolio; if the last three characters stay on stage, the exit should read '*Exeunt all but Romeo, Mercutio and Benvolio.*' But Romeo speaks shortly after the two Capulet men finish discussing their previous parties: Romeo will ask the '*Ser*' for the name of a particular lady (Juliet) and he will respond, 'I know not sir'. Thus Romeo (with the Servant, evidently) has either stayed on stage (with Mercutio and Benvolio) or left with them and come back in with the direction '*Enter all the guests . . .*' which must also include the servants, although they are not specifically mentioned.

These types of confusion in stage directions and speech-prefixes are typical of an author in the act of writing, especially in scenes such as these that have three sets of characters speaking only amongst themselves. After Shakespeare has occupied Romeo, Mercutio, Benvolio, their fellow Maskers and perhaps a musician in marching around the stage, he provides a short scene with four servants, then introduces a larger set of characters coming to the party. Only at this point does Romeo speak directly to the Servant. Unsurprisingly, then, Shakespeare has lost track of who has entered and exited when and where. Most likely he intended Romeo and his friends to be wandering around the stage during the servants' discussion and exeunt during the entrance of the other guests, naturally falling into the large group as they came in. Shakespeare is imprecise as to who exactly enters among 'all the guests and gentlewomen', which must include Lord Capulet, his cousin, Juliet, the Nurse and Tybalt, all of whom will speak in the scene, as well as Lady Capulet and others who would be expected to be on stage.

But such imprecision here, as well as previously in how many Maskers and Torchbearers accompany Romeo and his friends, demonstrates that Shakespeare is thinking, changing, sorting and figuring as he writes, still working out the storyline, the plot, the characters and other stage business. This is exactly what Heywood and Jonson are doing in their manuscripts of

The Captives and *The Entertainment at Britain's Burse*, and according to Robert Kean Turner, what Fletcher does in the 1647 Folio text of *A Wife for a Month*.[43] Although Shakespeare has not used formal act–scene notations here or elsewhere in his foul paper texts, he, like his contemporary dramatists, may instead have relied on 'exit' or 'exeunt' directions to signal the end of a scene.

What such imprecision shows us is what Shakespeare did and did not do in the act of composition. Like Heywood, Jonson and Fletcher, he produced slight errors, inconsistencies and loose ends, but he did not go back after composition and clean up or correct all of them, at least not in his foul papers. Shakespeare's apparent lack of correction suggests either that he prepared his own fair copy of his foul papers or that he assisted a scribe in doing so. That such confusing and imprecise foul paper copy could have been passed on to the censor and then corrected by a book-keeper or in rehearsal seems highly doubtful. Shakespeare would, then, have made his corrections in that fair copy, leaving his foul papers uncorrected, eventually offering the foul papers on behalf of himself and fellow sharers to printers in that condition to use as printers' copy. The fair copy would have gone to the Chamberlain's/King's Men who would send it to the Master of the Revels.

Confusions in speech-prefixes and stage directions are not the only signs of a composing author and of foul papers. Shakespeare is clearly reworking dialogue, from single words or images to entire speeches, throughout his first draft of *Romeo and Juliet*. One of the most noticeable duplications (that is, repeated passages) in the play appears at the end of 2.2 and the beginning of 2.3. Romeo and Juliet part in the famous balcony scene, with this passage:

> *Iu.* Sleep dwel vpon thine eyes, peace in thy breast.
> *Ro.* Would I were sleepe and peace so sweet to rest
> The grey eyde morne smiles on the frowning night,
> Checkring the Easterne Clouds with streaks of light,
> And darknesse fleckted like a drunkard reeles,
> From forth daies pathway, made by *Tytans* wheeles.
> Hence will I to my ghostly Friers close cell,
> His helpe to craue, and my deare hap to tell.
>
> *Exit.*

The exit direction is for Romeo, as Juliet must have left the stage on her last line, especially since she has kept the Nurse waiting and must go inside to keep her from coming out onto the balcony and seeing Romeo. Thus there is a missing exit direction for Juliet. But more interesting is the beginning of the next scene. It is not marked as a new scene; but this would not be unusual, for Shakespeare apparently did not usually separate scenes in his foul papers either with a horizontal line or Latin tags such as 'Finis', followed by 'Imprimis' for the next scene or act. Instead he may have thought the 'Exit' direction sufficient. Immediately after the *'Exit'* direction for Romeo, suggesting the end of one scene (because no characters are left on stage), there appears this direction and dialogue:

> *Enter Frier alone with a basket.*
> *Fri.* The grey-eyed morne smiles on the frowning night,
> Checking the Easterne clowdes with streaks of light:
> And fleckeld darknesse like a drunkward reeles,
> From forth daies path, and *Titans* burning wheeles:
> Now ere the sun aduance his burning eie,
> The day to cheere, and nights dancke dewe to drie,
> I must vphill this osier cage of ours,
> With balefull weedes . . .   (sig. D4v)

The Friar continues this speech for several lines before Romeo enters and confesses his love for Juliet.

This new scene and the Friar's speech begin with four lines nearly identical to those spoken by Romeo at the end of the previous scene. It seems both awkward and repetitive for both men to speak the same lines consecutively. In the reported Q1 text, in fact, the lines, although slightly variant, are given only to the Friar. However, this does not prove that Shakespeare originally wrote the lines for the Friar. The reporters or assemblers of the manuscript behind Q1 might have forgotten to assign the lines to Romeo in their text, or the lines may have already been cut in Romeo's speech to suit provincial playing. The fact remains that both versions appear in the foul papers. For this duplication (sometimes called a repetition bracket) there are a number of possible explanations:

1 Shakespeare originally wrote the lines for Romeo, and the printer of Q2 reprinted them accidentally, especially if his eye skipped up when setting the type for the Friar's speech.
2 Shakespeare originally wrote the lines for the Friar, and the printer accidentally printed them with some minor alteration in the wrong place, especially if his eye skipped down when setting the type for Romeo's speech. After realising what he had done, he printed them again for the Friar in the right place.
3 Shakespeare originally wrote the lines for Romeo but changed his mind and gave them to the Friar instead, slightly revising them. His deletion mark for the lines in Romeo's speech was either ignored or overlooked by the printer. This printer did recognise Shakespeare's mark for where to add the lines to the Friar's speech, probably because they were added not in the text but in the margin or on an inserted slip or sheet of paper. As we know from Heywood's foul papers, author's deletion marks can consist only of a vertical line and can easily be overlooked.

4   Shakespeare originally wrote the lines for the Friar but changed his
    mind and gave them to Romeo instead, slightly revising them. His
    deletion mark for the lines in the Friar's speech was either ignored or
    not seen by the printer. This printer did recognise Shakespeare's mark
    for where to add the lines to Romeo's speech, especially since they were
    probably added not in the text but as an afterthought in the margin or
    on an inserted slip or sheet.
5   Shakespeare wrote the lines for both Romeo and the Friar, revising them
    slightly in the second version, for the Friar.
6   Shakespeare wrote the lines for both the Friar and Romeo, revising them
    slightly in the second version, for Romeo.

The majority of editors since 1623 have argued that Numbers 3 or 4 are the
only possibilities, and have been nearly evenly split between the two. Their
arguments have usually been based on their judgements about the poetic
quality of the lines.[44] If juxtaposed (with the Romeo-version first and the
Friar-version second) the lines can easily be compared:

> The grey eyde morne smiles on the frowning night,
> The grey-eyed morne smiles on the frowning night,

> Checkring the Easterne Clouds with streaks of light,
> Checking the Easterne clowdes with streaks of light:

> And darknesse fleckted like a drunkard reeles,
> And fleckeld darknesse like a drunkard reeles,

> From forth daies pathway, made by *Tytans* wheeles.
> From forth daies path, and *Titans* burning wheeles:

Some scholars have decided which version was written second by deciding
which is better, assuming, probably incorrectly, that Shakespeare only
revised to 'improve' his text rather than to change it in some way.

   Differences in spelling cannot provide any clues here as to which version
is 'more Shakespearean'—that is, originating from the author and not a
book-keeper or printer—as these two passages do not record any uniquely
Shakespearean spelling. Nor was it standard for authors, including
Heywood, who left manuscripts in their own hand to spell the same word
exactly the same way in every occurrence. Printers could also vary their
spelling of the same words. As to the quality of the differences between versions, the first two lines have only incidental variants—in spelling, for
example. With the third and fourth lines are either an incidental or substantive variant, with 'Checkring' (that is 'checkering', meaning 'variegating',
but with a dropped syllable to fit the meter) and 'Checking' ('stopping').
'Check-ring' used as a noun, meaning a type of animal harness, is also

current to Shakespeare's time, but it does not fit the context. If both words are the same and it is a matter of Shakespeare's or the printers' accidentally adding or omitting an 'r' in either word, the variant would be incidental. However, the variant is probably not due to the printers' mistaking Shakespeare's handwriting if he spelled the word with an 'r', as it is a distinctive letter in secretary hand and would probably not have been mistaken for another letter. 'Checkring' and 'Checking' are in fact much different in sense, so the variant, whatever its origin, is substantive. Certainly 'checkering' is what is meant here from the context, so 'Checking' would be an error (or the first version that Shakespeare corrected in the second version). However, in lines 5 and 6 is a substantive variant: 'darknesse fleckted' (that is, darkness 'bent' or 'turned') versus 'fleckeld darknesse' (that is, 'spotted' or 'unblemished' darkness) which suggest slightly different meanings and images (here a printer may have confused a handwritten 't' with an 'l' in 'fleckeld').

In lines 7 and 8 appears the most interesting substantive variant, 'From forth daies pathway, made by *Tytans* wheeles' versus 'From forth daies path, and *Titans* burning wheeles'. Here is a deliberate and careful revision, as the addition of one or more syllables required a deletion of one or more syllables in the line, in order to keep the pentameter (both lines have ten syllables). Some may find the version in line 8 to be more poetic, especially in the image of the 'burning' wheels, as Titan is a poetic name for the sun, or some may prefer 'daies pathway' to 'daies path'. Scholars can try to deduce from Shakespeare's poetic patterns which version was the first or second. But they would also have to judge whether the lines are more characteristic of Romeo, who has already demonstrated his poetic prowess, or of the Friar, who has not yet done so but proves to be a powerful speaker throughout the next acts.[45] Shakespeare may have thought it necessary to character and plot development, uniquely in this play, that the Friar repeat Romeo's language and poetic imagery as soon as Romeo has left the stage to show a symbiotic, shared relationship between the two, whose minds may work together. The strongest evidence that Shakespeare meant both to stand is that this particular duplication has not been 'corrected' in the Q3 or F texts although others have.[46]

Yet, another uncorrected duplication appears in Q2 5.3, again in Romeo's speech as he commits suicide over Juliet's body:

> Why are thou yet so faire? I will beleeue,
> Shall I beleeue that unsubstantiall death is amorous,
> And that the leane abhorred monster keepes
> Thee here in darke to be his paramour?

The second line is hypermetric; that is, it has too many syllables for a pentameter line, most probably suggesting that Shakespeare reworked it during or after composition. He probably first wrote the speech like this:

> Why are thou yet so faire? I will beleeue,
> That unsubstantiall death is amorous . . .

As he wrote, however, Shakespeare apparently changed the assertion 'I will beleeue' into the question 'Shall I beleeue?', writing these three new words into the margin of the line beginning 'That unsubstantiall death'. When the printer set his copy from the foul papers he printed the verse line exactly as he saw it (perhaps ignoring a small deletion mark in the first line beside 'I will beleeue'):

	Why are thou yet so faire? I will beleeue, |
Shall I beleeue	That unsubstantiall death is amorous
	And that the leane abhorred monster keepes
	Thee here in darke to be his paramour?

This speech is not corrected in the later Folio text but is reprinted as hypermetric verse, so this is a duplication that Shakespeare, or his company, either overlooked or decided to keep. Romeo is distraught at this point, so his dialogue may need to reflect his refusal to 'beleeue' anything. Shakespeare may similarly have revised his famous Queen Mab speech,[47] and the rest of the Q2 text shows other examples of loose ends, false starts and inconsistencies.[48]

The Chamberlain's Men do not seem to have remained wholly antagonistic to the printing of Q1 for they may have allowed the Q2 printer to use a few sections of Q1 to print the later text.[49] For example, much of the Nurse's dialogue in Q2 1.3 is incorrectly printed in italic type, as it is in Q1, possibly because it was written in italic hand by one of the compilers of the Q1 manuscript, while the other compiler(s) used standard secretary hand. The King's Men were content to reprint the Q2 text in 1609 largely as it stood and then reprinted it again basically unaltered in the Folio. But while the F text does not show any major corrections it does contain some odd omissions, such as the Prologue to Act 1. It is not clear why the King's Men did not use the company's book or another corrected theatrical manuscript to print *Romeo and Juliet* in the magnificent Folio, instead of reprinting such a badly printed text. It is possible that the company book did not survive in 1622, when the Folio type was set. In addition to losing properties and costumes when the Globe theatre burned down in 1613, the company may have lost some of its company books, including *Romeo and Juliet*. Or this book may have been lost due to other factors. However, some Folio plays were apparently printed from company books (which could have dated from before or after 1613), so the Globe fire may be a convenient but not always definitive excuse for the transmission of some less than perfect Shakespearean texts after 1613. Besides, foul papers, fair copies and company books were primarily acting texts, not literary texts, so any theory that an acting company would have had to prepare or maintain copies eventually suitable for readers is insupportable from the kind of records kept by Henslowe and other theatrical businessmen.

The most likely conclusion is that the original 'book' of *Romeo and Juliet*, based on the foul papers and serving as the basis for the manuscript behind Q1, was lost at some point before 1622, as was the book of *Bonduca* owned by the same company. This manuscript of *Romeo and Juliet* may have contained corrections of some, but not all, of the duplications and other inconsistencies. During his lifetime, Shakespeare and his company were unperturbed, if not content, that an early authorial version of the play reached readers in 1599 and 1609 with its errors intact. Thus Shakespeare, like his King's Men colleagues Jonson and Middleton, may have seen his play-texts as fluid, variable and far from stable, whether in manuscript or print. In the case of Q2, Q3 and F *Romeo and Juliet*, the text was transmitted directly, and palpably, from the author to the audience, with little non-authorial interference or intervention.

Shakespeare apparently did not assume that he looked less than perfect, flawless or sacred in the act of composing a play or in transmitting it to literary readers. Regardless of its errors and inconsistencies, the uncorrected Q2/F text can be played successfully in the theatre. At least seventeen other plays were almost certainly printed from Shakespeare's foul papers, as this list shows:

Q1	Q2	Folio
Titus Andronicus	*Hamlet*	*The Taming of the Shrew*
Love's Labour's Lost		*1 Henry VI*
A Midsummer Night's Dream		*2 Henry VI*
Richard II		*3 Henry VI*
2 Henry IV		*The Comedy of Errors*
Much Ado About Nothing		*Henry V*
Troilus and Cressida		*All's Well that Ends Well*
King Lear		*Antony and Cleopatra*

All these plays show to varying degrees similar authorial errors, false starts, loose ends, duplications, inconsistencies and other confusions in plot, setting, character, dialogue, speech-prefixes and stage directions as in *Romeo and Juliet*. The following plays also show noticeable authorial revisions during or after composition: Q1 *Love's Labour's Lost*, Q1 *A Midsummer Night's Dream*, Q1 *Othello*, Q1 *The Two Noble Kinsmen*, Q2 *Hamlet*, F *Julius Caesar*, F *The Taming of the Shrew* and F *1 Henry VI*.[50] Plays such as *King Lear*, with surviving texts printed both from foul papers and partially or wholly from a theatrical book to which Shakespeare contributed at some point, reveal even more about Shakespeare's later revision practices.

The transmission of Shakespeare's texts, like those of Heywood, Jonson and Middleton, shows an early modern dramatist returning to reclaim his plays after their performances and printing. In essence, dramatists supported their plays throughout their transmission, preparing them for their use by contemporary and later theatre personnel as well as theatrical, and in some cases, reading audiences. Shakespeare, like his fellow dramatists, knew that plays would circulate primarily through and in performance, not in manuscript or print, but it is through all three types of this circulation that the author emerges and remains an essential contributor to the various textual and theatrical productions of his text.

Notes

Introduction: 'What is writ by hand we reverence more'

1 Such an argument is implicit in Andrew Gurr's generalisation in *The Shakespeare Company, 1594–1642* (Cambridge: Cambridge University Press, 2004), p. 2, that 'the company bought the play from the author and did with it whatever they pleased'. However, his argument is less extreme than those of theatre historians E. K. Chambers and G. E. Bentley (see Chapter 1) that a dramatist worked under the tyranny of an acting company which dismissed him as soon as his foul papers of a contracted play were 'surrendered' (to use a term common to these scholars). Some of Gurr's theories in this book contradict his more generous views of dramatists in *The Shakespearean Stage, 1574–1642* (Cambridge: Cambridge University Press, 1980), since reprinted numerous times in successive editions. Manuscript scholars such as W. W. Greg, R. B. McKerrow and A. W. Pollard used their comprehensive study of extant dramatic manuscripts to establish a more liberal view of the relationship between dramatists and acting companies. These textual scholars argued that, at the least, a company dramatist such as Shakespeare could work closely with company personnel on any given play up to the submission of the fair copy, either his own or that completed by a scribe with his assistance, but not afterward. See, for example, Greg's arguments in *The Shakespeare First Folio* (Oxford: Clarendon Press, 1955), pp. 106–59, which incorporate McKerrow's and Pollard's theories.

2 See Dedication, *The Works of Mr William Shakespear*, ed. Nicholas Rowe (London: Jacob Tonson, 1709), 1:sig. A2 and 'Some Account of the Life of Mr William Shakespear', p. vi, in which Rowe appears to have had access to original theatrical documents as well as anecdotes about Shakespeare; and 'The Preface of the Editor', *The Works of Shakespear in Six Volumes*, ed. Alexander Pope (London: Jacob Tonson, 1725), 1: xvii, xix, including Pope's discussion of the difference between the original manuscripts and 'the Prompter's Book'. Pope specifically notes, 'I have seen one [quarto] in particular (which seems to have belonged to the playhouse, by having the parts divided with lines, and the Actors names in the margin) where several of those passages were added in a written hand, which are since to be found in the folio' (p. xvii). He also appears to have access to other theatrical documents.

3 On the role of eighteenth- and nineteenth-century Shakespearean editors, see, for example, *Mr William Shakespeare his Comedies, Histories, and Tragedies*, ed. Edward Capell, 10 vols (London: Dryden Leach, 1767–8); The *Plays and Poems of William Shakespaere*, ed. Edmond Malone, 10 vols (London: H. Baldwin, 1790); and Samuel T. Coleridge, *Lectures 1808–1819: On Literature*, ed. R. A. Foakes, 2 vols (London: Routledge and Kegan Paul, 1987).

4 Greg provides a revealing discussion of how his arguments differ from those of

preceding and succeeding new bibliographers in 'The Present Position of Bibliography', reprinted in *Collected Papers*, ed. J. C. Maxwell (Oxford: Clarendon Press, 1966), pp. 207–25. Also see E. A. J. Honigmann's interesting discussion of how his own theories fit into those of four generations of new bibliographers in 'The New Bibliography and its Critics', in *Textual Performances: The Modern Reproduction of Shakespeare's Drama*, ed. Lucas Erne and Margaret J. Kidnie (Cambridge: Cambridge University Press, 2004), pp. 77–93.

5 See John Heminge and Henrie Condell's 'To the great Variety of Readers', *Mr William Shakespeares Comedies, Histories, & Tragedies. Published according to the True Originall Copies* (London: Isaac Jaggard, and Ed. Blount, 1623), sig. A3^r.

6 Greg's extraordinarily important and comprehensive study of manuscripts led him to comment on this growing rivalry between scholars working in bibliography and those in textual criticism. In 'Bibliography—an Apologia' (*Collected Papers*, pp. 239–66), he indeed apologised for the fact that unlike textual critics, bibliographers generally marginalised manuscripts in discussing the transmission of the text because 'bibliography is the study of books as material objects. For bibliography to be a serious study it is necessary that books should be objects of importance.' In this type of study, manuscripts, as Greg acknowledges, have little importance because the bibliographer's 'concern is with the whole history of the text, and to him the author's original is but one step in the transmission. It may be the most important step—of course, in the majority of cases it is the only important one—but that is a question dependent upon outside considerations that do not strictly concern the bibliographer' (p. 257). Greg also argued in his essay '*The Escapes of Jupiter*', that the manuscript of this play 'adds one more to the indubitable instances of revision to be taken into account by those who seek to minimize the practice' (*Collected Papers*, p. 176). In *The Shakespeare First Folio* and elsewhere, however, he repeatedly minimised Shakespeare's practices as a reviser. Perhaps Greg's solution to the domination of textual critics by bibliographers was to exclude Shakespeare from textual criticism—that is, from sharing the practices by other dramatists seen in their extant manuscripts—and instead to feature Shakespeare mainly in bibliography.

7 See, for example, Paul Werstine's citation of Fredson Bowers's discussions of 'manuscript copy' for printed texts in Wertine's repeated attacks on Greg's work in 'Plays in Manuscript', in *A New History of Early English Drama*, ed. John D. Cox and David Scott Kastan (Columbia: Columbia University Press, 1997), p. 493. Although Werstine claims that his 16-page essay presents the results of his study of 'a great number of the extant manuscripts' of the period (p. 495), he uses a small selection of manuscripts rather than a 'great number' and frequently misrepresents them. For example, he states that Heywood's autograph manuscript of *The Captives* is not foul papers because it was 'copiously' annotated by another hand. On the contrary, this hand annotates occasionally and certainly not copiously, confining itself largely to marginal additions to stage directions, such as writing 'cleere' at the end of a scene to clear the stage. In addition, the repeated places in the manuscript in which Heywood has rubbed out words before the ink had dried and rewritten them clearly show Heywood changing his mind in the act of composition and not in the act of recopying (see Chapters 3 and 4, pp. 94–9 and 112–16). Werstine also misrepresents other manuscripts, including Heywood's autograph manuscript of *The Escapes of Jupiter* and the two scribal manuscripts of Middleton's play *Hengist, King of Kent, or The Mayor of Queenborough*, from which I recently set two editions of the play, including one for the Malone Society Reprints series.

8 When I sought his advice in 1990 about some hitherto unnoticed pencil markings that I had found in a well-known dramatic manuscript, Fredson Bowers wrote to me: 'I have had so little experience with mss. (in fact practically none

except for editing 2–3 simple ones) that I am of no help' (Bowers, Letter to Grace Ioppolo, dated 17 January 1990). Of course, Bowers did use manuscripts during his long and very distinguished career, particularly those of modern novelists such as William Faulkner and F. Scott Fitzgerald. But this may be what misled him, because the manuscripts of modern novelists are not transmitted in the same ways as dramatic ones, particularly those in the early modern period.

9 In sum, the study of authorial dramatic manuscripts and their progress into print became solidified and normalised in the early and mid-twentieth century into the literary disciplines of textual criticism (the physical examination of authorial documents, including manuscripts and printed texts) and bibliography (the study of printed texts and their forms). These scholars' seemingly united aim became the establishment of the 'ideal' text. That is, they wanted to recover (or to be more precise, reconstruct) the supposed text that a great author like Shakespeare or Jonson wrote but which no longer survived, due to non-authorial 'corruption' and 'interference', and which had never quite reached his literary audience, particularly the scholars' generation of readers. As a result of their search for the ideal text, these men and their successors decided to study the history and circumstances of the writing and printing of the less than ideal, and 'corrupt', surviving texts of these dramatists' plays. One of the many reasons for this focus on Shakespeare is that studying the non-Shakespearean material required special skills (in reading 'secretary' handwriting, for example) and access to rare and non-circulating material in particular libraries and record offices. See Greg's discussion of these points in 'The Rationale of Copy-Text' (*Collected Papers*, p. 378), in which he rebukes editors who should have been 'more familiar with works transmitted in manuscript'.

10 Howard-Hill, Introduction, *A Game at Chess* (Manchester: Manchester University Press, 1993), p. 6.

11 Jerome J. McGann, *The Textual Condition* (Princeton, N.J.: Princeton University Press, 1991), p. 4.

12 Margreta de Grazia, 'The essential Shakespeare and the material book', *Textual Practice*, 2 (1988), p. 71. On the failure of these types of uninformed textual arguments, see Stanley Cavell, 'Skepticism as Iconoclasm: The Saturation of the Shakespearean Text', in *Shakespeare in the Twentieth Century*, ed. Jonathan Bate, Jill L. Levenson, Dieter Mehl and Stanley Wells (Newark, Del.: University of Delaware Press, 1998), pp. 231–47.

13 The rise and dominance of literary theory, although tied to a variety of social upheavals in the 1960s and 1970s, coincides with the period in which the last of the new bibliographers in the Greg–Bowers generations ceased to teach or publish widely. Thus the considerable, and perhaps overwhelming, power that they had exerted from the early to the mid-twentieth century over the discipline and the profession of literary studies in general, insisting, for example, that all postgraduate students of literature be required to take a 'new' bibliography course, had ceased.

14 See, for example, the various essays in *Women in the Renaissance: Selections from English Literary Renaissance*, ed. Kirby Farrell, Elizabeth H. Hageman and Arthur F. Kinney (Amherst, Mass.: University of Massachusetts Press, 1988), and in *English Manuscript Studies 1100–1700*. Volume 9: *Writings by Early Modern Women*, ed. Peter Beal and Margaret J. M. Ezell (London: The British Library, 2000); also see Margaret J. M. Ezell, *Writing Women's Literary History* (Baltimore, Md.: Johns Hopkins Press, 1993).

15 The most notable of these is Jeffrey Masten, whose publications focus on 'authorship' and 'authority' while privileging a homosexual reading of the early modern theatre. His central contention is that early modern 'dramatic authorship emerges from the publishing house and only indirectly from the theatre'

('Playwriting: Authorship and Collaboration', in *A New History of Early English Drama*, p. 371). Masten appears to be able to make this assertion because, with the exception of a few cursory generalisations, he does not discuss dramatic texts in manuscript form, even though he purports to detail how authors wrote, collaborated and submitted their handwritten dramatic texts to playhouse personnel. His lack of knowledge of manuscripts, and manuscript culture, is most obvious in his incorrect claims about the placement of hands in the manuscript of *Sir Thomas More* (see Chapter 4, p. 104). Masten does not appear to know that 'authorship' in this age emerges for dramatists, as with many poets and prose writers, with manuscripts, which in this age could circulate and constitute an alternative form of 'publication' which was not dependent on print. Thus Masten's general arguments for the 'inappropriateness of an authorially based canon in this period' before dramatists' works were in print (*Textual Intercourse* [Cambridge: Cambridge University Press, 1997], p. 10) are insupportable. In *Shakespeare, Co-Author: A Historical Study of Five Collaborative Plays* (Oxford: Oxford University Press, 2002), particularly the long appendix entitled 'Abolishing the Author? Theory *versus* History' (pp. 506–41), Brian Vickers offers a comprehensive discussion of other serious errors in Masten's arguments. For example, Vickers shows that 'Foucault's theory of the author not "emerging" until the eighteenth century, and of authors having no sense that they owned their work before the introduction of the copyright laws, lacks any historical validity'. Vickers concludes of Masten's work, 'although purporting to offer a historical account, it failed to examine the primary evidence for authorship, contained on plays' title pages, in the Stationers' Register, in Henslowe's Diary, and in Sir Henry Herbert's licensing book. Simply to open these sources is to notice not just the presence of the author but his centrality, in creating the play-texts without which no theatrical production could take place' (pp. 399–400, 539). To Vickers's list of primary evidence that Masten failed to examine for authorship, I can add manuscripts. MacDonald P. Jackson, a leading expert in attribution studies, rightly blames Masten's 'lack of practical experience' in textual study for allowing him to make 'misleading' and uninformed attacks on those with such experience (*Defining Shakespeare: 'Pericles' as Test Case* [Oxford: Oxford University Press, 2003], pp. 6, 8). Also see Jeffrey Knapp's attack on Masten in 'What is a Co-Author', *Representations*, 89 (2005), pp. 1–29.

16 Masten's uninformed arguments about how authors and collaborators wrote their plays have been widely quoted, for example in claims made by Douglas A. Brooks. Although repeatedly claiming to take up 'drama and authorship' in the playhouse and the printing house, Brooks offers no discussion of manuscripts at all, except for a brief footnote on my own study of dramatic manuscripts; see Brooks, *From Playhouse to Printing House: Drama and Authorship in Early Modern England* (Cambridge: Cambridge University Press, 2002), p. 232, note 45. Brooks confines himself throughout the book to a study of *printed* play-texts only, yet he claims to cover comprehensively, for instance, Heywood's career as the sole author of numerous plays and as collaborator or reviser of other plays. Brooks's dubious claim that 'no playwright in the period wrote more about the vicissitudes of dramatic authorship than Heywood' allows him to set Heywood up as the standard representative of the author who can only speak in and through print. However, Brooks ignores entirely Heywood's autograph manuscripts of *The Captives* and *The Escapes of Jupiter* and his autograph additions and revisions to the manuscript of *Sir Thomas More*. Readers of Brooks's book would be left to conclude that these plays did not belong to Heywood's canon, or that if they did they do not rate attention or discussion in terms of his career or habits. In this case Brooks follows Masten, whom he cites heavily, in ignoring the very manuscripts that reveal Heywood providing an inordinate amount of

original and unique information on how he wrote, revised, altered, corrected, amended and collaborated as a major dramatist of the age.

17 Greg, *Dramatic Documents from the Elizabethan Playhouses* (Oxford: Clarendon Press, 1931), p. 190.

18 Leah Marcus applies such criteria in 'The Veil of Manuscript', delivered as a lecture in a plenary session of the 2001 Shakespeare Association of America conference. She first complains that seeking out manuscripts will not resolve our understanding of the transmission of dramatic texts. In an echo of the argument that manuscripts are 'enabling figments of the imagination', she states that 'Shakespeareans in particular, deprived of even a single precious holograph of a poem or play, invest in the lost evidence with almost apocalyptic status as authorial witness'. Marcus then offers a case history of the problems of assigning authority to manuscripts and authors by using a 'scribal' manuscript (British Library Cotton MS Titus C.vi, ff. 410r–411v) among the papers of Henry Howard, Earl of Northampton (1540–1614) of the final speech of Queen Elizabeth I before Parliament on 19 December 1601. Marcus claims that the manuscript 'is not in Northampton's own hand, or so my historian friends assure me'. On the basis of this assertion, she builds the argument that Northampton 'dictated his recollection of the speech to a secretary shortly after its delivery by the queen', thereby producing a 'memorial reconstruction' of it. Although acknowledging that 'this hand, so far as we know, has nothing to do with Shakespeare', she concludes that 'it serves to tell us' that even if we had Shakespeare's manuscripts, their 'interpretive cruxes' would not render them particularly useful ('The Veil of Manuscripts', *Renaissance Drama*, n.s., 30, pp. 115, 118–20; this volume of essays was co-edited by Masten). Although Marcus implies that a manuscript text derives no meaning from being written but from being read, she reads the Northampton manuscript incorrectly. The hand is indeed Northampton's, as a comparison with numerous other manuscripts and drafts in Northampton's distinctive and idiosyncratic hand in the same volume and elsewhere makes clear. Marcus's failure to identify Northampton's hand undermines her argument that he was 'dictating' the speech to a scribe. Her conclusion that, as there is no other surviving draft of the Queen's speech, Northampton must have been reconstructing the speech from memory is also faulty. Northampton had access to royal speeches, letters and proclamations that were copied and circulated in court circles. Marcus also errs in arguing that the text 'does not show the typical signs of having been copied from a previous manuscript but instead has an unusual pattern of revision'. In fact, the 'pattern' of revision looks fairly typical of Northampton's other manuscripts, and some alterations in this speech may not be revisions but corrections of words that he wrote out incorrectly due to eyeskip error in copying from another manuscript. Northampton's repeated and continual circulation of such texts in manuscript, particularly as presentation copies, constituted for him a form of publication that he preferred over publication in print. On this point, see H. R. Woudhuysen, *Sir Philip Sidney and the Circulation of Manuscripts 1558–1640* (Oxford: Clarendon Press, 1996), pp. 102–3. Marcus thus fails to comprehend Northampton's insistence on manuscript authority and makes an unwarranted assumption that scribes routinely distanced a text from its author. It is therefore especially ironic that Marcus uses Northampton's handwritten papers to argue throughout that manuscript texts offer more problems than they solve in deciphering textual transmission.

19 On the impact of this faulty contention, see G. Thomas Tanselle's important book, *Literature and Artefacts* (Charlottesville: Bibliographical Society of the University of Virginia, 1998), pp. 309ff.

20 For a discussion of this subject, see Seán Burke's excellent book, *The Death and*

Return of the Author: Criticism and Subjectivity in Barthes, Foucault and Derrida (Edinburgh: Edinburgh University Press, 1992).

21 For example, in *Shakespeare as Literary Dramatist* (Cambridge: Cambridge University Press, 2003), especially pp. 158–64, 259–61, Lukas Erne depends far too much on the textual 'transmission' theories of Masten and Brooks in attempting to place his study of Shakespeare's printed texts in the context of selected dramatic manuscripts. In fact, Erne works backward from printed texts and then limits himself to very brief discussion, mostly drawn from printed facsimiles, of those manuscripts that he claims are 'playbooks'. He notes the number of cuts in some of them, without examining how and by whom those manuscripts were copied, corrected, annotated, revised, circulated, let alone cut. In the process Erne shows no expertise on how those and other surviving manuscripts were written, transmitted or circulated, thereby rendering his conclusions on the 'circulation' of Shakespeare's manuscripts unreliable.

22 Orgel, *The Authentic Shakespeare and Other Problems of the Early Modern Stage* (London: Routledge, 2002), p. 35. His arguments first appeared in 'What is a Text', *Research Opportunities in Renaissance Drama*, 24 (1981), pp. 3–6.

23 For manuscripts and performance records of Oxford and Cambridge University plays, see the *Records of Early English Drama* volumes for Oxford and Cambridge. For manuscript plays produced by members of the upper-middle classes or aristocrats, see, for example, the manuscripts of John Newdigate of Arbury Hall, Warwickshire, England, discovered by Peter Beal in the 1970s and discussed in print by T. H. Howard-Hill in 'Another Warwickshire Playwright: John Newdigate of Arbury', in *Renaissance Papers* (1988), pp. 51–62; and the manuscripts of William Percy at Alnwick Castle, Northumberland, England. The Malone Society Reprints series has also produced a number of facsimile editions of non-professional plays of the period.

24 Bowers, *On Editing Shakespeare* (Charlottesville: University of Virginia Press, 1966), p. 13.

25 Greg, *The Shakespeare First Folio*, p. 106.

26 'Prompter's Book' is the term used repeatedly by Pope in his Preface to his 1725 edition, *The Works of Shakespear in Six Volumes*, 1: xvii, xix, and appears to be borrowed from the theatrical personnel whom he consulted.

27 It was Greg who first argued, in *Dramatic Documents from the Elizabethan Playhouses*, that only fifteen 'promptbooks' are extant. His tally has been accepted by several succeeding scholars such as T. H. Howard-Hill in 'Marginal Markings: The Censor and the Editing of Four English Promptbooks', *Studies in Bibliography*, 36 (1983), pp. 168–77.

28 Gurr, in *The Shakespeare Stage, 1594–1642*, p. 121, appears to follow Greg in assuming of eighteen of these scribal manuscripts, representing plays from the Chamberlain's/King's Men repertory, that they are 'mostly versions of the writer's text designed for private study'. There is no evidence to support this generalisation.

29 Study of Marlowe's texts always comes at a disadvantage, as his plays were heavily revised by later dramatists or adapters after his death, and although his plays remained profitable in the repertories of companies financed by Henslowe and Alleyn (as noted in Henslowe's Diary, for example), we have no evidence of how Marlowe himself worked with theatrical personnel such as theatre owners, actor-sharers and book-keepers. On these points, see, for example, Roslyn L. Knutson, 'Influence of the Repertory System on the Revival and Revision of *The Spanish Tragedy* and *Dr. Faustus*', *English Literary Renaissance*, 18 (1988), 257–74. Also see Knutson, 'Marlowe Reruns: Repertorial Commerce and Marlowe's Plays in Revival', and David Bevington, 'Staging the A- and B-Texts of *Doctor Faustus*', in *Marlowe's Empery: Expanding His Critical Contexts*, ed. Sara

Munson Deats and Robert A. Logan (Newark, Del.: University of Delaware Press, 2002), pp. 25–42, 43–60. Scott McMillin and Sally-Beth MacLean, *The Queen's Men and their Plays* (Cambridge: Cambridge University, 1998), discuss Marlowe in the context of how other dramatists reacted to him. I am not certain that the fragment of *The Massacre at Paris* (Folger Shakespeare Library MS J.b.8), which some scholars claim to be in Marlowe's hand, is authentic.

30 This point has persuasively and repeatedly been made in the last two decades, particularly by Peter Beal, Harold Love, Arthur F. Marotti, H. R. Woudhuysen, and most recently David McKitterick. See Beal, *Index of English Literary Manuscripts 1450–1700*, 2 vols (London: Mansell, 1980–93), shortly to be made into an electronic database accessible on the internet, and *In Praise of Scribes: Manuscripts and their Makers in Seventeenth-Century England* (Oxford: Clarendon Press, 1998); Love, *Scribal Publication in Seventeenth-Century England* (Oxford: Clarendon Press, 1993); Marotti, *Manuscript, Print, and the English Renaissance Lyric* (Ithaca, N.Y.: Cornell University Press, 1995); Woudhuysen, *Sir Philip Sidney and the Circulation of Manuscripts 1558–1640*; and McKitterick, *Print, Manuscript and the Search for Order 1450–1830* (Cambridge: Cambridge University Press, 2003). Beal and Woudhuysen have both discussed how the circulation of plays in manuscript form gave them a form of authority, as does Richard Dutton, in 'The Birth of the Author', *Texts and Cultural Change in Early Modern England*, ed. Cedric C. Brown and Arthur F. Marotti (Basingstoke: Macmillan Press Ltd, 1997), pp. 164ff. In Chapters 4 and 5 I will argue that many manuscript plays circulated among collaborators and theatrical colleagues of the original author(s), but not widely elsewhere.

31 Sir Christopher Sibthorp, *A reply to an answere* (Dublin: 1625), cited by David McKitterick, *A History of Cambridge University Press, I: Printing and the Book Trade in Cambridge 1534–1698* (Cambridge: Cambridge University Press, 1992), p. 2.

32 '*Sed quae scripta manu, sunt veneranda magis*', translated from the Latin by Edmund Blunden in 'Some Seventeenth-Century Latin Poems by English Writers', *University of Toronto Quarterly*, 25 (1955–6), p. 11. The truism, or general assumption, behind Donne's observation remains valid even though his comment appears in a slightly playful context in a Latin poem in which he is welcoming a manuscript copy sent by his friend Richard Andrews to replace a book that Donne had lent him and which Andrews's children had ripped up. Also see Hilton Kelliher, 'Donne, Jonson, Richard Andrews and The Newcastle Manuscript', *English Manuscript Studies 1100–1700*, Volume 4 (London: The British Library, 1993), pp. 135–73. Kelliher points out that 'coming from a poet who reached his audience almost wholly through manuscript transmission, and whom contemporary miscellanies show to have been far and away the most popular of the age, this veneration of the handwritten text was no mere pleading to suit the circumstances' (p. 134).

33 The only change I make is to supply in italics missing letters of the alphabet, including those omitted in standard secretary-hand abbreviations, when necessary. Otherwise I reproduce the material as originally written.

34 Orgel, *The Authentic Shakespeare*, p. 35.

1 'As good a play for y^r publiqe howse as euer was playd': dramatists and authorship

1 Bentley, *The Profession of Dramatist in Shakespeare's Time*, p. vii.
2 Bentley, *The Profession of Dramatist in Shakespeare's Time*, pp. 48, 37. He bases Henslowe's poor opinion of dramatists solely on Henslowe's attack on Ben Jonson after his murder of the actor Gabriel Spencer during a duel, with whom

Henslowe had a close friendship, which he did not have with Jonson. Henslowe employed Jonson for some years after the death of Spencer. As R. A. Foakes points out, W. W. Greg helped to institutionalise the incorrect view that Henslowe was a 'kind of Scrooge, concerned only for profit' who was antagonistic to those, including dramatists, with whom he worked. See Preface, *Henslowe's Diary*, ed. R. A. Foakes, 2nd edn (Cambridge: Cambridge University Press, 2002), p. viii; this 2nd edition, cited throughout this book, supersedes and corrects the 1st edition, jointly edited by Foakes and R. T. Rickert in 1961.

3   Orgel, *The Authentic Shakespeare*, p. 35.

4   Bentley drew selectively on his own work in *The Jacobean and Caroline Stage*, 7 vols (Oxford: Clarendon Press, 1941–68) and in E. K. Chambers's *The Elizabethan Stage*, 4 vols (Oxford: Clarendon Press, 1923). Chambers does not generally imply that relationships between dramatists and their employers were antagonistic or hostile, although he does see dramatists as under the control of acting companies. The work of Greg and other textual scholars suggests that relationships between dramatists and acting companies were more co-operative and generous. This split may derive from the fact that textual scholars draw their theories primarily from dramatic manuscripts, which record or suggest the views of authors, rather than from other types of theatrical records kept by entrepreneurs, upon which theatre historians draw. On this type of scholarly split, see Greg, 'Bibliography—an Apologia' (*Collected Papers*, pp. 239–66).

5   In total, the theatrical material can be found in the following volumes: **Alleyn Papers, MS No. I**: Alleyn's Letters/Papers on English Drama and Stage and the History of the Fortune Theatre, 1559–1662; **Alleyn Papers, MS No. II**: Henslowe's and Alleyn's Letters and Papers as Joint Masters of the Royal Game of Bears, Bulls and Mastiff Dogs, 1598–1626; **Alleyn Papers, MS No. III**: Alleyn/Henslowe General Correspondence, 1577–1626; **Alleyn Papers, MS No. IV**; **Alleyn Papers, MS No. V**: Legal and Miscellaneous Papers of Alleyn and Family, 1461–1611, 1612–26; **MS No. VII, Henslowe's Diary and Account-Book**, 1592–1609; **MS No. VIII, Alleyn's Memorandum Book**, 1594–1616; **MS No. IX, Alleyn's Diary and Account-Book**, 1617–22; **Alleyn Papers, MS No. XVIII**: Miscellaneous Papers, 1330–1662; **MS No. XIX**, 'Plott' (prompter's outline) of the second part of the play *The Seven Deadly Sins*; **MS No. XX**, Text of the play *The Telltale*; **Manuscripts, Second Series, 100**: 323 deeds; **Muniments, Section I**: The Theatre and Bear Garden documents, 1546–1662; **Muniments, Section 2**: further leases, deeds and receipts.

6   See Foakes and Rickert's discussions of monies earned by Henslowe in his various businesses in the Preface to the 1st edition of *Henslowe's Diary*, pp. xxxii–xliv.

7   The Henslowe and Alleyn archive includes their correspondence or other evidence of interaction with monarchs and their families (Elizabeth I, James I, Queen Anne, Prince Henry, Charles I); chancellors, privy councillors and courtiers (the Secretary of State, Sir Robert Cecil; the Lord Treasurer, Sir Thomas Howard; the Lord High Admiral, Charles Howard; the Earl of Pembroke, William Herbert; Sir Francis Bacon; Sir Edward Coke; Sir Christopher Hatton; Lord Strange; Lord Buckhurst; Lord Hunsdon, Henry Carey, the Lord Chamberlain and patron of Shakespeare's acting company; and George Villiers, the Duke of Buckingham; among many others); the Master of the Rolls (Sir Julius Caesar); church leaders (various Bishops of London, and John Donne, Dean of St Paul's and Alleyn's second father-in-law); foreign ambassadors (Count Gondomar); local London officials (various lord mayors, sheriffs and

local councillors) as well as Masters of the Revels (Sir Edmund Tilney and George Buc).

8 Named joint 'Masters of the Royal Game of Bears, Bulls and Mastiff Dogs' by James I, Henslowe and Alleyn also staged such blood sports as bull- and bear-baiting at their theatres, including the Bear Garden, or other venues, and the full records for the costs and financial returns of these types of events are also in the Dulwich archive. With the blood sports records, their papers further emphasise Henslowe and Alleyn's near monopoly on presenting and profiting from public and private entertainment in London, at court, and the provinces in this period. In fact, they turned these events into a substantial income 'with a social flourish that guaranteed them eminent social standing amongst the London citizenry and many noblemen of the period as well'. See S. P. Cerasano, 'Edward Alleyn (1566–1626), Thomas Dekker (1570?–1641?) and Samuel Rowley (d. 1633?)', in *'The Pen's Excellencie': Treasures from the Manuscript Collection of the Folger Library*, ed. Heather Wolfe (Washington, DC: The Folger Shakespeare Library, 2002), pp. 81–4; also see Cerasano, 'The Patronage Network of Philip Henslowe and Edward Alleyn', *Medieval and Renaissance Drama in England*, 13 (2001), 82–92. For biographical information on Henslowe and Alleyn, see Cerasano's entries on them in the new *Oxford Dictionary of National Biography*. For a bibliography on recent work on Henslowe and Alleyn, see Foakes's Preface to the 2nd edition of *Henslowe's Diary*, pp. xi–xii.

9 *English Professional Theatre, 1530–1660*, ed. Glynne Wickham, Herbert Berry and William Ingram (Cambridge: Cambridge University Press, 2000), p. 102.

10 On the impact of this 'duopoly', see Gurr, *The Shakespearean Stage, 1574–1642*, pp. 9, 42ff.

11 Gurr, *The Shakespeare Company, 1594–1642*, p. 89.

12 See Andrew Gurr, *The Shakespearian Playing Companies* (Oxford: Clarendon Press, 1996), p. 357.

13 On Heywood and Beeston, see Bentley, *The Jacobean and Caroline Stage*, 4:554–7, 363–70; on Phillips, see Chambers, *The Elizabethan Stage*, 2:333. On Brome, see Chapter 2. Neil Carson alone suggests that Heywood worked with Derby's Men; see *A Companion to Henslowe's Diary* (Cambridge: Cambridge University Press, 1988), p. 65, but he does not provide a full reference for this statement. For a contemporary review of *The Witches of Lancashire*, see *English Professional Theatre, 1530–1660*, ed. Wickham, Berry and Ingram, pp. 619–20.

14 Theatre historians have especially used Henslowe's extensive records to examine the business of playing from the point of view of theatre owners, managers and actors. See, for example, S. P. Cerasano, including 'Philip Henslowe, Simon Forman and the Theatrical Community of the 1590s', *Shakespeare Quarterly*, 44 (1993), 145–58; Roslyn L. Knutson, including *Playing Companies and Commerce in Shakespeare's Time* (Cambridge: Cambridge University Press, 2001), and 'The Commercial Significance of the Payments for Playtexts in Henslowe's Diary, 1597–1603', *Medieval and Renaissance Drama in England*, 5 (1991), 117–63; and Carol Chillington Rutter, including *Documents from the Rose Playhouse* (Manchester: Manchester University Press, 1984; rpt 1999). Yet, with the exception of Edmond Malone, W. W. Greg, G. E. Bentley, R. A. Foakes, Neil Carson and a few others, most scholars, whether theatre historians, 'new' or old bibliographers, or theorists, have failed for nearly three centuries to use these records to examine the business of playwriting from the point of view of the dramatist. Malone was the first to use Henslowe's papers to school himself in the possible routes of transmission of

an Elizabethan/Jacobean play-text. He published his conclusions after examining some of the documents, most notably the Diary, in his 'Historical Account of the English Stage' in his 1790 edition of Shakespeare's plays, 10 vols (London: H. Baldwin). Some of the documents he had seen have since disappeared, but are reprinted along with other documents in his 1821 edition of Shakespeare. J. P. Collier also used the archive and was later charged with having made a number of forged entries in the Diary and other documents. For a history of the archive, including a discussion of Collier's forgeries, see George F. Warner, Introduction, *Catalogue of the Manuscripts and Muniments of Alleyn's College of God's Gift at Dulwich*, 2 vols (Longman's, Green, and Co., 1881), 1:v–liv. Greg and Foakes (with the late R. T. Rickert) used the information gained from their editions of the *Diary* and other papers in their textual scholarship. Foakes and Rickert's 1st edition (Cambridge, 1961) corrected the errors of Greg's *The Henslowe Papers* (2 vols, London, A. H. Bullen, 1907), and Foakes's 2nd edition corrects other errors. J. Payne Collier's edition (London, 1845) contains his forgeries and is unreliable. The Foakes and Rickert edition is now the standard edition, but it long remained out of print until reprinted in 2002, solely under the editorship of Foakes.

15 In *The Shakespearean Stage, 1594–1642*, p. 102, Andrew Gurr cites records from 1595–7 in Henslowe's *Diary* to argue that even the most popular plays 'would be put on stage not more often than once every month or so'. Roslyn Knutson notes in 'The Repertory', in *A New History of Early English Drama*, p. 468, that 'a "typical" stage run, whether for a new play or a revival, appears to be one in which the play was performed eight to twelve times over four to six months'. However, the records vary enormously, with some plays performed more or less often than Gurr's and Knutson's typical runs. On possible Sunday performances, see Foakes and Rickert's Preface to the 1st edition of *Henlsowe's Diary*, p. xiii.

16 Bentley, *The Profession of Dramatist in Shakespeare's Time*, p. 25.

17 I arrived at this figure by adding up the number of plays listed in the index of plays in Foakes's modern edition of the *Diary*.

18 That so many plays mentioned by Henslowe do not survive in manuscript or print does not mean that they were not completed, for his payments to license and provide costumes or wine at their first readings, and his box-office receipts for their performances between 1591/2 and 1597, comprise a performance history for the plays.

19 Chambers, *The Elizabethan Stage*, 1:366.

20 Knutson, 'The Commercial Significance of the Payments for Playtexts in Henslowe's Diary', 1597–1603, pp. 117–63. Also see Rebecca Rogers and Kathleen E. McLuskie, 'Which Early-Modern Playing Companies Were Commercially Successful?', *Research Opportunities in Renaissance Drama*, 43 (2004), 54–74.

21 Chambers, *The Elizabethan Stage*, 3:289.

22 Dulwich College MS 7:23^r, 37^{r-v}. For transcriptions see *Henslowe's Diary*, 2nd edition, ed. Foakes, pp. 50, 72, 73, 323. For all the Henslowe–Alleyn manuscripts, I use my own transcriptions of the originals in Dulwich College but provide references in the notes to printed transcriptions. I wish to thank Dulwich College's Keeper of Archives, Dr Jan Piggott, for allowing me to use the collections, the Governors of Dulwich College for allowing me to quote from them, and Peter Beal, S.P. Cerasano, R. A. Foakes and Alan H. Nelson for their advice on particular matters in the archive.

23 Although Henslowe records payments to almost all the major professional dramatists of the age, Shakespeare is never mentioned in the *Diary*. However, early in his career, Shakespeare did write for acting companies, including Sussex's and Pembroke's Men, whom Henslowe financed or earned income

from in his theatres, so Shakespeare must have had some contact with Henslowe.

24 Dulwich College MS 1: Article 81. Photographic reproductions of all these letters and other Henslowe documents are available without transcriptions in *The Henslowe Papers*, ed. R. A. Foakes, 2 vols (London, Scolar Press, 1977), 2:70–92; Foakes's page numbers correspond to the manuscript article, *not* the page numbers. Transcriptions of the letters were also made by Edmond Malone in his 1821 edition of the works of Shakespeare, by John Payne Collier in *The Alleyn Papers* (London, 1843), and in Greg's *The Henslowe Papers*, pp. 70–85; all three have occasional errors.

25 In *The Profession of Dramatist in Shakespeare's Time*, pp. 88–110, Bentley suggests that schoolmasters' annual salaries were in the range of £20–£30. However, Peter Davison has very kindly provided me with documentary evidence from the period suggesting that provincial schoolmasters in Marlborough and elsewhere were paid far less than Bentley estimates, more in the range of £6–£10, at least in the 1590s.

26 Knutson, 'The Commercial Significance of the Payments for Playtexts in Henslowe's Diary', 1597–1603, p. 127.

27 Dulwich College MS 7:96^r, 109^r; *Henslowe's Diary*, ed. Foakes, pp. 187, 207.

28 Dulwich College MS 7:105^v, 93^r; *Henslowe's Diary*, ed. Foakes, pp. 200, 180.

29 Dutton, *Licensing, Censorship and Authorship in Early Modern England* (Basingstoke: Palgrave, 2000), p. 96.

30 Dulwich College MS 7:54^r; *Henslowe's Diary*, ed. Foakes, p. 105.

31 Dulwich College MS 7:105^r; *Henslowe's Diary*, ed. Foakes, p. 199.

32 Chambers, *The Elizabethan Stage*, 2:379.

33 Dulwich College MS 7:67^v, 68^r; *Henslowe's Diary*, ed. Foakes, pp. 131–2.

34 It is extremely difficult to believe that Henslowe allowed others access to his Diary while he was absent, thus these entries were made in the Diary while Henslowe was present.

35 Dulwich College MS 7:65^r; *Henslowe's Diary*, ed. Foakes, p. 126.

36 For example, in this period an engrossed (i.e. formally scribally prepared) deed is commonly referred to as a 'book', even if written on a single membrane of vellum, for it is a complete and finished, not to mention official, text in itself. The term 'play-book', also used repeatedly in the period, can mean a printed, as well as manuscript, text of a play. Hence Edward Dering's list of 'playbookes' that he had purchased between 1619 and 1624 appears to refer to printed editions, even though he also purchased dramatic manuscripts; see T. N. S. Lennam, 'Sir Edward Dering's Collection of Playbooks, 1619–1624', *Shakespeare Quarterly*, 16 (1965), 145–53. But, once again, the term is used to refer to a finished and complete text; when used for a dramatic text the understanding is that the 'book' had been or could or would be used in the theatre. For further information on contemporary manuscript terminology, see Peter Beal's forthcoming *A Dictionary of Manuscript Terms* (Oxford: Oxford University Press).

37 National Archives C2/Eliz./D11/49; *English Professional Theatre, 1530–1660*, ed. Wickham, Berry and Ingram, pp. 234–5.

38 Dulwich College MS 1: Articles 70, 71.

39 Dulwich MS 1: Article 92.

40 See Chambers's analysis of Henslowe's bail payments in *The Elizabethan Stage*, 1:374.

41 Dulwich College MS 7:106^v; *Henslowe's Diary*, ed. Foakes, p. 203.

42 Dulwich College MS 1: Article 24; *Henslowe's Diary*, ed. Foakes, pp. 285–6.

43 Dulwich College MS 7:105^v, 106^v; 1: Article 37; *Henslowe's Diary*, ed. Foakes, pp. 200–3, 296.

44 Walter Burre, 'To his Many ways endeared friend Master Robert Keysar', in *The Knight of the Burning Pestle* (London: Walter Burre, 1613), sig. A2ᵛ.

45 See *Poetaster*, ed. Tom Cain (Manchester: Manchester University Press, 1995), p. 69, note on 0.2, in which Cain links the character of Envy to Marston's character of the same name in *Histriomastix*.

46 Dulwich College MS 7:46ʳ; *Henslowe's Diary*, ed. Foakes, 90.

47 Dulwich College MS 1: Article 84.

48 Dulwich College MS 7:65ʳ; *Henslowe's Diary*, ed. Foakes, p. 126. Also see Henslowe's payments of 10 shillings each to Daye in 1601 'after the playnge of the 2 parte of strowde' and to Dekker 'ouer & a bove his price of his boocke called A medysen for A cvrste wiffe' on 27 September 1602 (Dulwich College MS 7:86ᵛ, 116ʳ; *Henslowe's Diary*, ed. Foakes, pp. 168, 216). See Bentley, *The Profession of Dramatist in Shakespeare's Time*, pp. 128–35. As Bentley notes (pp. 130, 132), Davenant's play *The Playhouse to be Let* (1663), states that the 'poets used to have the second day', as did Malone who saw Henry Herbert's licensing book, now lost.

49 Dulwich College MS 7:105ʳ, 109ᵛ; *Henslowe's Diary*, ed. Foakes, pp. 199, 208.

50 Alleyn notes in his Diary that he had agreed to Massey's urgent request to help him secure a loan in 1613, and sold him a share in the lease of the original Fortune Theatre in 1618 and the new Fortune Theatre in 1622. Alleyn also had Massey over for dinner at his house three times in 1621 and 1622. In May 1621, Alleyn paid Middleton 5 shillings for bringing him a 'book'. This amount also seems too small for even a first or interim payment for a playbook, and may refer instead to the purchase of one of the printed books which Alleyn records. Dulwich MS 1: Article 67, MUNIMENTS 1: Articles 56, 58, MS 9. For partial transcriptions of these manuscripts, see Warner, *Catalogue of the Manuscripts and Muniments of Alleyn's College of God's Gift at Dulwich*, vol. 1.

51 *The Defence of Conny catching* (London, 1592), sig. C3ʳ⁻ᵛ; *Henslowe's Diary*, ed. Foakes, p. 16.

52 Dulwich MS 7:7; *Henslowe's Diary*, ed. Foakes, p. 16.

53 Dulwich MS 1: Article 86.

54 Dulwich College MS 1: Article 2; *Henslowe's Diary*, ed. Foakes, p. 273.

55 On 16 May 1598 Henslowe paid Martin Slater £7 for 'v boockes', the last of which he delivered on 18 July. On 19 September 1601 Henslowe paid Alleyn 40 shillings for *The Wise Man of West Chester*, which Bentley takes to be Munday's old play of *John a Kent and John a Cumber*. It is possible that, although not known as an author, Slater wrote or collaborated in the writing of the plays, and Alleyn's payment may be a reimbursement of money already paid out to another author for a new play on Henslowe's behalf. Henslowe also paid Alleyn £6 for three books on 18 January 1602. See Dulwich College MS 7:45ᵛ, 47ᵛ, 93ᵛ, 96ʳ; *Henslowe's Diary*, ed. Foakes, pp. 89, 93, 181, 187. For another disputed case of the ownership of used play-books, see the case of *Richard Perkins et al.* v. *Robert Lee*, National Archives C2 James I/P16/14, transcribed in *English Professional Theatre, 1530–1660*, ed. Wickham, Berry and Ingram, pp. 239–41.

56 Bentley, *The Profession of Dramatist in Shakespeare's Time*, pp. 86–7.

57 See, for example, National Archives C21 James 1/P16/14; transcribed in *English Professional Theatre, 1530–1660*, ed. Wickham, Berry and Ingram, pp. 239–41.

58 See, for example, Dulwich College MS 1: Article 106, transcribed in *English Professional Theatre, 1530–1660*, ed. Wickham, Berry and Ingram, pp. 218–20.

59 Dulwich College MS 7:51ʳ, 119ʳ; *Henslowe's Diary*, ed. Foakes, pp. 100, 222.

60 Dulwich College MS 7:105ʳ, *Henslowe's Diary*, ed. Foakes, p. 199.

61 Dulwich College MS 7:120ʳ; *Henslowe's Diary*, ed. Foakes, p. 224. For a discus-

sion of Chettle's professional relationship with Henslowe, see Neil Carson, *A Companion to Henslowe's Diary*, pp. 62–3.

62 Dulwich College MS 7:119^v; *Henslowe's Diary*, ed. Foakes, p. 223.

63 Dulwich College MS 7:114^r; *Henslowe's Diary*, ed. Foakes, p. 213.

64 Dulwich MS 7:53^v; *Henslowe's Diary*, ed. Foakes, p. 105.

65 Dulwich MS 7:231^r; *Henslowe's Diary*, ed. Foakes, p. 241. There is nothing unusual about this exclusive contract, judging from another still extant for William Kendall, whom Alleyn bound on 8 December 1597 for two years. The full contract, written in Alleyn's hand, states, 'mnd [i.e. memorandum] y^t [that] this 8th of december 1597 my father philyp hinshlow hiered as A Covenauant servant william kendall for ii years after The statute of winchester w^t ii single penc A[nd] to geue hym for his sayd servis everi week of his playing in london x^s & in ye Cuntrie v^s, for the wch he covenaunteth y^e for space of those ii yeares To be redye att all Tymes to play in ye howse of the sayd philype & in no other during the sayd Terme wittnes my self the writer of This E Alleyn'. British Library Egerton MS 2625, f. 9.

66 Dulwich MS 7:23^r, 52^v–53^v, 109^r, 114^r, 115^r–119^r, 120^r, 122^r; *Henslowe's Diary*, ed. Foakes, pp. 50, 102, 104, 207, 208, 213, 215–24, 226.

67 In *The Authentic Shakespeare*, p. 2, Stephen Orgel contends that the author had little or no say in any revisions to his texts, as 'the text belonged to the company, and the authority represented by the text—I am talking now about the *performing* text—is that of the company, the owners, not that of the playwright, the author. . . . The very notion of "the author's original manuscript" is in such cases a figment.'

68 See Tiffany Stern, *Rehearsal from Shakespeare to Sheridan* (Oxford: Clarendon Press, 2000), p. 84. She also argues that during rehearsal an author could exert 'directorial influence' or offer instruction to the actors (pp. 60ff.); but she envisions this collaboration ending after the first performance of a new play. However, judging from Henslowe's employment of dramatists for successive or concurrent plays, dramatists with whom his companies worked were in constant contact with those acting their plays. The dramatists could almost certainly be consulted during the revival of old plays if they were in the process of completing new ones at the same time for the same companies.

69 Dulwich College MS 1: Article 26, 7:65^r; *Henslowe's Diary*, ed. Foakes, p. 288, 126. I transcribe and discuss this outline in Chapter 3.

70 Dulwich College MS 1: Article 32, 7:86^r–87^r, 92^r–94^r, 104^r; *Henslowe's Diary*, ed. Foakes, pp. 167–70, 178–82, 198, 294.

71 Dulwich College MS 1: Article 33, 7:86^{r-v}; *Henslowe's Diary*, ed. Foakes, pp. 295, 167–8.

72 On this point, also see Stern, *Rehearsal from Shakespeare to Sheridan*, pp. 60ff.

73 Dulwich College MS 7:37^v, 43^v; *Henslowe's Diary*, ed. Foakes, pp. 73, 85.

74 Dulwich College MS 7:45^r; *Henslowe's Diary*, ed. Foakes, p. 88.

75 In a letter dated 10 June 1613 (Dulwich College MS 1: Article 79), Daborne tells Henslowe, 'I can this weeke deliuer in ye last word & will y^t night they play thear new play read this', repeating this promise, 'when I read next week I will take ye 40^s'.

76 Vickers, *Shakespeare, Co-Author*. For discussions of dramatic collaboration in this age, see Vickers; also see Harold Love, *Attributing Authorship: An Introduction* (Cambridge: Cambridge University Press, 2002), and various articles and books by MacDonald P. Jackson, Cyrus Hoy and R. V. Holdsworth.

77 'To the Reader', in *The English Traveller* (London: Robert Raworth, 1633), sig. A3^r.

78 See Bentley's discussion of these points in *The Profession of Dramatist in Shakespeare's Time*, pp. 27–8.

79 See Knutson, '*Love's Labor's Won* in Repertory', *Publications of the Arkansas Philological Association*, 11 (1985), 45–57.
80 Jonson, Dedication, *Sejanus, His Fall* (London: G. Eld for Thomas Thorpe, 1605), sig. ¶2ᵛ.
81 Dulwich MS 1: Article 100.
82 Dulwich MS 1: Article 78.
83 See Charles Sisson, '*Keep the Widow Waking*: A lost play by Dekker', *The Library*, Ser. 4, 8 (1927), 2 pts, 39–59; 233–59.
84 National Archives, STAC 8/31/16; for reproductions and transcriptions, see Sisson, '*Keep the Widow Waking*: A lost play by Dekker', pp. 257–9; also see *English Professional Theatre, 1530–1660*, ed. Wickham, Berry and Ingram, pp. 582–3.
85 For discussion of how particular dramatists wrote collaboratively, see Cyrus Hoy, 'The Shares of Fletcher and His Collaborators in the Beaumont and Fletcher Canon (I–VIII)', *Studies in Bibliography*, 8 (1956), 128–46; 9 (1957), 143–62; 11 (1958), 85–106; 12 (1959), 9–116; 13 (1960), 77–108; 14 (1961), 45–67; 15 (1962), 71–90; and Jackson, *Defining Shakespeare*.
86 Dulwich MS 7:46ʳ⁻ᵛ; *Henslowe's Diary*, ed. Foakes, pp. 90–2.
87 *Henslowe's Diary*, ed. Foakes, p. 320.
88 For a discussion of Shakespeare's collaborative habits, see Vickers, *Shakespeare, Co-Author* and Jackson, *Defining Shakespeare*.
89 Dulwich MS 1: Article 81.
90 Dulwich College MS 7:114ᵛ; *Henslowe's Diary*, ed. Foakes, p. 213.
91 Dulwich College MS 7:94ᵛ; *Henslowe's Diary*, ed. Foakes, p. 184.
92 Dulwich MS 1: Article 92.
93 At least twenty-six letters, play-contracts, bonds and receipts are in the Dulwich College collection and one is in the British Library (Egerton MS 2623). Others may be elsewhere.
94 This is Greg's contention in *Henslowe's Diary, Part II: Commentary* (London, 1908), p. 142, but I see no reason to support this view, as Daborne treats the two plays separately in his correspondence.
95 Greg accepts F. G. Fleay's identification of the unnamed play as *The Honest Man's Fortune* in *Henslowe's Diary, Part II: Commentary*, p. 142.
96 Victoria and Albert Art Library Dyce MS 25.
97 See Mark Eccles, 'Brief Lives: Tudor and Stuart Authors', *Studies in Philology*, 79 (1982), pp. 29–30.
98 Most of the information that exists about Daborne's life and career derives from these letters to Henslowe. Other records suggest that he was a 'sizar' (an undergraduate student exempted from paying fees), at King's College, Cambridge, in 1598, from which he probably took the Master of Arts degree noted on the 1655 quarto title-page of his play *The Poor Man's Comfort*. The date of his attendance in 1598 would place his year of birth between 1580 and 1583. Daborne was married to Ann (or Agnes) Younger around 1602, by whom he had at least one child, a daughter, mentioned in one of the letters as delivering Daborne's manuscripts or other papers to Henslowe. Daborne had taken up residence with his first wife and his daughter in Shoreditch in his father-in-law's house by 1609, at which time some of his in-laws attempted to evict them. For biographical information on Daborne, see Baldwin Maxwell, 'Notes on Robert Daborne's Extant Plays', *Philological Quarterly*, 50 (1971), 85–98; Wayne H. Phelps, 'The Early Life of Robert Daborne', *Philological Quarterly*, 59 (1980), 1–10; Eccles, 'Brief Lives: Tudor and Stuart Authors', pp. 28–36; and Daniel J. Vitkus's 'Introduction' to his edition of *Three Turk Plays from Early Modern England: Selimus, A Christian Turned Turk and The Renegado* (New York, 2000), p. 23. Also see Greg, *Henslowe's Diary,*

Part II: Commentary, pp. 141–3; and Gurr, *Shakespearian Playing Companies*, pp. 357, 400.

99 See Chambers, *The Elizabethan Stage*, 2:246–60; and Bentley, *The Jacobean and Caroline Stage*, 1:176.

100 Bentley argues in *The Jacobean and Caroline Stage*, 1:176, that Henslowe controlled the company by 'keeping them in his debt through questionable means', judging from articles of grievance filed against Henslowe in 1615; also see Dulwich College MUNIMENTS 1: Article 52, MS 1: Article 106; transcribed in *English Professional Theatre, 1530–1660*, pp. 217–20.

101 See Greg, *Henslowe's Diary, Part II: Commentary*, pp. 20, 23; William Rendle, 'Henslowe', *The Genealogist*, n.s. 4 (1887), 157.

102 Dulwich College MS 1: Article 69.

103 Dulwich College MS 1: Article 75.

104 Dulwich College MS 1: Article 73.

105 Dulwich College MS 1: Article 74.

106 Dulwich College MS 1: Article 78.

107 Dulwich College MS 1: Article 89.

108 Dulwich College MS 1: Article 80.

109 British Library Egerton MS 1994. See Kenneth Palmer's Introduction, *The Poor Man's Comfort by Robert Daborne* (Oxford: Oxford University Press, 1955), p. xii, for discussion of this manuscript; also see Peter Holloway, 'Scribal Dittography: Daborne's *The Poor Man's Comfort*', *The Library*, ser. 6, 3 (1981), 233–9.

110 Maxwell, in 'Notes on Robert Daborne's Extant Plays', p. 90, assigns it a date of 1610–14, and Palmer argues for a date of 1615–17 in his Introduction to *The Poor Man's Comfort by Robert Daborne*, p. xi.

111 Daborne concluded his career as Dean of Lismore, Ireland, in 1621 and died on 23 March 1628. The eloquent rhetoric, complex arguments and ingratiating pleas for emotional and financial sustenance that he offers to Philip Henslowe in his 1613–14 letters were perhaps excellent practice for his later profession. Mary Bly argues in her book *Queer Virgins and Virgin Queans on the Early Modern Stage* (Oxford: Oxford University Press, 2000), pp. 135–9, that Daborne deliberately removed 'homoerotic' and 'sodomitical' material apparent in the sources when he wrote *A Christian Turned Turk*.

112 Dulwich MS 1: Article 76.

113 S. P. Cerasano, 'Competition for the King's Men?: Alleyn's Blackfriars Venture', *Medieval and Renaissance Drama in England*, 4 (1989), 173–86. Also see Eccles, 'Brief Lives: Tudor and Stuart Authors', pp. 29–32.

114 Dulwich College MS 1: Articles 73, 91.

115 Dulwich College MS 1: Article 94.

116 Dulwich College MS 1: Article 76.

117 Dulwich College MS 1: Article 79, 82.

118 Dulwich College MS 1: Article 83.

119 See Cerasano, 'Competition for the King's Men?: Alleyn's Blackfriars Venture'.

120 Dulwich College MS 1: Article 84.

121 Dulwich College MS 1: Article 89, 91.

122 Dulwich College MS 1: Article 96.

123 See Bentley, *The Jacobean and Caroline Stage*, 2:403; also see *Henslowe's Diary*, ed. Foakes, pp. 330, 332. In his 1687 will, William Cartwright the younger, son of William Cartwright the Jacobean actor, donated to Dulwich College his collection of one hundred manuscript plays, including *The Wizard* (British Library Additional MS 10306). He probably also donated the volume now catalogued as British Library Egerton MS 1994 which contains autograph and/or scribal manuscripts mainly from the 1620s and 1630s of *The Elder Brother*, *Dick of Devonshire*, *The Captives*, *The Escapes of Jupiter* (also known as *Calisto*),

Edmond Ironside, Charlemagne, The Fatal Marriage, Thomas of Woodstock (also known as *Richard II*), *The Lady Mother, Juno's Pastoral, The Two Noble Ladies and the Converted Conjuror, The Tragedy of Nero, Lovers Changeling Change, The Launching of the Mary* (also known as *The Seaman's Honest Wife*), as well as Daborne's *The Poor Man's Comfort.* Some of these plays were performed by companies financed by Henslowe and/or Alleyn. William Cartwright the younger was both a bookseller and an actor, associated with Salisbury Court when it housed Queen Henrietta's Company in the late 1630s and early 1640s. He could have assembled this volume of plays in either or both of his professions, bequeathing it and other manuscripts to Dulwich, perhaps in recognition of the plays' origins with Henslowe or Alleyn and/or to build on the archive Alleyn had already established there. See Eleanore Boswell, Introduction, *Edmund Ironside or War Hath Made All Friends* (Oxford: Oxford University Press, 1928), p. x. Cartwright also donated a number of actors' portraits to Dulwich College; they are now at the Dulwich Picture Gallery.

124   Dulwich College had a substantial library of plays by the eighteenth century, when staff gave David Garrick a 'collection of old plays', probably including *The Wizard* and other early modern dramatic manuscripts. Later, George Steevens and Edmond Malone, among others, borrowed Dulwich manuscripts which they failed to return. Among items from Malone's library that he left to the Bodleian Library, Oxford, are several manuscripts, including *The Witch* (Malone MS 12), purchased in the 1800 sale of Steevens's library, and *A Game at Chess* (Malone MS 525). Malone also purchased in the Steevens sale the theatrical plots of *Frederick and Basilea* and *The Dead Man's Fortune* (British Library Additional MS 10449), which almost certainly had come from Dulwich College. However, Dulwich College staff succeeded in reclaiming the anonymous play *The Telltale* (Dulwich College MS XX) and the plot of Part II of *The Seven Deadly Sins* (Dulwich College MS XIX), in which it was wrapped, from the 1825 sale of the library of James Boswell the younger, the executor of Malone. John Payne Collier also borrowed Dulwich manuscripts that were sold or dispersed, and he was accused of forging entries in Henslowe's 'Diary' and other Dulwich papers. John Philip Kemble and Alexander Dyce were just two of the many others whose collections of early modern play manuscripts and quartos may have included items originally housed at Dulwich College. Their collections, like those of Garrick, Steevens, Malone and Collier, are now at the British Library, the Victoria and Albert Art Library, the Folger Shakespeare Library and the Henry E. Huntington Library, among other archives. A few fragments removed from Henslowe's Diary and Alleyn's correspondence at Dulwich can now be found in the British Library, the Folger Library and Belvoir Castle, having been acquired in the late nineteenth and the early twentieth centuries. See the notes in British Library MS Egerton 2623. Also see W. W. Greg, 'A Fragment from Henslowe's Diary', *The Library*, ser. 4, 19 (1938), 180–4, and Joseph Quincy Adams, 'Another Fragment from Henslowe's Diary', *The Library*, ser. 4, 20 (1939), 154–8. At the very least, such collections remind us that even in the eighteenth and nineteenth centuries scholars were determined to collect as much *manuscript* evidence as possible in order to understand the role of dramatists and the transmission of the text in the early modern playhouse.

2 'You give them authority to play': dramatists and authority

1 Bentley, *The Jacobean and Caroline Stage*, 2:363.
2 Chambers, *The Elizabethan Stage*, 2:302.
3 National Archives (formerly PRO) Req. 2/662. For transcriptions (with only a

few minor errors) of this document and Brome's response, see Ann Haaker's excellent article, 'The Plague, the Theater and the Poet', *Renaissance Drama*, n.s. 1 (1968), pp. 283–306; she provides a history of the use of these documents, noting that C. W. Wallace discovered them among National Archives records and that his transcriptions are among his papers in the Wallace Collection at the Henry E. Huntington Library. However, the Wallace Collection has been re-catalogued since Haaker saw it, and Wallace's transcript of the Hearon–Brome case can now be found in Wallace Collection Box 9, Shelfmark BV13b. Also see Bentley, *The Profession of Dramatist in Shakespeare's Time*, pp. 112–15, and Berry, in *English Professional Theatre 1530–1660*, ed. Wickham, Berry and Ingram, pp. 657–64.

4 National Archives Req. 2/723.
5 Haaker, 'The Plague, the Theater and the Poet', pp. 295ff.
6 See Bentley, *The Profession of Dramatist*, pp. 116–19.
7 E. K. Chambers, *William Shakespeare: A Study of the Facts and Problems*, 2 vols (Oxford: Clarendon Press, 1930), 1:429–50.
8 Bentley, *The Jacobean and Caroline Stage*, 2:525, 539 and *passim*.
9 This is the description of the Court of Requests in the National Archives' online catalogue (accessed at www.nationalarchives.gov.uk).
10 Dulwich MS 7:68; *Henslowe's Diary*, ed. Foakes, p. 132.
11 National Archives C2/James I/A6/21; see Berry, in *English Professional Theatre 1530–1660*, ed. Wickham, Berry and Ingram, pp. 553–9.
12 'To the Reader', in *The English Traveller* (London: Robert Raworth, 1633), sig. A3ʳ.
13 National Archives LC 5/134/178, 5/135. W. W. Greg provides a transcript of both letters in *Collections Vol. II. Part III* [N. 71 in the Malone Society Reprints Series] (Oxford: Oxford University Press, 1931; rpt New York: AMS Press, 1985), pp. 384–5, 398–9.
14 British Library Additional MS 10449, Dulwich College MS XIX. One other, the dubious *England's Joy*, survives in print as a broadsheet, with the story fully summarised. For a discussion of plots see Greg, *Dramatic Documents from the Elizabethan Playhouses*.
15 For a discussion of the expansion of these directions in *The Battle of Alcazar*, see Foakes, 'Henslowe's Rose/Shakespeare's Globe', in *From Script to Stage in Early Modern England*, ed. Peter Holland and Stephen Orgel (Basingstoke: Palgrave Macmillan, 2004), p. 15.
16 For Richard Burbage's connection to Alleyn, see Scott McMillin, 'Building Stories: Greg, Fleay, and the Plot of *2 Seven Deadly Sins*', *Medieval and Renaissance Drama in England*, 4 (1989), 53–62.
17 Dulwich MS 1: Article 26, 7:65; *Henslowe's Diary*, ed. Foakes, pp. 126, 288.
18 Greg, *Dramatic Documents from the Elizabethan Playhouses*, pp. 70–93. For a timely discussion of the clues to staging found in plots, see Foakes, 'Henslowe's Rose/Shakespeare's Globe', pp. 11–31.
19 Dulwich College MS 7:51ᵛ; *Henslowe's Diary*, ed. Foakes, p. 100.
20 Another such author-plot, written no earlier than 1627, survives for a play enti-tled *Philander, King of Thrace*, and provides an outline of the first three acts, with Acts 4 and 5 unfinished. However, of the six pages of this manuscript, two are taken up with long summaries of the 'Cittyes and Townes and places of Thrace' as well as its rivers and regions. The outline also includes an analysis of the ancient Greek myth that serves as a basis for the play's story. Such an outline suggests a literary, amateur author at work, with the leisure to digress into geo-graphical study and outlines. See Joseph Quincy Adams, 'The Author-Plot of an Early Seventeenth Century Play', *The Library*, ser. 4, 26 (1945), 17–27.
21 Greene, *The Historie of Orlando Furioso* (London: John Danter for Cuthbert Burbie,

1594); Greg, *Two Elizabethan Stage Abridgements: The Battle of Alcazar & Orlando Furioso* (Oxford: Clarendon Press, 1923), pp. 133–4. Greg offers a parallel text of the part and the printed play on pp. 142–201.

22 Dulwich MS 1:138.

23 See Chambers, *The Elizabethan Stage*, 3:327–30.

24 Greg, *Dramatic Documents from the Elizabethan Playhouses*, pp. 179–80.

25 Greg, *Dramatic Documents from the Elizabethan Playhouses*, p. 176.

26 Greg, *Two Elizabethan Stage Abridgements: The Battle of Alcazar & Orlando Furioso*, p. 127.

27 David Carnegie discusses four other extant parts from university productions in the 1610s in 'Actors' Parts and the "Play of Poore"', *Harvard Library Bulletin*, 30 (1922), 5–23.

28 In at least one amateur performance of a miracle play in this period, the book-keeper is called the 'ordinary': 'the players conne not their parts without booke, but are prompted by one called the Ordinary, who followeth at their back with the booke in his hand, and telleth them softly what they must pronounce aloud'. See Richard Carew, *The Suruey of Cornwall* (London: S. S. for John Jaggard, 1602), sig. 71^v.

29 Shakespeare, *The Tragoedy of Othello, The Moore of Venice* (London: N. O for Thomas Wilkley, 1622), sig. C1^v.

30 For a study of such a case, see Leslie Thomson, 'A Quarto "Marked for Performance": Evidence of What?', *Medieval and Renaissance Drama in England*, 8 (1996), 176.

31 On records kept by playgoers of their activities, see Ann Jennalie Cook, *The Privileged Playgoers of Shakespeare's London, 1576–1642* (Princeton: Princeton University Press, 1981); Andrew Gurr, *Playgoing in Shakespeare's London* (Cambridge: Cambridge University Press, 1987); and S. P. Cerasano and Marion Wynne-Davies, *Renaissance Drama by Women: Texts and Documents* (London: Routledge, 1996). This latter text also includes editions of plays written by women.

32 Bodleian Library MS Ashmole 208.

33 Although the originals are difficult to access or use, many of these documents were transcribed in the twentieth century by the theatre historian Charles Wallace, and his transcriptions are now among the collections of the Henry E. Huntington Library.

34 National Archives C2/James I/P16/14, transcribed in *English Professional Theatre, 1530–1660*, ed. Wickham, Berry and Ingram, pp. 239–41; also see Bentley, *The Profession of Dramatist*, p. 86.

35 The standard guides for early modern English theatre history material, much of it drawn from manuscript records, include those by W. W. Greg, E. K. Chambers and G. E. Bentley. More material can be accessed by using printed or online transcriptions and reference indexes, such as Wickham *et al.*'s *English Professional Theatre, 1530–1660*; the individual *REED* volumes; and Peter Beal's *Index of English Literary Manuscripts 1450–1700*, shortly to be made into an electronic database accessible on the internet. More general indexes of historical records include the appropriate series of *The Calendar of State Papers, Domestic* and of the *Historical Manuscripts Commission*, particularly for the Salisbury, De L'Isle, and other families who took an interest in or commissioned theatrical performances. As more of these manuscript catalogues and indexes become available in searchable online databases, and as more of the records themselves become digitised, the secrets held by previously inaccessible manuscript records will greatly enlarge our understanding of dramatists and their texts and contexts.

36 For example, in 1604, Sir Walter Cope wrote to his employer, Sir Robert Cecil, at that time Viscount Cranbourne, with Richard Burbage, whom he has sent

for, at his side. Cope had been seeking 'players Iuglers & Such Creatures but fynde them harde to fynde', leaving notes for them to contact him. Finally Cope reports that 'burbage ys come & sayes ther ys no new playe that the quene hath not seene but they haue Revyvd an old one Cawled Loves Labour lost, wch for Wytt & mirth he sayes will please her exceedingly And Thys ys appointed to be playd to Morowe night at my Lord of Southamptons vnless you send a wyrtt to Remove the *Corpus Cum Causa* to yor house in [the] Strande'. It is not clear here whether the legal joke about using a writ to move the 'body with cause' is Cope's or Burbage's. Cope concludes: 'Burbage ys my messenger Ready attendynge yor pleasure'. Hatfield House CP 189/95; for a transcript see *Historical Manuscripts Commission: Report on the Manuscripts of the Earl of Salisbury*, 24 vols (London: His Majesty's Stationery Office, 1883–1976), 16:415; hereafter cited as *HMC: Salisbury*. Cope, in fact, miswrote the first word in the play's title and had to trace it over to get it right, suggesting that even though the play had been printed by 1598, and in performance for some time before that, he was evidently unfamiliar with it in 1604. That Burbage, an actor, theatre-sharer, and company-sharer served as a personal messenger to Cecil, the most powerful non-royal official in the kingdom, demonstrates the pervasive presence of the theatre industry. That Cope had left numerous messages for Burbage and his rival company-managers to 'seek' him because he had been unsuccessfully trying to hire actors and needed to organise this performance also implies that actors sometimes had the upper hand, as in any supply-and-demand business deal. Presumably, as this performance was to be staged at the London home of Southampton, personal friend and patron of Shakespeare, the dramatist would also have joined the cast or been present in some other capacity. Another close friend of Southampton, Robert Devereux, second Earl of Essex, also hosted numerous private play performances in his London home, Essex House. For example, on 14 February 1598, Essex, later executed by Elizabeth I as a traitor in 1601, and his guests complained of having 'had 2 plaies which kept them up till 1 aclocke after midnight'. *Historical Manuscripts Commission: Report on the Manuscripts of Lord De L'Isle & Dudley preserved at Penshurst Place*, 4 vols (London: His Majesty's Stationery Office, 1925–42), 2:322; hereafter cited as *HMC: De L'Isle*.

37 Sir Gerard Herbert to Sir Dudley Carleton, National Archives SP14/107, 109; for transcriptions, see *Calendar of State Papers, Domestic Series, James I, 1619–1623*, ed. M. A. Everett Green (London: Longman, Brown, Green, Longmans & Roberts, 1858), pp. 26, 47), hereafter *CSP*. Also see F. D. Hoeniger's discussion of Sir Gerald Herbert's comments on this performance at Whitehall in his Introduction to his Arden edition of *Pericles* (London: Methuen & Co. Ltd, 1963), p. lxvi.

38 Hatfield House CP 114/58; *HMC: Salisbury*, 17:605.

39 Hatfield House CP 144/272; 144/271; 144/267; *HMC: Salisbury*, 18:209, 19:136, 490–2.

40 Hatfield House CP Bills 22; *HMC: Salisbury*, 24:149–50.

41 Even more broad and comprehensive sets of manuscript records for public, private or provincial performance before aristocrats, or less socially elevated audiences, can be found in numerous regional record offices in the United Kingdom. Such documents have been painstakingly transcribed and collected in volumes of the *Records of Early English Drama* (REED), each of which offers material pertaining to theatrical production in individual cities, counties or regions. The volumes for Oxford and Cambridge especially track the many university productions, some of which, like *The Second Part of the Return from Parnassus*, mock London professional dramatists or their plays.

42 For these comments and others, ranging from idolatrous to envious, see Jonson,

'To the memory of my beloued, the AVTHOR MR. WILLIAM SHAKE-SPEARE', in the *Mr. William Shakespeares Comedies, Histories, & Tradedies* [*sic*] (London: Isaac Jaggard and Ed. Blount, 1623), sig. A4^{r-v}, and *Timber, or Discoveries* and *Conversations with Drummond*, in *Ben Jonson*, ed. C. H. Hereford and Percy and Evelyn Simpson, 11 vols (Oxford: Clarendon Press, 1925–52), 8:584, 1:138, 133.

43 National Library of Scotland Adv. MS 33.3.19, ff. 25^v–31^r, first published in *The Works of William Drummond, of Hawthornden* (Edinburgh: James Watson, 1711).

44 These tracts include Stephen Gosson's *The Schoole of Abuse* (1579) and *Playes Confuted in fiue Actions* (1582), Philip Stubbes's *Anatomy of Abuses* (1583), John Rainold's *Th'Overthrow of Stage-Playes* (1599) and William Prynne's *Histriomastix* (1633), to name just a few. For extracts from a variety of contemporary documents on theatre, see Chambers, *The Elizabethan Stage*, pp. 184–259.

45 Heywood, *An Apology for Actors*, (London, Nicholas Okes, 1612), sig. F3^{r-v}.

46 *Henslowe's Diary*, ed. Foakes, pp. 218–19.

47 Webster, 'To his beloued friend Maister Thomas Heywood', in Heywood, *An Apology for Actors*, sig. A2^{r-v}.

48 *Dictionary of National Biography* (Oxford: Oxford University Press, 1975), 1:1240.

49 Hopton, in Heywood, *An Apology for Actors*, sig. A1^v.

50 Shakespeare, *A Midsommer nights dreame* (London: Thomas Fisher, 1600), sig. G2^v. J. Dover Wilson proposed that the mislineation throughout this long speech in the 1600 Quarto edition, printed from foul papers, which is corrected in the 1623 Folio, suggests that, sometime after composition, Shakespeare had added the dramatist to the list of madman and lover who use imagination to create 'more than coole reason euen comprehends'. See 'The Copy for *A Midsummer Night's Dream*, 1600', in *A Midsummer Night's Dream*, ed. A. Quiller-Couch and J. D. Wilson (Cambridge: Cambridge University Press, 1924), pp. 85ff.

51 All quotations are from my edition of *Hengist, King of Kent, or The Mayor of Queenborough*, in *Thomas Middleton: The Collected Works* (Oxford: Oxford University Press, 2006). For a transcription of the manuscript-text, see also my Malone Society edition, *Hengist, King of Kent, or The Mayor of Queenborough by Thomas Middleton* (Oxford: Oxford University Press, 2003).

52 Quarto 2, sig. F2^v.

53 Quarto 2, sig. G4^r. See Gurr, *The Shakespearean Stage, 1574–1642*, p. 87.

54 Moseley, 'The Stationer to the Reader', in *Comedies and Tragedies written by Francis Beaumont and John Fletcher* (London: Humphrey Moseley, 1647), sig. A3^v; Burr, *The Knight of the Burning Pestle* (London: Printed for Walter Burre, 1613), sig. A2^r.

55 Walkley, 'To the Right Worshipful and Worthy Knight, Sir Henry Nevill', in *A King and No King* (London, Thomas Walkley, 1619), sig. A2^v.

56 Lowin and Taylor, 'The Dedication To the Honored Few Lovers of Dramatic Poesy', *The Wild-Goose Chase* (London: Humphrey Moseley, 1652), sig. A2^r.

57 See my discussion of these points in *Revising Shakespeare* (Cambridge, Mass.: Harvard University Press, 1991), pp. 146–54.

58 Jonson, *Epicoene, The Workes of Beniamin Jonson* (London, William Stansby, 1616), p. 527. Further references will be made parenthetically in the text.

59 For a succinct discussion of Jonson's debt to Horace, see Tom Cain, Introduction, *Poetaster* (Manchester: Manchester University Press, 1995), pp. 10–14.

60 Jonson, *Poetaster* (London: M. L., 1602), sigs. L2^{r-v}.

61 Jonson, *Poetaster*, in *The Workes of Beniamin Jonson* (London, W. Stansby 1616), p. 348.

62 Jonson, *Bartholmew Fayre, The Workes of Benjamin Jonson*, 2nd vol. (London: Richard Meighen, 1640), Epilogue, ll. 3–8.

63 See Peter Beal, 'Massinger at Bay: Unpublished Verses in a War of the Theatres', *The Yearbook of English Studies*, 10 (1980), 190–203, for a transcript and discussion of the verses.

64 National Archives, STAC 8/31/16; for reproductions and transcriptions, see Sisson, '*Keep the Widow Waking*: A lost play by Dekker', pp. 257–9; also see *English Professional Theatre, 1530–1660*, ed. Wickham, Berry and Ingram, pp. 582–3.

65 See Beal, 'Massinger at Bay: Unpublished Verses in a War of the Theatres', p. 201.

66 Marston, *The Dutch Courtesan* (London, Printed by T. P. for Iohn Hogdgets, 1605), sig. A2^r.

67 In the Prologue, Momus comments, 'What is presented here, is an old musty showe, that hath laine this twelfe-moneth in the bottome of a coale-house amongst broomes and odd shooes, an inuension that we are ashamed of, and therfore we haue promised the Copies to the Chandlers to wrappe candles in.' In Act 1, Scene 2, Ingenioso complains about the fee offered to him by the printer Danter, '40 Shillings? a fit reward for one of your reumatick poets, that beslauers all the paper he comes by, and furnishes the Chaundlers with wast papers to wrap candles in'. *The Second Part of the Return from Parnassus* (London, Printed by G. Eld for John Wright, 1605).

68 Meres states in *Palladis Tamia* (London: P. Short, 1598), 'As *Plautus* and *Seneca* are accounted the best for Comedy and Tragedy among the Latines: so *Shakespeare* among ye English is the most excellent in both kinds for the stage; for Comedy, witnes his *Gentlemen of Verona*, his *Errors*, his *Loue labors lost*, his *Loue labours wonne*, his *Midsummers night dreame*, & his *Merchant of Venice*: for Tragedy his *Richard the 2. Richard the 3. Henry the 4. King Iohn, Titus Andronicus* and his *Romeo and Juliet*'.

69 See Gurr, *The Shakespearean Stage, 1574–1642*, pp. 135ff.

70 Middleton, *The Masque of the Inner Temple* (London, 1619), sig. B3^r.

71 This was surely the case with *The Merry Wives of Windsor*, probably written to celebrate a feast of the Order of the Garter before Elizabeth I at Windsor Palace. Shakespeare then reworked to suit a wider audience at the Globe (and perhaps revised again later for private performance before King James). See Ioppolo, *Revising Shakespeare*, pp. 118–21.

72 See Andrew Gurr, who particularly insists in *The Shakespearean Stage, 1574–1642*, p. 103, that dramatists wrote to suit their companies' personnel and venues. Also see Knutson's discussion in *The Repertory of Shakespeare's Company, 1594–1613* (Fayetteville: University of Arkansas Press, 1991).

73 National Archives STAC 8/8/2; also see Herbert Berry's discussion of the case in *English Professional Theatre, 1530–1660*, ed. Wickham, Berry and Ingram, pp. 314–16.

74 On the composition history of these plays, see the individual textual introductions in Stanley Wells, Gary Taylor *et al.*, *William Shakespeare: A Textual Companion* (Oxford: Clarendon University Press, 1987; rpt New York: W. W. Norton and Company, 1997), pp. 175–8, 197–9, 217–18, 228–32.

75 See Knutson, 'The Repertory', in *A New History of Early English Drama*, p. 471.

76 See *Henslowe's Diary*, ed. Foakes, pp. 55–8, 59.

77 For a discussion of such cruxes, see Ioppolo, *Revising Shakespeare*, pp. 94–103.

3 'The fowle papers of the Authors': dramatists and foul papers

1 P. Werstine, 'Plays in Manuscript', in *A New History of Early English Drama*, ed. John D. Cox and David Scott Kastan (Columbia: Columbia University Press, 1997), pp. 481–97; N. W. Bawcutt, 'Renaissance Dramatists and the Texts of Their Plays', *Research Opportunities in Renaissance Drama*, 40 (2001), 1–24. Also

see E. A. J. Honigmann's response to Werstine in 'The New Bibliography and its Critics', in *Textual Performances: The Modern Reproduction of Shakespeare's Drama*, ed. Lucas Erne and Margaret J. Kidnie (Cambridge: Cambridge University Press, 2004).

2 Chambers, *The Elizabethan Stage*, 2:60.

3 Chambers, *The Elizabethan Stage*, 1:271.

4 No one has successfully undermined Greg's argument that the play is in Knight's hand. See Introduction, *Bonduca* (London: Oxford University Press, 1951), pp. v–vi.

5 See J. Gerritsen's discussion of Knight's theatrical activities in Introduction, *The Honest Man's Fortune* (Groningen, Germany: J. B. Wolters, 1953), pp. xxiii–xxvi.

6 British Library Additional MS 36758, F 24. For a complete transcription of the play, see Greg's edition of *Bonduca*.

7 Victoria and Albert Art Library Dyce MS 10. For a transcription of the manuscript, see G. M. Pinciss and G. R. Proudfoot, *The Faithful Friends* (Oxford: Oxford University Press, 1970).

8 Cited from John Pitcher, Introduction, *Hymen's Triumph* (Oxford: Oxford University Press, 1994), p. xviii.

9 Woudhuysen, *Sir Philip Sidney and the Circulation of Manuscripts 1558–1640*, pp. 223ff.

10 Samuel Schoenbaum, *Shakespeare's Lives* (Oxford: Oxford University Press, 1993), p. 82.

11 Bowers, *On Editing Shakespeare*, p. 13. Also see his article, 'Authority, Copy and Transmission in Shakespeare's Texts', in *Shakespeare Study Today*, ed. Georgianna Ziegler (New York: AMS Press, 1986), pp. 7–36.

12 British Library Egerton MS 1994.

13 Billingsley, *The Pens Excellencie or The Secretaries Delighte* (London: George Humble, 1618), sigs. C3ʳ–D4ʳ. This manual was frequently reprinted in the seventeenth century.

14 Cocker, *The Pen's Triumph* (London: Samuel Ayre, 1658), sigs. B1ᵛ–B4ʳ. Cocker also wrote and illustrated a number of other books on penmanship which were frequently reprinted, including *The Pens Transcendence* (London, 1657), *The Guide to Penmanship* (London: John Ruddiard, 1664) and *Englands Pen-man* (London, 1665). A British Library copy (shelfmark 1268.a.12) of the second edition of Billingsley's book *A Coppie Booke Containing varieties of Examples of all the most Curious hands written* (London: Thomas Dainty, 1637) is bound up with a copy of Cocker's manual.

15 Billingsley, *The Pens Excellencie or The Secretaries Delighte*, sig. A3ᵛ.

16 For a discussion of women's manuscripts, see *English Manuscript Studies, Volume 9: Writings by Early Modern Women*, ed. Peter Beal and Margaret J. M. Ezell.

17 On secretary hand, see Giles E. Dawson and Laetitia Kennedy-Skipton, *Elizabethan Handwriting 1500–1650: A Guide to the Reading of Documents and Manuscripts* (London: Faber and Faber, 1966); Jean F. Preston and Laetitia Yeandle (formerly Kennedy-Skipton), *English Handwriting 1400–1650: An Introductory Manual* (Binghamton, N.Y.: Medieval & Renaissance Texts & Studies, 1992); Anthony G. Petti, *English Literary Hands from Chaucer to Dryden* (London: Edward Arnold, 1977).

18 The terms 'upper case' and 'lower case' are properly applied only to printed and not handwritten letter forms; 'capital' or 'majuscule' and 'small' or 'minuscule' are applied to handwritten letter forms.

19 Cocker, *The Pen's Triumph*, sig. B3ᵛ.

20 See throughout the 'Hulton Letters' (British Library Additional MS 74286).

21 Henry E. Huntington Library MS EL 34 B 17.

22 R. B. McKerrow, 'The Relationship of English Printed Books to Authors' Manuscripts during the Sixteenth and Seventeenth Centuries: *The 1928 Sandars Lectures*', ed. Carlo M. Bajetta, *Studies in Bibliography*, 53 (2000), pp. 23, 26.

23 *Henslowe's Diary*, ed. Foakes, pp. 107, 110–11.

24 Chettle, 'To the Gentlemen Readers', *Kind-Harts Dreame* (London: William Wright, 1592), sig. A4ʳ.

25 McKerrow, 'The Relationship of English Printed Books to Authors' Manuscripts during the Sixteenth and Seventeenth Centuries, p. 39.

26 R. B. McKerrow's *An Introduction to Bibliography for Literary Students* (Oxford: Clarendon Press, 1927), and Philip Gaskell's *A New Introduction to Bibliography* (Oxford: Oxford University Press, 1972), pp. 74–5, discuss paper-making.

27 For this information I thank Mrs. Ruby Reid Thompson, a paper historian who has presented her findings at a number of conferences.

28 This is Gurr's calculation from figures provided by Betty R. Masters; see *The Shakespeare Company, 1594–1642*, p. 103, note 39.

29 For example, see the case I outline for the Portland scribal manuscript of *Hengist, King of Kent* (copied *c.* 1640) in my Malone Society Reprints edition of the play (Oxford: Oxford University Press, 2003). The tightness of the modern binding prohibits any close examination of the original binding, and thus it is not possible to say with certainty whether the sheets are bound in a series of separate bifolia or are quired, or contain any half sheets other than the *dramatis personae* list. As the scribe was most likely copying from a theatrical 'book', he would have been able to determine how many leaves in all he would need to use, so, in theory, he could have quired all the leaves before he began writing. However, the bifolium numbering suggests that the scribe worked with one folded sheet at a time before they were sewn together. One other feature in the manuscript would support this view. The scribe has sometimes written so far into the right margin of recto pages that his markings continue slightly on to the next recto page (as in f. 4). Occasionally, his markings, particularly in ruling off-stage directions or act–scene notations, stray on to the previous recto page. This was probably due to the top recto page of the bifolium springing back and getting caught in his ruler as he was writing on the bottom recto page (as in f. 7). Every occurrence of these two types of stray marking is within a single bifolium; thus the scribe appears to have worked with individual, unbound, bifolia throughout. This type of unquired construction of the manuscript is fairly common in the period.

30 On the characteristics of the Diary and other contemporary account books, see S. P. Cerasano, 'Henslowe's "Curious" Diary', *Medieval and Renaissance Drama in England*, 17 (2005), 72–85.

31 British Library MS Egerton 2625, f. 9.

32 British Library Cotton MS Tiberius E. X.

33 Cocker, *The Pen's Triumph*, sigs. B1ᵛ–B4ʳ.

34 Cocker, *The Pen's Triumph*, sig. D4ʳ.

35 S. P. Cerasano and Marion Wynne-Davies provide records of women's participation in drama in their book *Renaissance Drama by Women: Texts and Documents*.

36 Arthur Brown, Introduction, *The Lady Mother by Henry Glapthorne* (Oxford: Oxford University Press, 1959), p. vi.

37 Fredson Bowers, for example, argues that Shakespeare wrote his own fair copies, and Gary Taylor argues that he did not. See Taylor's discussion of Bowers in his 'General Introduction' to *William Shakespeare: A Textual Companion*, p. 12.

38 British Library Manuscript Loan 98. See also Antony Hammond and Doreen Delvecchio, 'The Melbourne Manuscript and John Webster: A Reproduction and Transcript', *Studies in Bibliography*, 41 (1988), 1–32; National Archives SP 14/44/62*.

39 British Library Egerton MS 1994.

40 Alnwick Castle MS 507.

41 Heywood, *The Exemplary Lives and Memorable Acts of Nine the Most Worthy Women of the World* (London: Tho. Cotes for Richard Royston, 1640), sig. FF4ᵛ.

42 Honigmann makes this argument in his seminal book, *The Stability of Shakespeare's Text* (London, E. Arnold, Ltd, 1965), pp. 200–6.

43 As Arthur Brown, in his preface to his Malone Society Reprints edition of *The Captives by Thomas Heywood* (Oxford, 1953), p. xii, notes, it is 'unlikely' that there was ever a rougher authorial draft behind this foul paper manuscript. Also see Greg's discussion of the play as foul papers in *The Shakespeare First Folio*, p. 109.

44 British Library Egerton MS 2828.

45 Each leaf is now separately set within window-mounts. The leaves are no longer conjugate with one another and the original quire formation is not clear. Thus the manuscript can no longer be collated in its original form. It has also suffered some slight water damage. However, very little of the text has been lost and this does not affect its status as a foul paper manuscript.

46 Thomson, 'A Quarto "Marked for Performance": Evidence of What?', p. 177.

47 For a full discussion as well as a complete transcription of this manuscript, see Brown's Malone Society Reprints edition.

48 A. Dessen and L. Thomson, Introduction, *A Dictionary of Stage Directions in the English Drama 1580–1642* (Cambridge: Cambridge University Press, 1999), pp. viii–ix. In addition, they note: 'Who would be a better judge of what could or could not be accomplished by the players than an experienced writer who had seen many of his plays move from script to stage?' (p. x).

49 H. R. Woudhuysen, 'A New Manuscript Fragment of Sidney's *Old Arcadia*: The Huddleston Manuscript', in *English Manuscript Studies 1100–1700, Volume 11: Manuscripts and their Makers in the English Renaissance*, ed. Peter Beal and Grace Ioppolo (London: The British Library Press, 2002), pp. 52–69.

50 See Greg's discussion of Fletcher's uncertainties during his composition of *Bonduca* in his preface to his Malone Society Reprints edition, p. xiii; and C. J. Sisson's discussion of Massinger's composition practices in his preface to his Malone Society edition of *Believe as You List* (Oxford, 1928), pp. xiii–xv. For further discussion of Heywood's revision of at least one other play, see Madeleine Doran and W. W. Greg's Introduction to *If You Know Not Me You Know Nobody Part II* (Oxford: Oxford University Press, 1935), pp. xv–xviii.

51 The fragment, British Library Loan MS 98, was found at Melbourne Hall in Derbyshire in 1986 by Edward Saunders. Antony Hammond and Doreen Delvecchio followed Pryor in attributing the text to Webster, while I. A. Shapiro attributed it to James Shirley because the text resembles that in his play, *The Traitor*. See Beal, *Index of English Literary Manuscripts 1450–1700*, Vol. 2, part 2, p. 347, and Hammond and Delvecchio, 'The Melbourne Manuscript and John Webster: A Reproduction and Transcript', pp. 1–32.

52 For example, see R. B. McKerrow, 'The Elizabethan Printer and Dramatic Manuscripts', *The Library*, ser. 3, 12 (1931), 253–75; R. C. Bald, 'The Foul Papers of a Revision', *The Library*, Ser. 4, 26 (1946), 37–50; Greg, *The Shakespeare First Folio*, pp. 109ff.; and Robert Kean Turner, 'Revisions and Repetition-Brackets in Fletcher's *A Wife for a Month*', *Studies in Bibliography*, 36 (1983), 178–90.

53 Bentley, *The Jacobean and Caroline Stage*, 4:339.

4 'A fayre Copy herafter': dramatists and fair copies

1 See E. A. J. Honigmann's important discussion of this subject in *The Stability of Shakespeare's Text*.

2 Huntington Library MS 500.

3 In 'Play Identifications: *The Wise Man of West Chester* and *John a Kent and John a Cumber*; *Longshanks* and *Edward I*, *Huntington Library Quarterly*, 47 (1984), 1–11, Roslyn L. Knutson states that Chambers misread the date as 1596, Greg misread the date as 1595, and I. A. Shapiro correctly read it as 1590. However, the flourish still visible at the top of the last number in this date in the manuscript (Huntington Library MS 500) makes clear that it is a 5, not a 0. Hence the date is 1595.

4 For a transcription of this manuscript, see Muriel St. Clare Byrne's Malone Society Reprints edition of *John a Kent & John a Cumber* (Oxford: Oxford University Press, 1923); also see her Introduction, pp. 2, 14, 24, 34, 46.

5 Dulwich MS 7:10^r–14^v, 15^v, 21^v, 27^{r-v}, 93^v; *Henslowe's Diary*, ed. Foakes, pp. 26–34, 36, 47, 59, 60, 181.

6 British Library MS Lansdowne 807. On the debate on identifying the manuscript's hand as authorial, see Henry D. Jantzen's Introduction, *The Queen of Corsica by Francis Jaques 1642* (Oxford: Oxford University Press, 1989), pp. v–ix.

7 Wells, Textual Introduction, *Antony and Cleopatra*, in Wells and Taylor *et al.*, *William Shakespeare: A Textual Companion*, p. 549.

8 See John Jowett's Introduction to the play in Wells and Taylor *et al.*, *William Shakespeare: A Textual Companion*, pp. 288–9, in which he discusses the compositors' difficulty with the foul papers and debates critics' theories on the use of Q1 to print Q2. Also see G. Blakemore Evans's Textual Analysis in his edition of the play (Cambridge: Cambridge University Press, 1984), pp. 206–12.

9 British Library Harley MS 7368.

10 Greg, *The Shakespeare First Folio*, p. 109. On Hand D as Shakespearean foul papers, also see E. A. J. Honigmann, '*Sir Thomas More* and Asylum Seekers', *Shakespeare Survey*, 57 (2004), 225–35, and 'Shakespeare's Deletions and False-Starts', *The Review of English Studies*, 56 (2005), 37–48.

11 Petti, *English Literary Hands from Chaucer to Dryden*, p. 87.

12 Scott McMillin, *The Elizabethan Theatre and The Book of Sir Thomas More* (Ithaca, N.Y.: Cornell University Press, 1987), pp. 144–7. Thomas Merriam recently extended earlier arguments of E. A. J. Honigmann and McMillin that Munday was predominantly a copyist rather than the composer of the play. Merriam argues that Munday's portions of the manuscript suggest he was fair-copying another author's text to pass it off as his own, rather than composing or fair-copying his own text. Merriam claims Munday did so 'to create a provocation in order to injure a theatre company under suspicion because of its patron, its playwrights, and its daring and popular presentations on the public stage'. Merriam, 'The Misunderstanding of Munday as Author of *Sir Thomas More*', *The Review of English Studies*, 51 (2000), 540–81. However, Merriam's failure to compare Munday's autograph characteristics with those of authors and scribes, as foul and fair copyists, in the numerous other extant manuscripts of the period (relying instead, evidently, on Malone Society reprints of the play-texts) provides a weak foundation on which to build his case. Instead, Munday's contributions in the *More* manuscript are his fair copies of his own foul papers either as sole or as joint author, closely resembling his practice in his fair copy manuscript of *John a Kent and John a Cumber*. Only by surveying all extant authorial fair copies could Merriam command as much information as would be necessary to promote Munday's work as copyist rather than composer in the *More* manuscript.

13 The failure to study the original details of this manuscript results in the kind of incorrect argument presented by Jeffrey Masten that 'as the manuscript of *Sir Thomas More* complexly suggests, early modern playwrights were far less

interested in keeping their hands, pages, and conversation [i.e. sexual intercourse] separate than are the twentieth century critics who have studied them' (Masten, 'Playwrighting and Collaboration', in *A New History of Early English Drama*, p. 361). In fact, in this collaborative manuscript, only Heywood, who acted as later corrector of Munday's original work, shares any space at all with another dramatist. On fol. 10^v and 11^r *only* Heywood has marginally added in three places brief lines for the Clown, whose presence Munday had not included in the scene. Heywood also makes additions on separate sheets. Heywood's alterations call attention to his own separate work, clearly written after Munday has ceased to work on the text, and do *not* show any individual or mutual interest in sharing 'hands, pages, and conversation'. All the major and the other minor additions in the play, with the exception of those annotations made by the 'book-keeper' and the censor, are written either on *additional* pages or on the other side of the pages written by Munday. In every occurrence in which an additional sheet was pasted onto Munday's text, as in fols. 6^r, 11^v and 14^r, the original text on which they were placed was heavily deleted with large X's. That is, Munday's work was made illegible and was therefore expunged before the work of each of his collaborators replaced it. Thus, contrary to Masten's chimerical statement, the early modern dramatists who acted as Munday's collaborators, including Dekker, Chettle, Heywood and, probably, Shakespeare, insisted on keeping their hands, pages and conversation separate in this particular manuscript. Each author in *The Book of Sir Thomas More* demanded separate space that was entirely his own, probably in an attempt to display his own individual capabilities as a form of recognition or competition.

14 The manuscript requires special permission for viewing from the British Library and is usually given to readers a few leaves at a time, each of which is under 'Perspex' (lucite). If studied in microfilm or photocopy form, it is nearly impossible to discern that the numerous strikeouts and other deletions in the three pages are in a hand and ink other than that used by Hand D. I am very grateful to the staff of the British Library Manuscripts Room for allowing me special permission to see all the leaves at the same time on several occasions in the last fifteen years.

15 Petti, *English Literary Hands from Chaucer to Dryden*, p. 87.

16 University of Aberystwyth Brogyntyn MS 1942; Bodleian Library Malone MS 12.

17 I use Greg's line numbers in his transcription of the pages in his Malone Society edition (pp. 73–9).

18 See Petti, *English Literary Hands from Chaucer to Dryden*, p. 6.

19 See for example Taylor's reluctance to accept the argument that Folio *Comedy of Errors* was printed entirely from foul papers because its 'act-divisions are difficult to attribute to undivided foul paper copy'; also John Jowett's claim that 'act divisions would probably not be a feature of Shakespeare's foul papers for *Measure* (or the original prompt-book), whereas act intervals would be usual in later theatrical performance' (in Wells and Taylor *et al.*, *William Shakespeare: A Textual Companion*, 266, 468). Such claims are made repeatedly throughout the textual introductions in this work by all the editors. Taylor repeats this argument in *Shakespeare Re-shaped*, co-written with John Jowett (Oxford: Clarendon Press, 1993), pp. 3–8.

20 For a discussion of such notations, see Robert K. Turner, 'Act-End Notations in Some Elizabethan Plays', *Modern Philology*, 72 (1975), 238–47.

21 Wells, Textual Introduction, *Twelfth Night*, in Wells and Taylor *et al.*, *William Shakespeare: A Textual Companion*, p. 421.

22 On these scribes' extreme faithfulness to their copy, see my essay, 'Revision,

Manuscript Transmission and Scribal Practice in Middleton's *Hengist, King of Kent, or, The Mayor of Queenborough*', *Critical Survey*, 7 (1995), 319–31. Also see the Introduction to my Malone Society Reprints edition of *Hengist, King of Kent, or, The Mayor of Queenborough*.

23   British Library Egerton MS 1994; Boswell, Introduction, *Edmund Ironside or War Hath Made All Friends* (Oxford: Oxford University Press, 1928), p. vi.

24   William B. Long, 'Stage-Directions: A Misinterpreted Factor in Determining Textual Provenance', *TEXT: Transactions of the Society for Textual Scholarship*, 2 (1985), 121–37.

25   Bowers, *On Editing Shakespeare*, p. 18.

26   Peter W. M. Blayney, 'The Printing of Playbooks', in *A New History of Early English Drama*, ed. John D. Cox and David Scott Kastan (Columbia: Columbia University Press, 1997) p. 419, n. 18.

27   Beal, *In Praise of Scribes*, p. 69.

28   Moseley, 'The Stationer to the Reader', in *Comedies and Tragedies written by Francis Beaumont and John Fletcher* (London: Humphrey Moseley, 1647), sig. A2ᵛ.

29   Edward Dering paid £2 for two copies of the 1623 Shakespeare First Folio; the prices for a Folio volume may, of course, have risen considerably by 1647. See T. N. S. Lennam, 'Sir Edward Dering's Collection of Playbooks, 1619–1624', pp. 145–53.

30   Brown, Introduction, *The Captives by Thomas Heywood*, ed. Arthur Brown (Oxford: Oxford University Press, 1953), pp. xi–xii.

31   Thomson, 'A Quarto "Marked for Performance": Evidence of What?', p. 177.

32   Brown, Introduction, *The Captives by Thomas Heywood*, p. xii,

33   Greg, *The Shakespeare First Folio*, p. 95.

34   Victoria and Albert Art Library, Dyce MS 9.

35   *The Dramatic Records of Sir Henry Herbert*, ed. Joseph Quincy Adams (New Haven: Yale University Press, 1917), p. 30; *The Control and Censorship of Caroline Drama: The Records of Sir Henry Herbert, Master of the Revels 1623–73*, ed. N. W. Bawcutt (Oxford: Clarendon Press, 1996), pp. 57–9, 160.

36   Greg, *The Shakespeare First Folio*, p. v.

37   British Library Lansdowne MS 807. For a discussion of this text, see Greg's Introduction, *The Second Maiden's Tragedy, 1611* (Oxford: Oxford University Press, 1910).

38   Wiltshire Record Office MS 865. See John H. P. Pafford and W. W. Greg's Introduction to *The Soddered Citizen* (Oxford: Oxford University Press, 1936), p. viii.

39   Alnwick Castle MS 507.

40   See G. R. Proudfoot's portion of J. W. Lever's Introduction, which he finished after Lever's death, in *The Wasp or Subject's Precedent* (Oxford: Oxford University Press, 1976), p. xix.

41   See J. W. Lever's Introduction, finished by G. R. Proudfoot, to *The Wasp or Subject's Precedent*, pp. viii ff. This superb introduction demonstrates how much we can learn from reading and analysing all the physical aspects of a dramatic manuscript.

42   *The Dramatic Records of Sir Henry Herbert*, ed. Adams, p. 21; *The Control and Censorship of Caroline Drama*, ed. Bawcutt, pp. 183, 185.

43   See Greg's many studies of dramatic manuscripts; Proudfoot's work, especially as editor or general editor of various Malone Society Reprints editions of early modern plays; Beal's two-volume, four-part *Index of English Literary Manuscripts 1450–1700*, and Woudhuysen, *Sir Philip Sidney and the Circulation of Manuscripts 1558–1640*, pp. 134–45.

44   Cardiff (Wales) Central Library MS 4.12, f. 10ᵛ, 16ᵛ.

45 See H. Littledale and W. W. Greg's preface and notes to their Malone Society Reprints edition of *The Welsh Embassador* (Oxford: Oxford University Press, 1920), pp. vii, 1.

46 Victoria and Albert Art Library Dyce MS 10.

47 See Kathleen Marguerite Lea, *The Parliament of Love* (Oxford: Oxford University Press, 1929), p. xiii.

48 Lea, Introduction, *The Parliament of Love*, p. xiii.

49 The term is Lea's in her Introduction, *The Parliament of Love*, p. xv.

50 Alnwick Castle MS 507.

51 W. L. Renwick and W. W. Greg, Introduction, *John of Bordeaux or The Second Part of Friar Bacon* (Oxford: Oxford University Press, 1936), p. vii. They also contend that the second hand may be the same as in the plots of *The Seven Deadly Sins* and *The Battle of Alcazar*.

52 Renwick and Greg, Introduction, *John of Bordeaux*, p. viii.

53 See Renwick and Greg, Introduction, *John of Bordeaux*, p. viii.

54 See Renwick and Greg, Introduction, *John of Bordeaux*, p. viii.

55 Dulwich College MS 7:108^v; *Henslowe's Diary*, ed. Foakes, p. 207. Another entry on 29 December (MS 7:109; *Diary*, p. 207) notes that Chettle has also been paid for a prologue and epilogue for the court, but the play is not specified. He may have collaborated with or taken over from Middleton in providing these pieces for *Friar Bacon and Friar Bungay*.

56 Quarto 1, sig. E4^v.

57 Other types of books, including those serving as copy for printed editions, can show the same type of non-intrusive annotation by a book-keeper. A copy of an undated edition (*c.*1603) of *A Looking Glass for London and England* (first printed in 1594), a play which originally belonged to the Queen's Men and then to Prince Charles's Men, has theatrical annotations in an early seventeenth-century hand. Written in two or more hands over a period of time, these annotations include entrance and exit directions, cues for properties, music and other stage effects. They also include at least one note to 'Clear' the stage at a scene's conclusion, similar to the book-keeper's annotations in Heywood's autograph manuscript of *The Captives*. The text also shows cuts and marginal additions. Charles Read Baskervill argues that these types of properties and effects used suggest professional performance in London, but 'the changes are very few and as brief as possible', with the printed stage directions given preference. What is particularly clear is that other directions that we might now consider necessary for stage action have not been added, nor have obviously 'corrupt' lines of dialogue been corrected. Baskervill concludes that 'clearly the prompter in the company or companies using this book was not expected to concern himself with details of the text'; Baskervill, 'A Prompt Copy of *A Looking Glass for London and England*', pp. 50–1.

58 See Richard Dutton, *Mastering the Revels: The Regulation and Censorship of English Renaissance Drama* (Iowa City: University of Iowa Press, 1991), p. 94.

59 British Library Egerton MS 2623.

60 See Dutton, *Mastering the Revels*, pp. 145–55.

61 Albert Feuillerat, *Documents Relating to the Office of the Revels in the Time of Queen Elizabeth* (Louvain: A. Uystpruyst, 1908), p. 52.

62 See Chambers, *The Elizabethan Stage*, 4:229–33.

63 For an illustration of this manuscript (Lambeth Palace Library MS 4267, f. 2) and a partial transcription of it, see the Sotheby's English Literature and History sale catalogue, 16/17 December 1996, pp. 46–7.

64 Bentley, *The Profession of Dramatist in Shakespeare's Time*, 150. He cites other documents of the period, including acting company licences, that demand that new plays be submitted to the censor.

65 *The Dramatic Records of Sir Henry Herbert*, ed. Adams, p. 21; *The Control and Censorship of Caroline Drama*, ed. Bawcutt, pp. 182–3. Also see T. H. Howard-Hill, 'Crane's 1619 "Promptbook" of *Barnavelt* and Theatrical Processes', *Modern Philology*, 86 (1988–9), 146–70.

66 *The Control and Censorship of Caroline Drama*, ed. Bawcutt, p. 44.

67 *The Dramatic Records of Sir Henry Herbert*, ed. Adams, pp. 19–21; *The Control and Censorship of Caroline Drama*, ed. Bawcutt, pp. 182–3.

68 See Bawcutt's discussion of this point in *The Control and Censorship of Caroline Drama*, ed. Bawcutt, p. 43.

69 Introduction to 1st edition, *Henslowe's Diary*, ed. Foakes, p. xxix.

70 Dulwich College MS 7:54^r, 67^r, 69^r; *Henslowe's Diary*, ed. Foakes, pp. 106, 130, 134.

71 Dulwich College MS 7:20^r, 23^v, 81^v, 83^v, 44^r, 47^v, 63^r; *Henslowe's Diary*, ed. Foakes, pp. 44, 51, 86, 94, 121, 162, 164.

72 See Feuillerat, *Documents Relating to the Office of the Revels in the Time of Queen Elizabeth*, p. 401.

73 *The Dramatic Records of Sir Henry Herbert*, ed. Adams, p. 19; *The Control and Censorship of Caroline Drama*, ed. Bawcutt, p. 172.

74 Bentley, *The Profession of Dramatist in Shakespeare's Time*, p. 154.

75 *The Dramatic Records of Sir Henry Herbert*, ed. Adams, p. 25; *The Control and Censorship of Caroline Drama*, ed. Bawcutt, p. 142.

76 *The Dramatic Records of Sir Henry Herbert*, ed. Adams, pp. 34–5; *The Control and Censorship of Caroline Drama*, ed. Bawcutt, p. 182.

77 *The Dramatic Records of Sir Henry Herbert*, ed. Adams, p. 22.

78 *The Dramatic Records of Sir Henry Herbert*, ed. Adams, p. 23; *The Control and Censorship of Caroline Drama*, ed. Bawcutt, p. 204.

79 Dutton, *Mastering the Revels*, p. 1.

80 National Library of Scotland Adv. MS 33.3.19, f. 27^v; *Conversations with Drummond*, in *Ben Jonson*, ed. C. H. Hereford and Percy and Evelyn Simpson, 11 vols (Oxford: Clarendon Press, 1925–52), 1:140.

81 The conflicting evidence of what punishment the three men were subjected to is discussed by R. Van Fossen in Introduction, *Eastward Ho!* (Manchester: Manchester University Press, 1979), 4–7. He concludes from extant letters of Chapman and Jonson that the censorship of the play came after rather than before performance, and that the 'booke' had not received the 'allowance' of the Lord Chamberlain. However, it is not clear whether it had been shown to Tilney, the current Master of the Revels, before this episode of censorship took place.

82 See 'Life of Jonson' in *Ben Jonson*, ed. Hereford and P. and E. Simpson, 1:38–9.

83 Dutton, *Mastering the Revels*, p. 90.

84 *The Works of Thomas Nashe*, ed. R. B. McKerrow, 5 vols (Oxford: Basil Blackwell, 1904–10), 3:153–4.

85 Cited in 'Life of Ben Jonson', in *Ben Jonson*, ed. Hereford and P. and E. Simpson, 1:15–16.

86 Hatfield House CP 114/58; *HMC: Salisbury*, p. 605.

87 *The Dramatic Records of Sir Henry Herbert*, ed. Adams, p. 19; *The Control and Censorship of Caroline Drama*, ed. Bawcutt, p. 177.

88 *The Dramatic Records of Sir Henry Herbert*, ed. Adams, p. 21; *The Control and Censorship of Caroline Drama*, ed. Bawcutt, p. 184.

89 Turner, 'Revisions and Repetition-Brackets in Fletcher's *A Wife for a Month*', p. 190.

90 Jonson sometimes employs cultural or popular stereotypes of actors as wastrels or scoundrels. For such stereotypes, see Wickham *et al.*, *English Professional Theatre 1530–1660*, pp. 157–210.

91 *The Tragedy of Philotas* (London: M. Bradwood for Edward Blount, 1607); on this case of censorship, see Bentley, *The Profession of Dramatist in Shakespeare's Time*, pp. 168ff.

92 Gurr, *The Shakespearean Stage, 1574–1642*, pp. 51–2.

93 Dutton, *Licensing, Censorship and Authorship in Early Modern England*, p. 39.

94 Cited by Bentley in *The Profession of Dramatist in Shakespeare's Time*, p. 175.

95 *Collections, Vol. II, Part II*, ed. W. W. Greg (Oxford: Oxford University Press, 1923), p. 149.

96 British Library MS Harley 7368. For a transcription of this manuscript see Greg's edition of *The Book of Sir Thomas More*.

97 British Library Additional MS 18653, f. 5ᵛ.

98 British Library, Egerton MS 1994, f. 349ᵛ.

99 For a discussion of this manuscript, see John Johnson, Introduction, *The Launching of the Mary* (Oxford: Oxford University Press, 1933).

100 *The Dramatic Records of Sir Henry Herbert*, ed. Adams, p. 19; *The Control and Censorship of Caroline Drama*, ed. Bawcutt, pp. 171–2.

101 Dulwich MS 1:81.

102 *The Dramatic Records of Sir Henry Herbert*, ed. Adams, p. 21; *The Control and Censorship of Caroline Drama*, ed. Bawcutt, p. 183.

103 For a discussion of Herbert's fairly typical treatment of one manuscript, see John Henry Walter's preface to *The Launching of the Mary*, p. x.

104 For the continuing debate on the play staged on this occasion, see Blair Worden, 'Which play was performed at the Globe theatre on 7 February 1601?', *London Review of Books*, vol. 25, no. 13, 10 July 2003, pp. 22–4, and succeeding issues with letters to and from Worden and Frank Kermode.

105 *The Second part of Henrie the fourth* (London: V. S. for Andrew Wise and William Aspley, 1600), sig. L1ᵛ. We lack such direct, contemporary, external or internal evidence of censorship in other Shakespearean plays. However, over the years, critics have investigated the possibility of censorship in numerous others, including *Hamlet, King Lear* and *Othello*, as well as other history plays, including *Richard III* and one or more of the *Henry VI* plays. Such arguments for censorship are usually made to explain difficult, nonsensical or inept readings, gaps, cruxes or lacunae in Quarto and Folio texts, or they are based on post-Jacobean sensibilities of what would have given offence. All that we can say with certainty is that Shakespeare crossed the boundaries with at least the two *Henry IV* plays. See Bentley, *The Jacobean and Caroline Stage*, 3:119. The early Quartos of *Richard II* may lack the deposition scene for a variety of reasons not stemming from the censor's demands, either at the time of licensing or after performance. Shakespeare's company may have themselves withheld the scene from the stage, thereby practising their own censorship, or they may not have included it in the printer's copy for the first three Quartos, as some have argued. It is even possible that the scene may not have been written until after 1598.

106 *The Dramatic Records of Sir Henry Herbert*, ed. Adams, p. 19; *The Control and Censorship of Caroline Drama*, ed. Bawcutt, p. 177.

107 *The Dramatic Records of Sir Henry Herbert*, ed. Adams, pp. 19–20; *The Control and Censorship of Caroline Drama*, ed. Bawcutt, p 180.

5 'Plaide in 1613': authorial and scribal manuscripts in the playhouse

1 See Cyrus Hoy's discussion of the shares of each collaborator in his Textual Introduction to his edition of *The Honest Man's Fortune*, in *The Collected Works of Beaumont and Fletcher*, gen. ed. Fredson Bowers, 10 vols (Cambridge: Cambridge University Press, 1966–96), 10:3–4. Also see Gerritsen's Introduction to his edition of the play.

2 Victoria and Albert Art Library Dyce MS 9.
3 Hoy argues in his Textual Introduction to his edition (p. 5) that the manuscript must have been copied from foul papers (also see Gerritsen's Introduction to his edition, p. xliii). But it could have been copied from a manuscript at any stage of the play's transmission; in any event, the foul papers appear to have been difficult to read.
4 Hoy, Textual Introduction, *The Honest Man's Fortune*, p. 9.
5 Victoria and Albert Art Library Dyce MS 10.
6 See Greg, Introduction, *Bonduca by John Fletcher*, pp. vii–ix. R. B. McKerrow discusses four signs of a book-keeper at work in a manuscript: warnings of actors or properties to be made ready; mentions of character or properties appearing later in a scene; actors' names as a 'gloss'; and characters entering before the proper time. See 'The Elizabethan Printer and Dramatic Manuscripts, pp. 270–3.
7 See G. M. Pinciss and G. R. Proudfoot, Introduction, *The Faithful Friends* (Oxford: Oxford University Press, 1975), pp. x–xii, xv.
8 See J. H. P. Pafford, Introduction, *The Soddered Citizen* (Oxford: Oxford University Press, 1936), p. viii.
9 British Library Egerton MS 1994.
10 On the manuscript's characteristics, see John Henry Walter and W. W. Greg's edition of *Charlemagne or the Distracted Emperor* (Oxford: Oxford University Press, 1938), pp. vi–viii.
11 See Foakes and Gibson's discussion of these points in Introduction, *The Telltale*, p. vii. William B. Long argues that the manuscript is 'a scribal copy of the playwright's holograph that was used as a theatrical playbook which was now being prepared as a reading copy for a private person, or for some other nontheatrical use', in 'Dulwich MS. XX, *The Telltale*: Clues to Provenance', *Medieval and Renaissance Drama in England*, 17 (2005), p. 183.
12 See Francis W. Steer, *A History of the Worshipful Company of Scriveners of London* (London and Chichester: Phillimore & Co. Ltd, 1973), p. 68.
13 This manuscript is part of the Henslowe–Alleyn archive at Dulwich College, London and may have been associated with either or both men, especially if it was among the manuscripts donated by William Cartwright. A non-authorial appropriation appears at the beginning of this manuscript, where another hand has written 'mine' in the left margin of the first speech, perhaps to claim the manuscript or the speech as personal property. As the manuscript spent some years outside Dulwich College, eventually being reclaimed from James Boswell the younger's library in the early nineteenth century, the claim of 'mine' may not be contemporary to the manuscript.
14 Sisson, Introduction, *Believe as You List by Philip Massinger 1631* (Oxford: Oxford University Press, 1928), p. v.
15 See Sisson, Introduction, *Believe as You List*, p. xiii, for further discussion of these points.
16 British Library Egerton MS 2828, f. 29^v.
17 Sisson, Introduction, *Believe as You List*, pp. xxv–xxvi.
18 Sisson, Introduction, *Believe as You List*, pp. xvii–xxi. He demonstrates why the manuscript took this circuitous and non-linear route of progress, and further details the play's authorial revision.
19 See Woudhuysen, *Sir Philip Sidney and the Circulation of Manuscripts 1558–1640*, pp. 207–391; also see Harold Love, *Scribal Publication in Seventeenth-Century England*; and Beal, *In Praise of Scribes*.
20 Greg argued that this manuscript is a scribal fair copy of foul papers, and he identified three other hands in it, an author's, the censor's and book-keeper's, who added stage directions, some of which include actors' names. See Greg,

Introduction, *The Second Maiden's Tragedy 1611*, ed. W. W. Greg (Oxford: Oxford University Press, 1910), pp. vi–vii.

21 This 'fair' copy is far from fair (the complaint made by Herbert at the end of *The Launching of the Mary*), for it contains a number of authorial corrections as well as additions and revisions, written out on small sheets and pasted over the replaced passages. The extra sheets were most likely added after Herbert objected to the original passages and demanded changes to the manuscript, although the other revisions and corrections may have been made at another time. So, all of the alterations may not have been made at once. See Greg, Introduction, *The Second Maiden's Tragedy 1611*, pp. viii–xii.

22 Arthur Brown, Introduction, *The Lady Mother by Henry Glapthorne* (Oxford: Oxford University Press, 1959), p. xiii.

23 Brown, Introduction, *The Lady Mother by Henry Glapthorne*, pp. vii–ix, xiii.

24 'Amateur' is Bentley's term; see *The Jacobean and Caroline Stage*, 4:475.

25 Andrew Gurr, *The Shakespearean Stage; 1574–1642*, pp. 41–2, 45–6. See also *The Shakespeare Company, 1594–1642*, p. 13.

26 I am very grateful to Herbert Berry and to Andrew Gurr for clarifying very complicated issues relating to the three consortia for me. See Berry's discussion of these financial arrangements in *English Professional Theatre 1530–1660*, ed. Wickham, Berry and Ingram, pp. 493–5, 502–3. He accepts that the financial shares for the first Globe were similar to those documented for the second Globe, hence the Burbages had larger shares than other investors, including Shakespeare. Gurr is more cautious in *The Shakespeare Company, 1594–1642*, pp. 85–119.

27 See Gurr, *The Shakespearean Stage 1574–1642*, pp. 193–4. This argument is contradicted in Gurr's *The Shakespeare Company, 1594–1642*, p. xiv, in which he states that 'even Shakespeare, himself a company co-owner and a performer of his own scripts, never expected his texts to be transferred to the stage as he wrote them. The company did what it pleased with its scripts, as on more than one occasion Jonson, Webster and other writers lamented.' Whatever the company did with the scripts, the members could and did consult dramatists still attached to the company, as extant manuscripts show. On rehearsal, also see Stern, *Rehearsal from Shakespeare to Sheridan*.

28 Gurr, *The Shakespearean Stage, 1574–1642*, p. 85.

29 See R. C. Bald and Arthur Brown, Introduction, *The Knave in Grain 1640* (Oxford: Oxford University Press, 1961), p. vii.

30 Huntington Library MS HM 741.

31 See Ioppolo, *Revising Shakespeare*, pp. 65–70.

32 See Laurie E. Maguire, *Shakespearean Suspect Texts: The 'Bad' Quartos and their Contexts* (Cambridge: Cambridge University Press, 1996), who provides a history of 'New Bibliographical' theories for the provenance of the so-called 'bad' quartos; and Peter W. M. Blayney, *The Bookshops in Paul's Cross Churchyard* (London: The Bibliographical Society, 1990), who has convincingly argued in this essay and elsewhere that what we have long accepted as a 'pirated' text is in fact not a product of printer theft but collusion.

33 See Bentley, *The Jacobean and Caroline Stage*, 5:1100–1.

34 British Library Egerton MS 1994.

35 Greg, '*The Escapes of Jupiter*', in *Collected Papers*, p. 169. For a transcription of the manuscript, see Henry D. Jantzen's edition of *The Escapes of Jupiter by Thomas Heywood* (Oxford: Oxford University Press, 1978).

36 Greg, '*The Escapes of Jupiter*', p. 173. Greg further argues that 'this play adds one more to the indubitable instances of revision to be taken into account by those who seek to minimize the practice' (p. 176).

37 Victoria and Albert Art Library, Dyce Pressmark 25.A.106; Folger Shakespeare

Library STC 17634/copy 1; 17636/copy 1; 17640.2/copy 1; 17641/copy 1; 17642/copy 3. See Greg, 'Massinger's Autograph Corrections in *The Duke of Milan*, 1623', and 'More Massinger Corrections', in *The Collected Papers of Sir Walter Greg*, pp. 110–13, 120–2.

38 Malone Society *Collections*, Vol. 2, Part 3, 384.

39 Nottingham University Library MS PwV20. For a discussion of the manuscript's features, see the Introduction to my Malone Society edition of *Hengist, King of Kent*, pp. v–xvii.

40 The Portland–Nottingham copy of *Hengist, King of Kent* has inkblots made by the scribe at the time of copying that are mixed with gold flecks, so the paper was already gilt-edged before the scribe began to write.

41 Moseley, 'The Stationer to the Reader', in *Comedies and Tragedies written by Francis Beaumont and John Fletcher*, sig. A3^r.

42 The manuscripts are housed at Alnwick Castle, Northumberland and elsewhere, including the Huntington Library (see MS HM 4, for example); also see *English Professional Theatre, 1530–1660*, ed. Wickham, Berry and Ingram, p. 317.

43 British Library Lansdown MS 807, f. 1^{r-v}.

44 Greg, 'The Bakings of Betsy', *The Library*, ser. 3, 2 (1911), pp. 225–59. Greg's view of Warburton has become standard. However, judging from Warburton's editorial comments in his 1747 reissue of Pope's edition, *The Works of Shakespear*, ed. Alexander Pope and William Warburton, 8 vols (London: Printed for J. and P. Knapton *et al.*, 1747), he appears to have been serious about studying the documents of the period.

45 Lennam, 'Sir Edward Dering's Collection of Playbooks, 1619–1624, pp. 145–53.

46 No manuscript that served as printed copy for a play from this period is extant. Greg discusses a manuscript used as printer's copy for a translation of Ariosto's *Orlando Furioso* in 'An Elizabethan Printer and his Copy', reprinted in *Collected Papers*, pp. 95–109.

47 See Greg and F. P. Wilson, Introduction, *The Witch* (Oxford: Oxford University Press, 1950), pp. vii ff.

48 National Library of Wales, Aberystwyth, Brogyntyn MS II.42.

49 See T. H. Howard-Hill, Introduction, *Sir John van Olden Barnavelt by John Fletcher and Philip Massinger* (Oxford: Oxford University Press, 1980), pp. vi–vii.

50 Howard-Hill, Introduction, *Sir John van Olden Barnavelt*, p. ix.

51 Howard-Hill, Introduction, *Sir John van Olden Barnavelt*, p. x.

52 Howard-Hill, Introduction, *Sir John van Olden Barnavelt*, p. xi.

53 Margaret McLaren Cook and F. P. Wilson, Introduction, *Demetrius and Enanthe* (Oxford: Oxford University Press, 1951).

54 See T. H. Howard-Hill, *Ralph Crane and Some Shakespeare First Folio Comedies* (Charlottesville: University of Virginia Press, 1972).

55 See Wells's and Taylor's Textual Introductions to these plays in *William Shakespeare: A Textual Companion*, pp. 601, 604.

56 Also see James Hirsh, 'Act Divisions in the Shakespeare First Folio', *PBSA*, 96 (2002), 219–56.

57 Richard Knowles, 'How Shakespeare Knew *King Leir*', *Shakespeare Survey*, 55 (2002), 29–34.

58 John Pitcher, Introduction, *Hymen's Triumph* (Oxford: Oxford University Press, 1994), p. xxiv.

59 See Sarah Poynting, *The Shepherd's Paradise* (Oxford: Oxford University Press, 1997), pp. xiii–xiv.

60 Poynting, Introduction, *The Shepherd's Paradise*, p. xv.

61 Beal, *Index of English Literary Manuscripts 1450–1700*, 1:2, 283–93.

62 *The Dramatic Records of Sir Henry Herbert*, ed. Adams, p. 21; *The Control and Cen-*

sorship of Caroline Drama, ed. Bawcutt, pp. 182–3. Also see T. H. Howard-Hill, 'Crane's 1619 "Promptbook" of *Barnavelt* and Theatrical Processes', *Modern Philology*, 86 (1988–9), pp. 146–70.

63　Bentley, *The Profession of Dramatist in Shakespeare's Time, 1590–1642*, pp. 15–16.

64　See the Introduction to my Malone Society edition of *Hengist, King of Kent*, pp. vi–vii.

65　Evans, 'Note on the Text' of *Coriolanus*, *The Riverside Shakespeare* (Boston: Houghton Mifflin, 1974), p. 1437.

66　See Greg, *The Shakespeare First Folio*, p. 401.

67　See Greg, *The Shakespeare First Folio*, p. 399.

68　Bowers, *On Editing Shakespeare*, p. 26.

69　See Blayney's discussion of similar points about the interconnectedness of printers' shops in 'The Printing of Playbooks'.

70　Jowett, Textual Introduction, *1 Henry IV*, in Wells and Taylor *et al.*, *William Shakespeare: A Textual Companion*, pp. 329–30.

71　Jowett, Textual Introduction, *1 Henry IV*, 329; Greg, *The Shakespeare First Folio*, p. 264.

72　Jowett, Introduction, *2 Henry IV*, in Wells and Taylor *et al.*, *William Shakespeare: A Textual Companion*, p. 352.

73　Greg, *The Shakespeare First Folio*, p. 268.

74　British Library Harley MS 7650.

75　Worcester College, Oxford, MS Plays 9.21.

76　See Hilton Kelliher, 'Donne, Jonson, Richard Andrews and The Newcastle Manuscript', pp. 150, 145. Also see Anthony Johnson and H. R. Woudhuysen, Introduction, *The Country Captain by William Cavendish Earl of Newcastle* (Oxford: Oxford University Press, 1999), p. xiv, who discuss the identification of the hands in *The Country Captain* by W. W. Greg, Peter Beal and Kelliher.

77　Johnson and Woudhuysen, Introduction, *The Country Captain*, pp. xiv, xvii.

78　Greg, *The Shakespeare First Folio*, p. 296.

79　Jowett, Textual Introduction, *Julius Caesar*, in Wells and Taylor *et al.*, *William Shakespeare: A Textual Companion*, p. 386.

80　Taylor, Textual Introduction, *Richard III*, in Wells and Taylor *et al.*, *William Shakespeare: A Textual Companion*, p. 229.

81　On authorial revision in the Shakespeare canon, see the introductions to the individual plays in *William Shakespeare: A Textual Companion*, and Ioppolo, *Revising Shakespeare*.

6　'It sprang from ye Poet': Jonson, Middleton and Shakespeare at work

1　Hatfield House CP 114/58; National Archives SP 14/16/30; British Library Cotton MS Julius C. III, f. 222. For a discussion of extant examples of Jonson's hand, see Beal, *Index of English Literary Manuscripts 1450–1700*, Vol. 1, Part 2, p. 233.

2　Knowles, 'Cecil's shopping centre', *TLS*, 7 February 1997, pp. 14–15; and 'Jonson's *Entertainment at Britain's Burse*', in *Re-Presenting Ben Jonson: Text, History, Performance*, ed. Martin Butler (Basingstoke: Macmillan, 1999), pp. 114–51.

3　National Archives, SP MS 14/44/62*. The first page of the manuscript was stamped as '144' but has been renumbered in pencil.

4　For a discussion of Cecil's treatment of Ralegh's home and the designs of these buildings, see Lawrence Stone, 'Inigo Jones and the New Exchange', *Archaeological Journal*, CXIV (1957), 103–21.

5　Hatfield House CP Bills 35/7, 35/1, Box U/2; National Archives MS State Papers

Venetian 11/497. In 1968, Scott McMillin discussed these documents in 'Jonson's Early Entertainments: New Information from Hatfield House', *Renaissance Drama*, n.s. 1 (1968), 153–66.

6 As cited by McMillin, 'Jonson's Early Entertainments', p. 157.

7 See Knowles, *TLS*, p. 14.

8 Wilson's letter in full appears as the following: 'We haue not bene vnmindfull of this busines we haue sought out diuers toyes whervpo*n* conceits are ministred, yett doth not the towne afford such plenty as we expected, the partyes requyre mony to buy them, or some other apointm* who shall buy them, I tell the*m* they shall haue mony, and being trifles it skells not much. The deseigne is to haue three persones only actors according to yo* lo*ps* conceit. The first shall represent the keeper who from the stayre foote to the place of shewe, shall geue entertaynm* by familiar speech in discoursing vpon the place and what it is, and what it is not, thervpon taking occation to taxe the diuers ydle coments that hath ben vpon it since it was begone, w*ch* doubtlese the king hath herd of, & by this tyme he shalbe come to y*e* place Att the first opening, they wold haue lowd musick of Cornetts & such lyke, to erect the more the intendem* Then, the other two *personati* shall beginn to play ther Montebanke tricks, first in talking one to an other after ther fashion, and then to discorse vpon, & to distribute ther tryfles wher in they desyre to knowe the best & most of the best that shold be ther. Whylst this toyes are in hand they wold haue the Montebank to haue a visard as they vse to haue and all this while those things of prise to be couered w*th* curtaynes. When ther torne comes to be spoken of, he shall vnmaske as a marchant that sell not *merces adulterinas* and then make such a presentm* of them as the things & *per*sons deserue This is shortly the subiect w*ch* according to yo* lo*ps* invention they haue framed thers, and doe promise (as fathers that are most in loue w*th* ther yongest chyld) to make it an admirable & pleasing spectacle. The conclusio*n* they wold haue with soft musick and a songe in the midle windowe next Duresm yard as the king shalll returne y* way // yo* lo*ps* most bonde seruant Tho: Wilson. Salsb. howse 31 Mar. 1609'. Hatfield House CP 195/100; *HMC: Salisbury*, 21:37.

9 McMillin, 'Jonson's Early Entertainments', pp. 161–2.

10 McMillin, 'Jonson's Early Entertainments', pp. 157–8, argues that Jonson celebrates the 'endeavors of shopkeeping at Britain's Burse, with the royal family assembled near a sign which said "all other places give for money, here all is given for love", which might have seemed inimical to a poet who always liked cant as readily as he eventually disliked the Earl of Salisbury. Perhaps the satirical impulse which produced *The Alchemist* a year later began to form in April of 1609.'

11 Stone, 'Inigo Jones and the New Exchange', p. 116.

12 Knowles, *TLS*, p. 15.

13 Knowles, *TLS*, p. 15.

14 Knowles, 'Jonson's *Entertainment at Britain's Burse*', p. 122.

15 Knowles, *TLS*, p. 15.

16 Hatfield House Cecil CP 144/271–2.

17 Knowles, 'Jonson's *Entertainment at Britain's Burse*', p. 131.

18 I wish to thank Peter Beal, Peter W. M. Blayney, R. A. Foakes, Alan H. Nelson, S. P. Cerasano and Laetitia Yeandle for answering my queries about this manuscript. For samples of Jonson's hand that match Hand A in this manuscript I especially thank the late James Riddell, a specialist on Jonson's manuscripts and printed canon, who accepted the hand in the first part of *The Entertainment* as Jonson's.

19 John Pitcher, Introduction, *Hymen's Triumph by Samuel Daniel* (Oxford: Oxford University Press, 1994), pp. vii and x. Pitcher continues, 'as he hurried to write new choruses and a prologue for the performance text, and to provide manu-

script copies of this for the actors and possibly the Lord Chamberlain too, Daniel would also arrange for another copy to be made for the bride, as promptly as possible, either from his working papers or from an early draft'. When the text was presented to the bride and also when published in 1615, Daniel had deleted a song.

20 British Library Additional MS 64875, f. 37ʳ; Coke Papers Vol. 6. I am indebted to Peter Beal for this reference in the Coke papers.

21 For a list of manuscripts pertaining to *The Entertainment at Prince Henry's Barriers*, see C. E. McGee and John C. Meagher, 'Preliminary Checklist of Tudor and Stuart Entertainments: 1603–1613', *Research Opportunities in Renaissance Drama*, 27 (1984), 92–3.

22 The *Britain's Burse* Hand A particularly resembles that in a less than formal dedication to a copy of 1605 Quarto 1 of *Sejanus* that was catalogued in the Huth sale catalogue, 7 July 1914, and sold to the Huntington Library (shelfmark RB 60659).

23 Field's mostly italic hand in his letter to Henslowe (Dulwich College MS 1: Article 68) bears little resemblance to any of the hands in the manuscript of *The Entertainment at Britain's Burse*.

24 This concluding poem appears as follows:

> if to yoʳ eare it wonder bring
> To heer Apollos statue singe
>   Gaynste natiuers lawe
>   Aske this great kinge
> And his faier Queene, whoe are the proper cause
>   It is not wisdomes power aloue
>   Or Beauties that cane moue a stone
>   But both so high
>   In this great king
> And his faier Queen do strike the harmony
>   which harmony hath power to touch
>   The dulleste earth, and makes it such
>   As I ame nowe
>   To this great king
> And his faier Queene, whome now to playes knowes how
>   Excepte wᵗʰ sylence which inded
>   doth trueste admiration breed
>   And that cam I
>   To this beste kinge
> And his beste Queene in my last notes & dye.   (f. 147ʳ)

25 Hatfield House CP Bills 35.

26 Hatfield House CP Bills 35/7, 35/1, 35/1a; *HMC: Salisbury*, 24:168.

27 Knowles, 'Jonson's *Entertainment at Britain's Burse*', p. 127.

28 McMillin, 'Jonson's Early Entertainments', p. 160.

29 T. H. Howard-Hill, Introduction, *A Game at Chess* (Manchester: Manchester University Press, 1993), p. 6.

30 Trinity College MS O.2.66; Huntington Library MS EL 34.B.17.

31 British Library Lansdowne MS 690; Bodleian Library MS 525; Folger Shakespeare Library MS V.a.231.

32 Folger Shakespeare Library MS V.a.342.

33 Howard-Hill, Introduction, *A Game at Chess*, p. 5.

34 See Jean Shami, '"Twice a Day on the Banke Side"?: A Contemporary Report on Middleton's *A Game at Chesse*', *Notes and Queries*, 243 (1998), 367–70.

35 British Library Egerton MS 2623, f. 28ʳ.

36 National Archives State Papers 14/171, f. 558^{r-v}; for this and other transcriptions, see the appendices to Howard-Hill's 1993 Manchester University Press edition; also see *English Professional Theatre, 1530–1660*, ed. Wickham, Berry and Ingram, pp. 615–16.

37 *The Dramatic Records of Sir Henry Herbert*, ed. Adams, p. 29; *The Control and Censorship of Caroline Drama*, ed. Bawcutt, p. 152 (also see pages 153–4).

38 For discussion of the play's textual and performance history, see R. C. Bald, Introduction, *A Game at Chesse* (Cambridge: Cambridge University Press, 1929); Susan Zimmerman, 'The Folger Manuscripts of Thomas Middleton's *A Game at Chesse*: A Study in the Genealogy of Texts', *Papers of the Bibliographic Society of America*, 76 (1982), 159–95; T. H. Howard-Hill, 'The Author as Scribe or Reviser? Middleton's Intentions in *A Game at Chess*', *TEXT* 3 (1987), 305–18; Ioppolo, *Revising Shakespeare*, pp. 70–7; and Howard-Hill's Introduction to his 1993 Manchester University Press edition of *A Game at Chess*.

39 Dutton, *Licensing, Censorship and Authorship in Early Modern England*, pp. 155, 157; Howard-Hill, Introduction, *A Game at Chess*, p. 9.

40 See Howard-Hill, Introduction, *A Game at Chess*, pp. 4ff, and Ioppolo, *Revising Shakespeare*, pp. 75–6.

41 As I have discussed in my Malone Society Reprints edition of this play, it was written around 1619 and was revised at least after composition and after performance. Both manuscripts, which vary in incidentals and not susbstantively, were copied from the same company book showing identical cuts, using a vertical line in the margin, in the dialogue of the character Roxena. When the text was eventually printed in 1661 these portions of the text do not appear. The Quarto text reduces the number of characters, cuts lines by female characters, and presents a briefer conclusion to the play's final scene, possibly to make it suitable as a companion play to *The Birth of Merlin*. As Bald has noted, the Quarto omits 175 lines found in the manuscripts while adding 25 lines not found in the manuscripts. Yet, if the play was revised shortly after its composition, as represented by cuts in the manuscript text, it may have been revised again. Rather than overtly reacting to, or ignoring censorship, Middleton shows a pattern of revision in which he very neatly cut passages within speeches with as little alteration as possible of the surrounding dialogue.

42 See John Jowett's Introduction to the play in Wells and Taylor *et al.*, *William Shakespeare: A Textual Companion*, pp. 288–9, in which he discusses the compositors' difficulty with the foul papers and debates critics' theories on the use of Q1 to print Q2. Also see G. Blakemore Evans's Textual Analysis in his edition of *Romeo and Juliet* (Cambridge: Cambridge University Press, 1984), pp. 206–12.

43 Turner finds irregular portions that 'reveal Fletcher actually at work on the play, revising perhaps at the actors' behest but more likely changing his mind during the original act of composition about how the action should proceed and rewriting accordingly. Some of the revised sections contain repetition-brackets— entire or partial duplications of a line at some distance from its incorrect first appearance—a characteristic of revised texts long known of but recently not much discussed.' 'Revisions and Repetition-Brackets in Fletcher's *A Wife for a Month*', pp. 178–9.

44 See for example Evans's argument that the Friar's speech represents a 'rather careless revision' cancelling the first version in Romeo's speech (Textual Analysis in his Cambridge edition, p. 211). Evans astutely notes, 'whichever version is preferred all editors produce an eclectic text of the lines'. See also Jowett's earlier discussion of editorial arguments about this duplication in Textual Introduction, p. 295 and his later discussion in 'Addressing Adaptation in *Measure for Measure* and *Sir Thomas More*, in *Textual Performances: The Modern Reproduction of*

Shakespeare's Drama, ed. Lucas Erne and Margaret J. Kidnie (Cambridge: Cambridge University Press, 2004), p. 65.

45 As Randall McLeod, who champions 'unediting', argues, Shakespeare may have wanted both versions to stand together, and thus he did not delete one, or judge one better than the other, or find one defective and tried to 'improve' it. McLeod (under the name Random Cloud), 'The Marriage of Good and Bad Quartos', *Shakespeare Quarterly*, 33 (1982), 421–31.

46 One of these corrected duplications appears in Romeo's speech in 3.3, as printed in Q2:

> This may flyes doe, when I from this must flie,
> And sayest thou yet, that exile is not death?
> But Romeo may not, he is banished.
> Flies may do this, but I from this must flie:
> They are freemen, but I am banished.

The last two lines do not appear (and were probably cut rather than accidentally omitted) in F (the later text), but not Q3 and Q4; the first two lines do not appear in the Q1 text (which would have been a cut version of the first original text, Q2). Perhaps Shakespeare or his colleagues made the correction, which eventually was printed in the Folio, during some later performance, preferring the later version. Because the duplication appears in Q4, printed from Q3, it may not have been cut in performance, with or without Shakespeare's participation, but was cut only in the Folio printer's copy of the play, a marked-up copy of Q3. Thus the cut is a later literary correction, designed to suit a later reading audience, rather than a theatrical revision. The duplication may not have been noticeable or incongruent during performance.

47 The Queen Mab speech is printed as prose in all the texts except Q1, even though it is obviously written as poetry in iambic pentameter. Not surprisingly this jumbled speech appears in 1.4, the same scene in which Shakespeare was undecided about which characters are on stage when, and what exactly they do if they are on stage. Here is the first portion of the speech in the foul paper Q2:

> *Mer.* O then I see Queene Mab hath bin with you:
> She is the Fairies midwife, and she comes in shape no bigger then
> an Agot stone, on the forefinger of an Alderman, drawne with
> a teeme of little ottarmie, ouer mens noses as they he asleepe . . .

The speech should have been printed like this in Q2 and the later texts:

> *Mer.* O then I see Queene Mab hath bin with you:
> She is the Fairies midwife, and she comes
> In shape no bigger then an Agot stone,
> On the forefinger of an Alderman,
> Drawne with a teeme of little ottarmie
> Ouer mens noses as they he [be] asleepe . . .

The most logical explanation for misprinting this obviously poetic speech as prose is that Shakespeare was reworking the entire speech as he wrote and added extra words in the margins or interlinearly; that is, above the lines or on inserted sheets. The manuscript behind the Q1 text had been corrected at some point, again probably without Shakespeare's participation. Thus the Q2 printer, working quickly, set the text as he saw it in the manuscript, sometimes uncertain about where to insert extra words or lines. The King's Men failed to correct it in the Folio text.

48 For example, Shakespeare uses the Chorus to open Acts 1 and 2 and then drops it, either forgetting or declining to use it in the other three acts.

49 See John Jowett, in Wells and Taylor *et al.*, *William Shakespeare: A Textual Companion*, p. 289.

50 See the various introductions to the plays in Wells and Taylor *et al.*, *William Shakespeare: A Textual Companion*. Also see the Introductions to *The Second Part of King Henry the Fourth 1600*, ed. Thomas L. Berger (Oxford: Oxford University Press, 1990), pp. xi–xiii, and *A Midsummer Night's Dream 1600*, ed. Thomas L. Berger (Oxford: Oxford University Press, 1995).

Select bibliography

Adams, Joseph Quincy, ed. *The Dramatic Records of Sir Henry Herbert.* New Haven, Conn.: Yale University Press, 1917.

Bald, R. C. 'The Foul Papers of a Revision'. *The Library,* ser. 4, 26 (1946), 37–50.

Bawcutt, N. W., ed. *The Control and Censorship of Caroline Drama: The Records of Sir Henry Herbert, Master of the Revels 1623–73.* Oxford: Clarendon Press, 1996.

—— 'Renaissance Dramatists and the Texts of Their Plays'. *Research Opportunities in Renaissance Drama,* 40 (2001), 1–24.

Beal, Peter. *Index of English Literary Manuscripts 1450–1700.* 2 vols. London: Mansell, 1980–93.

—— *In Praise of Scribes: Manuscripts and their Makers in Seventeenth-Century England.* Oxford: Clarendon Press, 1998.

Beal, Peter and Margaret J. M. Ezell, ed. *English Manuscript Studies 1100–1500, Volume 9: Writings by Early Modern Women.* London: The British Library, 2000.

Beal, Peter and Grace Ioppolo, ed. *English Manuscript Studies 1100–1700, Volume 11: Manuscripts and their Makers in the English Renaissance.* London: The British Library, 2002.

Bentley, G. E. *The Jacobean and Caroline Stage.* 7 vols. Oxford: Clarendon Press, 1941–68.

—— *The Profession of Dramatist in Shakespeare's Time, 1590–1642.* Princeton, N.J.: Princeton University Press, 1971.

Blayney, Peter W. M. *The Bookshops in Paul's Cross Churchyard.* London: The Bibliographical Society, 1990.

—— 'The Printing of Playbooks'. In *A New History of Early English Drama.* Ed. John D. Cox and David Scott Kastan. Columbia: Columbia University Press, 1997, pp. 383–422.

Bowers, Fredson. *On Editing Shakespeare.* Charlottesville: University of Virginia Press, 1966.

—— 'Authority, Copy and Transmission in Shakespeare's Texts'. In *Shakespeare Study Today.* Ed. Georgianna Ziegler. New York: AMS Press, 1986, pp. 7–36.

Burke, Seán. *The Death and Return of the Author: Criticism and Subjectivity in Barthes, Foucault and Derrida.* Edinburgh: Edinburgh University Press, 1992.

Carson, Neil. *A Companion to Henslowe's Diary.* Cambridge: Cambridge University Press, 1988.

Cerasano, S. P. 'Competition for the King's Men?: Alleyn's Blackfriars Venture'. *Medieval and Renaissance Drama in England,* 4 (1989), 173–86.

—— 'Philip Henslowe, Simon Forman and the Theatrical Community of the 1590s'. *Shakespeare Quarterly,* 44 (1993), 145–58.

—— 'The Patronage Network of Philip Henslowe and Edward Alleyn'. *Medieval and Renaissance Drama in England*, 13 (2001), 82–92.

Cerasano, S. P. and Marion Wynne-Daviesl, ed. *Renaissance Drama by Women: Texts and Documents*. London: Routledge, 1996.

Chambers, E. K. *The Elizabethan Stage*, 4 vols. Oxford: Clarendon Press, 1923.

—— *William Shakespeare: A Study of the Facts and Problems*, 2 vols. Oxford: Clarendon Press, 1930.

Cook, Ann Jennalie. *The Privileged Playgoers of Shakespeare's London, 1576–1642*. Princeton, N.J.: Princeton University Press, 1981.

Dawson, Giles E. and Laetitia Kennedy-Skipton. *Elizabethan Handwriting 1500–1650: A Guide to the Reading of Documents and Manuscripts*. London: Faber and Faber, 1966.

Dessen, Alan and Leslie Thomson. *A Dictionary of Stage Directions in the English Drama 1580–1642*. Cambridge: Cambridge University Press, 1999.

Dutton, Richard. *Mastering the Revels: The Regulation and Censorship of English Renaissance Drama*. Iowa City: University of Iowa Press, 1991.

—— *Licensing, Censorship and Authorship in Early Modern England*. Basingstoke: Palgrave, 2000.

Ezell, Margaret J. M. *Writing Women's Literary History*. Baltimore, Md.: Johns Hopkins Press, 1993.

Farrell, Kirby, Elizabeth H. Hageman and Arthur F. Kinney, ed. *Women in the Renaissance: Selections from English Literary Renaissance*. Amherst, Mass.: University of Massachusetts Press, 1988.

Feuillerat, Albert. *Documents Relating to the Office of the Revels in the Time of Queen Elizabeth*. Louvain: A. Uystpruyst, 1908.

Foakes, R. A., ed. *The Henslowe Papers*, 2 vols. London: Scolar Press, 1977.

—— ed. *Henslowe's Diary*. 2nd edn. Cambridge: Cambridge University Press, 2002.

—— 'Henslowe's Rose/Shakespeare's Globe'. In *From Script to Stage in Early Modern England*. Ed. Peter Holland and Stephen Orgel (Basingstoke: Palgrave Macmillan, 2004), pp. 11–31.

Gaskell, Philip. *A New Introduction to Bibliography*. Oxford: Oxford University Press, 1972.

Greg, W. W., ed. *The Henslowe Papers*. 2 vols. London: A. H. Bullen, 1907.

—— *Two Elizabethan Stage Abridgements: The Battle of Alcazar & Orlando Furioso*. Oxford: Clarendon Press, 1923.

—— *Dramatic Documents from the Elizabethan Playhouses*. Oxford: Clarendon Press, 1931.

—— *The Shakespeare First Folio*. Oxford: Clarendon Press, 1955.

—— *Collected Papers*. Ed. J. C. Maxwell. Oxford: Clarendon Press, 1966.

Gurr, Andrew. *The Shakespearean Stage, 1574–1642*. Cambridge: Cambridge University Press, 1980.

—— *Playgoing in Shakespeare's London*. Cambridge: Cambridge University Press, 1987.

—— *The Shakespearian Playing Companies*. Oxford: Clarendon Press, 1996.

Haaker, Ann. 'The Plague, the Theater and the Poet'. *Renaissance Drama*, n.s. 1 (1968), 283–306.

Hammond, Antony and Doreen Delvecchio. 'The Melbourne Manuscript and John Webster: A Reproduction and Transcript'. *Studies in Bibliography*, 41 (1988), 1–32.

Honigmann, E. A. J. *The Stability of Shakespeare's Text*. London: E. Arnold, Ltd, 1965.

—— 'The New Bibliography and its Critics'. In *Textual Performances: The Modern Reproduction of Shakespeare's Drama*. Ed. Lucas Erne and Margaret J. Kidnie. Cambridge: Cambridge University Press, 2004.

Howard-Hill, T. H. *Ralph Crane and Some Shakespeare First Folio Comedies*. Charlottesville: University of Virginia Press, 1972.

—— 'Marginal Markings: The Censor and the Editing of Four English Promptbooks'. *Studies in Bibliography*, 36 (1983).

—— 'The Author as Scribe or Reviser? Middleton's Intentions in *A Game at Chess*'. *TEXT: Transactions of the Society for Textual Scholarship*, 3 (1987), 305–18.

Ioppolo, Grace. *Revising Shakespeare*. Cambridge, Mass.: Harvard University Press, 1991.

—— 'Revision, Manuscript Transmission and Scribal Practice in Middleton's *Hengist, King of Kent, or, The Mayor of Queenborough*'. *Critical Survey*, 7 (1995), 319–31.

Jackson, MacDonald P. *Defining Shakespeare: 'Pericles' as Test Case*. Oxford: Oxford University Press, 2003.

Kelliher, Hilton. 'Donne, Jonson, Richard Andrews and The Newcastle Manuscript'. *English Manuscript Studies 1100–1700, Volume 4*. London: The British Library, 1993, pp. 135–73.

Knutson, Roslyn L. *The Repertory of Shakespeare's Company, 1594–1613*. Fayetteville: University of Arkansas Press, 1991.

—— 'The Commercial Significance of the Payments for Playtexts in Henslowe's Diary, 1597–1603'. *Medieval and Renaissance Drama in England*, 5 (1991), 117–63.

—— *Playing Companies and Commerce in Shakespeare's Time*. Cambridge: Cambridge University Press, 2001.

Lennam, T. N. S. 'Sir Edward Dering's Collection of Playbooks, 1619–1624'. *Shakespeare Quarterly*, 16 (1965), 145–53.

Long, William B. 'Stage-Directions: A Misinterpreted Factor in Determining Textual Provenance'. *TEXT: Transactions of the Society for Textual Scholarship*, 2 (1985), 121–37.

—— 'Dulwich MS. XX, *The Telltale*: Clues to Provenance'. *Medieval and Renaissance Drama in England*, 17 (2005).

Love, Harold. *Scribal Publication in Seventeenth-Century England*. Oxford: Clarendon Press, 1993.

—— *Attributing Authorship: An Introduction*. Cambridge: Cambridge University Press, 2002.

McGann, Jerome J. *The Textual Condition*. Princeton, N.J.: Princeton University Press, 1991.

McKerrow, R. B. *An Introduction to Bibliography for Literary Students*. Oxford: Clarendon Press, 1927.

—— 'The Elizabethan Printer and Dramatic Manuscripts'. *The Library*, ser. 3, 12 (1931), 253–75.

—— 'The Relationship of English Printed Books to Authors' Manuscripts during the Sixteenth and Seventeenth Centuries: *The 1928 Sandars Lectures*'. Ed. Carlo M. Bajetta. *Studies in Bibliography*, 53 (2000), 1–65.

McKitterick, David. *Print, Manuscript and the Search for Order 1450–1830*. Cambridge: Cambridge University Press, 2003.

McLeod, Randall (Random Cloud). 'The Marriage of Good and Bad Quartos'. *Shakespeare Quarterly*, 33 (1982), 421–31.

McMillin, Scott. *The Elizabethan Theatre and The Book of Sir Thomas More*. Ithaca, N.Y.: Cornell University Press, 1987.

—— 'Building Stories: Greg, Fleay, and the Plot of *2 Seven Deadly Sins*'. *Medieval and Renaissance Drama in England*, 4 (1989), 53–62.

McMillin, Scott and Sally-Beth MacLean. *The Queen's Men and their Plays*. Cambridge: Cambridge University Press, 1998.

Marotti, Arthur F. *Manuscript, Print, and the English Renaissance Lyric*. Ithaca, N.Y.: Cornell University Press, 1995.

Orgel, Stephen. *The Authentic Shakespeare and Other Problems of the Early Modern Stage*. London: Routledge, 2002.

Petti, Antony G. *English Literary Hands from Chaucer to Dryden*. London: Edward Arnold, 1977.

Preston, Jean F. and Laetitia Yeandle. *English Handwriting 1400–1650: An Introductory Manual*. Binghamton, N.Y.: Medieval & Renaissance Texts & Studies, 1992.

Rutter, Carol Chillington. *Documents from the Rose Playhouse*. Manchester: Manchester University Press, 1984; rpt 1999.

Sisson, Charles. '*Keep the Widow Waking*: A lost play by Dekker'. *The Library*, ser. 4, 8 (1927), 2 pts, 39–59; 233–59.

Stern, Tiffany. *Rehearsal from Shakespeare to Sheridan*. Oxford: Clarendon Press, 2000.

Tanselle, G. Thomas. *Literature and Artefacts*. Charlottesville: Bibliographical Society of the University of Virginia, 1998.

Thomson, Leslie. 'A Quarto "Marked for Performance": Evidence of What?'. *Medieval and Renaissance Drama in England*, 8 (1996), 176–210.

Turner, Robert Kean. 'Act-End Notations in Some Elizabethan Plays'. *Modern Philology*, 72 (1975), 238–47.

—— 'Revisions and Repetition-Brackets in Fletcher's *A Wife for a Month*'. *Studies in Bibliography*, 36 (1983), 178–90.

Vickers, Brian. *Shakespeare, Co-Author: A Historical Study of Five Collaborative Plays*. Oxford: Oxford University Press, 2002.

Warner, George F. *Catalogue of the Manuscripts and Muniments of Alleyn's College of God's Gift at Dulwich*. 2 vols. [London]: Longman's, Green, and Co., 1881.

Wells, Stanley and Gary Taylor, with John Jowett and William Montgomery. *William Shakespeare: A Textual Companion*. Oxford: Clarendon Press, 1987; rpt New York: W. W. Norton and Company, 1997.

Wickham, Glynne, Herbert Berry and William Ingram, ed. *English Professional Theatre, 1530–1660*. Cambridge: Cambridge University Press, 2000.

Woudhuysen, H. R. *Sir Philip Sidney and the Circulation of Manuscripts 1558–1640*. Oxford: Clarendon Press, 1996.

—— 'A New Manuscript Fragment of Sidney's *Old Arcadia*: The Huddleston Manuscript'. *English Manuscript Studies 1100–1700, Volume 11: Manuscripts and their Makers in the English Renaissance*. Ed. Peter Beal and Grace Ioppolo. London: The British Library, 2002, pp. 52–69.

Index

eBooks – at www.eBookstore.tandf.co.uk

A library at your fingertips!

eBooks are electronic versions of printed books. You can store them on your PC/laptop or browse them online.

They have advantages for anyone needing rapid access to a wide variety of published, copyright information.

eBooks can help your research by enabling you to bookmark chapters, annotate text and use instant searches to find specific words or phrases. Several eBook files would fit on even a small laptop or PDA.

NEW: Save money by eSubscribing: cheap, online access to any eBook for as long as you need it.

Annual subscription packages

We now offer special low-cost bulk subscriptions to packages of eBooks in certain subject areas. These are available to libraries or to individuals.

For more information please contact webmaster.ebooks@tandf.co.uk

We're continually developing the eBook concept, so keep up to date by visiting the website.

www.eBookstore.tandf.co.uk